P9-CDV-581

The UN Secretary-General and the Maintenance of Peace

NUMBER FOUR

Columbia University Studies in International Organization

EDITORS

LELAND M. GOODRICH

WILLIAM T. R. FOX

THE UN Secretary-General AND THE Maintenance of Peace

by LEON GORDENKER

COLUMBIA UNIVERSITY PRESS
NEW YORK AND LONDON, 1967

Leon Gordenker is Professor of Politics and Faculty Associate at the Center of International Studies, Princeton University, and Lecturer in Government in the Department of Public Law and Government at Columbia University.

Library of Congress Catalog Card Number: 67-15254
Printed in the United States of America

COLUMBIA UNIVERSITY STUDIES IN INTERNATIONAL ORGANIZATION

This series of monographs was initiated to provide for the publication under University auspices of studies in the field of international organization undertaken and carried out, in whole or in part, by members of the Columbia Faculties or with the assistance of funds made available under research programs of the University. Work in this field has been substantially assisted by grants from the Rockefeller and Ford Foundations.

The series is not intended to provide a systematic coverage of the field of international organization nor is it anticipated that volumes will appear with any set regularity. The value of the contribution which the monograph makes to knowledge and understanding of the role of international organization and its functioning in the world in which we live will be the dominant consideration in determining inclusion.

The series is published under the joint editorship of Leland M. Goodrich and William T. R. Fox, with Andrew W. Cordier and Louis Henkin acting in an advisory capacity.

The other books in this series are *Controls for Outer Space,* by Philip C. Jessup and Howard J. Taubenfield, *The United Nations Emergency Force,* by Gabriella Rosner, and *UN Administration of Economic and Social Programs,* edited by Gerard J. Mangone.

FOREWORD

Professor Gordenker's study of the role of the United Nations Secretary-General in the maintenance of peace was initially undertaken as a study of the Secretary-General's total role in the organization. He soon discovered, however, that this was too large a subject for one book and chose to concentrate on what undoubtedly has been the most publicized, if not the most important aspect of the Secretary-General's work. The Secretary-General's role in the maintenance of peace has received a great deal of attention from scholars during recent years, particularly since Dag Hammarskjöld took a conspicuous role in connection with the establishment of UNEF. Though a considerable amount of scholarly writing on the subject has accumulated, up to now no one has attempted a comprehensive and detailed analysis of the Secretary-General's peace-keeping role in its manifold aspects over the total period of the United Nations' existence. It is with a view to meeting this real need that Professor Gordenker undertook the preparation of this book.

That the role of the Secretary-General in the maintenance of peace should be considered sufficiently important to justify the attention it has received, and more particularly the writing of a book, is one striking indication of the difference between the United Nations' approach to peace and that of the League of Nations. No scholar in the thirties would have seriously thought of undertaking this kind of study for the League Secretary-General. Quite apart from the consideration that the materials for such a study would not have been readily available because of the manner in which the Secretary-General performed his more limited responsibilities, the Covenant did not explicitly place on the League's chief administrative officer the responsibilities that the Charter accords to the United Nations Secretary-General, nor did the practice of the League in the two decades of its active functioning do much to alter the situation.

Only now in the light of the striking development of the role of the United Nations Secretary-General—carried to its highest point by Hammarskjöld but maintained with quiet determination and substantial success by his successor—has the attention of scholars been turned to a reexamination of the role of his League counterpart. Even access to materials not hitherto available is not likely to alter to any great extent the contrast between the peace-keeping roles of the two Secretaries-General, the responsibilities placed upon them and assumed by them, the powers they exercised, and the manner in which they discharged their responsibilities.

Over a period of less than a half-century, a great change has taken place in the conception of the role of the top-ranking international civil servant in the keeping of peace, and in the practical importance attached to his work in this field. Professor Gordenker's study contributes to the elucidation of this development.

LELAND M. GOODRICH

Columbia University
New York, N.Y.
November, 1966

PREFACE

The United Nations and the whole generation that lived through World War II as children and young men and women have grown to maturity together. The world organization has been their familiar companion in times of international political strife and, for an increasing number, a friend in the effort to gain economic and social well-being and the rights of man. Above all, the United Nations still functions in its limited and erratic way to foster the maintenance of international peace.

Yet the United Nations often displays a curiously insubstantial quality. Its organs sometimes deal with crises and conflicts only by discussing procedure, and sometimes fail to deal with them at all. Sometimes enthusiastic resolutions substitute for real cooperation among governments, and sometimes cool, logical argument masks hot irrationality outside the United Nations. Representatives of member countries sometimes win a dash of fame in the United Nations, only to retire into diplomatic obscurity elsewhere. The governments of member states often change, and the leading statesman of yesterday's General Assembly is today's political cipher or tomorrow's villain.

In such circumstances, the Secretary-General of the United Nations, as was anticipated at the San Francisco Conference and before, does symbolize the world organization and gives a concrete quality to its lengthy decision process. The three men who have held the post until now have on a number of occasions exerted dramatic leadership. They spoke to and perhaps for the peoples of the world. They sought and carried out important work in efforts to maintain the peace. And they managed the routine functions necessary to any political organization.

As a member of the wartime generation who was associated closer than most with the United Nations during its formative years, I have felt an interest, as natural as breathing and thinking, in the world organization and the maintenance of peace. That is one motive for writing this book. Another is the intellectual and practical need to seek understanding of the official who so often symbolizes the United Nations.

My interest in this subject was fired even more by the contrasts between the sullen atmosphere around the office of Secretary-General when Trygve Lie left it in 1953, and its brilliance after Dag Hammarskjöld carried off the complicated maneuver that helped to end the Suez crisis in 1956. It was after that that the Secretary-General often was compared (with whatever scant basis) with the President of the United States. Later Hammarskjöld himself suggested such a comparison.

A concept developed by Richard Neustadt for his study of the United States presidency, *Presidential Power*, gave me much help when work on this book began in 1961. His work suggested the idea of "influence" which I have employed throughout the following pages. A concept which emphasizes process rather than formal, legal characteristics, it has been far more useful than a comparison of the office of Secretary-General with that of the United States President.

My other intellectual debts are even greater. I owe much to Professor Leland M. Goodrich of Columbia University, and to my colleagues in the Center of International Studies and the Department of Politics at Princeton University. Dr. Gabriella Rosner Lande and Professor Samir Anabtawi were kind enough to give me extensive comments.

I am also indebted to a long list of former colleagues in the United Nations Secretariat, whose ideas, advice, and sometimes opposition, have contributed to this book. The late William M. Jordan of the Department of Political and Security Affairs was particularly helpful in making suggestions for improving an early version. To publish other names here perhaps would embarrass some of the international civil servants; I am therefore preserving the anonymity of those who so kindly put up with my questions and patiently criticized my views. It need hardly be said that the mistakes here are mine.

Financial and clerical support for this study came from Columbia

University, the Center of International Studies of Princeton University, and the Princeton University Committee on Research in the Humanities and Social Sciences. I am greatly indebted to all of them. Miss M. Bos Bakker of Leiden University and Mr. H. Gajentaan, then a student at Utrecht University, gave me valuable research assistance at an early stage. Mr. Taylor Reveley, then a student at Princeton University, provided indispensable help at a later stage. My gratitude is also due Mrs. A. van den Elshout and Mrs. Gloria Mason for expert typing.

My wife and children bravely bore the burdens of living with an author and deserve full credit for a major contribution.

LEON GORDENKER

Princeton, N.J.
February, 1967

INTRODUCTION

This study deals with the office of the Secretary-General of the United Nations and the influence of its incumbent on the process taking place when the international organization becomes involved in issues relating to the maintenance of peace and security. It concentrates on those issues in which the use of armed force either has occurred or may not be far distant. It leaves aside such long-term factors as the control of armaments, or economic and social development.

The underlying proposition for research is that the Secretary-General can act within narrow but undefined and shifting limits, and his independent actions influence the course of international politics but never at a constant level. The configuration of international politics always modulates his actions and his influence. So do his character, energy, intelligence, and style. His independent actions may generate precedents that have dual results. In similar circumstances he may attempt similar actions and achieve equal or even greater influence. Or he may reach a limit which can provoke attack from opponents who might derive other conclusions from the precedents.

Taking as given the existence of an international political environment, this study also accepts as a fact the imperfection of the United Nations as an authoritative organization of states and men. It aims at finding out how the Secretary-General fits into the context of international politics and influences its course and that of the organization, and concentrates on activities centering in his office.

The United Nations possesses a unique quality as the only international organization with general purposes and worldwide membership. It therefore mirrors the problems of the vast and the miniscule nations, the powerful and the weak, the contentious and the quiescent, the rich and the poor. But the United Nations is a complex organization that has no real existence except as an outgrowth of the agreement of its members, which are states and not individual persons. Individuals usually have importance in the work of the United Nations only as representatives of member governments.

Yet the office of Secretary-General has a personal flavor. The man who holds that office stands alone as an elected official who serves the international organization in all its activities.[1] He receives his post by means of a special process involving both the Security Council, always nervous with great-power contention, and the General Assembly, ponderous, encompassing, sometimes monotonous in its endless diplomatic maneuver and yet always alive with the variety of its composition.

The selection process and the Charter place this person at the head of a main organ of the United Nations, the Secretariat. At times the Secretary-General and his immediate entourage take actions which hardly involve the rest of the Secretariat. On other occasions, the Secretary-General's work takes on meaning only because his subordinates can execute decisions. But he bears full responsibility for their actions, and for this reason this study concentrates on the Secretary-General, rather than on the Secretariat as a whole.

In a unique organization, the Secretary-General holds an office unique among international bodies. It has no precise contemporary or historical counterpart. But if the office of Secretary-General can be taken as the direct descendant of its forerunner in the League of Nations, it differs as a son may from his father. The scope of the League's activities was narrower, especially in the field of peace and security, than that of the United Nations. Nor did the League have to cope with the consequences of a Cold War, an unarrested expansion of new means of destruction, or a colonial revolution. For the Secretary-General of the United Nations, all of these developments provide the background against which he works.

The breadth of subject matter with which the United Nations deals provides a source of contrast between the office of Secretary-General and those of the heads of Specialized Agencies, which perform expressly limited duties in what are presumed to be nonpolitical fields. The Secretary-General, moreover, heads a bigger staff than any in the Specialized Agencies.[2]

The office of Secretary-General differs sharply from familiar high posts in national governments. The Secretary-General has few functions in the creation or recitation of the myths which underlie nationalism and patriotism. Nor does he have a constituency to give strength to his views and contest those of a rival. His administration collects no taxes, bears no arms, and issues almost no orders having general effects. The Secretary-General, in short, heads neither state nor government.

Even superficial acquaintance with the office of Secretary-General and the work of its holders leads readily to the conclusion that it is a source of influence on the formation of international organization policy. Such a conclusion, however, begs the question of how this influence is exerted, when, and in what circumstances. Clearly the constitutional provisions of the Charter for suppressing the use of violence give him a role. Furthermore, the history of the United Nations, marked by such incidents as the Korean conflict and the interventions in Suez and the Congo, contains persuasive examples of the Secretary-General's influence on high politics.

In this analysis of the development of the office of the Secretary-General of the United Nations and its influence, emphasis has been placed on matters of peace and security not because no other issues have importance, but because even a study limited to the influence of the Secretary-General in these matters involves a massive record and a great variety of political and administrative techniques.

The many activities of the Secretary-General, each of them offering opportunities for influence, can be classified under headings which provide a convenient analytical framework. They are the idea of the office, the routine and representational activities of the Secretary-General, his political functions, and the general administrative functions of his office.[3]

By tracing the origins of the office of Secretary-General and the expectations of those who designed and held it, the first step toward understanding his influence can be taken. This historical investigation will give depth and form to the present, for the past holds the present office partly in bondage, and the expectations of yesterday soon begin to resemble the norms of today.

The activities of the Secretary-General which fall under the rubric of routine administration on the whole have mainly technical content and significance. But even those administrative matters which seem most routine, such as budgeting operations on which the members have agreed, as in Suez or the Congo, involve important political judgments.

In carrying out his representational functions, the Secretary-General speaks or acts publicly on behalf of the organization. Such representational activities may be inspired by a hope of influencing the course of events and policy decisions. Other representational acts have a purely formal character but nevertheless may bear on the decision-making process.

The direct political functions of the Secretary-General derive in the first instance from the "quite special right" [4] given the Secretary-General under Article 99 of the Charter. This right may put him in at the beginning of any peace-breaking incident which could come to the Security Council. The implications of this right make the Secretary-General an integral part of the entire discussion and action on any matter of peace and war in the Security Council.

The Secretary-General's general administrative duties also may have effects on the formation of United Nations policies. He has been given administrative tasks far beyond the expectations of the drafters of the Charter or the experience of the League of Nations. Under Article 98, the deliberative organs may assign "other duties" to the Secretary-General. In carrying out these assignments, the Secretary-General has given new breadth and political content to the general administrative category of his functions.

Each of the men who has held the office of Secretary-General has left his imprint on it. Because the Secretaries-General were human beings, their records include elements of impulse, lack of logic, and imperfect knowledge. No student can be confident of his explanations of these human manifestations, but to omit observing them would leave as false a picture as would a reading only of the Charter in attempting to understand the work of the United Nations.

This endeavor to provide an orderly view of an office which has caught the imagination of millions of people and of many of their leaders must then take into account the complexity of individuals, of governments, and of political aspirations and failures. The record of two decades of development and change provides a firm basis for study. But the past provides no reason to believe that the office of Secretary-General is now permanently molded. It provides every reason to believe that the office will be subject to further development and redefinition.

ABBREVIATIONS USED IN TEXT

ANC	Armée Nationale Congolaise
ILO	International Labor Organization
ONUC	L'Organisation des Nations Unies au Congo
OPI	Office of Public Information
UNCACK	United Nations Civil Assistance Command
UNCOK	United Nations Commission on Korea
UNCURK	United Nations Commission for the Unification and Rehabilitation of Korea
UNEF	United Nations Emergency Force
UNFICYP	United Nations Force in Cyprus
UNIPOM	United Nations India-Pakistan Observation Mission
UNKRA	United Nations Korean Reconstruction Agency
UNMOGIP	United Nations Military Observer Group in India and Pakistan
UNOGIL	United Nations Observation Group in Lebanon
UNRRA	United Nations Relief and Rehabilitation Administration
UNRWA	United Nations Relief and Works Agency for Palestine Refugees
UNSF	United Nations Special Force
UNTEA	United Nations Temporary Executive Authority
UNTSO	United Nations Truce Supervision Organization
UNYOM	United Nations Yemen Observation Mission

CONTENTS

PART ONE

The Idea of the Office

CHAPTER I

MODELS FOR SAN FRANCISCO

The delegates at San Francisco had some choice of concepts from the past when they set about designing the office of the United Nations Secretary-General. These concepts were divided along two main lines. The first pointed to the Secretary-General as the humble servant of the assembled delegations. The other indicated his office as a fount of ideas and a vigorous arm for executing decisions.

In the first view, the office of the Secretary-General is identified with the concept of the passive secretariat, an idea that has deep roots in national political practice. Civil servants in modern states do not formally participate in policy decisions unless bidden to do so by ministers of the government who bear responsibility for policy recommendations and decisions. Civil servants may prepare material for policy decisions, but they seldom decide matters by themselves. After decisions are made they execute the policy, again under the direction of a responsible minister.

The concept of an initiating secretariat has even less foundation in traditional diplomatic practice than in national governments. Servants of national governments sometimes do influence policy formation. The Under-Secretary in the British Foreign Office consults closely with his chief, makes suggestions regarding policy, and frequently takes part in negotiations. The role of civil servants in the formation of French government policies certainly was at least as great under the Third and Fourth Republics as in Britain. In the United States government, civil servants participate even more directly in the policy process. In part, this results from the appointment of leading officials for political reasons. In part it reflects the special nature of the office of the President, which both initiates national policies and actively directs the entire federal civil service. And in part it derives from the practices of Congress, which involve civil servants in appearances before committees and in lobbying for decisions acceptable to the President.

Diplomatic practice lacks the clarity and completeness of a national governmental scheme. Typically, a diplomatic conference has available no permanent civil service to prepare its documents and do such tasks as translating and printing. These services must be organized on an *ad hoc* basis and usually require the participation of technicians from several foreign offices and governments. In addition, the diplomatic conference consists only of formally equal representatives of formally equal sovereigns. It cannot take corporate decisions but only reach agreements, which activate no organized administration. Rather, execution is left to national governments. Frequently, diplomatic conferences end with agreements that require no execution and no continuously functioning civil service but only the announcement of attitudes on an important issue.[1]

The delegates at San Francisco who relied primarily or exclusively on traditional diplomatic practice favored a Secretary-General who was an amanuensis. This attitude was reinforced by the usual diplomatic view that the politics of the national government, with its ability to interfere with the lives of its citizens, differs in kind from international politics with its emphasis on independence of action for all states.

Yet national governments had increasingly bound themselves with commitments to international organizations during the previous century. These organizations ranged from primitive to sophisticated in the design of their deliberative bodies and executive organs. Many of them had permanent secretariats engaged in carrying out international work in the months and sometimes years between meetings of representative organs. The League of Nations and the International Labor Organization created well-developed, skillful secretariats, independent of any national service. They exerted influence on the policy process far beyond the limits of a traditional diplomatic conference. Their histories, experiences and examples were available at San Francisco as the basis for an active, leading secretariat for the new organization.[2]

The Model of the League of Nations [3]

The conferees at Versailles who drafted the League of Nations Covenant regarded such administrative questions as the nature of a secretariat as distinctly secondary and subordinate. That this should be so was hardly surprising, for the conferees broke much new ground in outlining an international organization to maintain peace. There was little to guide them in creating a secretariat. The earlier international public unions had developed no clear and undisputed appreciation of the role of their staffs. And the extensive unofficial discussions which took place in Great Britain and the United States during World War I failed to restate scattered earlier activities of international experience into a doctrine for an international secretariat of the kind that developed under the League Covenant.

Official study groups produced textual suggestions for the League Covenant, mainly during the summer and autumn of 1918. Perhaps the earliest definite suggestion relating to a secretariat came from a French governmental commission, which showed more interest in a military staff than in a civil service. The first official British draft of the Covenant, the product of the Phillimore Commission, did not even mention the subject of a secretariat. Nor did the first attempts by Colonel Edward H. House and President Woodrow Wilson. The most influential suggestion before the Versailles conference came from General Jan Christiaan Smuts. In his seminal proposals for the League of Nations he projected a permanent secretariat, which was to keep alert to disturbances anywhere and to acquire firsthand information about them. A secretariat always appeared in subsequent drafts but not in well defined terms.

As the peace conference got under way in January, 1919, the idea of endowing the proposed secretariat with leading responsibility in political affairs was talked about seriously. The Greek statesman, Eleutherios Venizelos, was approached about taking the post of "chancellor of the League of Nations." Venizelos declined and the grandiose title of chancellor disappeared, to be replaced with the more mundane Secretary-General, a literal translation from the French terminology of diplomatic conferences. Most of the texts proposed to the conference looked to the creation of a much less ambitious office than was envisaged for Venizelos. The idea and scope of the projected secretariat caused no real controversy at the peace conference, and as a result the delegates accepted a plan the implications of which scarcely had been fully explored.

The terms of the Covenant of the League of Nations regarding the Secretariat were cast in uninformative and rather indefinite language. Nevertheless, the earlier discussion of a chancellor with political responsibilities, and the French suggestion of a general staff, indicated that the thinking of the conferees had not been completely cast in traditional molds. Against this background, the laconic terms of the Covenant meant that the nature of the office of Secretary-General and its development was to be determined by the character, ideas, and activities of its first occupant, quite as much as by its constitutional framework. Moreover, the office had not been so defined as to exclude proponents of novel ideas. This was shown by the offer of the post to Sir Maurice Hankey, who had been the master organizer of wartime cooperation around meetings of experts. He could have been expected to organize the Secretariat on intergovernmental, representational lines, in accordance with his war experience, rather than as an independent international civil service. In the end, Hankey rejected the invitation and the nomination went to Sir Eric Drummond.

The first Secretary-General had come to the attention of the inner circle of the peace conference because of his competence and because of his interest in the League. He was eager for the appointment and accepted it at once. Drummond remained at the head of the League Secretariat for 13 years, shaped its structure and character, and left a model that had to be taken into account in planning any future international organization.

Sir Eric Drummond had won the admiration of his diplomatic colleagues in Britain and abroad at a time when Foreign Office standing was at its pinnacle. He was a member of a civil service that understood how it could be influential and how responsibility was distributed within a government. This civil service helped to protect its own independence by discretion in word and in action: these were public servants, but not public personages.

From this concept it was but a step to Drummond's idea of the international civil service. Nothing like it had ever existed in an international organization, but it was scarcely revolutionary in the light of the independence and integrity of the British civil service. The new Secretary-General planned a secretariat which would be made up of the most qualified men of all countries. These Secretariat members would not take instructions from any government.

They and he were to be public servants for the world community. His plans established him as master in his office and his independent Secretariat was accepted by his masters, the Assembly and the Council. If every government did not always loyally support the independent civil service as it operated, none was able to destroy the principle.[4]

While Drummond behaved with the circumspection and intelligence of an Under-Secretary of the Foreign Office, he also had to act in some limited respects as a minister. There was no one else to do so. The Secretary-General was appointed by and reported to international bodies whose functions in regard to the operations of the Secretariat were legislative. Drummond found himself acting as prime minister when the Assembly and the Council dealt with matters of concern to the administration and operation of the staff but not when it shaped substantive policy. Furthermore, as soon as the Secretary-General offered his budget or his suggestions on an administrative policy, he lost his prime minister's status and once again was a civil servant, for he had no organized party to support him in the legislative organs. He alone answered his critics and defended his plans and budgets. His ministerial role included leadership and responsibility, but excluded real political power.

To lack political power did not necessarily mean that the Secretary-General would lack political influence. In a number of ways, the provisions of the Covenant and the rules of procedure of the organs provided a framework within which he could express opinions, make choices, and direct work. With these possibilities he could exert some influence on the work of the League.

The Covenant assigned certain ministerial duties to the Secretary-General, such as registering treaties, summoning emergency meetings of the Council at the request of a member, or collating documentation submitted by members in connection with a dispute not submitted to third-party settlement. These duties offered chances for discussions with governments regarding their precise intentions. A request for clarification is an old diplomatic device for opening up discussion of a question. Drummond did use such opportunities as occasions on which his advice could be sought. When it was sought, he offered it.

More highly charged with political content was the provision of the Covenant that in connection with the submission of a dispute to the Council, the Secretary-General should arrange for a full investigation. In making such arrangements, the Secretary-General and his staff could shape the entire investigation. They could select the personnel, devise the methods, establish the limits of action, and control the drafting of the report. This provision of the Covenant did not result in the blossoming of Secretariat influence. In part this was because the Council usually met so promptly that there was no time for a full investigation, and in part it was because the rapporteur system and informal consultations made an independent, formal investigation by the Secretariat unnecessary.

The Secretary-General did exercise his rights under this provision of the Covenant when China applied to the Council early in 1932 for assistance against the Japanese onslaught. Drummond immediately organized a committee of consuls at Shanghai, where one of his trusted subordinates was on a mission at the time. The information received passed into the hands of the Council members, although it did not have a marked influence on them.

By far the most important base on which the political influence of the League Secretariat could be built rested in the provision of the Covenant instructing the Secretary-General to act in that capacity at all meetings of the Assembly and the Council. Symbolically, at least, the Secretary-General took part in all of the political and administrative discussions of the League's decision-taking organs. From the point of view of members, the Secretary-General could be consulted as an expert on the deliberations, and if his talents extended to political advice, this too might be sought with a degree of eagerness that depended on his abilities.

Both the Council and the Assembly adopted rules of procedure which gave some definition to the function of the Secretary-General. With the approval of the President of the Council or the Assembly, the Secretary-General drew up provisional agendas. Since the Secretariat had expert knowledge of the functioning of the organization and the presidencies shifted from one delegate to another, a real opportunity to exercise influence was available to the Secretary-General.

The Assembly also extended to the Secretary-General a marked and important opportunity to exercise direct pressure on the proceedings. He was given the right to speak on his own initiative in any committee or subcommittee, and could address the plenary session of the Assembly on invitation from the President. In the Council the rules of procedure gave the Secretary-General no such right. But his presence at the Council table clearly indicated that he might find opportunities to address the meeting, as did his duty of investigating disputes. In addition, the rules of procedure of both organs provided for several classes of communications which could be sent by the Secretary-General to the member states. If he could address them, even if only when instructed to do so, the clear inference of a high standing in international affairs could be drawn.

Finally, the Assembly decided that the Secretary-General should submit to it an annual report on the work of the organization. This report soon became the basis for general debate. Here again was a point at which the Secretary-General could intervene in discussion, since it would be his report which served as a base for the proceedings. Furthermore, the report itself could be the vehicle by which the Secretary-General made known his views.

These procedural features were designed with the assistance and advice of Drummond and his small corps of aides during the first weeks of the League's infancy. Thus the Secretary-General had an early influence on the functioning of the Assembly and the Council. Presumably the Secretary-General faced his work with full awareness of the potentialities for influencing the conduct of League business.

Drummond could invariably be seen at sessions of the Assembly and the Council, but he was seldom heard. The interventions of the Secretary-General almost never fell outside of the field of budget and administration. And even on that subject, so important for the operation of the Secretariat, most of the work was confined to closed sessions.

Sir Eric's activities behind the scenes contrasted sharply with his public work. He viewed his role as that of a diplomatic adviser and confidant for those who sought him out. He regarded such work as effective and always more telling than a speech, which might convince no one and rob him of his diplomatic prestige. He managed to maintain a reputation for impartiality and shrewdness. His own evaluation of these activities was that they were fully as successful as a more open and dramatic approach would have been.

There is no reason to suspect that a discreet approach to the secretary-generalship necessarily produced a generally weak and colorless influence on the proceedings of the League. On the contrary, Drummond took the initiative on some occasions, as in the Leticia dispute of 1933, when he permitted himself to give the British and Dutch representatives dealing with the matter a lecture on the responsibilities of their governments. But even here, he waited until the delegates had shown themselves reluctant to go farther.

Drummond's conduct of his office left some members of the League dissatisfied, notably Italy and Germany. For four years beginning in 1928, the Assembly debated the role of the Secretariat in the League's activities. In a sense, this debate was a tribute to the prestige that Sir Eric had built into the Secretariat. The Italian and German delegates opposed the manner in which the work of the Secretariat was guided, and suggested that a committee of under-secretaries-general, of which they would each name one, might form a governing board.[5] They based their opinion on the view that "the political influence of the Secretariat, and especially of its principal officers, is, in fact, enormous and it would be a mistake to close our eyes to this fact." In the end, any alteration of the senior staff was refused by the Assembly before Sir Eric's expected retirement in 1933.

Ironically, Italy, one of the leaders in the attempt to restrict Sir Eric Drummond's political influence, later was involved in one of the most notable—and confused—attempts by a Secretary-General to exercise initiative. Drummond's successor, Joseph Avenol, tried in 1936 to bring Italy back to the League. To do so, he traveled to Rome on his own initiative and sounded out Mussolini, who set conditions. The Secretary-General subsequently made a notable intervention in the League Council, but failed to convince it of the usefulness of his efforts. At the same time, he brought himself under a cloud of suspicion as a trimmer, which his resignation in even more disturbing circumstances in 1940 did not dissipate.[6]

Avenol, a French finance ministry official who had specialized in administration for a decade as Drummond's deputy, later complained that his predecessor's pattern had thwarted his own conception of the office. Whatever the strength of the second Secretary-General's penchant for initiative, his first task with political overtones came with the reorganization of the Secretariat in 1933.

The reorganization, decreed by the Assembly, in fact tended to reaffirm the special rights that the great powers (originally France, Great Britain, Italy, and Japan) had insisted on having in the nomination of leading officials of the League. In addition, several top posts now were given to officers from lesser countries, in effect emphasizing the principle of wide geographic representation. But neither the new officials nor the old credited Avenol's leadership as they had Drummond's. One former under-secretary flatly says that Avenol's record had been marred by grave faults and sympathy with French reactionaries.[7] The final chapter of Avenol's incumbency remains somewhat murky, but it is obvious that he never attempted another *démarche* so dramatic as his visit to Mussolini.

The record of the two Secretaries-General of the League shows a mixture of innovation and unused capacity, developments partly based on the personal attributes of the officeholders, and partly a reflection of the confused political situation of a world skidding into war. Drummond had invented the international civil service for the League, but concentrated on indirect influence while leaving undeveloped the powers which might have given him a more leading public role. His successor claimed and perhaps sometimes showed more public flamboyance, but with insensitive timing. Drummond's indirect course had necessarily to be largely passive, for it depended on the willingness of delegates to bring problems to him. No long-range program could be developed through such procedures, although it is likely that the freedom he gave to his technically-minded officials resulted in rapid and full development of the League's capacity in unexplored fields of economic and social cooperation. In proposing and directing a long-range program, Avenol certainly fared no better.

The Model of the International Labor Organization

While the League of Nations took shape in the negotiations of the statesmen at Paris, a group of labor leaders and social welfare specialists formed the League's sister agency, the International Labor Organization (ILO).[8] As in the case of the League, negotiations for the ILO gave scant attention to provision for a secretariat. Almost absent-mindedly the founding conference provided in the ILO Constitution that the new body should have a permanent secretariat called the International Labor Office, which would be headed by a Director.

What came out of the Paris deliberations, conducted under pressure and without regular schedules or participation of all the members of the Labor Commission of the peace conference, resembled the League pattern only incidentally. The ILO would operate through complex, hierarchical administrative arrangements. An International Labor Conference would meet to set general policy; it would appoint a Governing Body, which would supervise the International Labor Office and appoint its Director. The Director would report to the Governing Body, which like the Conference was to be made up of government, labor, and management representatives in the pattern that became a distinguishing characteristic of the organization. Thus, the bare constitutional bones implied that the Director would work firmly under the control of the representatives of governments and policy-making groups.[9]

The ILO Constitution named the Office as a principal part of the new agency. The Director was to attend all meetings of the Governing Body and serve as Secretary-General of the International Labor Conference. He could speak by invitation. The Director was to appoint the staff, giving attention to geographical distribution and including women among his subordinates. Specific functions were assigned. The Office had the task, as did the League Secretariat for the Assembly, of preparing the agenda of the Conference, and was to collect statistics and make studies of industrial life and labor, especially on matters to be brought before the Conference. It was instructed to publish a periodical on labor. It could carry out investigations ordered by the Conference and also execute any other tasks assigned it by the Conference. It had the express right to communicate with the specialized government departments dealing with labor and industrial problems (not exclusively the foreign affairs departments) as channels of communication, and also had the right of aid from the League's Secretary-General where it could be given.

Finally, the Secretary-General was to receive from the Director reports accounting for expenditures.

These constitutional provisions closely followed a British draft which had been the basis of discussion at the Paris conference. The officials who prepared the draft had had considerable experience with international cooperation in labor matters, and they displayed a practical attitude at the conference. It could be expected then that the conception of the Director's role would not differ markedly from that which guided Sir Eric Drummond. If this expectation were true, the future Director would be a public servant and would operate within careful limits and with a highly pragmatic style. It would have been no surprise to find the new Director chosen from the ranks of civil servants.

No sense of urgency seemed to hurry the choice, for with a temporary Secretary-General, the first International Labor Conference met and chose the first Governing Body. Meanwhile, the temporary Secretariat gathered experience and became the logical recruiting ground for the new post. By the time the Governing Body met in the summer of 1919, a British civil servant, Harold Butler, who had a reputation for brilliance, and a French *fonctionnaire,* Arthur Fontaine, who had also been involved in the Paris conference and in earlier labor cooperation, led the field as candidates. Fontaine failed to give a clear indication of his wishes and was elected chairman of the Governing Body, removing him from the list of candidates. Butler's chances, however, were not enhanced by the selection of an Englishman as Secretary-General of the League. At this point the name of Albert Thomas appeared, and this Socialist who served France as wartime Minister of Munitions received the appointment as Director of the International Labor Office.[10]

Albert Thomas' background contrasted with that of Drummond, Butler or any other British civil servant about as much as one could imagine possible. This was a dynamic, flamboyant personality, an orator, a controversial writer, a member of the French Parliament and of the government. He proved himself an innovator and in doing so invented a pattern for the Directors of the International Labor Office which has never been abandoned. The first Director of the Office took his place as a man in the public eye and remained one until his greatly lamented death.

As Director of the International Labor Office, Thomas was ever in evidence in ILO meetings, intervening even during exchanges of insults by hotheaded delegates to the International Labor Conference. He soon made it clear that he was the guiding spirit of the Governing Body, and managed eventually to win the ill will of some delegates who did not appreciate his boldness. His annual report to the Governing Body became the channel for a broadcast of his views on social problems.[11] It contained specific proposals, advice, cautions, and wide-ranging comments. A special time during the meetings of the Conference was set aside for discussing it; this practice is still followed.

Thomas insisted on the independence of the ILO and on his own management of the staff. The relationship of the ILO with the League never became as close as the Treaty of Versailles and the Paris negotiations implied it should be. The provision of the ILO constitution for review of the organization's budget by the League Council assumed no importance. Thomas and his staff, at the same time, developed rapidly and profoundly the system of dealing directly with the government departments concerned with ILO matters and bypassing foreign offices. Moreover, the Office did not hesitate to maintain contact with nonofficial bodies in both labor and management fields.[12]

These contacts and Thomas' broad exploration and thought brought exciting agendas, well prepared by expert staff work, before the Governing Body and the Conference. The ILO moved ahead with the preparation of labor conventions, bringing an unheard-of degree of international regulation and standards to matters which could easily have been regarded as outside the purview of such an agency. These conventions and the deliberations of the various organs and special conferences, moreover, did not represent in Thomas' view mere reactions to existing complaints. Rather, the Director and his staff regarded them as part of a program which under their guidance the ILO could carry out. Unquestionably, the International Labor Office and Albert Thomas had a great influence and leading position in the work of the organization. After Thomas' death in 1932, the tradition of leadership was carried on by his successors, who included such impressive figures as Harold Butler, who had been Deputy Director; E.J. Phelan; and John Winant.

Thomas and Drummond, side-by-side in Geneva, furnished a record of two very different approaches to the task of heading an international secretariat. These two pioneer international officials began their work with limited constitutional instructions and rights. Both stood in the shadow of a diplomatic past which hardly seemed to encourage a great deal of initiative. Despite that shadow, Drummond brought the enlightened idea of international civil service, and Thomas introduced incandescent leadership.

The early experience of the League and the ILO demonstrated that the head of an international secretariat that dealt in any way with political questions would inevitably become involved with their substance. He could stand aside from political problems only by becoming a mere cipher. The degree of involvement, however, was not constant. It depended on the constitutional provisions of the organization, the administrative structure of its secretariat, and the personal views of its head. These views varied greatly. They tended to be a distillation of the knowledge, careers, and personalities of the chief officials.

The two approaches in Geneva to the work of directing international secretariats could hardly have been in greater contrast. Neither could the mature image of the office of the Secretary-General and that of the Director. Each approach achieved its successes. Each did something to demonstrate to the statesmen at San Francisco in 1945 something about the limits of the activities of international officials.

CHAPTER II

THE MODELS MODERNIZED

The fifty countries that would emerge from World War II as victors required two months at San Francisco in the spring of 1945 to draft the United Nations Charter. It came forth neither full-blown from the ashes of war nor as a foreordained heir of the League Covenant. But the models inherited from the first great international organization for peacekeeping were modernized.

Four time stages can be discerned in this modernizing process. Unofficial but influential talks had begun well before the first official drafts were completed by the United States Department of State in mid-1943. United States planning and less-publicized discussions in the United Kingdom, the Soviet Union, and China contributed to the second stage, which was achieved in the Dumbarton Oaks Conference in the autumn of 1944. The third stage was that of the San Francisco Conference. A final stage of detailed planning took place in the meetings of the Preparatory Commission in London in the winter of 1945 and the subsequent first part of the first session of the General Assembly.

In each stage, certain issues with regard to the office of Secretary-General emerged. The first and most general related to its political status and expectations. Other issues were more concrete and included the selection of the Secretary-General, his term of office and its degree of autonomy, and the appointment of senior officials of the Secretariat. The official planning and negotiations did not deal uniformly or even comprehensively with these issues. Planners and delegates, sensitive to the horrifying war around them, concentrated on problems of international peace and security. The office of Secretary-General might well have been viewed as a secondary, largely administrative matter. In any case, the powers and potential of the Secretary-General held no central focus of attention at the San Francisco Conference, where the discussion of the office was thin and incomplete.

Two different points of view seem to have led to the omission of detailed discussion of the authority and influence of the office. The first foresaw the office of the Secretary-General as subordinate to other, deliberative organs. The other regarded the draft texts as an adequate distillation of earlier experience. Only after the San Francisco Conference had passed its work to the Preparatory Commission for further elucidation did the office of Secretary-General receive sharper definition.

Wartime Beginnings

Unofficial discussions, in which former high officials of the League of Nations were involved, pointed toward an expansion of the political importance of the Secretary-General of any new peace-keeping organization. Groups brought together by the Royal Institute of International Affairs in London and by the Carnegie Endowment for International Peace in Washington both urged going well beyond League practice. This consensus had special poignancy because of the fact that Drummond was a participant in the British discussion. The Washington group assumed that the new chief administrative officer would be a United States national, since that country would be a principal supporter of the postwar organization.[1]

Much of the common currency of the League Secretariat was reissued in these reports, which were placed in the hands of official planners in Washington and London. Some of the boldest thinking of 1919 was revived. The unofficial planners projected a Secretary-General who would have functions appropriate for Venizelos had he become chancellor of the League. In effect, the reports held that despite general admiration for Drummond's methods, his powers would be insufficient for the postwar world. They looked forward to giving institutional and public character to the private and diplomatic methods and results attributed to Drummond, while fully retaining his idea of an international civil service.

The United States undertook an elaborate planning effort for the postwar organization.[2] The drafts prepared by the Department of State eventually became the basis of discussion at Dumbarton Oaks, and therefore must be considered as especially influential in reaching the decisions embodied in the Charter. From the first, the State

Department planners agreed with the unofficial study groups on the need for a politically potent chief permanent official.

The Draft Constitution of June, 1943 proposed giving the chief officer—then called general secretary—the permanent chairmanship of the peace-keeping Council. In case of an actual or threatened breach of the peace, he could convene the Council and call on the parties to desist. The Staff Charter of August, 1943 titled the chief officer "director-general," and proposed giving him duties similar to those of the earlier draft. When an outline of these papers was put before Franklin D. Roosevelt after the Teheran Conference, he suggested a new higher level post, called "moderator." As in the earlier proposals, the moderator would be a statesman of international reputation, but Roosevelt's idea emphasized his freedom to act as chairman of political bodies and as a conciliator who, by overcoming disagreements among permanent members, might increase the flexibility of a Council limited by the requirement of great-power unanimity. When further discussions failed to clarify the role of the moderator, the suggestion disappeared. So did provisions giving the chief officer the right to act as chairman and to place matters involving peace and security on the agenda of the Council.

Although the early State Department drafts sharply revised the League idea and even exceeded the scope of unofficial suggestions, in the rush to prepare for Dumbarton Oaks the planners returned to a simpler conception, closely conforming to the League model as it had evolved in practice. This meant that plans for freeing the chief officer from administrative supervision of the Secretariat in favor of greater political participation also disappeared.

Regarding the selection of the chief officer, the State Department planners suggested that he be appointed by the Assembly with the approval of the Council, so safeguarding the rights of the great powers to block an objectionable nomination. The project placed before the Dumbarton Oaks Conference did not contain radical alterations of the League ideas, and it omitted administrative details.

During the Dumbarton Oaks talks,[3] China and the United Kingdom secured acceptance of the idea that the Secretary-General should be authorized to put before the Council any matter which he thought would affect peace and security. With such a provision, no state would necessarily have to take responsibility for involving the international organization in the consideration of charges against another state. The Secretary-General could act on his own initiative before the Council. But no attention was given to providing him with a similar possibility in the General Assembly.

The United States draft and the Chinese suggestions foresaw an international civil service which would be widely recruited. But beyond this, only the Chinese paper attempted to specify the nature of the Secretary-General's immediate staff. Its suggestion for six deputy secretaries-general, rather in the style of the League of Nations, did not win support and disappeared.

Finally, the method for selecting the Secretary-General caused discussion. Consistently with its conception of the dominant role of the great powers, the Soviet Union proposed that the Security Council recommend to the General Assembly the name of a Secretary-General. This differed somewhat from the United States draft, which provided that the Council concur in the election of the Secretary-General by the Assembly. The difference was one of emphasis, and when the majority appeared willing to accept the Soviet view, the United States did so also.

As far as the Secretary-General and his office were concerned, the four powers (China, Great Britain, the Soviet Union, and the United States) completed their preparations for San Francisco at Dumbarton Oaks. Little controversial language had been injected into the original United States draft, and the generally conservative tone remained. The Secretary-General would have only one important new power, which was to provide an alternative to a governmental complaint as a means of bringing a matter before the Council.

Consensus at San Francisco

The Dumbarton Oaks draft sketched the powers and functions of the office of Secretary-General only in broadest outline.[4] The San Francisco Conference [5] had the right to change it in principle and to fill out its details. In fact, the delegates devoted little attention to the principles underlying the office of Secretary-General. The nearest they came to a fundamental examination was a discussion of broadening its powers to call attention to possible dangers to the peace. Much more time was spent in examining methods of appointing the Secretary-General and on proposals for the nomination of the top officials of the organization.

The politically-oriented provision to permit the Secretary-General to call threats to or breaches of the peace to the attention of the Security Council attracted no adverse criticism whatever in the San Francisco Conference. Two small countries, Venezuela and Uruguay, originated unsuccessful attempts to give the Secretary-General yet wider authority to engage the attention of the United Nations in matters of peace and security. Venezuela proposed giving him the option of bringing matters of peace and security before either the General Assembly or the Security Council. The proposal received some support, but encountered the convincing argument that the Secretary-General would be intolerably burdened if he had to choose between two major organs of the United Nations.

The Uruguayan proposal sought the extension of the Secretary-General's area of discretion from peace and security matters to any violation of the Charter. This idea would have greatly broadened the Secretary-General's political concern. It won considerable support, but not enough for adoption. Opposition to it was led by the United Kingdom, supported by Canada and New Zealand, on the grounds that it would have given wider scope to the Secretary-General than to member states, which could bring only matters of peace and security before the Security Council. Another line of argument held that to give the Secretary-General such wide authority would place him in a most difficult position.[6]

The defeat of the Venezuelan and Uruguayan proposals led to the unanimous approval of the text at the committee level. With editorial revision it became Article 99 of the Charter. The Secretary-General would have limited access to the Security Council, but could deal with highly important matters of peace and security. To this extent the model of the office based on the League of Nations experience was updated.

Procedures for nominating the Secretary-General have a number of political implications, even though they do not define the political role of the office. To the degree that the Secretary-General has independent powers, the interest in obstructing or promoting certain candidates increases. In any case, his appointment would be reviewed by one or more of the principal organs of the organization. The wider his support in these organs, the more free would he be to develop the role of the Secretariat and his own influence. If he really was an alternative channel by which the Security Council could be seized of a dispute, his support by the great powers would permit him to function with independence and dispatch. With such backing, the Secretary-General would be in a position to build trust upon trust and could be well informed and impartial.

Broad support might have to be obtained at a price. The Secretary-General might have to be all things to all men in order to keep it. His policies might deliberately be kept weak and vacillating in order to avoid alienating support. This might be particularly true in his relations with the General Assembly, where a broad spectrum of interests obviously would be represented.

Nevertheless, only a few members of the San Francisco Conference offered suggestions for more detailed provisions in the Dumbarton Oaks draft relating to the appointment of the Secretary-General. These suggestions dealt mainly with the involvement of the Security Council in the appointment process. Several small powers, including Australia, Ecuador, Honduras, Liberia, New Zealand, and Uruguay, proposed reserving to the General Assembly the entire decision on the naming of the Secretary-General. Uruguay also wanted a provision for a slate of three candidates from which the Assembly would elect the chief officer. Mexico and Venezuela were willing to give the Council a role, Venezuela pointing out that only with the approval of the Council could the Assembly make an efficacious choice.

The Soviet Union brought in a plan for the election of a great-power national for a two-year term, after which he would be ineligible for immediate reelection. The proposal for short tenure without the possibility of reelection drew criticism from the British and Chinese. The Soviet representative proved willing to compromise, and the Big Five proposed an amended text which provided for election of a Secretary-General by the General Assembly on the recommendation of the Security Council for a term of three years.[7] He would be eligible for reelection.

This proposal by the powers sponsoring the resolution failed to meet the main criticism voiced by the small states. The sponsoring powers' suggestion meant that the Security Council would not only have a role in the selection process but would also control the nomination of candidates. From the point of view of the great powers, this procedure reflected political reality, but to many of the smaller states, it meant control by the society of great powers. Finally, the question of how the proposed Security Council action related to the Yalta voting formula, which provided for unanimity of the permanent members of the Security Council on substantive matters, was not immediately clear from the proposed text.

In the subsequent debate, which included procedural complications that need not be examined here, the sponsoring powers clung to their insistence on making the Security Council an indispensable part of electing the Secretary-General. The United States gestured in the direction of the critics by proposing that the text read that the Council nomination should be by a majority of seven members. On the issue of voting, the Soviet representative argued that provisions for the composition of the Security Council majority were needless, since a majority of seven members implied the concurrence of the five permanent members. The Belgian representative, who had submitted a text which specified that the majority need not include the permanent members, urged that the Charter unambiguously state that there should not be a veto on the election of the Secretary-General.

In the final consideration of the election procedure, the difference between the great powers and their critics stood out sharply. France, Great Britain, and the Soviet Union argued that since the election of a Secretary-General fell into the category of important questions, it was subject to the veto. In addition, the British and Soviet representatives pointed out that a Secretary-General needed the support and confidence of the great powers. In a placating speech, the United States delegate claimed that the General Assembly had a veto on the Security Council action, which was only a nomination. This, he asserted, would ensure that the Secretary-General would have the necessary confidence of both bodies, although the Security Council's support was more important since that body met continuously.

The main challenge, flung down by Belgium, the Netherlands,

Canada, and Australia, concerned the independence of the Secretary-General and the influence of great-power agreement on the acceptability of a man of marked individuality. The Dutch representative expressed fear that only a nonentity could be persuaded to take the office, while Australia and Belgium warned that the independence of the Secretary-General would be jeopardized. Australia later declared itself willing to accept the reasoning presented by the United States at Dumbarton Oaks, and no longer opposed the idea of great-power agreement on a Secretary-General. India also accepted this idea, arguing that the nonpermanent members of the Council would change while the Secretary-General and the permanent members needed a long-term working relationship, which could be guaranteed by requiring the concurrence of the great powers in the selection of a chief officer. In the end, efforts to alter the Security Council voting procedure with regard to the Secretary-General or to omit the Council from the nominating process failed.

The Netherlands did succeed in getting the acceptance of proposals to omit any definition of the term of office, and to emphasize the administrative nature of the office by substituting "appointment" for "election" by the General Assembly.

The means by which top-level officials of the Secretariat were to be appointed raised questions of import for the role and influence of the Secretary-General. A chief officer who could choose his subordinates on his own responsibility would be able to organize a strong, cooperative and responsive group of advisers to increase his own influence.

If, on the other hand, the Assembly were to elect his closest associates, they would have a standing not far removed from his own. Even if he were required merely to present his subordinates for the approval of the Assembly, something of his freedom of action would be dissipated, since he would have to select persons to whom the minimum objections would be made. If the Security Council were involved in this process of approval or given exclusive authority, his ability to select a staff of his own design would be still further reduced. Finally, a prescription that the immediate subordinates of the Secretary-General should be selected on the basis of geographical or political qualification would mean reduction of the chief officer's prestige and control from another direction.

The question of the extent of the Secretary-General's freedom of choice with regard to his staff was related to how he was chosen and what political influence he should have. If he was to be chosen by the General Assembly alone, the great powers would be likely to insist on specifying the number and role of his subordinates. On the other hand, if the Security Council was to have an important share in the process of choosing the Secretary-General, the great powers might feel less need to have a hand in the appointment of his subordinates.

A Soviet-originated proposal by the sponsoring powers served as the pivot of the debate. It sought to flesh out the Dumbarton Oaks text with provisions for the appointing of four deputy secretaries-general by the General Assembly and the Security Council. It raised questions regarding the independence of the chief officer, administrative efficiency, and the geographical distribution of appointments.

The proposal produced little enthusiasm, but met with cogent criticism, in which Canada led. The Canadian delegate maintained that the Secretary-General would find it difficult to carry out his duties if he could not select his four deputies. The delegate feared that important decisions would have to be taken by a five-man committee, and he asserted that appointment by the Council and the Assembly of deputy secretaries-general would violate the principle of international civil service. The representative of New Zealand pointed out that such a plan made it likely that the entire top level of the Secretariat would be drawn from the permanent members of the Security Council. Moreover, since there was no proposal to make the deputies eligible for reelection, the entire scheme would guarantee instability. The five great powers reconsidered their proposal. The Soviet Union proved willing to agree to the suggestion that the deputy secretaries-general should be eligible for reelection and that there should be a total of five, one of whom would serve as alternate to his chief while the others would be delegated to particular organs.

Some support for the new proposal was evidenced, based on arguments that deputies would be needed to perform specialized functions for the main United Nations organs. As for the principle of international civil service, supporters of the amended proposal claimed that the international character of the Secretariat would be protected since the deputy secretaries-general would be elected in the same way as the Secretary-General.

The altered proposal came under attack from a number of directions. One argument held that no one could foresee how many deputies would be needed and that this was a decision best made later by the General Assembly. A number of representatives reiterated that to elect the deputies would interfere with the international character of the Secretariat. Others flatly favored the appointment of any deputies by the Secretary-General, on the grounds that he might otherwise be deprived of an efficient relationship with his subordinates.

Indications of division appeared during renewed consultations among the Big Five. The United States, seeking a compromise, urged that the chief officer have the responsibility of appointing his deputies, subject, however, to the approval of the organ with which each would be associated. The British representatives scorned even a compromise, and argued the same sort of case presented earlier by Canada. But the Soviet Union clung to its insistence on the appointment of deputy secretaries-general by election.

In the end, the conference fell back on the language of the Dumbarton Oaks proposal, and refused either to provide for deputy secretaries-general or for a definite number to be elected by the General Assembly and the Security Council. This decision left the problem of staffing the top level of the Secretariat to a later stage. It meant also that the small powers by a slight margin—for there were divisions in their ranks—had repelled the great-power attempt to ensure national composition of the immediate staff of the Secretary-General. This small-power victory had real significance, in view of the general opinion that a national of one of the great powers would become Secretary-General, with the consequence that the other great powers would insist on the appointment of their nominees to the second level in order to ensure balance and cooperation.

The decision to avoid constitutional provisions regarding deputy secretaries-general fitted in with the acceptance of the Dumbarton Oaks provision that the Secretary-General should be the chief administrative officer, and ensured a centralized administration. The

Secretary-General would have full responsibility for the staff. This course accorded both with the example of the League of Nations and the recommendations of former League officials.

Although the draft designating the Secretary-General as chief administrative officer caused no controversy, examination of his status and duties resulted in important additions at San Francisco. In order to avoid the listing of specific duties, it was decided that the language of the Charter should be kept broad enough to cover all political and administrative functions without repeating instructions referred to elsewhere in the Charter, e.g., registration of treaties. A text emerged which provided that the Secretary-General should act in that capacity at all meetings of the principal organs; he would also submit an annual report to the General Assembly.

To these general provisions a still more significant addition was made. The chief officer was to carry out "such other functions as are or may be entrusted to him by the Organization." This idea eventually became part of Article 98 of the Charter. It must have appeared at the time as the logical complement of the Secretary-General's service to deliberative organs. Yet the language was broadly permissive. It touched directly on the authority granted the Security Council in the field of enforcement measures, and on the wide possibilities open to it and the General Assembly in the peaceful settlement of disputes and other aspects of keeping the peace. It might well have been more thoroughly discussed in order to create expectations for the future.

The same lack of controversy and thorough discussion characterized the elaboration of the Dumbarton Oaks provision for an international secretariat. Canada took the lead in examination of the drafts, submitting texts which provided that international civil servants might neither seek nor receive governmental instructions. A further provision would obligate member governments to respect the exclusively international character of the work of the Secretary-General and his staff and not to attempt to influence them. These provisions became Article 100 of the Charter, and reflect insistence on the international status of the Secretariat and a desire to strengthen its independence of member governments. Thus, Drummond's innovation of an international civil service became a constitutional principle for the United Nations.

Another Canadian proposal, accepted with no difficulty, established a basis for selecting the international civil service. It was the provision, which now appears in Article 101, to the effect that the staff should be appointed under regulations designed by the General Assembly and in conformity with the highest standards of efficiency, competence, and integrity. A further suggestion introduced the idea that "due regard" should be paid to the principle of broad geographical distribution in recruiting the staff. This entire text reflected the hopes of the small and middle powers that the Secretariat would not be preempted by the great powers.

Planning by the Preparatory Commission

The signing of the United Nations Charter in June, 1945 fixed the results of the San Francisco Conference in final form. The conference also established a Preparatory Commission to complete specific planning for the new organization. Its work,[8] carried out in London and mainly in the Commisssion's Executive Committee, yielded a much more articulated picture of the office of Secretary-General, which found approval during the first session of the General Assembly, held in London early in 1946.

As in the earliest unofficial discussions of the new world organization, the ideas of former officials and delegates in the League of Nations proved influential during the Preparatory Commission stage. The membership of the Commission and its Executive Committee included such figures of League days as Philip Noel-Baker, and the subcommittee which drafted most of the texts relating to the Secretary-General and his staff had as its chairman Adrian Pelt, the last director of the League's information section and then a Netherlands representative. Its secretary was Martin Hill, an Englishman who had been in the League Secretariat. A draft report produced by Pelt and Hill on the character and organization of the United Nations Secretariat survived three stages of discussion, and was accepted without alteration or much controversy. What disagreement there was centered on the administrative structure of the Secretariat and on the term of office of the Secretary-General.

The Preparatory Commission moved far toward a specification of how important a figure the Secretary-General would be. While it was decided not to define the characteristics of the man who should be appointed, his task was described in such terms as to extend the tacit decision, made at San Francisco, that the chief officer should be blessed with high political ability and experience. The Pelt-Hill draft emphasized that the Secretary-General would have political duties requiring "the exercise of the highest qualities of political judgment, tact and integrity." It underscored the significance of Article 99 as giving the Secretary-General powers unique in the history of international organizations. It pointed toward an expansion of his political role by remarking that he could bring *any* matter, even beyond disputes and situations, before the Security Council if he saw in it a danger to peace and security. On this basis, the Pelt-Hill draft ventured the prophecy that the Secretary-General might have "an important role to play as mediator and as an informal adviser of many Governments, and will undoubtedly be called upon from time to time, in the exercise of his administrative duties, to take decisions which may justly be called political."

This general view of the Secretary-General is remarkable in two ways. First, it incorporates the lessons which the officials of the League believed they had learned from their work in Geneva. Second, it produced strong support and no overt opposition. No government, no matter how desirous of maintaining the fullest independence in foreign affairs, saw in this neatly-drafted passage any real danger to itself.

With regard to the representational functions of the Secretary-General, the Pelt-Hill report postulated that the United Nations could not prosper without "the active and steadfast support of the peoples of the world." "But the Secretary-General, more than anyone else," the draft continued, "will stand for the United Nations as a whole." The Secretary-General, it was said, would have to embody the principles and ideals of the Charter with the implied aim of gaining popular support. The new importance imputed to this public role may have reflected, as much as anything else, Pelt's close association with the League's Information Section. Whatever its ultimate source, this sketch of a public personality for the Secretary-General added greater depth to his role as an influence in political and security matters.

Some of the Secretary-General's functions, said the Pelt-Hill draft, might be delegated to subordinates. But he would subject all to his supervision and control, "the ultimate responsibility" remaining "his alone." Were the Secretariat to do a major task well, therefore, the legal, official, political, and representational aspects of the work would be credited to the Secretary-General; were the Secretariat to be found lacking, the blame would be his.

The report deals with day-to-day functions of the Secretary-General in a much more routine fashion. He would have general administrative tasks and certain specified ones in relation to the principal organs. Since he would be the channel of communication with the United Nations and its organs and would have to prepare for and administer the decisions taken by the organs, he would have a general coordinating function. But the political content of these functions was not spelled out. He would be responsible for choice of staff, and his leadership would determine the character and efficiency of the Secretariat as a whole. It was also assumed that he would have primary responsibility for preparing a budget under the financial regulations to be designed by the General Assembly.

Taken as a whole, the view of the Secretary-General adumbrated in the Pelt-Hill report represents that of a highly influential public official, whose views on the policy questions before the organization would be felt at every juncture. Not only would he have administrative responsibility with its manifold opportunities to interpret general policies, but he would also draw up the budget. He would represent the organization before the public and would have the opportunity to publicize the ideas which he considered important. He would have the right to bring any matter affecting peace and security before the Security Council, and moreover would have the chance to advise and mediate behind the scenes. The slender structure of office designed at San Francisco now had taken on considerable bulk.

The first attempt within the Preparatory Commission structure to determine the term of office of the Secretary-General reproduced the earlier difficulties at San Francisco. Terms ranging from three to ten years were suggested. Further discussion finally produced a compromise on a five-year appointment, with the possibility of renewing the appointment for one further term. The basis of the compromise seems to have been that on the one hand a Secretary-

General might remain in office for ten years, as the League's chief officer had, while on the other hand his term would not be so long as to negate altogether for some years the control implicit in an imminent election. Although the recommendation was made without opposition, Czechoslovakia, the Soviet Union, and Yugoslavia made known certain reservations. The decision represented a concession to the views of the small powers, which had argued at San Francisco that the Secretariat ought to be stable as well as independent.

A similar view of the independence of the Secretariat lay behind recommendations in regard to the organization of the Secretariat and the immediate staff of the Secretary-General. Yet the Preparatory Commission could not avoid reinstating at least some features of the great-power proposal that they should in effect appoint deputy secretaries-general.

The Pelt-Hill report set out a grading system for officials subordinate to the Secretary-General. The highest rank was to be that of Assistant Secretary-General. Each Assistant Secretary-General would head a department of the Secretariat, of which there were to be eight. It was also recommended that one of the Assistant Secretaries-General be designated to act as deputy to the Secretary-General whenever he might be absent or otherwise unable to carry on his work. Even though the possibility that the Secretary-General might remove himself from his functions was alluded to, no consideration was given to the contingency that the members might want him removed. The United Kingdom at one juncture submitted a paper suggesting a procedure for the suspension and dismissal of the Secretary-General. It was withdrawn almost immediately, apparently because most delegates believed that he could not in any case continue in office in the face of opposition by the permanent members of the Security Council.

These features caused considerable controversy and dissent. The Soviet Union proposed a separate secretariat for each main organ of the United Nations, and three service departments—administrative and financial, legal, and public information—to carry out common functions. Andrei A. Gromyko, the Soviet delegate, referred to his proposal as based on an "organic" principle, and said that his general attitude would be conditioned by the recommendation adopted on the structure of the Secretariat.

The Soviet proposal would have had the effect of putting the individual secretariats under greater influence and control from the organs they served than from the Secretary-General. The prevailing view sought to organize the Secretariat around general functions but did not entirely reject the organic principle, since a department for the maintenance of international peace and security, which would be engaged mainly with the business of the Security Council, was projected. The same might be said of the Department of Trusteeship and Information from Non-Self-Governing Territories, although the latter half of its title represented subject matter for the General Assembly. Two departments were proposed to deal with matters within the purview of the Economic and Social Council. For the General Assembly—the organ with the widest scope of any—a projected central bureau was to provide the immediate managing staff. The Assembly's coordinative function would be supported by the departments of the Secretariat.

A series of compromises smoothed away the conflicts concerning the administrative structure. These included bargains over who should be placed in the posts of Assistant Secretary-General. Because there were eight posts, the great powers could each have one of their nationals at the top administrative level, even if, as was becoming increasingly likely, the Secretary-General was to be chosen from among the small powers.

As for the Soviet demand for an "organic" scheme for the Secretariat, the United States representative eventually announced that he had been much impressed with the cogency of a Soviet argument that since the Security Council would be in permanent session and would deal with delicate matters, it should have its own service unit. He professed himself willing now to accept this idea and to drop his earlier bid for appointment of an under-secretary-general. This would leave the Secretariat, in his new view, with six substantive departments and two service units, the economic and social departments remaining separate. Thereupon, the Soviet delegate agreed to the creation of a department within the Secretariat to serve the Security Council instead of an altogether separate secretariat for it. If such a department were recommended, he told the committee, then he would agree that there should be separate economic and social departments. The revised United States scheme, which was accepted, now envisaged a liaison and conference services unit, and an administrative and financial service, to replace the earlier projected personnel and administration and treasury departments. The central bureau disappeared.

The basis of the bargain represented in this decision lay in offering the Soviet Union the opportunity to nominate the Assistant Secretary-General to head the department serving the Security Council. Four posts would be filled by nationals of the other permanent members of the Security Council, while the remaining offices would be held by nationals from among the smaller powers. To give the political and security post to a Soviet national fitted with the Soviet preoccupation with the role of the Security Council. At the same time, with the allocation of almost all anticipated functions to various departments and the elimination of the central bureau, the Secretary-General would have control of his staff only through the medium of political appointees. Thus, the design projected at London in many respects revived the sponsoring powers' proposal at San Francisco to write into the Charter provisions for a limited number of deputies to the Secretary-General, each of whom would head an important part of the staff. It also represented a considerable adaptation of the Executive Committee's proposal in the direction of the Soviet minority position.

Much of the remaining planning by the Preparatory Commission fell into the technical realm, dealing with such matters as staff regulations and rules for financial administration. Important decisions were taken, however, to safeguard the international character of the Secretariat. With a minimum of discussion, the Preparatory Commission not only affirmed the international nature of the Secretariat but also urged that no part of it should be made up of representatives of governments. The discussion also made it clear that even if there were no prohibition against hiring staff members for short terms, after which they would return to their governments, this should occur only exceptionally. The new Secretariat, like that of the League, was intended to be primarily a career service. Staff members were not to retain civil service or other status with governments for more than two years, and must decline to accept any national honor or remuneration while working in the international civil service. Furthermore, any official who chose to run for public office would have to resign.

These negative restrictions were combined with a conception of positive loyalty to the United Nations which would, however, involve no conflict with national loyalty since a "higher interest" (so reminiscent of League propaganda) would be served. "A broad international outlook and a detachment from national prejudice and narrow national interests," would be necessary for international officials. They would submit themselves to the exclusive authority of the Secretary-General and the discipline of his service, observing "the utmost discretion" about their business and not publishing or making public pronouncements except with permission of the Secretary-General.

The Secretariat would be recruited, as the Charter said, on the basis of competence and integrity with due regard to a wide geographical distribution. How to square these two requirements of Article 101 of the Charter was a principal problem for the Preparatory Commission.

In fact, the Preparatory Commission could not do so. To give heavy emphasis to either standard tends to eliminate the other. No generally accepted formula could either be designed or agreed upon to weight each factor. The Preparatory Commission reacted by leaving to the Secretary-General great discretion in setting up selection criteria for the staff. He would get some assistance from an International Civil Service Commission, the creation of which engaged much attention in the Preparatory Commission stage.

Despite the care with which the nature of the Secretariat and its protections were described, the precise execution of the plans posed a controversial and troublesome question for the Secretary-General and the organization. Moreover, the arrangements to distribute the Assistant Secretary-General posts would always remain as an argument for giving greater weight to political factors, expressed in the deceptive terms of geographical distribution, than to the presumably objective standards of civil service recruitment.

CHAPTER III

THE APPOINTMENT PROCESS

The process by which the Secretary-General is chosen has wide ramifications. It requires the concurrence of the two principal organs of the United Nations. In one of these, the Security Council, the agreement (or lack of it) of the permanent members controls all progress toward an appointment. After election, the Secretary-General needs the continued favor or acquiescence of both the Security Council and the General Assembly if he is to act without impediment. Consisting of national representatives, they may make their decisions independently of the Secretary-General, even though he may influence their work.

Because the Security Council must act to recommend a candidate for Secretary-General to the General Assembly, the permanent members of the Council necessarily must agree, or at least acquiesce. This produces negotiation and bargaining. Once a recommendation has been agreed upon by the Big Five in the Security Council, four more approving voices must be obtained before a recommendation can be adopted.[1] Although it seems unlikely that elected members would often coalesce to deny the wishes of the permanent members, such a situation could arise if the small states believed that a nomination for Secretary-General grew out of an unwillingness to consider their special interest in the matter.

It is conceivable that the Security Council could find it necessary to consult with leading representatives in the General Assembly or to bargain with them on the choice of a Secretary-General. This situation could arise if the Security Council tentatively decided on a candidate about whom reaction in the General Assembly was uncertain or who had only marginal support there. In such a case, members of the Security Council and their supporters in the General Assembly could well embark on a campaign of persuasion.

An incumbent Secretary-General wishing reappointment could be influential in both the Security Council and the General Assembly. His past record would be reviewed by the member governments. His actions in matters of security just before the expiration of his term might have special weight. At the same time, through informal conversations, he could presumably reach understandings with the members. And there is no prohibition against the Security Council's asking a Secretary-General for his views on issues before the organization or his approach to the office. Similar requests could conceivably be made by the General Assembly.

The rules of procedure of both the Security Council and the General Assembly reinforce the basis of bargaining created in the Charter.[2] The Security Council generally meets in public. To do otherwise requires a specific decision, but for the recommendation of a Secretary-General, closed meetings of the Council are obligatory. If public meetings force delegates to take positions which can be altered only with difficulty, private meetings increase the likelihood of face-to-face negotiation and offer the possibility of making suggestions without embarrassment.

The nominations of Trygve Lie, Dag Hammarskjöld, and U Thant emerged from meetings of the Security Council, the privacy of which was far from perfect. Delegates managed to convey at least the names and some of the discussions to the press. Such leaks of information tend to inject a greater element of uncertainty into the bargaining and to attract possibly extraneous pressures.

The General Assembly's rules of procedure would lead one to think that a process similar to that in the Security Council was foreseen. But the General Assembly in fact has never considered or discussed the nomination of a Secretary-General in either an open or a closed meeting. It has rather proceeded directly to a vote by a secret ballot. The voting has taken place in open sessions.[3]

The fact that the rules and practice of the General Assembly exempt the appointment of a Secretary-General from open discussion encourages consultation and negotiation among the members, for there is no opportunity to take a public position. In fact, the ease with which votes have been taken in the General Assembly on the appointment of the Secretary-General leaves no doubt that the necessary bargains are struck well before it is necessary to take and record a formal vote.

Trygve Lie

The first session of the United Nations General Assembly opened in an air of expectancy and drama on January 10, 1946, at London. A preliminary step was the election of a President. Earlier planning left an impression that the first President of the Assembly might have special importance for the future of the United Nations, because he might give one of the principal organs—which included representatives of all member countries—personal leadership and a distinctive political flavor at a crucial moment. For the sake of public impressions as well as for the efficient conduct of business, it was essential that a person of prestige and competence be elected. He would need such qualities as diplomatic skill, experience with international meetings, wide acquaintance among statesmen, and the support of many governments. These qualifications would also make a good Secretary-General.

Two names came to the fore at the opening meeting of the session. One of them was that of Paul-Henri Spaak, Foreign Minister of Belgium, prominent Socialist and expert politician. The other, publicly proposed by the Soviet Union despite the diplomatic awkwardness and procedural prohibition of nomination speeches, was Trygve Lie, Foreign Minister of Norway, also a Socialist and a prominent member of the wartime government-in-exile in London. Either of these men had the prestige and background necessary for the presidency of the General Assembly.

Despite Soviet opposition Paul-Henri Spaak won the post by a narrow margin. He was strongly supported by the British government, which had also indicated an unfavorable attitude toward Lie. The United States had originally backed Lie, but failed to press its case. The outcome of the election meant that some three weeks later Spaak presided over the election of his erstwhile rival to the office of Secretary-General.[4]

The appointment of Lie as Secretary-General came about officially in accordance with a strict ritual. No nominations were publicly made either in the Security Council or the General Assembly. The Council met in private session on January 30, 1946, and recommended Lie's name and his only to the General Assembly. On the following day, the General Assembly voted on the recommendation without discussion and adopted it by 46 votes to 3.

But back of the ritual lay countless discussions and much hard bargaining. The United States, the Soviet Union, and the United Kingdom came to the General Assembly with lists of candidates. Lie was first on none of these lists, which were revised after the election of Spaak to the presidency of the General Assembly. The British inclined at first to General Dwight D. Eisenhower and Gladwyn Jebb, the able Executive Secretary of the Preparatory Commission. The French apparently put forward the name of Henri Bonnet, Ambassador to the United States and a power in prewar international cultural cooperation. First on the United States list was Lester Pearson of Canada, while the Soviet list was headed by Stanoje Simić, Foreign Minister of Marshal Tito's Yugoslav government.[5] Lie was in the second place on both the Soviet and the United States lists.

Candidates who were great-power nationals soon were eliminated, an event foreshadowed in discussions in the Preparatory Commission and at San Francisco. It was striking but natural at the time that most of the names on the lists were those of Europeans.

The candidacy of Pearson drew considerable attention. As an individual, he had both the prestige and experience for the post. The case of Simić was more doubtful, for even in what remained of war time camaraderie, it was unlikely that a Communist would have been accepted as Secretary-General by the members of the United Nations. The Soviet Union in the end declared Pearson unacceptable on the basis of the argument that since the headquarters of the world organization was to be in North America, a European should be selected. The United States refused to accept Simić, and proposed Lie as its candidate after Pearson had been rejected. France acceded to Lie's nomination and so did the United Kingdom after Ernest Bevin, then Secretary of State for Foreign Affairs, had listened to strong pleas on behalf of his brother Social Democrat.

The negotiations preceding Lie's nomination emphasized the primitive political fact that the office of Secretary-General, itself not innocent of potentially influential features, could not be filled without attention to the wishes of the great powers. Their support of a statesman of a small country was, however, not a simple act of free will. Rather it represented the mutual checking of each other's influence by the United States and the Soviet Union and also the insistence by the small powers that no great-power national should fill the highest permanent office of the United Nations. From the point of view of the Secretary-General taking office, the bargaining augured that the great powers could never be overlooked. At the same time, it meant that the first Secretary-General was obligated to no single great power. This indicated that he had an area of maneuver in setting up his administration and in deciding on policies for it. It also meant that he could act as if he had strong great-power support, even though he would not necessarily be able to rely on it in all circumstances.

As an experienced politician, Lie no doubt regarded the calendar of his first term with some bemusement. He approached its end with a record on which arguments for the renewal of his appointment could be based. If he had made enemies—and he had incurred the wrath of the Chinese and of some of the Arab states by the beginning of 1950—he certainly also had made friends. By late 1949 the Secretary-General received indications of positive support for his reappointment. Among his backers were several of the great powers. It was apparently commonly assumed that Lie would be available, and that his reappointment would encounter no insuperable obstacles.

But the Secretary-General had in the first instance to decide whether he would be a candidate for reappointment. No matter what his decision, the course he should follow remained somewhat unclear. Drummond had not sought or been offered a second term. Moreover, there was some misgiving about, not to say open opposition to, another term for Lie. In these circumstances, how far could he go in making public his own desires? Any slightly equivocal statement would be interpreted as standard for a politician who desired to display due modesty. But if he took a flat position of refusal to run again, his own ability to direct his staff and to influence the course of yet unknown events during the remainder of his term might be reduced. Furthermore, such a course could encourage a flood of speculation and campaigning that could conceivably involve the office of Secretary-General in intense partisanship in the Security Council and the General Assembly.

Lie's first public response to the corridor gossip and informal encouragement to hope for another term came during a press conference in December, 1949. He has since declared that his mind was made up not to serve as Secretary-General again and that he so informed his family.[6] To the press corps he said:

> When I have completed my term of service as Secretary-General I shall be very happy to have been able to serve the United Nations for five years, and I am not a candidate for re-appointment.[7]

It soon became known that Britain, France, and the United States had decided that no one but Lie would be acceptable in a post which, they thought, he had managed competently. Nationalist China had made plain its stiff opposition, a result of the Secretary-General's comments on the status of the Taipeh government. Lie believed that he had the support of the Soviet Union, which was, however, boycotting the Security Council in protest against the presence of Nationalist China. Assuming that Nationalist China could be persuaded not to veto the reappointment, it seemed likely in June, 1950 that the compromise choice of 1946 would be repeated.

The unexpected North Korean attack on the Republic of Korea brought a sharp reaction from the Secretary-General, who called it a breach of the peace. This statement was followed by vituperative personal attacks on Lie in the Moscow press, which scarcely more than a month earlier had welcomed his visit to the Soviet capital. The denunciations created much doubt about what would happen. Furthermore, when the General Assembly began meeting in September, the Soviet delegation shunned any talk about the reappointment of Lie.

The meetings of the Security Council during September and October, 1950 disclosed no basis for a bargain. Lie actively kept himself informed of the developing situation, and even exerted some influence on the tactics used by his supporters and enemies. The Soviet Union openly opposed a plan, then being bruited about the United Nations lounges, to have the General Assembly simply extend Lie's term another two or three years without reference to the Security Council; at the same time, the Soviet representative refrained from flatly stating that he would veto the Secretary-General's candidacy for a new nomination. But this restraint soon turned into a veto, which, incidentally, relieved the Nationalist Chinese delegate of the necessity of doing anything more than abstaining.

While this was going on, the Secretary-General pressed the delegates of the Western powers for precise statements of their views. He went so far as to draft a letter, which he showed unsigned to certain representatives, insisting that he was not available for another term. Such tactics no doubt had the effect of forcing maximum expressions of confidence from the delegates presumed to be favorable to Lie and of impelling them to seek ever sharper instructions from their governments. Stopping short of a public statement, the Secretary-General nevertheless was using his position to influence the electoral process.

The Soviet Union played a solitary, provocative, and obstructive role. Its initial position, which involved the use of the veto, gave way to a new invitation to bargain over other candidates. This tactic was adopted when it became increasingly likely that the General Assembly could be induced to extend the Secretary-General's term. Yakov A. Malik even expressed Soviet willingness to accept Carlos Romulo, the outspokenly anti-Soviet statesman from the Philippines, Luis Padilla Nervo of Mexico, Sir Benegal N. Rau of India, or Charles Malik of Lebanon.

The Soviet attempt to resurrect negotiations had some effects. While there was insufficient interest in General Romulo or Dr. Malik to ensure their endorsement by the Security Council, Padilla Nervo did have a serious chance, providing that the United States reneged on its hardening commitment to Lie. The favorable response to Lie's candidature—he had received nine favorable votes in the initial consideration by the Security Council—shifted because of the regional appeal of the Soviet candidates and in response to the argument that the normal functioning of the organization should have priority and that an effective Secretary-General needed the backing of the great powers. If such a candidate could be found, this argument ran, he should be given the recommendation in preference to one who had a permanent member stiffly opposing him.

The most remarkable effect of the Soviet course came in the second of the two private (but leaky) meetings of the permanent members convoked because of the difficulties in the Council. With histrionic emphasis, Warren Austin, speaking for the United States, threatened the use of the veto to prevent the Council from recommending anyone but Lie. Austin declared:

> I do not believe a veto will become necessary, but the great moral principle of the unity of the free powers is at stake and I do not fear to use whatever means I can to maintain that unity.[8]

The United States stand forced the Council into a position of being unable to accept any candidate but Lie and of being equally unable to recommend him to the General Assembly. This impasse found the United States in the curious position of implicitly agreeing in principle with the Soviet Union that the person holding the office of Secretary-General was more important than the office itself.

The intense dispute in the Security Council had provided more than enough time to plan action in the General Assembly to extend Lie's term by three years. Austin's statement soon was followed by the collapse of further Soviet delaying tactics in both the Council and the General Assembly. On October 31 and November 1, 1950, the General Assembly took up a 14-nation draft resolution to extend the Secretary-General's term, and passed it with 46 votes in favor, five against, and eight abstentions. The majority exceeded by one vote that which Lie later declared as the minimum he required to stay in office.[9]

The debate in the General Assembly [10] served as an opportunity for the Soviet Union and its supporters to reiterate that their objection to Lie was on the one hand personal and on the other hand linked to his views. Not only was he unfit for office, in the Soviet view, but also he had supported the North Atlantic Treaty Organization, and such "illegal" creations of the vast majority of the General Assembly as the Interim Committee, the Commission on Korea, and that on the Balkans. Even the previously favored Twenty-Year Peace Plan became a blotch on Lie's record. Finally, Andrei Y. Vishinsky and his miniscule group of supporters promised that they would not deal with Lie if the General Assembly acted to extend his term of office.

While the United States based most of its argument in favor of the resolution it had cosponsored on legal considerations, Austin made clear that his government backed the Secretary-General for his personal qualities and because of his faithful service. The basic legal argument propounded by the sponsors of the resolution was that since the General Assembly originally set the term of office on its own authority it had the right to alter its original decision and extend the time period.

Lie, by this time committed to serving if the General Assembly should call on him to do so, explained his understanding of the vote:

> In the present circumstances, I feel that I am under an obligation to the United Nations not to refuse your mandate continuing me in office. . . . The United Nations cannot function effectively unless the Secretariat acts in the collective interest of the United Nations as a whole, and in the collective interest only. . . .
>
> I shall do my part towards the maintenance of similar relations with all the Member governments—without exception—during the next three years.[11]

His final effort to make clear to the Soviet Union that he looked forward to a resumption of once cordial relations, or at least a relationship of mutual tolerance, was answered by a complete Soviet boycott. The Soviet boycott was matched by the other members of the Soviet bloc. They addressed communications to the "United Nations Secretariat," and deliberately excluded the Secretary-General from social functions. Far more important was the fact that the Secretary-General no longer had normal business contacts with the Soviet group. The work of the Secretariat went on, and Lie took his usual place at the Security Council table and the General Assembly dais. But no longer could he take full part in conversations involving Cold War problems or put forward plans which would require the acquiescence or support of the permanent members of the Security Council. The work of his office was inhibited.[12]

Over a long period, this situation could not be tolerated, either by the Secretary-General or the members of the organization. Two alternative courses of action existed. On the one hand, the Secretary-General might resign, either before or after a replacement for him was found. In 1950 the Soviet Union gave sufficient support to a number of candidates, so that the basis for a deal seemed to exist. The United States might retract its threat to use the veto against any candidate but Lie if he were given an honorable opportunity to resign. On the other hand, the majority—and it would have to be a large one—could attempt to strengthen the Secretary-General's prestige by issuing declarations of commendation and confidence on every possible occasion. Such a consistent favoring of Lie would either induce the Soviet Union to relent its boycott, or, more likely, would risk further isolating the Soviet Union, perhaps even driving it from the organization.

During the autumn of 1952, Lie made his own choice. He decided to resign, continuing his functions until a successor could be chosen.[13] In making this decision he consulted only a few governmental figures. The British and French governments apparently were informed well in advance of the actual resignation, and the United States only after it was too late to secure a reversal. Thus, Lie's principal backer in the struggle for his reappointment had little opportunity to counsel him to continue in office, although by this time its once-blazing enthusiasm had cooled.

Lie's speech of resignation surprised the General Assembly and even his own immediate staff. The short statement on November 10, 1952 included a letter he had sent to Lester Pearson, then President of the General Assembly, in which he said that his decision had not been made public until the foreign ministers of all the permanent members of the Security Council had come to New York. It was made at a time, he said, when he could leave without damaging the United Nations and when it would be better for the organization, which he had agreed to continue to serve in 1950 because of the circumstances created by the aggression in Korea. He did not "want the position of Secretary-General to hinder in the slightest degree any hope of reaching a new understanding that would prevent world disaster," and thought a new man might be helpful. He insisted that no reason other than those stated had caused his resignation, thus denying that he was bowing to Soviet pressure.

Whatever his motives or his personal feelings about the Soviet attack on the office of Secretary-General, by resigning Lie could not help securing for the Soviet Union the simplest of its goals. The failure of the General Assembly to generate a flood of sentiment for keeping the first Secretary-General in office, and the immediate hunt for a successor, enhanced the Soviet success.

In these circumstances, even if Lie had attempted to influence the choice of his successor his efforts would most likely have been in vain. He had a strong preference for Pearson as the next Secretary-

General, but the Canadian statesman was scheduled for election to the presidency of the General Assembly. The holder of that office labors under a handicap as a candidate for the secretary-generalship. Furthermore, an endorsement by Lie might only have made Pearson's support among the Western European powers all the more suspicious to the Communist group.

Dag Hammarskjöld

Although long lists of candidates for the post of Secretary-General appeared immediately in the press and in corridor conversations at United Nations headquarters, five months were required to select a new chief administrative officer.[14] The lists contained most of the former candidates—Romulo, Padilla Nervo, Pearson, Spaak, Rau—and a few new ones—Nasrollah Entezam of Iran, Mrs. Vijaya Lakshmi Pandit of India, Charles Malik of Lebanon, Dirk U. Stikker of the Netherlands, and Erik Boheman of Sweden. Lie recalls that 17 names appeared on the lists. He does not seem to have tried to sponsor any candidate, or, if he did, it made little impression.

When the Security Council finally met, long after the foreign ministers of the Big Five had consulted, three names officially were proposed. The United States suggested Romulo, Denmark nominated Pearson, and the Soviet Union backed Stanislaw Skrzeszewski. The first two nominations clearly were serious. The Soviet Union's suggestion could not have been intended as more than "a stalking horse," and not a very effective one at that, for the Polish Foreign Minister's attainments, however estimable, had not penetrated beyond the Eastern bloc. No candidate got the necessary recommendation. Romulo received five affirmative votes, two negatives, and four abstentions; Skrzeszewski got one favorable vote, three negatives, and seven abstentions; and Pearson came closest to wide support with nine favorable votes, one abstention, and a Soviet veto.

The next meeting of the Security Council to consider a recommendation saw an effort by the Soviet Union to gain approval for Mrs. Pandit. This may have reflected not only the beginning of a willingness to accept a compromise candidate but also the start of a "thaw" in Soviet policy. Mrs. Pandit as a candidate would have seemed to appeal to many diverse groups and governments. She had risen to eminence in a land where members of her sex usually have a subordinate position; and she came from a former colony which endeavored to play a role of leadership in international politics. Furthermore, she was known to the members of the United Nations, since she had served as President of the General Assembly and was a familiar figure on the Indian delegation. But this was not yet the compromise which would carry the day, for the Security Council rejected her in a secret ballot by two favorable votes, one negative, and eight abstentions. The permanent members were then asked to continue their consultations, but they produced neither nominations nor recommendations at two subsequent Security Council meetings.

Finally, on March 31, 1953, the search for a compromise candidate ended when France nominated Dag Hammarskjöld, the Minister of State of Sweden. This suggestion was supported by the United Kingdom. The Security Council recommended Hammarskjöld by 10 votes to none with one abstention, and a surprised civil servant in Sweden found on April 1 that the rumors of the day before had turned into reality. He had dismissed the rumors as unfounded, but accepted the fact of the Security Council's nomination as a personal honor and obligation. The General Assembly appointed Hammarskjöld by 57 votes with one against and one abstention on April 7, and three days later he stood before the delegates to take his oath of office.

In several ways, the appointment of Hammarskjöld resembled that of his predecessor eight years earlier.[15] It followed the rejection of a strong candidate in Pearson and a stalking horse in Skrzeszewski. Hammarskjöld, like Lie, was a European, chosen over any Latin American or Asian possibility, although in this case a serious nomination of an Asian had been made. Both were citizens of small countries and both had achieved cabinet rank. Both had studied law. Neither had engaged in strong anti-Communist activities or actively supported pro-American policies. Nor had either Lie or Hammarskjöld achieved a wide popular recognition on the international scene.

But the political situation into which Hammarskjöld was appointed differed markedly from that of 1946. The job of Secretary-General was no longer novel. The Secretariat existed and had developed an important role. Its chief and his subordinates had been deeply involved in the effort to meet aggression in Korea, and they had also dealt with such intractable matters as Palestine, the Greek guerrillas, the Berlin blockade, the breakdown of colonial empires, and the growing problems of economic development. The Secretary-General himself had come under attack for his activities. The outlook into an uncertain future in 1946 seemed benign in retrospect, compared to the sourness of the political situation within the United Nations in 1953, even after the death of Stalin.

Yet the bargaining process, set in both instances in the same constitutional and procedural framework, had an essential similarity. In 1953, as in 1946, the great powers consulted and negotiated to find an acceptable candidate. In both cases, agreement was reached on a candidate who had not been outstanding at the beginning of discussions; the first-rank candidates had failed to win approval; the candidates themselves had little or no direct influence on their selection; and both men won almost unanimous approval in the General Assembly once the Security Council had made its recommendation.

On the personal plane, the choice of 1953 differed greatly from that of 1946. Lie had climbed to cabinet level by the electoral ladder and the trade-union movement. Hammarskjöld was the youngest of four sons of a conservative former prime minister who brought to his family the sense of *noblesse oblige* that befitted a duty-bound line of public servants. Hammarskjöld's upbringing took him closer to the Royal Academy of Sweden than to the Marxist-influenced trade unions in Lie's Norway. Hammarskjöld was still studying in aristocratic Uppsala University when Lie had begun to lift himself to the top of the union and Socialist Party hierarchies. Lie pursued most of his prewar ministerial career in the Ministry of Justice, while Hammarskjöld dealt mainly with general economic problems as Under-Secretary of the Ministry of Finance and Chairman of the Riksbank. The war shoved Lie into the foreign ministry where he tasted military defeat and government-in-exile, while Hammarskjöld in neutral Sweden took part in a government that sought never to provoke an attack by the Germans. During the war years he began studying the shape of the postwar economy for the Socialist government. Lie approached the burgeoning warfare programs of his country as a trade-union lawyer and politician, while Hammarskjöld planned as a top-level bureaucrat.

In international relations, the two Secretaries-General had had quite different experiences. Lie's main tasks in foreign affairs came during the wartime years, when he brought Norway's merchant fleet into the hands of the grateful United Nations alliance and when he took part, as head of his government's delegation, in the drafting of the United Nations Charter. Hammarskjöld began to deal with foreign affairs in Sweden by the economic route. His brilliance as an economic manager and planner made him a natural choice as a Swedish negotiator of postwar trade agreements with the United States and as a participant in the creation and operation of the Marshall Plan agencies in Western Europe. A sharp mind and an analytical flair soon called him to the attention of the technicians who flocked to Paris. He moved out of the finance ministry and into the foreign ministry, where he became Secretary-General and in 1951 Vice Minister and a member of the cabinet, still concentrating on economic questions.

Both men had touched Soviet foreign policy but in different ways. Lie had visited Moscow in 1921, 1934, and 1944, and during the last stay signed an agreement, identical with those reached with the United States and the United Kingdom, on arrangements for the liberation of Norway. He had fought Norwegian Communists, some of them close to the Russians, in the labor movement and had been responsible for decisions on asylum for Trotsky. Hammarskjöld had had little direct contact with Communists in a country where they are of negligible importance, and had his main encounter with Soviet diplomacy only in 1952, when he was in charge of the foreign ministry during a vacation of Foreign Minister Oesten Undén. Soviet aircraft shot down a Swedish plane at that time, and Hammarskjöld directed a sharp protest to Moscow. Of the two men, it seems likely that Lie was far better known to the Kremlin than was his successor.

As personalities, Lie and Hammarskjöld differed as much as their social and political backgrounds suggest. Lie's ponderous directness contrasted with Hammarskjöld's subtlety and complex attitudes. The Norwegian's undisguised interest in the substance of political questions differed from Hammarskjöld's cautious, even dissimulating, approach. Lie spoke in short, simple phrases. Hammarskjöld employed a complex syntax and an allusive style. Lie, although a lawyer, acted a politician. Hammarskjöld, a political administrator who grew up in a tradition where the cabinet leads and the legislature discusses, let the Swedish preference for juridical justifications pervade his explanations. Lie remembers New York for the warmth of its personal relationships, while Hammarskjöld saw the same city as an artistic capital in which his fondness for literature and fine arts could come into full play. Lie found much happiness in the company of his wife and two daughters. Hammarskjöld was a bachelor. Finally, whatever his mental qualities may have been, Lie never gave the impression that he was a brilliant thinker, while Hammarskjöld unfailingly impressed his listeners with his intellectual sparkle.

As the end of Hammarskjöld's first term grew near, his wide recognition as a man of inventiveness, discretion, and trust exceeded that accorded his predecessor. Moreover, Soviet policy had grown more tolerant toward the United Nations, while the United States continued generally to give strong support to the organization. The pressure of the two superpowers held within bounds the resentment of the British and French governments after their failure in the Suez adventure. Despite the obvious pitfalls, Hammarskjöld managed to keep his appearance of impartiality, and instead of attracting the enmity of the great powers had earned their goodwill.

In these circumstances, the reappointment of Hammarskjöld [16] was practically a foregone conclusion. Soon after the 1957 session of the General Assembly opened, the Security Council met on September 26 in a private session. One short meeting was all that was required for the Council, whose members had found preliminary consultation easy this time, to reach its decision to recommend Hammarskjöld for another five-year term. Later on the same day the General Assembly voted, by 80 to none with one invalid ballot, to reappoint him. Sir Leslie Munro, President of the General Assembly, sounded the dominant note when he said that Hammarskjöld was "surely our supreme international civil servant."

During his second term, Hammarskjöld's already deep involvement in policy-making and operations to maintain the peace continued without cease. Although at the time of reappointment the Soviet Union and its allies did not fail to remark the growth in importance of the office of Secretary-General, whatever protests they chose to make remained polite and without virulence. But shortly after Hammarskjöld undertook great responsibilities, which his own suggestions had outlined, in an attempt to return stability to the Congo, the Soviet Union began a flamboyant and determined attack on him personally and on the conduct of his office. This attack had an unmistakable bearing on his prospects for reappointment at the end of a term which was to expire in 1963.

To force Hammarskjöld out of office and thus to control not only his activity but also to influence that of his successor became Soviet policy. Its executor was the most prestigious politician in the Soviet Union, Nikita S. Khrushchev. Khrushchev's extreme position found admirers only in the Communist camp. Although other governments had numerous doubts about the Congo policy, only the Soviet Union and its allies focused their wrath on the Secretary-General.

The Soviet campaign against Hammarskjöld passed through three stages. In the first, beginning in August, 1960, and continuing until September 23, the day Khrushchev addressed the General Assembly, Soviet delegates insisted that the Secretary-General had failed to carry out the instructions of the Security Council, especially in regard to relations with the Congolese government headed by Patrice Lumumba. The second stage began with the Soviet Premier's famous troika proposal, which in effect would have changed the office of Secretary-General into a three-member college and ensured the disappearance of Hammarskjöld from it. Finally, with the murder of Lumumba in February, 1961, the Soviet Union announced that in view of the Secretary-General's facilitating the death of the Congolese political leader, it would no longer have anything to do with Hammarskjöld.

During the first stage of the Soviet attack, Valerian A. Zorin, Soviet Deputy Minister of Foreign Affairs, used language strongly reminiscent of the earlier denunciation of Lie.[17] Although Soviet spokesmen at that time did not refer to Hammarskjöld's possible reappointment, it took little insight to understand that so long as he maintained his policy in the Congo and the Soviet Union insisted on its position, he had no chance to serve another term. Any possibility that a mutual accommodation might be reached the next year vanished when Khrushchev laid out in the most authoritative fashion what the Soviet Union thought about a Secretary-General who supported "colonialists" in the Congo. "We do not, and cannot, place confidence in Mr. Hammarskjöld," the Soviet leader declared. "If he himself cannot muster the courage to resign in, let us say, a chivalrous way, we shall draw the inevitable conclusions from the situation." [18] Thus, the Soviet Union sought to influence the next election for the post of Secretary-General by changing the nature of the office, and in any case by keeping Hammarskjöld out of it. Finally, the boycott against dealings with Lie was repeated for Hammarskjöld.

After such attacks Hammarskjöld found himself, as Lie had ten years before, the supporter of a policy endorsed by the majority of the United Nations, the proponent of a protected, international but active role for the Secretary-General, and the subject of a Soviet boycott of unlimited nature. There was no attempt to extend his term, as had been done in the case of Lie. Just before discussions preliminary to the appointment of a Secretary-General should have begun, Dag Hammarskjöld crashed to his death in the Zambian bush in an aircraft which was bringing him on a negotiating mission to Katanga.

The death of Hammarskjöld, deplored by all members of the United Nations, created an unprecedented situation. The late Secretary-General's term had another eighteen months to run. The practice of leaving an assistant in charge, recommended long before by the Preparatory Commission, had lapsed. There was no provision for a deputy secretary-general either in the Charter or in the resolutions of the General Assembly. At a time when the demands on the executive instruments of the United Nations were at their height, the Secretariat had neither a chief nor unanimity of support from the great powers.

To add to the complications, the Soviet Union's demands for the reorganization of the Secretariat had opened the question of the very nature of the office of Secretary-General. While these radical demands had been staved off by the tenacious Secretary-General and by a majority unwilling to tinker with a useful administrative machine, Hammarskjöld's death cast doubt on whether the precedents he had sought to create could endure. Facing the need to provide some chief administrative officer, the General Assembly might be responsive as never before to schemes for reorganizing the Secretariat. At the same time, because the Soviet proposals would require an amendment to the Charter, which could be adopted only with the consent of all five great powers and two-thirds of the member states,[19] the Soviet camp now had the power to wreck the organization by refusing either to accept a successor to Hammarskjöld or anything less than a troika.

The uncertainty caused by Hammarskjöld's death, the necessity for speedy administrative adjustments, the unknown limits of the Soviet position, and the impetus to bargaining contained in the arrangements for the appointment of a Secretary-General, all combined to make negotiations imperative. Several approaches to the problem immediately suggested themselves. The Security Council might recommend the appointment of a Secretary-General to the General Assembly in the normal procedure. But this would assume that the Soviet Union had changed its position. An Acting Secretary-General might be appointed to fill out the unexpired term. He could perhaps be appointed by the General Assembly alone and certainly on the recommendation of the Security Council. A number of approximations to the troika might be imagined. An interim administrative council might be agreed to by the General Assembly with a membership roughly in line with the Soviet division of the world into three camps. A Secretary-General might be appointed with the understanding that he would seek advice from a formal or informal advisory committee representing three or more geographical or ideological divisions. Finally, the understanding of 1946 regarding Lie's immediate subordinates had indicated that the position of the Under-Secretaries (until 1954 titled Assistant-Secretaries General) might also enter the negotiations.

Negotiating to fill the post of Secretary-General was mechanically easier than it might have been, simply because Hammarskjöld died just before the General Assembly began its sixteenth session. Immediate reactions of the delegates, as explained to the press, inclined toward the appointment of a stopgap Secretary-General, who perhaps might even be the President of the General Assembly. The exact terms at first were unclear, but some delegates evidently believed that a mere coordinator of the Secretariat might suffice until a full-term head was found.

Mongi Slim, the Tunisian Ambassador who had worked closely with Hammarskjöld in developing a Congo policy and who had been influential in the Lebanon case, immediately became a leading possibility as a coordinator.[20] His candidacy received full support from the small countries. At the same time, he had long been the agreed candidate for the presidency of the General Assembly. The first reaction from the United States government brought word of President John F. Kennedy's intention to intervene personally to protect the office of Secretary-General, while Moscow hinted that it would be a good time to proceed with establishing a troika. France let it be known that it opposed Slim because of his activities while his government tried to take over the Bizerte base.

Slim reacted in a remarkable manner. Just before his election as President of the General Assembly by a unanimous vote, he showed reluctance to accept an appointment as Acting Secretary-General by the action of the General Assembly alone. He wanted the backing of the Security Council and preferred not to involve himself in a dispute between the two great powers. His attitude resulted in a return of attention to the normal Charter processes. If the Security Council had to act, a full-term officer might as well be selected. But even if only a temporary chief executive was to be chosen, at least the process would be a familiar one.

The United States then launched a specific proposal. Secretary of State Dean Rusk urged a temporary appointment in order to give time to seek agreement on a full-term Secretary-General. "The General Assembly," Rusk said, "has full authority to make such a provisional appointment." But no specific candidate was suggested. Slim did not relent in his insistence on action by the Security Council. Meanwhile the Soviet Union sought to avoid the appointment of an acting officer. It broached the idea of a four-man directorate of Under-Secretaries, one of whom would be elected chairman. No new appointment, presumably, would be required.

By the beginning of October everything but the appointment of a full-term Secretary-General had been responsibly suggested. Yet the situation was altogether rigid, as the result of the positions taken by the great powers. Some signs of a possible approach to the problem of succeeding Hammarskjöld appeared when representatives of the United States and the Soviet Union began to hold private discussions.[21] The British, French, Soviet, and United States delegates had held an unsuccessful talk as early as September 26, apparently at the instigation of Nathan Barnes, a Liberian who was then President of the Security Council. Barnes' initiative represented only one of a series of moves by smaller powers to arrange a compromise.

During the next month, repeated meetings of Soviet and United States representatives made it clear that both governments would accept the appointment of an interim Secretary-General as the basis of negotiations. U Thant of Burma emerged as the most acceptable candidate, and Slim's chances faded as he became increasingly engaged in the management of the General Assembly and as objections were raised to his simultaneously filling the administrative post.

The bargaining between the United States and the Soviet Union centered on the number of Under-Secretaries who should serve on the Acting Secretary-General's staff. The Soviet Union at first proposed three—one from its own country, one from the United States, and one from Asia or Africa—who would act in "a spirit of concert." The Soviet statement on the subject also implied that the Security Council must act on the chief officer's election, and explicitly denied seeking a veto over the appointment of the deputies. While the United States rejected this idea, the small states explored a proposal made earlier by Hammarskjöld for five officials with the revived title of Assistant Secretaries-General at the political level. The United States proved unwilling to make specific the number of Under-Secretaries, but it favored more than three, so long as the Acting Secretary-General could consult them at will rather than by necessity. The United States also announced its acceptance of U Thant.

This suggestion was followed by a series of talks between Soviet and United States representatives, during which the Soviet Union proposed that the Acting Secretary-General should define his policy before his appointment. This provision was rejected by the United States government. By the middle of October another point remaining to be resolved was whether there should be four or five Under-Secretaries. It was already agreed that their ranks should include a United States national, a Russian, a Latin American, and an African, while Western Europe might or might not be represented. The Acting Secretary-General would presumably be an Asian; he would be an interim officeholder; and he would be appointed on recommendation of the Security Council.

U Thant

The leading candidate now began to exert an influence on the terms of his appointment.[22] One of Thant's early interventions in the bargaining involved a specific list of Under-Secretaries. He proposed naming five men already in the Secretariat. Valerian A. Zorin objected that the Soviet Union would require six, including a representative from another Eastern European country as well as from the Soviet Union.

As the dissension between the Soviet and United States representatives remained unresolved, Thant let it be known that he was preparing further proposals of his own. In discussions with the Soviet and United States delegations he indicated unwillingness to commit himself to appoint either five Under-Secretaries, the number the United States now favored, or seven, the number projected by the Soviet Union. Furthermore, he wanted the authority enjoyed in the past by the Secretary-General, and said as much in a public speech.

On November 1, Adlai Stevenson stated that the United States reluctantly agreed to the appointment of as many Under-Secretaries as the acting chief officer thought necessary; the latter should be left with the right to "settle this question as he sees fit and inform the General Assembly after his election." Thant had been consulted before this statement was made, and his reluctance to commit himself had no doubt been instrumental in producing it. The Soviet Union agreed with it after Thant talked at length with Zorin. France and Britain, kept informed of the negotiations, acceded to the new formula.

Earlier conversations between Thant and representatives of the United States and the Soviet Union had produced agreement that he would make his policy statement regarding his chief assistants before the General Assembly and not before the Security Council. A formula was found to define the relationship of the Acting Secretary-General with his subordinates. He was to consult with them "in a spirit of mutual understanding." The phrase represented a retreat from the troika principle and yet emphasized that the new chief officer would take command in a different setting from that of his predecessors.

The Security Council acted on November 3, 1961 to turn the

agreements of its permanent members into a recommendation to the General Assembly. On the same day, the General Assembly by unanimous vote appointed Thant Acting Secretary-General to fill out Hammarskjöld's term. He took the oath of office before the Assembly, and declared:

In my new role I shall continue to maintain . . . [an] attitude of objectivity and to pursue the ideal of universal friendship. . . . [T]he international climate can hardly be described as sunny. . . . I shall need, in the first instance, the wholehearted support, friendly understanding and unstinting cooperation from [the delegates.] [23]

The new Acting Secretary-General said that he intended to select some principal advisers from among the present Under-Secretaries, or from outside their ranks. The first would be Ralph Bunche and Georgy P. Arkadev, both Under-Secretaries and each a citizen of one of the superpowers. "It is my intention," he said, "to work together with these colleagues in close collaboration and consultation in a spirit of mutual understanding." Using this last phrase, he reiterated the precise formula of the Russo-American understanding on the interim appointment.

U Thant [24] creates an impression of firm determination and softspoken assurance. He appears at home in the complex web of United Nations politics. As Acting Secretary-General he was the first Asian and Buddhist to reach the highest office of the Secretariat. His selection emphasized the new importance of the non-European states in the United Nations and pointed toward a new pool of "neutral" governments from which international civil servants might be sought.

In a primarily agricultural, underdeveloped country, Thant was able, as the son of a landowner, to get a Western education. His studies were accomplished entirely in Burma and connected with Europe through the ruling British and through the tone they set at the University of Rangoon. There he made a friend of U Nu, later to be Prime Minister of Burma, and both of them taught English and history at Pantanaw High School, where Thant had been a student. While Lie and Hammarskjöld were climbing administrative ladders Thant was dealing with his pupils and leading a busy life as a freelance political journalist.

In addition to experience with a colonial regime, which neither

Lie nor Hammarskjöld knew, Thant lived through the military occupation of his country by Japan. During that time, except for some months as a government official in the educational field, he taught school. Soon after the war's end Thant became public relations chief for the Anti-Fascist People's Freedom League, and in 1948, after Burma secured independence, became government press director. He was also writing and publishing books on Burmese history and public affairs. His connection with the United Nations began in 1952, when he served as a delegate to the General Assembly. By 1955, when he attended the Bandung Conference of African and Asian states, he had gotten a taste of foreign affairs. In 1957 he became his government's permanent representative to the United Nations.

Fifty-two years of age at the time of his appointment, U Thant had less extensive foreign affairs experience than either of his predecessors, had held lesser governmental ranks, and could not match in any respect Hammarskjöld's reputation in the field of economics. He had a studious bent which contrasted with Lie's pragmatic approaches. He had had no experience with the democratic politics of Europe and North America. Yet like Lie he was primarily a politician rather than an administrative technician, and like him plainspoken and forthright. The colonial setting, which served as his political cradle, gave him a special insight into the problems of the former colonies and the underdeveloped countries. During his tenure as Burma's representative to the United Nations he was identified with the uncommitted nations, among whose representatives he had considerable prestige. At the time of his appointment he had had far more experience with the United Nations than either Lie or Hammarskjöld.

The first six months of Thant's term as Acting Secretary-General gave the members of the United Nations and the world at large an opportunity to assay the organization's interim replacement for Hammarskjöld. By the beginning of May 1962, press articles began to speculate about whether the General Assembly would accept the Acting Secretary-General for a full five-year term. Member governments had only a little more time to make their decisions on the question, for the 1962 session of the General Assembly would have to decide on the future holder of the office of Secretary-General after the expiration of Thant's interim appointment in April 1963.[25]

If Thant sought appointment as the Secretary-General for a full term, the six months before the opening of the General Assembly in mid-September 1962 offered him strategic opportunities to influence the election process. Whether or not he deliberately set out to win the appointment, his actions during that period unquestionably had the favorable effects that an office-seeker would ardently desire. During the summer he traveled to Eastern and Western Europe and Latin America, making speeches, appearing in press conferences, and conferring with governmental leaders in Sweden, Denmark, England, Ireland, France, Norway, Switzerland, Finland, Brazil, the Soviet Union, Czechoslovakia, Poland, and Austria. He also conferred with President Kennedy in Washington.

Nor were his utterances merely saccharine. Immediately after visiting Khrushchev at Yalta, for example, he recorded a radio message to the Soviet people in which he stated that if they had the facts on the Congo operation they would hold a very different opinion of it. The Soviet government censored the passage, indicating that it was perfectly aware of the opposition of the Acting Secretary-General to its policies.

Thant denied that he was soliciting the post. But it was perfectly clear that the future of the office figured importantly in his conversations. By the beginning of August he admitted in a news conference that he had thought of the conditions which must be met before taking a job that two months earlier he said he would be happier not having. "Before I make up my mind," the Acting Secretary-General declared, "I want to be pretty sure whether I shall have the necessary means at my disposal to discharge the obligations and responsibilities entrusted to me by the various organs of the United Nations." He insisted, moreover, that he would accept the office only if he had solid support for his peace-keeping policies from the members.

Some of that support was volunteered early. Adlai Stevenson broadly hinted as early as the end of May that the United States was committed to Thant for a full five-year term and had reason to be hopeful he would get it. By the end of August press accounts flatly stated that the Acting Secretary-General had full support from the Western European and North American governments. It could be assumed that he also had great strength as a candidate among the

African and Asian governments. Presumably the Latin American governments would be willing to accept him.

On the same day that the Acting Secretary-General held his pre-Assembly press conference, the Soviet newspaper *Pravda* published an article supporting the troika proposition. An American press report said that the Soviet bloc had raised the question of a two- or three-year term for Thant in consultation with other delegations, but a Soviet spokesman was quoted as saying that no decision had been reached in Moscow. By mid-October the Soviet attitude was still not completely clear. Foreign Minister Gromyko held one of his rare press conferences in New York and claimed that although the troika organization of the Secretariat had to come, the Soviet Union had no doubts about Thant's abilities to carry out the duties of Secretary-General.

At that point whatever consultations may have been in progress gave way to the crisis between the United States and the Soviet Union over Soviet missiles in Cuba. Following the relaxation of the crisis, consultations between the Soviet Union and the United States on the election of a Secretary-General bore fruit. A three-hour meeting at the Soviet delegation offices resulted in agreement on November 28 that Thant should be appointed to the office. Apparently some earlier consultations had remained inconclusive because of Soviet insistence that the liquidation of the Cuban crisis was a precondition to the choice of the Secretary-General. The Security Council met on November 30 and unanimously recommended to the General Assembly the appointment of Thant for a term to end on November 3, 1966, five years after his selection as Acting Secretary-General. The General Assembly immediately and unanimously accepted the recommendation.

While Thant's travels and speeches during the summer months certainly contributed to his acceptability, his role in the Cuban crisis and the easing of tension between the Soviet Union and the United States immediately following were probably decisive factors. Another source of prestige was the successful conclusion of negotiations he had initiated during the summer over the disposition of the Dutch colony in West New Guinea. In a brief address, Thant referred to the Congo, West New Guinea, and Cuba, and to his earlier hope that he might offer some service as a bridge between the Soviet Union and the United States. The 26 speeches of congratulation which followed his acceptance by the General Assembly left no doubt that the record of Thant's first year as chief administrative officer had been mainly responsible for his reelection.

Thant's Reappointment

The tactics followed by Thant during the last year of his first term greatly enhanced his influence on the expectations which member governments might have of the conduct of the office of Secretary-General. Although the question of whether he would succeed himself was put to him publicly early in 1966, he evaded giving a direct answer for months. By doing so, he avoided identification as a "lame duck" office holder.

At first Thant took the position that he should inform the Security Council of his decision by June so as to allow time to search for a successor. His own attitude began with a reluctance to take the office at all, and the simultaneous hope that if he did take office he would be able to settle the Congo problem, reduce tensions in the world, bring about a great power *rapprochement,* and see that the United Nations would develop into a really effective instrument to achieve the aims of its Charter.[26] His recurring, disappointed comments on the lack of progress toward a settlement in Viet Nam made it obvious that he perceived little reduction in political tensions in the Far East. Nor were promising solutions for the financial plight of the organization in sight. He could, however, view the United Nations peace-keeping mission in the Congo as concluded and could record useful responses to crises in Cyprus and Kashmir.

By June, Thant had changed his mind about making an announcement of his intentions. "Many friends and well-meaning Government representatives," he said, "advise me that if I decide one way or the other I should not announce it three or four months ahead of the expiry of my term."[27] The end of August, immediately before the General Assembly met, now was set as the appropriate time for a decision. The Secretary-General discussed his future with the representatives of many governments. He visited the Soviet Union and other European capitals and Latin America during the months before the end of his term, to gain further opportunities to discover governmental views on his position.

As the new deadline approached, it was clear that Thant had no implacable opposition to renewal of his appointment. The United States and the United Kingdom were known to favor his retaining the post, and the Soviet Union had made public no objection. France, known to oppose strong executive action by the Secretary-General, also exhibited no hostility to Thant's candidature. No flood of rumors about replacements appeared. A positive word from Thant would have assured him of reelection.

The Secretary-General nevertheless announced at the beginning of September that he would not offer himself for a second term.[28] Ostensibly, the decision was based on Thant's belief, often aired earlier, that no one should hold the office more than one term and that no one is indispensable. It was also understood that his family's attitude hardly encouraged him to look forward to another five-year term and that, in any case, he regarded the job as killing.

Yet his very statement points toward long-considered political reasons for his declining to serve again. The financial crisis remained. The United Nations Development Decade, given great importance by him, was falling far short of its aims. Above all, the struggle in Viet Nam disheartened Thant, who saw it as a cruel destruction of human life and a remorseless progress toward a major war. He furthermore expressed dissatisfaction with the exclusion of the Peking government from the United Nations, and with the lack of progress on disarmament. While he did point to some advances, the negative tone of his assessment could not be mistaken.

"To be candid," he added a few days later, "I feel that I have found it increasingly difficult to function as Secretary-General in the manner in which I wish to function, and secondly I do not subscribe to the view that the Secretary-General should be just a chief administrative officer, or, in other words, that the Secretary-General should be a glorified clerk." [29]

Meanwhile, the pressure on Thant to remain in office, earlier exerted in private, now became both more intense and more open as the representatives of great and small powers urged him to stay on. At first the only response, aside from his advice to the Security Council to look for a successor, was an indication that he would keep his office until the end of the General Assembly, by which time a new man could take over.[30]

This indication produced the extraordinary effect of a consensus in the Security Council on a statement which in effect promised Thant another full term if he would change his mind. The General Assembly, acting on the basis of the Security Council's statement, extended Thant's term of office until the end of the session but did so in a manner calculated to pay the warmest homage to the Secretary-General. Chief S. O. Adebo, the representative of Nigeria, sounded the prevailing tone when he spoke of "the hopes of the general membership that the successor to U Thant shall be U Thant." After receiving a standing ovation, the Secretary-General made a statement which might have been taken to indicate that his decision was not yet final.[31]

During the next month, Thant continued to come under heavy pressure to change his mind. But the expressions of support and confidence which his reluctance had elicited demonstrated that he too now had considerable capacity to make demands which could not be brushed aside. They were not.

By the end of November, the Security Council, then chaired by Arthur Goldberg of the United States, who took a leading role in the discussions, persuaded Thant to stay on—and not as a glorified clerk. The members of the Council specifically stated that "they fully respect his position and his action in bringing basic issues confronting the Organization and disturbing developments in many parts of the world to their notice, as he has done in his statement of 1 September 1966, to which they accord their closest attention." [32] The General Assembly subsequently accepted unanimously the Security Council's endorsement, and heard Thant explain that he had changed his mind in order to "serve the higher interests of the Organization and thus represent a positive factor in the current international situation." But he also remarked that he based his decision neither on new developments nor on any fond hopes that the aims set forth in his statement of September 1 would be achieved.[33]

Whether or not Thant received any formal or informal assurances of changes in governmental policies or actions that would help to bring about the harmony in international politics and peace in Viet

Nam that he so ardently sought, it is clear that he deeply influenced and shaped the terms on which he was reappointed. He furthermore achieved an unprecedented degree of deference both from the Security Council and the General Assembly.

Consequences of the Appointment Process

The election of the Secretary-General of the United Nations inescapably takes place in the conditioning atmosphere of world politics and brings into play forces which the organization has only slight ability to control. The institutional arrangements for the appointment process alone guarantee that policies of the major powers have to be taken into account. Therefore, the more active and influential a candidate promises to be or an incumbent has been, the greater is the likelihood that his views will be known on matters considered important by the great powers. When the policies of the great powers conflict, as they frequently have during the history of the United Nations, the process of appointing an active and able Secretary-General can be difficult indeed.

As a result of the special place of the Security Council in selecting the Secretary-General, no candidate may be appointed only for his personal qualifications, suitability, experience, talents at diplomacy, popular leadership, or any combination of these qualities which can be stated in advance. Rather, the great powers apply shifting, sometimes accidental, sometimes unfathomable, political criteria which need only be implied, never stated explicitly. Since the governments of the great powers are impelled to look long and hard at a proposed Secretary-General, the leading initial candidates so far have disclosed visible political blemishes, including in some cases that of nationality. They have given way to more obscure—but not necessarily less worthy—figures. None of the three incumbents had a firmly established public record or reputation on which firm predictions of behavior might have been based. Yet the great powers found it less difficult to agree—or to gamble—on these persons of vaguer reputation and unknown promise than they did on more familiar personalities.

Each appointment of a Secretary-General provides an occasion to define that office. The appointee's subsequent work and views help to give it further definition. The end of Lie's first term marked an attempt by the Soviet Union to secure a redefinition of the office more to its liking. Although failing in this aim, the Soviet Union nevertheless saw Lie resign before the end of his extended term and by implication was able to set conditions for the office when Hammarskjöld was appointed. The second Secretary-General managed his work in such a way as to win reelection by acclamation, only to lose the confidence of the Soviet Union before his second term had expired. His death made it unnecessary for the Soviet Union to carry its forcing tactics to a conclusion. But the appointment of Thant once more produced a reconsideration of the nature of the office. Thus, the necessity of going through an electoral process provides a clear, periodic opportunity for the members to attempt to revise the conception of the office of Secretary-General.

Moreover, the incumbent Secretary-General and the candidates for the office have some opportunity to influence the electoral process. The previous actions of an incumbent are, of course, considered by the member governments. It is possible for an office-holder to tailor some of his decisions with a view to building up a constituency among the members. From a contrary point of view, it is certain that a Secretary-General who does not take into account at least the views of the great powers certainly will not be reelected, no matter what moral claims may be made for his course.

Of the candidates for office, only Slim and Thant had strong, clear, and direct influences on the election process. In other elections, the opportunities were fewer, the consultations briefer, and the situations perhaps less fluid. But no individual can hope to exert really decisive pressure on any member government, especially that of a great power. He must bargain with the governments and perhaps play them off against each other, but be ready to surrender any ambition to office as a defense of his principles. As a result, the more elaborate the consultations before the appointment of a Secretary-General, the more restricted a conception of office he is likely to encounter. The lamentable attacks on Lie and Hammarskjöld demonstrate that the ability of an incumbent to reshape the conception of the office has definite limits. At the same time, they show the need for the Secretary-General to command adroit and practiced diplomatic skills.

CHAPTER IV

CONCEPTS OF THE OFFICE

Each Secretary-General forms his own concept of the office and of its scope and functions.

This idea must be fitted into a broad and somewhat vague description in Article 7 of the United Nations Charter. The article, primarily formal and legal in purpose, establishes the existence of the Secretariat on a plane of equality with other principal organs. Its reference only to the Secretariat and not to the Secretary-General seems to imply a legal distinction which has little political significance. Since the Secretary-General is principal officer of the Secretariat and bears responsibility for its activities, it is actually the Secretary-General who acts as a principal organ.[1]

Although Article 7 has only sporadically been cited as an important basis for the development of the office of Secretary-General, it does provide the concept of a prestigious and important legal position.[2] It is a novel position, since it elevates an international official to the eminence given to deliberative bodies made up of representatives of sovereign states. It could be argued that the Secretary-General with his staff has the same legal standing as any member state and probably a superior status, since the members act only collegially in United Nations institutions.

But such an argument flourishes only in a political vacuum. Of much more significance than the legal standing of the office of Secretary-General have been the ideas of its incumbents concerning its role in world politics, its functions in making and carrying out policies bearing on the maintenance of peace and security, and its place within the scheme of the United Nations Charter. The concepts put forward by the Secretary-General are tested and tempered in the continuous work of the office, and relate to its direct political functions by framing in doctrinal terms a view of the overt actions the Secretary-General may take. At the same time, such concepts connect with the administrative functions of the Secretary-General by elaborating his relationship to other principal organs.

The enunciation by the Secretary-General of his concepts of the office influences the work of the United Nations in a number of important ways. Conceptualization of past activities in rational terms encourages discussion and the formation of guidelines for future action. The reaction by member governments and observers helps to define the Secretary-General's sphere of activity and influence. The concepts discussed by the Secretary-General produce insights into his mode of thought and can thus become important considerations in the policies of member governments toward the United Nations.

Each holder of the office has deliberately put forward some articulated statements of doctrine. These have appeared most often in the *Introduction to the Annual Report of the Secretary-General on the Work of the Organization,* in his public speeches and articles, and in remarks at press conferences. Lie and Hammarskjöld also produced explicit concepts of the independence of the office in the face of challenges. Because Hammarskjöld, always articulate and a passionate intellectualizer, showed great interest in developing concepts of his office, his views provide a natural set of central themes for discussion.

The United Nations in World Politics

Each Secretary-General stoutly maintained the importance of the United Nations as a factor in international politics, but differed somewhat regarding the precise place the organization should have in the relations among its members. No one of them took the radical view that the United Nations should act as a general governing authority in the maintenance of peace and security. Each Secretary-General made the point that the United Nations is, in Hammarskjöld's formulation, "a living, evolving, experimental institution."[3]

Hammarskjöld conceived of the United Nations as "only a first approximation to the world order which we need and which one day must be brought about" and as "part of the great pattern of change of our time."[4] He readily admitted that the United Nations fell short of perfection but attributed this shortcoming to the "facts of international life in our age."[5] Nevertheless, an integrative trend could be discerned in the establishment and functioning of the United Nations. In his usual sensitive and complex style, he regarded the United Nations as

. . . an experimental operation on one of the lines along which men at present push forward in the direction of higher forms of an international society. It is obvious that we cannot regard the line of approach represented by the United Nations as intrinsically more valuable or more promising than other lines, in spite of the fact that, through its universality, it lies closer to or points more directly towards the ideal of a true constitutional framework for world-wide international cooperation, and notwithstanding the obvious weaknesses of regional approaches to such cooperation. However, if one cannot *a priori* give it higher value, it is, on the other hand, equally impermissible to regard it as less promising than experiments at present pursued on other lines. The effort carried on within and through the United Nations is an effort just as necessary as other experiments, and nothing short of the pursuit of this specific experiment with all our ability, all our energy and all our dedication can be defended. In fact, the effort seems already to have been carried so far that we have conquered essential new ground for our work for the future. This would remain true in all circumstances and even if political complications were one day to force us to a wholly new start.[6]

Hammarskjöld looked ahead to the evolutionary emergence of international institutions on the basis of a firmly established and irreversible progression which, in spite of references to other lines of advance, should have the primacy deserved by a target worthy of all energy and determination.

Lie, who unlike Hammarskjöld often and without hesitation spoke out strongly on controversial political issues, sought a more central position for the United Nations, which, he declared in 1950, "is the only real road to peace." [7] It was in the maintenance of peace that he found his principal measure of the success of the organization. Each year in the *Introduction* to the *Annual Report* he applied this gauge to the previous year's activities. While he never overlooked the deep divisions of the Cold War or the menacing portent of the outbreak of fighting in Korea, he nevertheless continued to hold the view that the United Nations could serve to promote peace.

Lie's most comprehensive remarks about the peace-keeping functions of the United Nations came in his *Annual Report* in 1951, after the Korean conflict and the attack on him personally by the Soviet Union. Noting that a threat of a third world war burdened the lives of the peoples of the world, he summed up the experience of his organization as a factor in political decisions:

> The first conclusion that emerges . . . is, surely, that the governments of Members have found it both wise and necessary to resort to the United Nations in their efforts to settle, ameliorate, or at least contain, most of the dangerous differences and disputes that have arisen among them since the end of the Second World War, including those directly involving the interests of the great powers. . . .
>
> A second conclusion to be drawn from the record of political activity is this: in spite of the lack of unanimity of the permanent members of the Security Council, United Nations action has resulted in bringing about the peaceful settlement of a substantial number of serious international issues in the first six years of its existence. In other cases not yet settled, United Nations action has prevented or halted armed conflict. . . .
>
> A third conclusion is that armed aggression anywhere, or the threat of armed conflict anywhere is, in fact as well as in theory, becoming more the concern of nations everywhere.
>
> Finally, there are the "United for Peace" resolutions, adopted by the General Assembly at its last session, which aim at the development of an effective collective security system which could immediately be set in motion in case of an emergency.[8]

This passage reflects Lie's central concern with international peace viewed as the avoidance of armed conflict and his consequent preoccupation with collective security and enforcement action. The effectiveness of the United Nations as an organizing center for collective avoidance and repression of violence was in his view the primary test of the organization.

Beyond claiming that the United Nations had a useful function in world politics, Lie attributed a still broader significance to it. In his last *Annual Report* he wrote:

> I am deeply convinced that a sober appraisal and an honest judgement of the present state of the world will lead to the conclusion that the very dangers and uncertainties of our times and the magnitude and diversity of the forces of disruption with which we must contend make the United Nations more important than ever in the struggle for peace and progress.[9]

In an assessment made four years earlier, Lie had gone further, asserting that the "United Nations has become the chief force that holds the world together against all the conflicting strains and stresses that are pulling it apart." [10] Moreover, Lie expressed the belief that what he called "the United Nations way" would be as right a generation hence in the effort to create a peaceful world as it had been at San Francisco.[11] He drew from his pioneering experience the lesson that the United Nations appropriately fitted the context of world politics, and either had or should have a guiding influence in maintaining peace. Unlike Hammarskjöld, the first Secretary-General espoused no vision of a pluralistic international system in which the United Nations was only one, but perhaps the most potent, of a number of progressive elements.

Like Hammarskjöld, Thant views the United Nations in the context of efforts to build a world order; and like Lie, he shows a high sensitivity to the Cold War. This sensitivity easily fits into the third Secretary-General's background as a delegate from nonaligned Burma. Thant equates the use of force with international anarchy. But power politics derives from four fundamental factors which cause world tensions. These are political ideologies, a passing phase; economic disparity, the greatest practical problem; unresolved colonial issues; and racial feelings, which he regards as contemptible and revolting.[11a]

He rejects the possibility of achieving world government either by a voluntary union or by conquest, remarking that:

> This leaves us with the necessity of having to try to form a world authority within the limitations of the present world set-up, across the barriers of the cold war. . . . Anything capable of mitigating the present anarchy would represent a valuable advance.[12]

Thant implies that the United Nations has such a role, serving as a world parliament and a "machinery for multilateral diplomacy." [13]

Thant appears to have approached Lie's conception of the United Nations, imperfect but existing as a central institution in the world political process, more closely than he does Hammarskjöld's pluralistic formulation. Although its peacekeeping methods might be improvised and fumbling, Thant declares that:

> . . . we have to develop it to deal with the modern antagonisms and dangers of our world until we can evolve more permanent institutions. There has been already a great advance in the world toward cooperation, mutual responsibility and common interest.[14]

He does not, however, avoid the fact that major issues are dealt with outside of the United Nations structure, and disclaims any belief in making the international organization the sole means for conducting diplomacy or the only place where problems could be solved. It is, rather, a novel means of diplomacy, Thant declares, which is always open. Moreover, he has seen many problems that were taken out of the United Nations context "finally come back . . . for debate, negotiations, compromise and ultimate settlement." [15]

Attempts by the United Nations to maintain peace represent in Thant's opinion vital steps in the direction of world order. "I am a firm believer in the organic development of institutions," he declares.[16] He remarked on another occasion that the United Nations had offered practical responses in a variety of crises and had thus enlarged its capacities to deal with emergencies.[17]

Hammarskjöld, and Lie before him, gave considerable attention in their statements and especially in the *Introductions* to their *Annual Reports* [18] to the growing importance of the liquidation of colonial empires and the related question of the universality of United Nations membership. Both agreed that the developing countries needed not only membership but special treatment from the international organization.

Within two years of taking office, Hammarskjöld could see the results of the "package deal" which admitted 16 new members to the organization. When he died, the membership of the organization had increased by more than 80 percent. Most of the new members had been colonies or had had their independence restricted in other ways. Hammarskjöld witnessed the culmination of the process of nationalism and drives for independence to which Lie had called attention as early as 1948. He had at first continued Lie's line of comment to the effect that without universal membership the organization could never serve its full purpose.[19] By 1956 he could remark of the emergence of a new nationalism that:

> Within the community of nations, so great a change in the political relationships must arouse deep emotions on all sides. Positions long vital to great nations are involved. And on the other side the intensity of aspirations for equal status creates pressures for extreme action. I am convinced that in this situation the United Nations could be a source of greater assistance to Governments than it has so far been. The give and take of public debate has been firmly established within the Organization and plays a valuable role in the determination of the common interest, but the resources for reconciliation, which the Organization can also provide, have not received equal recognition.[20]

At the same time, his comments on the declining colonial empires began to focus increasingly on Africa, in much the same way that Lie inevitably had been drawn to observe events in Asia. In 1956 he noted that Africa "is in a crucial state of transition." Political, economic, and social changes, he declared, were taking place at a more rapid rate than could be assimilated, while "a growing restiveness" was endemic elsewhere.[21] He thought that the United Nations, although limited in the possibilities for action in Africa, could be increasingly helpful. In his 1960 report, following the outbreak of violence and the involvement of the United Nations in a major effort in the Congo, Hammarskjöld gave much more attention to Africa. Warning of the influence of the Cold War and other divisive tendencies, the Secretary-General declared that "in the face of all this . . . the United Nations has, in the great task which it is facing in the Congo, appealed to 'African solidarity within the framework of the United Nations.' "[22]

The duty of the United Nations in Hammarskjöld's view went far beyond Lie's conception of containing and channeling conflict:

> The Organization must further and support policies aiming at independence, not only in the constitutional sense but in every sense of the word, protecting the possibilities of the African people to choose their own way without undue influence being exercised and without attempts to abuse the situation. This must be true in all fields—the political, the economic, as well as the ideological—if independence is to have a real meaning. Working for these purposes, the United Nations can build on the confidence of the best and most responsible elements of all the countries of the continent.[23]

At the same time, Hammarskjöld demanded responsible behavior from the African states.

During Thant's first term, more fragments of colonial empires reached independence, but those still in uncertain status—Rhodesia, South-West Africa, and the Portuguese colonies—still agitated the organization. The Secretary-General nevertheless refused to place all the blame on these disturbing elements for sudden and violent political change in Africa. "By no means all of the many problems that the African peoples are facing," he declared, "are of their own making, but few, if any of them can be solved except by the African countries themselves showing the qualities of maturity and restraint which they have often displayed."[23a]

Hammarskjöld's opinions in regard to Africa contain a remarkable evolution of ideas about regional organizations. Both he and Lie endorsed regional economic organizations under United Nations auspices. But both of them had also to form some judgment of the effect of regional political organizations outside the United Nations. Lie held office during the formation of the North Atlantic Treaty Organization, to which his own Norway adhered. Such regional self-defense organizations, which depended on a particular interpretation of Article 51 of the Charter, were widely viewed at the time as damaging to the United Nations and were the subject of considerable controversy in Europe.

Lie unhestitatingly endorsed the Marshall Plan in the *Introduction* to his 1949 *Report*.[24] Two years later, he attempted to show that regional defense arrangements—NATO had been the object of a great deal of strengthening effort during the war in Korea—could find a place in the United Nations system as complementary to the "primary obligation to join in defending world peace under the United Nations." [25] Hammarskjöld's view was perhaps more flexible and less unequivocally an edorsement of NATO, but was in fact rather similar in its insistence on a balance between regional and universal security arrangements.[26]

With the development of his views on Africa, Hammarskjöld seemed to have concluded that regional political arrangements (which were not long-term alliances) could be put together on an *ad hoc* basis within the organization, and that they were most appropriate for the areas with the least political experience. It is no doubt true that such arrangements would more easily prove effective within the United Nations structure than altogether outside it, for the states involved were in no position to attempt so powerful and elaborate an organization as NATO.

Thant's views of the effect of alliances on the United Nations diverge quite sharply from his predecessors'. He attributes alliances to the Cold War at its most extreme. Warning the West that it should appreciate the full significance of a change of political climate in the Soviet Union, he has said that a "concept of iron-clad alliances and a view of the world purely in terms of black and white was, in essence, the Western response to Stalinism." At the same time, he declared, the bipolarism of that era had given way to a multipolar situation as a result of the admission of the new members since 1956, turning the General Assembly into a "battleground of the cold war." Thant hopes that the General Assembly, already "the greatest public forum in the world today," might become even more effective as a center for harmonizing actions of members.[27]

Thant continues to voice deep concern with the problems of the emerging nations, emphasizing the material and technical aid they need from the highly developed countries in order to make their independence meaningful through rapid development.[28] He also expresses satisfaction with the progress toward self-government in certain remaining colonial areas with which United Nations bodies have been concerned.[29]

The Secretary-General, the United Nations, and World Politics

By discussing the importance of the United Nations in world politics, the Secretaries-General provided a context within which doctrines concerning their own roles could be developed. On one point they agreed completely: the Secretary-General, head of a principal organ, had a place in the process of deciding upon and carrying out policies intended to maintain peace. Moreover, because they served an organization which they unanimously regarded as active and responsive, they saw their own roles as active, alert, responsive, and sometimes initiating.

Hammarskjöld developed the most elaborate and sophisticated doctrines. These, as Lash points out, remained remarkably consistent from the beginning of his term of office, when he told reporters that the Secretary-General should be "active as an instrument, as a catalyst, perhaps as an inspirer—he serves." [30] At first Hammarskjöld guarded his words, leaving the impression with many observers that he would eschew political involvement. Yet the key to his views on the office of Secretary-General could be found in the cryptic "he serves." Hammarskjöld sought to serve by developing the functions of his office as far as his terms of reference and the world political configuration would permit him to do so. This was no neutral role, for international service requires

> . . . first and foremost the courage to be ourselves. . . . If this is the essence of international service, such service will expose us to conflicts. . . . Politics and diplomacy are no play of will and skill where results are

independent of the character of those engaging in the game. Results are determined not by superficial ability but by the consistency of the actors in their efforts and by the validity of their ideals.[31]

Whatever the content of the policies the Secretary-General followed, whether he would be a retiring civil servant or a dynamic diplomat, his inner convictions, his personal morality, would have a great share in shaping his work.

International civil servants who "have their own convictions and hopes, their own idealism," [32] have a creative capacity to introduce new ideas and influence member governments in the course of their work. "[T]he Secretary-General," said Hammarskjöld, "can to some extent exert influence on the frame within which it is his duty to accept responsibility for a sound development of the United Nations." The inspiration for this activity can only be the principles and aims of the United Nations, on behalf of which the Secretary-General personally and unspectacularly is engaged in "quiet diplomacy." But in this work, the guiding principle remains that of service to the community—"the inspiration and the challenge for all those who have to carry the responsibility of office." [33]

Implicitly the concept of "quiet diplomacy" guided Hammarskjöld in the successful negotiations to secure the release by China of some United States prisoners of war. But the trip was not unspectacular, with its personal involvement of the highest permanent officer of the United Nations in an attempt to breach a formidable diplomatic wall.

Hammarskjöld, always ready to formulate concepts, spoke of "quiet diplomacy" throughout his career, even when he publicly helped shape policies for the Security Council, as in the Suez or Congo cases, or when he closeted himself with Nasser or Lumumba. He amplified the content and setting of the term in his *Annual Report* to the General Assembly in 1956, when he viewed the United Nations as an instrument for negotiation "added to the time-honoured means of diplomacy." He said that "the greatest need today is to blunt the edges of conflict among the nations, not to sharpen them. If properly used, the United Nations can serve a diplomacy of reconciliation better than other instruments." While debate was necessary, the use of the "legislative procedures" to promote negotiations was also required. He continued:

In the diplomacy of world organization the quiet work of preparing the ground, of accommodation of interest and viewpoint, of conciliation and mediation, all that goes into the winning of consent to agreed solutions and common programmes, this forms a basis upon which the United Nations can become an increasingly influential and effective force. . . . There are, I believe, promising and practical opportunities for improving the practices and strengthening the institutions of the United Nations in this area of multilateral diplomacy. Especially in the past two years we have begun to explore these opportunities in a number of ways with generally positive results. I hope this evolution of emphasis and practice will be pursued and broadened in the future.[34]

Even if Hammarskjöld did not specifically mention his work as having contributed to the growth of conciliatory procedures, there was no mistaking his thought that it formed part of the new instruments of negotiation.

Hammarskjöld put these concepts to a strong test during the Suez crisis, when he left no doubt of his belief that he had the right to take part in the work of the United Nations to maintain peace and security. He declared to the Security Council, speaking on his own initiative on October 31, 1956, that had members not convened the Council following the Israeli attack and the Anglo-French ultimatum to Egypt, he would have used his rights—under Article 99 of the Charter—to do so. He formally told the Council that

. . . the Secretary-General has the duty to maintain his usefulness by avoiding public stands on conflicts between Member Nations unless and until such an action might help to resolve the conflict. However, the discretion and impartiality thus imposed on the Secretary-General by the character of his immediate task may not degenerate into a policy of expediency.

He then employed his special oracular style to take a public stand opposing the actions of the Israeli and British and French governments in attacking Egypt. His opposition was based on his position as "a servant of the principles of the Charter," the aims of which "must ultimately determine what for him is right and wrong." He reinforced his remarks by calling, in effect, for a vote of confidence, with the following comment: "Were the Members to consider that another view of the duties of the Secretary-General than the one here stated would better serve the interests of the Organization, it is their obvious right to act accordingly." [35]

This statement elicited an immediate show of confidence in Hammarskjöld. Nine of the 11 Council members explicitly told the Secretary-General that he had the support of their governments. These included the United States, the Soviet Union, France, and the United Kingdom as well as the smaller powers. Of the veto-wielders, only China maintained silence, as it had in 1950 on Lie's exercise of initiative.[36] In effect, Hammarskjöld not only had enunciated a doctrine which provided for influential and continuous involvement by the Secretary-General in the maintenance of the peace, but also had secured quite explicit recognition of the validity of this concept from the Security Council, including Britain and France, whose policies he strongly opposed, at a crucial time.

Upon his reappointment in 1957, he used the occasion to assess his past record and told the member governments that they could expect him to base his future actions on some of the more bold concepts which underlay his work.[37] By giving a more precise significance to the election—a significance which no member then denied—Hammarskjöld in effect provided a statement of his mandate from the General Assembly. As he saw the mandate, it was broader than anyone might have expected in 1945 and as broad as Lie would have wanted in his own vision of the office of Secretary-General.

The newly reappointed Secretary-General described his position as exacting as well as deeply rewarding, and saw as a first reason for gratitude "the privilege of working on terms of mutual confidence with all Governments and their representatives in international co-operation." In a much drier tone, he said that he had little to add and nothing to change in his interpretation of his office as made in the Security Council at the height of the Suez crisis and in his most recent *Annual Report on the Work of the Organization.*

Hammarskjöld then enunciated a more positive conception of his office than he ever had before. He remarked that in his Charter-based functions he must feel secure that his actions, even if they cut across principles of national policies, would not result in impaired confidence in his office. The Secretary-General, he said, should not be asked to act unless guidance can be found, either in the Charter or in a decision of a major organ. But within these limits, he said, it was the duty of the Secretary-General to use his office and the machinery of the Organization to the utmost "and to the full extent permitted at each stage by practical circumstances."

Beyond this mandate, Hammarskjöld said, there was an independent role for the office of Secretary-General:

> It is in keeping with the philosophy of the Charter that the Secretary-General should be expected to act also without such guidance, should this appear to him necessary in order to help in filling any vacuum that may appear in the systems which the Charter and traditional diplomacy provide for the safeguarding of peace and security.[38]

This statement marked the full flowering of a far-reaching conception of the office of Secretary-General, whose incumbent would engage in high-level diplomacy and would be guided by the Charter and his personal conscience to work for the cause of peace.

Hammarskjöld gave the name "preventive diplomacy" to his new concept of activity by the Secretary-General.[39] It comprises diplomatic action by the Secretary-General or an authorized representative to forestall the worsening of international friction and to keep it off the agendas of other United Nations organs where it might become a Cold War issue. It includes some of the many kinds of arrangements which have been lumped together under the heading of a "United Nations presence." [40]

Because the Secretary-General's "preventive diplomacy" relates to specific situations and is not the subject of instructions by the Security Council or the General Assembly, no single statement accurately defines it. But all approaches to a definition are based on the doctrine that the Secretary-General has a generalized responsibility emanating from Article 99. In addition, the fact that he has been given vaguely defined administrative tasks of high political content, which must be carried out on the basis of a personal interpretation of the terms of reference, has encouraged "preventive diplomacy."

After acting on his own initiative to send a mission—a United Nations presence—to Laos in 1958, Hammarskjöld further elaborated his doctrine of preventive diplomacy. He used his right to speak before the Security Council, which had neither asked him to report nor taken any action of its own in Laos.[41] Hammarskjöld's first explanation of his expansion of the functions of his office was rather bland. He regarded his actions in dispatching personal representatives at the request of governments as a further development in the course of furnishing good offices, a task with which the Secretary-General had been charged often. "Such actions by the Secretary-General," he wrote later, "fall within the competence of his office and are, in my view, in other respects also in strict accordance with the Charter, when they serve its purpose." He did not indicate how one decided whether the purposes of the Charter were indeed served, but he did point out that he had informed the members of appropriate organs and that he was setting no precedents, since formal decisions could be sought from the deliberative bodies.

The main significance of this evolution, he claimed,

> . . . lies in the fact that it has provided means for smooth and fast action, which might otherwise not have been open to the Organization. This is of special value in situations in which prior public debate on a proposed course of action might increase the difficulties that such an action would encounter, or in which a vacuum might be feared because Members may prove hesitant, without fuller knowledge of the facts or for other reasons, to give explicit prior support in detail to an action which, however, they approve in general terms or are willing should be tried without formal commitment.[42]

This passage contains some remarkable reasoning, for it seems to advocate a course which encourages the member states to support broad initiatives by the Secretary-General without taking any responsibility of their own. At the same time it might be asserted that this would be merely a conciliation function undertaken by the Secretary-General with tacit approval. It is difficult to see how he could do more than fact-finding if full knowledge were not available, but the passage strongly hints at a stouter effort than mere investigation.

An even more remarkable passage follows. Here Hammarskjöld explains that nothing has happened to change his relationship with the main organs of the organization. His actions were wholly dependent on governmental decisions, but yet greater ability to act in specific cases "within a latitude of independence in practice given . . . by . . . member governments for such cases" was to be expected. All this, he insisted, falls within the "scope of intentions reflected in Article 99" and points to methods which conceivably could become "part of a common law of organized international cooperation."[43] The creation of a common law based on novel functions for an office would seem in fact to mean that relationships were changing: could actions be entirely dependent on governmental approval when in fact such consent can be obtained only for vague projects for which no advance commitment is needed? There also remains the question of what happens when results which are displeasing to members of the deliberative organs are obtained by a Secretary-General.

In 1960 Hammarskjöld restated his views of diplomatic action by the Secretary-General in a broader context of preventive diplomacy, in which he also included such cases as Suez, Lebanon and Jordan, and the Congo. He reasoned in the *Introduction* to his 1960 *Annual Report* that since the United Nations could have little effectiveness in conflicts between the two great-power blocs, the Secretary-General would also find it perilous to his office to act. But efforts could be made to keep "newly-arising conflicts outside the sphere of bloc differences." He remarked that preventive diplomacy

> . . . is of special significance in cases where the original conflict may be said either to be the result of, or to imply risks for, the creation of a power vacuum so that it will not provoke action from any of the major parties, the initiative for which might be taken for preventive purposes but might in turn lead to counteraction from the other side. The ways in which a vacuum can be filled by the United Nations so as to forestall such initiatives differ from case to case, but they have this in common: temporarily, and pending the filling of a vacuum by normal means, the United Nations enters the picture on the basis of its noncommitment to any power bloc, so as to provide to the extent possible a guarantee in relation to all parties against initiatives from others.[44]

Thus, Hammarskjöld's conception of the vacuum which diplomatic action by the Secretary-General might fill evolved over a year from one caused by hesitation, either because of ignorance or possible outcome, to one produced by a lag in great-power involvement.

Hammarskjöld did not limit his concept of diplomatic action to the usual devices of persuasion, consultation, and probing. He also pointed out in his 1960 *Introduction* that there were possibilities for preventive diplomacy in the economic sphere, where factors of long-term determinative import operate.[45] He did not expand on the possibility that economic activities might provide a political tool to the organization and his office. But his action a year earlier in assigning a special representative to Guinea,[46] which had cut itself off from French assistance, indicated that he appreciated the economic aspects of diplomatic action. This was underlined in Laos, where his appointment of a Special Representative was clothed entirely in the mantle of economic assistance, although the Laotian government had phrased its calls for help primarily in political and military terms. Such an economic approach could be made only by stretching the usual terms of reference of the Resident Representative of the Technical Assistance Board almost beyond recognition.[47]

Lie had produced hardly a shadow of the doctrinal statements that were so characteristic of Hammarskjöld's tenure. In his case, the need to make pioneering decisions at the beginning of the life of an organization perhaps dictated a certain caution in conceptualizing his actions. Moreover, Lie does not seem to have had the cast of mind which would encourage elaborate general statements on the rights and duties of his office. Thant, however, inherited a great deal of doctrine from his predecessor and, unlike Lie as the first incumbent of the office, can refer to it whenever necessary.

Despite the scarcity of extended, formal reasoning about the role of the office of Secretary-General in influencing world politics, Lie offered both some clues to his ideas and some indicators for future development. He continually made specific references in his *Annual Reports*[48] to outstanding problems in world politics. These ranged from pleas to reduce the tension of the Cold War to quite specific comments on the disposition of the former Italian colonies, the control of nuclear and biological weapons, the future of Germany, and the value of the Marshall Plan. Such remarks indicate that he believed that the Secretary-General should be an active force in the search for means to keep the peace, but he did not follow through these general thoughts with further detail.

Lie also implied that the Secretary-General had a good offices function when in 1949 he offered such services to the great powers to facilitate consultations among them.[49] Furthermore, he enunciated in a primigenial way the doctrine that the Secretary-General could, as part of preventive diplomacy, dispatch representatives on fact-finding missions. He flatly claimed during the Security Council debate on the Greek frontier question in 1946 that if the Council did not act to investigate the situation, he had the right to do so in order to determine whether he should bring any aspect of the dispute to the attention of the Council.[50] This was a claim, according to Schwebel, that he had not "merely the right to make inquiries or investigations without authorization from United Nations organs but the right to initiate such investigations even in cases where the Security Council has decided not to look into the matter." [51] It is noteworthy that Lie's statement met no challenge, but it remained for Hammarskjöld to develop its full implications.

Lie believed that the Secretary-General had an important tool of political action in his influence on broad public opinion. He applied a "concept of a spokesman for the world interest" to his activities in office,[52] and Schwebel speaks of him as the voice of an "international synthesis." [53] The tone of his speeches accorded with this concept.

The role of spokesman for broad segments of unofficial opinion was one that Hammarskjöld explicitly eschewed. Although in his view the Secretary-General could try to resolve controversial questions without obtaining a formal decision of a deliberative organ, he had to do so on the basis of the Charter alone, not as a "kind of delphic oracle who alone speaks for the international community." [54] While Lie never claimed the role of oracle, his concept of speaking for a world interest must either be interpreted as based on a knowledge of the opinions of people, not just their governments, or else must derive from agreements of governments in the United Nations.

Although there is no doubt that Thant regards the office as rightfully involved in important political questions, at first he created this certainty by actions rather than doctrine. He has entered in negotiations over West New Guinea (now West Irian), Cuba, the Congo, Yemen, and Cyprus—all of them political situations in which a Secretary-General who did not conceive of his office as having a positive and even leading role in world politics could not become involved. He has elaborately saluted the work of his eminent predecessor as brilliant and worthy of the Nobel Peace Prize, and referred to his principles as admirable.

At the same time, Thant characterized Hammarskjöld's contribution as "unique, since it came at a time when the Organization itself was in its formative stage." [55] Thant is known to consider Hammarskjöld's concept of his office as a model, and has specifically endorsed the practice of quiet diplomacy in helping parties to disputes find their way to peaceful solutions.[56]

The extended period of uncertainty over whether Thant would be a candidate for reelection gave him a chance to develop more boldly than ever before his belief that the Secretary-General should be no glorified clerk. While he insisted on the right of the Secretary-General to engage in political activities, he also recognized that his practical possibilities depended on limited actual authority and power. That made it all the more important that his powers should be exercised conservatively—not frittered away on dramatic gestures but rather supported with hard work. Yet he declined any neutrality on moral issues and was attracted by the "moderator" concept, so hazily sketched by President Roosevelt during World War II.[56a]

The elaboration of Thant's views of his office retain a concreteness that recall Lie's approach more than Hammarskjöld's. His comments on international politics are specific and blunt and do not approach the intellectualized character of Hammarskjöld's doctrinal exercises.

The Independence of the Office

The major challenges by the Soviet Union and its allies to the continued tenure of Lie and Hammarskjöld produced defensive responses which emphasized the independence of the office of Secretary-General. They embody concepts of the Secretary-General as international civil servant.

Lie did not reply with lengthy doctrinal arguments to the Soviet attack and boycott following his support of United Nations intervention in Korea. Rather, he briefly stated that he regarded the vote to extend his term of office as "a reaffirmation . . . of the independence and integrity of the office of Secretary-General."[57] He indicated his belief that the office must have its own vitality, aside from the policies of members, in serving the interests of the organization.

In his final statement to the General Assembly, Lie indicated that Article 100 of the Charter, setting forth the international status and independence of the Secretariat, had an essential bearing on the integrity of his office.[58] He thus singled out a crucial issue. Hammarskjöld later made much of this point and based much of the defense of his views against Soviet pressure on the implications of Article 100.

After the intensifying Soviet criticism of Hammarskjöld's policies in the Congo and the subsequent troika proposition by Khrushchev, the Secretary-General declared that he would rather see his office "break on strict adherence to the principle of independence, impartiality and objectivity than drift on the basis of compromise." Criticism of the Secretary-General for standing by that principle, he said, "strikes the very office and the concepts on which it is based."[59] While the vast majority of the General Assembly greeted these comments with applause, the Soviet delegates pounded their desks in derision.[60]

As the sulphurous debate between the Secretary-General and the head of the Soviet government continued, Hammarskjöld was led to spell out in more detail a theory of a consensual basis for his office. He viewed the Soviet attack as referring to an institution, not a man. Because the Soviet Union wanted an arrangement which would make it impossible to have an effective executive, he said:

> By resigning I would, therefore, at the present difficult and dangerous juncture, throw the Organization to the winds. I have no right to do so because I have a responsibility to all those member states for which the Organization is of decisive importance—a responsibility which overrides all other considerations.
>
> It is not the Soviet Union or indeed any other big power which needs the United Nations for their protection. It is all the others. In this sense, the Organization is first of all their Organization, and I deeply believe in the wisdom with which they will be able to use it and guide it. I shall remain in my post during the term of office as a servant of the Organization in the interest of all those other nations as long as they wish me to do so.[61]

This statement echoed Lie's earlier defiance of Soviet pressure, and in addition formulated a concept of the duty of the Secretary-General to serve the smaller members of the United Nations before the powerful.

Hammarskjöld reacted to the subsequent Soviet boycott with a series of responses, the first of which took the form of a sophisticated lecture at Oxford University on May 30, 1961.[62] He gave special attention to the attitude of the international civil servant who undertook political responsibilities. He deftly analyzed the meaning of the Soviet premier's aphorism that "while there are neutral countries, there are no neutral men." His conclusion held that "the international official cannot be accused of lack of neutrality simply for taking a stand on a controversial issue when this is his duty and cannot be avoided." Such an official, who is protected by the law of the United Nations Charter, must check himself, as a judge does, to prevent his personal views from influencing his actions.

If the international civil servant is guided solely by the aims of his organization and by recognized legal principles, Hammarskjöld continued,

> then he can face the criticism which, even so, will be unavoidable. . . . [A]t the final test, this is a question of integrity, and if integrity in the sense of respect for law and respect for truth were to drive him into positions of conflict with this or that interest, then that conflict is a sign of his neutrality—and not of his failure to observe neutrality.

His argument, emphasizing personal integrity rather than loyalty to a political faith, fits into the still broader institutional discussion which constitutes Hammarskjöld's second articulated response to the Soviet challenge. This is contained in the *Introduction* to the *Annual Report of the Secretary-General on the Work of the Organization* put before the General Assembly late in the summer of 1961.[63] He thought of this document, published shortly before his death, as his political testament.[64] In its dignity, succinctness, and breadth, it serves as a fitting monument to a Secretary-General who did so much to create a doctrinal framework for his office.

Hammarskjöld divides the members of the United Nations into those who regard the organization as a "static conference machinery" and those who believe it should serve as a dynamic instrument for resolving conflict and developing forms of executive action aimed at forestalling or arresting conflict "in a spirit of objectivity and in implementation of the principles and purposes of the Charter." The proponents of the static conference machinery, clearly the Soviet group, Hammarskjöld judged as old fashioned, while the second, his supporters, he saw as progressive.

Hammarskjöld remarked that the Charter gave a disproportionate amount of attention to the features of the conference approach, which had been well understood at San Francisco, and less to the possibilities of executive action which in fact evolved from attempts by the deliberative organs to deal with security issues.

> Members have to a large extent used the possibility to request the Secretary-General to perform specal functions by instructing him to take the necessary executive steps for implementation of the action decided

upon. This has been done under Article 98 . . . and has represented a development in practice of the duties of the Secretary-General under Article 97. The character of the mandates has, in many cases, been such that in carrying out his functions the Secretary-General has found himself forced also to interpret the decisions in the light of the Charter, United Nations precedents and the aims and intentions expressed by the Members. . . . [H]e has had to shoulder responsibility for certain limited political functions, which may be considered to be in line with the spirit of Article 99 but which legally have been based on decisions of the main organs themselves, under Article 98, and thus the exclusive responsibility of Member States acting through these organs. Naturally, in carrying out such functions the Secretariat has remained fully subject to the decisions of the political bodies.[65]

Hammarskjöld reasoned that in order to function in this political context, the Secretariat must be organized on an international basis —not strictly necessary for the conference approach—and that the organization could not be satisfied with anything less. Thus, the troika demand was lumped with the conference approach as backward-looking. Finally, Hammarskjöld reiterated his belief that a neutral Secretariat was possible and that anyone of integrity who was not subjected to undue pressure could act in an "exclusively international" spirit and be guided by the principles of the Charter. This repeated in final form his earlier comments about neutral men and neutral nations.

Three Concepts of the Office

Three propositions serve as the foundation of the entire conceptual structure built up by the Secretaries-General. The first of these attributes to the United Nations a significant role in world politics. While Lie may have regarded that role as more central in the political process than did either of his successors, neither of the latter thought the organization should be quiescent or uninfluential in the face of a security issue.

Second, each Secretary-General believed that his office should have an important share in developing policies to maintain peace and security and should be involved in negotiations and actions following from such policies. Again, the three holders of the office differed in the degree of influence and its precise form.

Finally, each Secretary-General unequivocally held that his office should be independent of any political movement or bloc, and should head a truly international, as opposed to representative, civil service. The views expressed on this point differed not at all in kind and little in degree, although their expression varied with circumstances.

Lie enunciated each of the three foundations from which further conceptualization could proceed. His expression of concepts of his office remained rudimentary but nonetheless basic for creating further doctrine. Whether a more sophisticated doctrine could have been evolved at the beginning stage of the United Nations cannot be surely known, but in view of the sharp reactions to at least some of his public attempts to involve the office in matters of peace and security, it seems likely that a record of practice had to precede the theoretical elaboration undertaken by Hammarskjöld.

Hammarskjöld showed far and away the greatest proclivity for expression in conceptual terms of views of his office and of the actions he took in accordance with those views. In part, his willingness to trace a doctrine for his office must be attributed to his personal character, his intelligence, and his formation as a student of economics and as a civil servant working on such matters as central banking and fiscal and economic policy, which require rather abstract treatment. At the same time, the quite remarkable expansion of his office required conceptualization to become permanent.

Hammarskjöld obviously understood this function of conceptualizing and willingly engaged in it, as his speeches to nongovernmental groups and some of his official documents, notably his *Annual Reports* and his inaugural address at the beginning of his second term, indicate. It seems likely that his close reasoning and generalizations have helped to give lasting definition to the office of Secretary-General.

Certainly Hammarskjöld's successor proved ready to claim that he would base his work on the concepts spelled out during the eight years before he took office. At the same time, Thant indicated—by his comment that Hammarskjöld had done unique, formulative work—that he had no immediate plans for adding much to the concepts of the office thus far elaborated. It seems probable that Hammarskjöld developed concepts that are full and detailed enough to cover a wide range of future actions by an office of Secretary-General deeply engaged in efforts to maintain peace and security.

The conceptualization of the office of Secretary-General has become elaborate enough to indicate some of the limits of action which the chief executive officer will undertake in his own initiative. He must either have instructions by the Security Council or the General Assembly, or else be able to deduce authority directly from the provisions of the Charter. In the former case, he may be able to create extensive administrative mechanisms, while in the latter case he is more limited and confined largely to investigative and good offices functions. Nevertheless, in filling vacuums left by the inability of a deliberative organ to act, the Secretary-General could conceivably undertake far-reaching negotiations which would require a considerable staff engaged in supporting—but not direct—peacekeeping activities. He could thus create no United Nations Emergency Force (UNEF) on his own authority, but might be able to organize sizable and influential missions along the Laos pattern.

To the extent that the membership of the United Nations willingly accepts his concept of the office, the incumbent Secretary-General may act confidently. The consensus reflected in such acceptance opens the way to considerable influence on the part of the Secretary-General who is willing to take actions on his own initiative.

The concepts espoused by the Secretaries-General have not been unanimously accepted by the membership. One powerful group has absolutely opposed the formulations attempted by Lie and Hammarskjöld. Moreover, doctrinal statements by the Secretary-General have frequently been designed either to deal with an attack or to shield a controversial *démarche*. Even if such statements have won general acceptance, it is hazardous to separate them entirely from their context. The conclusion follows that the consensus behind a given doctrinal formulation may change, and the limits of the Secretary-General's influence could be radically retrenched.

The existence of a series of conceptual statements thus has a dual effect. Such formulations sum up earlier experience; they outline precedents. The existence of a precedent always may serve as an argument against further innovation. As further practice revalidates precedents, the latter can harden sufficiently to prevent any retrogression without a great struggle. Or they can serve as the foundation for further expansion of influence.

PART TWO

Routine and Representational Functions

CHAPTER V

INTERNAL ADMINISTRATION

As chief officer, the Secretary-General shapes the design of the administrative structure, has responsibility for the staff which he appoints and directs, and prepares the budget of the organization. He oversees the routine functions with which most of the staff is concerned.

From time to time even routine, technical duties have political implications and offer the Secretary-General or his immediate staff an opportunity to contribute to the policy of the organization and of member governments. The crises through which the office of Secretary-General passed in 1950 and in 1960 demonstrate that internal administrative functions have relevance to the maintenance of peace and security. Budgeting and finance bear directly on and reflect the peace-keeping operations in which the scope of the office of Secretary-General was so much broadened.

Administrative Head of the Secretariat

At the time the office of Secretary-General was formally established, the officially sanctioned view governing its internal administrative functions was that of highly centralized authority and responsibility. "The Secretary-General," said the Preparatory Commission unequivocally, "is the head of the Secretariat." To him is left the task of appointing, assigning, and instructing subordinates in the exacting work of an international team. In the General Assembly and other principal organs, "[h]e alone is responsible . . . for the Secretariat's work." [1] (See Appendix C.) If anyone can, he sets the tone of the Secretariat.

Because the United Nations Charter establishes an international civil service, the Secretary-General exercises authority in internal administration within that concept. This rules out an appointments policy which would build the Secretariat around the principle of representation of governments. The staff remains at his disposal only, and he or any subordinate is prohibited from accepting instructions from governments.

The pristine concepts spelled out by the Preparatory Commission hardly fit either the complexity of the real world of administration or the special problems of an international civil service. The Preparatory Commission betrayed a rather romantic view of the Secretary-General as commander of his organization. But even disciplined military establishments—let alone civil services with direct links to the political organs—often fail to respond with dispatch and enthusiasm to suggestions and orders. While the head of an administrative establishment may put heavy formal and informal pressures on his subordinates and even have the right to use sanctions, he is rarely willing to substitute fiat for persuasion.

Both the Secretary-General and his subordinates bring to the international civil service their national administrative conventions. Sometimes these contrast sharply. For example, English and French administrative structures require quite different procedures. At other times, the background and tradition of an official may depend entirely on the practice of nepotism, favoritism, and bribery. Some officials, moreover, come to the Secretariat from countries governed by authoritarian, centralized administrations which discourage independent initiative and inject doctrinal considerations into every function. Yet individuals with these diverse and perhaps incompatible administrative experiences must work together under the instructions of the Secretary-General.

The twenty-year experience of the League of Nations Secretariat furnished only inconclusive precedents and nothing like enough trained civil servants to man the new organization, which by the end of its first year had more than twice as many officials as ever worked for the League.[2] Most of them needed experience, training, and leadership. Yet they had almost immediately to handle observational duties in Greece, mediation in Palestine, and within the first five years, the conflict in Korea. These and succeeding assignments of even greater complexity would have challenged even a trained civil service. They made the internal administrative functions of the Secretary-General directly relevant to the maintenance of peace.

Although the United Nations Charter established the sole responsibility of the Secretary-General for the appointment and direction of the Secretariat, its organization into departments headed by officers of stature and influence suggests the possibility of the evolution of a collegial body. The agreement of these officers, at first titled Assistant Secretaries-General and now Under-Secretaries, would lend strength to the Secretary-General in the supervision of the Secretariat. Constant discord among them could be taken by member states as signifying a need to reexamine the decision made at San Francisco to allow the Secretary-General freedom in administering his staff. A prudent course then might involve careful efforts to achieve consensus. The use of the Under-Secretaries as a cabinet of which the Secretary-General was chairman offered one means of doing so. Thus the Secretary-General would be seen from the outside as chief, and by his colleagues closest to his own rank as chairman.

Even before the appointment of Lie, the permanent members of the Security Council decided to share out five of the eight assistant secretary-generalships in order to protect what they conceived to be their interests. This decision, which had no formal standing, limited the freedom of the Secretary-General to appoint his most important subordinates, and, moreover, fitted far better with the conception of the Secretariat as a representative organism than with that of an international civil service. Although theoretically all Assistant Secretaries-General would work only with the interests of the United Nations in view, at least five would yet owe their appointments to member governments. The presence of persons of enough prestige to be nominated by permanent members of the Security Council suggested that a collegial direction of the Secretariat might have important political advantages.[3]

The role of the Secretary-General as chief officer has nevertheless outbalanced tendencies toward collegial direction. A number of reasons underlie this development. The permanent members of the Security Council showed neither equal nor consistent interest in the appointment and performance of their nominees. The only discernible pattern is in the case of the Soviet nationals, who are replaced at regular intervals. The Secretary-General also has had considerably more choice than the agreement among the great powers suggests, and has had the opportunity in consultations to influence nominations. Then the Soviet Union has shown the most interest in having one of its nationals head the department which services only the Security Council and is not equally concerned with the work of the organization as a whole.[4] A United States national for many years had the top personnel and financial post, which only occasionally has relevance for political work.

Lie's comments do not indicate that the heads of his administrative departments in fact served as either the spokesmen of or ears for their own governments to an untoward degree. Nor is there any reason to believe that any of the Assistant Secretaries-General during Lie's tenure ever achieved the autonomous and disturbing positions of the Deputy Secretaries-General of the League of Nations. Even in the case of the Soviet nationals at the top level of the Secretariat, the most that could be said with assurance is that some Soviet nationals were closer to the Soviet delegation "than would appear proper," but the Secretary-General derived the advantage of having a high-ranking officer who knew a good deal about the intentions of the Soviet government.[5] There has, moreover, been no indication that the contributions of any given Under-Secretary were altogether indispensable.

Lie's administrative practice of giving his subordinates responsibility for internal management problems and concentrating himself on political matters also ran counter to any collegial trends. So did his practice of bringing together the Assistant Secretaries-General only for rather futile, if frequent, meetings. The department heads then had to busy themselves with technical matters and not with political roles. Reorganizations of the Secretariat under Hammarskjöld and Thant continued to strengthen the Secretary-General's leading position and to avoid pressures for collegial direction.[6]

Despite the emergence of the Secretary-General as a chief, the idea of a collegial management of the Secretariat died hard. It was revived in Khrushchev's troika proposal. This extravagant demand related directly to the growth of the Secretary-General's political influence, which the Soviet Union hoped to check.

The sheer vehemence with which the Soviet Premier made the proposal was bound to have a political effect, but would hardly result in reform of the Secretariat. Only the Soviet bloc proposed wholesale adoption of the principle. But several new members, including Ghana and Guinea, somewhat troubled by the predominance of European and North American officials serving in the Secretariat under permanent appointments, responded to the Soviet initiative with proposals that deputy secretaries-general acceptable to the West, the East, and the neutral group be appointed and invested with defined responsibilities.

This proposal appeared again in a more rationalized form in the Report of the Committee of Experts which the General Assembly established in 1959 to review the activities and organization of the Secretariat. The committee logically concentrated on the top level of the Secretariat. The Soviet member of the committee, predictably, reiterated the Soviet position favoring the troika. The experts from Egypt, Ghana, and India favored the creation of three new posts of deputy secretaries-general, whose incumbents would serve for one term only, supervise the work of the Secretariat from the highest level, and reflect "the main political trends in the world today." [7]

Hammarskjöld reacted strongly to suggestions of a collegial system. His view was that since the Charter provided for an international civil service with one chief administrative officer, anything else, which included the Indian and Ghanaian suggestions, would either infringe on the responsibilities of the Secretary-General or introduce a representative function which was contrary to the Charter. Either case, he insisted, would necessitate a change in the Charter.[8] He is known to have supported the view that whatever authority he had derived from his ultimate personal responsibility. Plans to dilute that personal responsibility through the introduction of a cabinet system, he argued, were based on reasoning from national analogies which, in the Cold War situation and whenever national interests clash, could not apply in the United Nations. Furthermore, according to Hammarskjöld's views, the failure of the Assistant Secretary-General level, when Lie held office, to provide a link between a one-man executive and the administrative ranks also showed the impossibility of a cabinet system. If it were intended only to provide an advisory body for the Secretary-General, Hammarskjöld could see little need for it and considerable danger of breakdown and retrogression.

The death of Hammarskjöld interfered with the efforts of those favoring the representation of "main political trends" within the Secretariat. But the collegial idea, once reintroduced, continued to have strong influences. It underlay the discussions of the number of Under-Secretaries to be appointed by Thant as Acting Secretary-General. He opposed the collegial principle, opting for Hammarskjöld's view that he needed broad and sole responsibility (or close to it) in order to carry out the duties of Secretary-General. Nor has he as a general practice brought his principal advisers together for discussions prior to decisions. On the contrary, he has assigned them specific functions and has sent of them away from headquarters for special missions.

Despite the durability of the collegial idea and the fortuitous support given it by the troika proposals, the Secretariat remains on the whole a unitary organization and the Secretary-General continues to deal with the deliberative organs as its responsible head. That he consults his colleagues goes without saying, but their views, however forceful or tuned to the needs of a national delegation, constitute influences, not vetoes.

The suppression and reemergence of the collegial proposal points to the importance of the top level of the Secretariat as a factor in the influence of the Secretary-General.[9] It has been organized along two main patterns. The first of these, applied by Lie in accordance with the plans of the Preparatory Commission, emphasized the devolution of responsibility for functional operations to top officials heading strong departments. The second, created in part out of the shortcomings of the first, emphasized the central position of the Secretary-General and provided him with closer associates for political work and more direct tools of management.

Lie's organization of the Secretariat was probably inevitably bedeviled by its own novelty. But beyond that, it also demonstrated persistent difficulties with coordination and with political functions. The first of these difficulties could be traced, as much as anything else, to the establishment of posts at two levels at the top of each department. An Assistant Secretary-General headed each department and immediately below him was a Top-Ranking or Principal Director. The Assistant Secretaries-General were to devolve administrative responsibilities upon their Principal Directors.

Although a clear distinction in principle could be drawn between the two ranks, in fact it gave way to varying practical expedients. In some cases, the Assistant Secretary-General left the management of his department largely to the Principal Director and devoted himself to policies and political liaison. In other cases, the two ranking officials collaborated to form a team. Sometimes the Principal Director of a department had closer links with the Secretary-General than did the department head. Such variation produces administrative clumsiness and not necessarily a great deal of influence for the Secretary-General, either in forming and directing internal policies or in advancing his views with other organs and governments.

Lie gave evidence of concern with both coordination and political functions in the Secretariat in his appointment, in 1948, of an Assistant Secretary-General with general coordinating functions and in his drastic reorganization proposal of 1952. The appointment of the super-coordinator, Commander R.G.A. Jackson, an experienced Australian who had held high posts in the United Nations Relief and Rehabilitation Administration (UNRRA), proved less than a success. Jackson's assignment as a troubleshooter lasted less than a year, during which his energy apparently exceeded the restraints imposed by an international service and by the prestige of his colleagues. No attempt was made by Lie to appoint another superior officer to act formally on his behalf to coordinate the coordinators.[10]

Neither the problem of coordination nor of political functions had been solved when Lie proposed, just before his resignation, a sweeping regrouping of the Secretariat under three deputy secretaries-general. These three senior officers would have the competence and experience to serve as top administrators and keep the Secretary-General from getting bogged down in detail. They would head up, respectively, the Departments of Political and Security Council Affairs, Trusteeship and Information from Non-Self-Governing Territories, and Public Information. These are the functions most relevant to the political role of the Secretary-General. All of the deputy secretaries general would have the confidence and respect of member governments; they could therefore assist in political matters. Routine responsibilities for administration would be turned over to the level of Principal Directors.[11]

Two important inferences can be drawn from Lie's reorganization scheme. First, the existing organization of the Secretariat, in Lie's opinion, drew the Secretary-General away from the possibilities of directly influencing the formation of policy in matters of peace and security. Second, although Lie praised the Assistant Secretaries-General, the ranking officers of the Secretariat had apparently been of less than maximum assistance in helping him in his efforts to form peace and security policies.

Hammarskjöld specifically rejected Lie's reorganization scheme, but proposed his own to meet the same problems of coordination and support in matters of maintenance of the peace that had troubled his predecessor. In order to improve coordination, he successfully sought permission from the General Assembly in 1954 to dismantle the old eight-department structure, replacing it with staff offices for personnel, finance, legal, and information functions under his direct supervision, and line departments headed by senior officials. The dual ranks at the top of the Secretariat gave way to the single title of Under-Secretary.[12]

Another proposal, the most novel of any in Hammarskjöld's suggestions, bore directly on his activities in the field of peace and security and set the pattern which, in general, still endures. He successfully urged the appointment of two Under-Secretaries for Special Political Affairs, who would have no administrative assignments as heads of departments. "The Under-Secretaries without department," he said, "will have assignments predominantly of a political character which also cut across the competence of several departments." [13] The Under-Secretaries for Special Political Affairs later took charge of such matters as the preparation and operation of the Atoms-for-Peace conferences and the day-to-day direction and management of UNEF and the United Nations Operation in the Congo (ONUC).[14]

Any official of Under-Secretary rank can be considered senior and influential enough to contribute something to the Secretary-General's equipment for dealing with matters of peace and security. Those assigned to functions directly relevant to the maintenance of peace or those who have influence in governmental circles can naturally contribute directly to the formation and execution of policies. Although the number of senior officials has grown large enough to cause some comment in the General Assembly,[15] it is by no means obvious that the top level of the Secretariat provides enough talent to support the Secretary-General in all enterprises. Furthermore, many officials of Under-Secretary rank either have highly specialized duties, such as the High Commissioner for Refugees, or else have a great deal of autonomy, as do the Executive Secretaries of the regional economic commissions.

The growth of politico-administrative functions and, in particular, the large-scale operation in the Congo caused Hammarskjöld to call for an expansion of the number of top-level officials. In the *Introduction* to his *Annual Report* in 1960, he declared:

> There is, generally speaking, within the Secretariat not enough of a diplomatic tradition or staff with training in political and diplomatic field activities to meet the needs which have developed over the years.[16]

When additional personnel for political activities were needed, as far as possible they were sought out and secured on short-term appointment or loan, which meant, of course, that after a brief period their experience became unavailable. Three past presidents of the General Assembly, whom Hammarskjöld had asked during the tense situation created by the Soviet attack to serve as a committee to advise him on the organization of the Under-Secretary level of the Secretariat, supported his proposal for increasing the number of high officials. Hammarskjöld also planned a further refinement of the Under-Secretary level to separate officials with political duties from those engaged in internal administration. The former would have the title of assistant secretary-general, while the latter would use the old title. The post of Executive Assistant was to become two, one of them an assistant secretary-general and the other a *chef de cabinet*. These reorganization plans were not carried forward because of Hammarskjöld's death.[17]

The appointment of Principal Advisers by Thant as a condition of his taking office only superficially deviated from the centralizing line taken by Hammarskjöld. In addition to appointing Bunche and Arkadev as Principal Advisers, he made three new appointments to fill out the list. These were Jiri Nosek of Czechoslovakia, G.K.J. Amachree of Nigeria, and the late Omar Loutfi of the United Arab Republic.[18] Later three more Under-Secretaries in the Secretariat received appointment as Principal Advisers.

Changes in the administrative structure of the top level of the Secretariat up to mid-1966 seem to have produced little that is really new. The number of Principal Advisers, affected by retirement and death, has not greatly augmented the senior staff available to the Secretary-General. It also seems true that the growing experience of the Secretariat and the seasoning of some of the senior officials in political matters may have to some degree reduced the immediate severity of the problems of coordination and perhaps of political support.[19]

The centralized supervision and control of the Secretariat, strengthened by the Hammarskjöld reforms, make it imperative that the Secretary-General have a personal staff to serve as his right hand, his eyes and ears. The Preparatory Commission did not anticipate the development of a personal office for the Secretary-General, but one nevertheless made its appearance as the Executive Office of the Secretary-General immediately after Lie's appointment.[20] It was at first headed by David Owen, who became Assistant Secretary-General for Economic Affairs during the first year of the organization, and then by Andrew W. Cordier, who remained in the post of Executive Assistant to the Secretary-General and in charge of the Executive Office until 1961, shortly before his retirement. The Executive Assistant at first had the rank of Principal Director, and after the Hammarskjöld reorganization, of Under-Secretary.

Aside from providing the obvious secretarial services for the Secretary-General, the Executive Office was immediately asked to engage in work which gave it an overview of the activities of the organization. To begin with, the Executive Office furnished the senior secretariat for, and managed the agenda of, the General Assembly. Since all work of the organization, whether by Secretariat or international organ, is reported to the General Assembly, the Executive Office therefore has access to information on all activities. The Executive Office edits the Secretary-General's *Annual Report on the Work of the Organization.* As a result, it is influential in composing a public face for the work of the entire Secretariat. In 1954, by appointing a Chief Editor, Hammarskjöld moved to bring the control of all United Nations publications, especially official documents, under closer scrutiny by his office.[21]

The Executive Office allocates the responsibilities approved by the General Assembly to the various departments. Such allocations are made occasionally by simple order, but are usually presented on the basis of the substance of a resolution and after consultation; that does not diminish the strategic importance of the Executive Office in the execution of General Assembly policies.

What was begun as a coordination function gradually grew into an officially recognized supervisory and planning task. Furthermore, as the General Assembly and the Security Council established field missions, their supervision and coordination became part of the work of the Executive Office. As a result, it is in constant and direct touch with United Nations activities in the most difficult and dangerous political situations.

In other important ways, the Executive Office remains in touch with political affairs. It has liaison duties with representatives of member states. In addition, it serves as the last check point for correspondence directed to member governments, and it has charge of relationships with other international organizations. Because of these strategic functions in dealing with governments, other organizations, and political matters, the Executive Office began to assume new duties as a link with the press and the public, and these public functions were eventually assigned officially to it. At various times, also, the Executive Office supervised the United Nations Library and bore direct responsibility for routine coordination with the Specialized Agencies.

The Executive Office has always included a high proportion of senior officials, as might be expected from the character of the work assigned to it. In fact, early in 1949 it underwent a reorganization intended to bring more senior personnel into its manning table. Moreover, since the Hammarskjöld reorganization the Secretary-General has had close at hand the Under-Secretaries for Special Political Affairs, to whom he could assign *ad hoc* tasks. New offices of personnel, the controller, and the legal counsel brought other high-ranking officers into closer relationship with the Secretary-General. Furthermore, when a Military Adviser was appointed after the beginning of the Congo operation, he became part of the Executive Office. It can therefore be concluded that the number of high-ranking officials in the Secretary-General's immediate entourage certainly increased along with his political activities.[22]

The formal official responsibilities of the Executive Office attain full significance only with the creation of informal working relationships and persistent patterns of thought and action. The success of the Executive Office in this accomplishment has provided the Secretary-General with substantial help in influencing and executing policy in matters of peace and security. A great deal of this assistance comprises the routine functions of the Executive Office; it is seldom completely visible. In other instances the personnel of the Executive Office have been given important temporary duties, which indicates that the Secretary-General places a high degree of trust in them.

Two aspects of the assignment given to the Executive Office make it a natural source of advice on policies to be supported and promoted by the Secretary-General. First, as coordinator of the work of the Secretariat, the Executive Office acts as the Secretary-General's "general staff." [23] It is apprised of and is a channel of communication for the Secretary-General's ideas with regard to the operation of the Secretariat. It assesses the capacities and limitations of the Secretariat and suggests to the Secretary-General suitable personnel for operational or developmental assignments.

As the Secretariat of the General Assembly and in liaison with the national delegations, the Executive Office receives a flow of information about the policies of the member governments. This is supplemented by additional material passed along through the Secretariat departments. The Executive Assistant has, therefore, frequently acted as coordinator of intelligence for the Secretary-General. At the same time, he and his staff often carry on negotiations with member governments on behalf of the Secretary-General. And later, if a public account of such activities becomes desirable or necessary or if the Secretary-General wishes to make a public matter of it, the Executive Office prepares or reviews the press statements or speeches which the chief administrative officer makes.

These activities by the Executive Office are easy to illustrate. Andrew Cordier became such a familiar figure at the left of the President of the General Assembly that his absence from his familiar place after his retirement, even though anticipated, seemed a sharp change to the "old hands" of United Nations business. He was renowned for his smooth and imperturbable leadership in managing the complex business of the General Assembly. Lie spoke of Cordier as his "strong right hand" throughout his term. The Executive Assistant constantly had negotiating tasks, including such important political dealings as those on Palestine and Korea. He traveled abroad frequently on administrative matters and in connection with his responsibility as coordinator of field missions. These trips brought him into further contact with governments.[24]

The political potential of the Executive Office became fully apparent with the outbreak of the Korean conflict. The allocation of Assistant Secretary-General posts among the permanent members of the Security Council meant that a Soviet national, Constantin Zinchenko, headed the Department of Political and Security Council Affairs in the Secretariat. In the midst of the Cold War, Zinchenko's position, dependent as it was on nomination by his government, became, as Lie vastly understates it, "difficult."

The Secretary-General's own position had its difficult aspects, too, for he personally was attempting to secure a novel and important place for his organization in directing the struggle to reverse the invasion of South Korea. This kind of high politics requires relationships of trust among all the participants and their staffs. In this situation a special unit in the Executive Office, in which Cordier took up a leading role, was created to deal with Korean affairs.[25] The Department of Political and Security Council Affairs and its Soviet head thus were altogether by-passed in the most important matter of peace and security yet to come before the United Nations.

Once the detour around the Security Council affairs department had been marked out, it was never forgotten. The Soviet Union, nevertheless, clung to its determination to have one of its nationals at the head of the department and protested that, as the Soviet member of the Committee of Experts on the Secretariat declared in 1961, "essential categories of political questions and the direction of political affairs had without justification been moved from the Department of Political and Security Council Affairs to the Office of the Secretary-General." [26] The same Soviet delegate, speaking in the General Assembly a year earlier, declared that operations had been taken out of the hands of the department because it was headed by a Soviet citizen. Operations, he insisted, are "exclusively in the hands of United States citizens working in the Secretariat. . . . This accounts for the fact that the Security Council decisions . . . are being carried out wrongly." [27]

Hammarskjöld replied sharply that:

> The Secretary-General is the only member of the administration which Members have chosen, by election, to bear political responsibility; he cannot delegate such responsibility, be it to a citizen of the Soviet Union

or a citizen of the United States, or indeed, a citizen of any other Member Country. . . . Were the Under-Secretary in charge of the Political Affairs Department, whoever he is, to be considered as automatically in charge of field operations, on his own personal responsibility, the logical conclusion would seem to be that he should be appointed with the approval of the main organs of the United Nations in analogy with the principle established in Article 97.[28]

Although Hammarskjöld might have gone farther than he needed in defending the principle of his responsibility for the Secretariat, it remains true that the Soviet nationals who have headed the Department of Political and Security Council Affairs have made little mark on the record of the Secretary-General in matters of peace and security. At the same time, with Cordier as Executive Assistant and Bunche as one of the two Under-Secretaries for Special Political Affairs, two United States nationals in the Secretariat did have an outstanding share in directing operations.

Because Hammarskjöld and Cordier soon established an excellent working relationship—"Anything of concern to Hammarskjöld was in Cordier's domain too"[29]—the Executive Office and its head were constantly involved in peace and security operations. The Suez negotiations and the creation of UNEF either had the personal attention of the Secretary-General or were in the charge of the Executive Office. While the Under-Secretaries for Special Political Affairs formally were separate from the Executive Office, their presence on the Secretary-General's floor and their close working relationships with him required that they function in close harmony with Cordier's group. As a result, the management of the Congo operation included uninterrupted participation by the Executive Assistant.[30] From time to time, as they were needed, other lower-ranking staff members whose expertise had particular relevance to a problem under consideration were brought into the Executive Office. For example, the late Hans Wieschoff of the Department of Trusteeship and Information from Non-Self-Governing Territories served as adviser on African politics.

Several effects on the rest of the Secretariat resulted from this centralization of political functions. The Department of Political and Security Council Affairs failed to develop influence, and this gave the Soviet Union opportunities for complaint. Other officials of the organization found themselves at a distance from concern with political problems, even if their work touched on them. Junior officials gained little experience in this area. It is less than clear that the handling of political problems, for which Hammarskjöld requested more personnel, became part of the routine of the bureaucratic mechanism of the United Nations. Rather, political affairs came to be regarded by many officials as the closely-held specialty of a small group, chosen personally by the Secretary-General without regard to organizational niceties. Some men of great capacities, including Sir Humphrey Trevelyan and Guillaume Georges-Picot, are said to have resigned from the Secretariat because of these working methods.[31]

During the last months of Hammarskjöld's tenure, changes were made in the structure of the Executive Office. Cordier, near retirement age and under criticism by the Soviet bloc for his nationality and for his actions in the Congo, resigned his powerful post in June, 1961. His letter to Hammarskjöld made it clear that his leaving was intended to make it easier to realign the top level of the Secretariat to take into account the new membership of the organization. He stayed on until February, 1962, in charge of General Assembly affairs. His other duties devolved on C.V. Narasimhan, who had come from the Economic Commission for Asia and the Far East to serve as Under-Secretary for Special Political Affairs. As projected in his comments on the report of the Committee of Experts, Hammarskjöld called Narasimhan his *chef de cabinet,* a title which remained attached to the office after Thant's appointment. When Cordier retired in 1962, Narasimhan assumed all of Cordier's former functions and the title of Principal Adviser as well. It can be taken for granted that the strategic and influential place of the Executive Office of the Secretary-General in no way declined upon this appointment.

Service as secretary to international deliberative organs is one of the most characteristic and long-practiced functions of the Secretary-General. Usually he personally attends meetings of the Security Council and plenary sessions of the General Assembly, at which the appropriate Under-Secretary actually functions as secretary. In other organs and committees, a high-ranking staff member, sometimes a veteran who has served for many years with the same body, is assigned as secretary.

These officials, usually the first to discuss agendas with delegates and always the ready advisers on procedures and legal questions, have a strategic position from which to observe and consult.[32] They frequently provide the Secretary-General with important information about political trends and are likely to be the officials who suggest that the Secretary-General should make an appearance in order to bring the prestige of his office and his person to bear on the proceedings.

In smaller deliberative bodies, the secretary may have a direct influence on the policy process when reports must be written. Even in the main committees of the General Assembly, where resolutions are drafted mainly by governmental representatives, the secretaries may make important private suggestions and have been known to propose specific amendments in open meetings. In bodies with mediatory or fact-finding duties, the secretary and his staff draft reports on the basis of the discussions. He comes to understand the instructions given by governments to their representatives, and therefore may be able to exercise persuasive powers or exert pressure on behalf of the Secretary-General.

In the case of private meetings of the Security Council or other deliberative bodies, the Secretary-General or his representative normally has the responsibility of drafting and issuing an official communiqué. The Secretary-General or his representative sometimes is asked to fill in the details of the communiqué by holding an unofficial press briefing. He therefore may find an opportunity to comment on possible public reaction to the content of an announcement, and his advice may to some extent influence decisions.

Some discretion with implications for the maintenance of peace is left to the Secretary-General in regard to the circulation of communications and the actions he may take on the basis of them. The Rules of Procedure of the Security Council provide that he shall bring to the attention of all representatives communications from states, organs of the United Nations, and himself concerning any matter for its consideration.[33] In some instances the circulation of a communication as an official document touches delicate political nerves. It may lend itself to a propaganda effort by a government or a private group. But to refuse to circulate the communication may bring the Secretary-General under criticism.

Several developments have taken place which affect the Secretary-General's discretion in circulating documents. In the Hyderabad case, in which Indian troops occupied the princely state in 1948, the Secretary-General circulated documents from the Hyderabad government under a note which stated simply that he was not in a position to determine whether he was obliged to do so and left it to the Council to decide. A year later he circulated an application for membership from the Democratic People's Republic of Korea (the Communist regime in North Korea) "for the convenience of the members . . . which desire to be informed of it." [34] Since then, a great number of documents have been reproduced at the request of governments for the information of the Council. The states involved call attention to problems which eventually may come before the Council, and at the same time get wider circulation for their views.[35] Such actions of the Secretary-General have usually caused no special discord and have left a wide area of discretion within which he may choose to put political material before the Council.

In the Congo case, the Secretary-General's decision (discussed in Chapter VII) to put his own letter before the Council rather than transmit two cables from the Leopoldville government had greater significance. The sharp discussion which followed made it clear that the Secretary-General's examination and assessment of communications could have a political impact.

Another class of communications, that dealing with accreditation of representatives to the Security Council, has a potentially high political content. The Secretary-General has the duty of examining the credentials of any delegate sitting with the Council.[36] So far he has treated this duty in a neutral and technical way, and after 1948 his report was no longer on the Security Council agenda, it being understood that it was approved unless an objection was made.

In case of doubt about the rightful government of a state following an insurrection, the Secretary-General may well have two sets of credentials in his hands. After the victory of the Chinese Communists, the potentiality of precisely such a situation obtained. Early in 1950 Lie received a cablegram from the Peking government, informing him that a representative had been appointed. The involved debate which followed in the Security Council and eventuated in the Soviet delegate's leaving the table (to begin an absence that endured until more than a month after the outbreak of hostilities in Korea) did not call into question the Secretary-General's routine function.

However, Lie used the Peking demand as the basis for a legal memorandum on representation in the Council. After it began to leak to the press, he had it circulated as a Security Council document. The memorandum argued that the difficulty in the Chinese case arose from linking representation with recognition by governments. Representation should be based on objective factors, such as whether the government in question could employ the resources and direct the people of the state so that the conditions of membership under the Charter could be fulfilled. The memorandum did not argue that the Secretary-General should decide when a revolutionary government has met the objective criteria described in it. Rather, such a decision would clearly be for the organ involved to make.

Even when members of the Council raised questions regarding credentials, as they did during the Hungarian case in 1956 and during the Iraqi revolution in 1958, the Secretary-General has assumed a reserved attitude.[37] In the latter instance, Hammarskjöld gave an opinion on whether the credentials of the representative of the revolutionary government were in order, once declaring that they were not and later, after circumstances had changed, stating that they were. The comments of the Secretary-General were entirely based on a juridical analysis and kept on a neutral plane. The decision was left entirely to the Council.

The duties of the Secretary-General with regard to credentials of representatives to the Security Council may then be taken as usually routine. If representation of a government does raise questions, the matter probably would be too delicate for the Secretary-General overtly to attempt to influence the immediate decision.

Of consistently greater political influence than the Secretary-General's concern with communications and credentials are his duties involving the agendas of United Nations organs. For the Security Council, he draws up a provisional agenda which must be approved by the President of the Council, who changes each month. The agenda may include only items which have been introduced by members or the Secretary-General or have not been disposed of previously.[38] For the General Assembly, the Secretary-General draws up a provisional agenda and has the right to list items he deems necessary. In the Security Council he has a similar right. It derives from Article 99 of the Charter, although since Hammarskjöld's report on his trip to Laos a general right to propose items for consideration seems to have been established. In the General Assembly his right to put items on the provisional agenda is unlimited.

The manner in which he exercises these rights contrasts sharply in the two organs. The Secretary-General has rarely introduced items in the Security Council. More frequently he lists items on the agenda of the General Assembly. Most of these concern the inner workings of the organization; but Lie, for example, introduced his twenty-year peace program to the agenda, and in 1958 Hammarskjöld successfully proposed that the General Assembly discuss the "Question of Disarmament." [39]

The involvement of the Secretary-General in drafting the provisional agendas for the two organs touches on his concern with the efficient conduct of work. He therefore may suggest such concrete steps as the consolidation of several items under one heading. His private suggestions guide the General Committee of the Assembly in allocating items among the main committees. Furthermore, the Secretary-General must remain alert to work implied for the Secretariat in proposed agenda items.

From such necessary technical conversations come "innumerable discussions on agenda items," in which the Secretary-General may express his views on the substance of what has been proposed. "If the item involves his own responsibility or a mandate placed on him, or the highest interests of the organization, or is crucial in preserving the peace," the former Executive Assistant to the Secretary-General writes, "he is morally obliged to play a maximum role in securing a sound outcome of the debate." [40]

Limitations on Personnel Direction

As chief of the Secretariat, the Secretary-General has a chance to develop something of a following, the influence of which cannot be entirely overlooked by member governments. If the Secretariat furnishes ideas, advice, information, and persuasiveness, the influence derived from his position as head of the staff may be increased. But a controversial situation within the Secretariat may not only deprive him of the benefits of good staff work but also open the way to attacks on his prestige and authority, with a concomitant lessening of influence in matters of peace and security.

Aside from the familiar administrative imperatives of protecting the prestige and welfare of his subordinates, the Secretary-General must act within limitations characteristic of the United Nations. The Charter charges him with the appointment of the Secretariat so as to meet "the highest standards of efficiency, competence, and integrity." But he is simultaneously instructed to pay "due regard . . . to the importance of recruiting the staff on as wide a geographical basis as possible."[41] Connected with this instruction is the involvement of the Secretary-General in problems of "loyalty" of staff members. Controversies over "loyalty" have proven quite poisonous to the prestige of the Secretary-General and to his firm control of the Secretariat.

Geographical distribution increasingly became a cause of controversy between the Secretary-General and a growing group of members as new countries were admitted to the United Nations. It was also connected by the Soviet Union to the troika proposal and demands for replacement of career international civil servants with personnel on short-term appointment. Pressure from the new members to have their nationals appointed to the Secretariat has resulted in greater use of temporary appointments.

Although all three Secretaries-General have had to spend much time explaining geographical distribution policies and answering criticisms, the results of repeated examinations by his own officials and by the General Assembly has left the matter in each administration roughly where it began. The Secretaries-General have maintained control over appointments and shifted the guidelines for geographical distribution only slightly. Their plans[42] for improving geographical distribution of the Secretariat in response to the wider membership in the organization have won approval in the General Assembly, indicating that their influence in this administrative issue remains high.

Insistence by member governments that their nationals ought to occupy posts in the Secretariat suggests that they do not entirely support the idea of an international civil service. The contrary principle of a staff whose membership duplicates that of the General Assembly so as to represent the ideas of each government lay behind Khrushchev's famous phrase that denied that there were neutral men.[43] The Soviet leader thus raised a question of the loyalty of the international civil servants. The issue was no novelty, for the United States has searched for Communists and spies among its nationals in the Secretariat and, in several ways, other governments have touched on the subject of loyalty.

If governments were to demand that international civil servants have detailed beliefs in accordance with their own, even the normal national elections, let alone more violent change, could cause endless difficulties for the Secretariat. No Secretary-General can afford to surround himself with refugee revolutionaries or eccentrics. Yet he can use his appointment power to please governments and still not incorporate merely somnolent bodies into the Secretariat, and he has usually sought to do so.

"[H]elp from governments in getting the best people was obviously necessary, and advisable, so long as my independence of judgement and decision was respected," Lie wrote.[44] This help could assist the Secretary-General in keeping clear of controversial persons, should he wish to do so. At the same time, governmental advice did tend to limit the Secretary-General's freedom of choice of personnel, for he could not ask for advice and then seem to refuse to heed it. Nor did he have more than a theoretical freedom of choice in other respects, for he never had a recruitment and personnel network to produce full slates of candidates for appointment on the basis of anything approaching perfect knowledge.

Lie found it impossible to please both the United States and those members of the General Assembly who criticized his policy of acquiescence in the investigation of United States members of the Secretariat during the McCarthyite hysteria. Hammarskjöld succeeded in working out with the United States administrative procedures which helped to calm the political turbulence around appointment of United States nationals in the Secretariat.[45]

In fact, the implied loyalty issue revived by the Soviet Union was secondary to the issue of control over the activities of the Secretariat. The Secretary-General's control had been strengthened by Hammarskjöld, over Soviet objections. By 1960 the unquestioned leadership of the staff by the Secretary-General had become an element in his ability to influence actions in the field of peace and security. Although the pressure brought by the Soviet Union and its allies on the Secretary-General was reduced after Hammarskjöld's death, the demand for a large number of highly responsive Soviet nationals (as well as those from other socialist countries) has never been renounced.

It is conceivable that the loyalty issue could again be raised by the Soviet Union as a means of interfering with the action of the Secretary-General. It seems less likely that the United States could easily do so, in view of the elaborate machinery to screen that country's employees; but the charges that the United Nations is a center for espionage could again be revived as a means of checking action by the United Nations and the Secretary-General.

The Budget Process and Finances

Ordinarily, neither budget nor finance has much to do with the maintenance of peace and security.[46] But from some issues of peace and security unusual budgetary and financial demands have arisen, impelling the Secretary-General to exert every possible influence on the policy-making process and imposing limits on his ability to maintain his influence and to carry out his own policies.

The budget document presented to the General Assembly each year issues from the Secretary-General and is his responsibility. The guidelines within which the budget is worked out are laid down by deliberative organs in which the Secretary-General to a greater or lesser extent is influential. The final approval of the budget is a matter for the General Assembly, and the Secretary-General may exert influence on that body at several junctures during the budget process.

Until the great expansion of peace-keeping functions assigned to the Secretary-General, only small percentages of the budget were directly linked to matters of peace and security. These typically included a field mission, or a commission, or perhaps the cost of a special meeting or conference involving governments in a dispute. Only the assignments undertaken by the Secretary-General in Suez and the Congo included expenditures which exceeded approximately an eighth of the regular budget of the organization.

Although the Secretary-General makes suggestions implying large expenditures in the economic and social field, leading from initiative to budgetary proposal, in the peace and security field he has done so very infrequently and with indifferent success. One example is Lie's suggestion of an international guard force, which became in the end an administrative adjunct with special abilities to deal with the problems of field operations.[47]

The process of budgetary consideration has sometimes induced sharp exchanges between the delegates and the Secretary-General. The usual practice, followed from the beginning by Lie and continued by Hammarskjöld and Thant, sees the Secretary-General introduce his budget personally in the Fifth Committee. On that occasion he defends any controversial items and tries to meet anticipated criticisms as well as those already projected by the Advisory Committee on Administrative and Budgetary Questions. The Secretary-General always presents a closely-pared, conservative budget. He takes the position that it has been stripped of waste and represents a minimum amount necessary to carry out the programs decided upon by the organs.

In any case, the Secretary-General and his staff control the principal documents; they are far better informed and have more expertness than the delegates, especially in a large committee setting. The Secretary-General can also rely to some extent on his prestige, as Thant did by pointing out that his views on the budget represented those of a principal organ and must therefore be weighed carefully and credited for the experience behind them. With such advantages he seldom finds it necessary to abandon proposals because of criticism, and can usually strike a bargain when his recommendations do not prevail.

The UNEF and ONUC issues produced a financial crisis in part resulting from attempts to use the budgetary route to prevent the Secretary-General from carrying out his policies to maintain peace. It also grew out of the vast expansion of an organization whose members had always insisted on a tight budget. The Secretary-General became deeply involved in the crisis because his policies were under attack, because he had to attempt to carry out approved programs for which financing was insufficient, and because he was bidden by the General Assembly to seek solutions.

In the case of UNEF, the cost for the first 14 months was some $30 million and later was stabilized at approximately $20 million a year. ONUC cost in the neighborhood of $10 million a month.

It was not the passage of the budget for UNEF and ONUC, for which the required two-thirds majority vote was always forthcoming, which caused the crisis. Rather it was the securing of finances and apportioning expenses among the members which produced it. As both Hammarskjöld and Thant pointed out, financing the approved work of the organization is the responsibility of the member governments, not of the Secretary-General.

Before UNEF, the Secretary-General's main function in financing related to voluntary contributions, which in the case of the United Nations Korean Reconstruction Agency (UNKRA) and the United Nations Relief and Works Agency for Palestine Refugees (UNRWA) had some connection with peace and security. He pressed member governments to contribute or to add to initial contributions.

The seeds of the financial crisis of 1960–1964, which became so severe at times that the Secretary-General could not be certain that the staff would be paid, began to sprout during the operation of UNEF. That peace-keeping force, he said, "is essentially a United Nations responsibility" and its financing must be construed as falling under Article 17 of the Charter.[48] In successfully asking the General Assembly, in 1956, to approve a Special Account for UNEF, Hammarskjöld used his budget-making powers to help lead to a decision on financing. "For the first time in history," Miss Rosner observes, "the principle of collective responsibility was established in regard to meeting the costs of an international security force."[49] The Secretary-General followed this line throughout the ONUC operation, and it did not go unchallenged in either the UNEF or ONUC cases.

Three kinds of challenges were raised during both experiences in which many members refused to pay assessments, even if they approved the policies for which financing was sought. The sharpest objection came from the Soviet group (joined by the Arab states in the UNEF case), which argued that the aggressors ought to be made to pay for the disturbances they had caused. The bills should be sent to Britain and France for UNEF, and to Belgium for the Congo. A further Soviet argument held that peace-keeping in any case was a matter for the Security Council and that it should deal with the financing, which could not be treated as apportionable under Article 17 of the Charter. The implications of this argument were that the General Assembly could not apply Article 19 of the Charter, which provides that in case any state falls more than two years in arrears in paying its contributions it may be deprived of its vote in the General Assembly.

The second and third kinds of challenges were related, in that they both referred to the magnitude of the new assessments. The Latin American countries, employing legal arguments, urged that the great powers should be assessed in accordance with their heavy responsibilities for the peace. The third challenge came from the smallest and poorest states, which did not so much object to collective responsibility as they did to the practicality and morality of their contributing any more in view of their poverty.

In fact, generous voluntary contributions to UNEF permitted adjustments in the assessment pattern to reduce the burden on the poorer countries and to move some distance in fact, if not in principle, to the goal sought by the Latin American countries. But by 1960, 42 governments had failed to contribute to the UNEF account and the ONUC operation for that year alone left a gap of $48.5 million to be filled. By September, 1964, the accumulated deficits had mounted to $113.3 million and the cash resources of the organization, even after numerous expedients, had fallen to $24.8 million. It was no wonder that Thant could tell the General Assembly that "the financial crisis has been one of my major preoccupations." [50]

The hand-to-mouth arrangements forced on the Secretary-General by the reluctance of some members to pay for peace-keeping necessarily drove him into issues of financing. Hammarskjöld reacted sharply, and personally posed the issue to the Fifth Committee in 1960, when he asked:

> Will this Organization face the economic consequences of its own actions and how will it be done? Further if it is not willing to face the financial consequences of its own decisions, is it prepared to change its substantive policies? There is no third alternative. It must be remembered that it is

not the Secretariat which carries the responsibility for costs caused by steps taken by the General Assembly or the Security Council.[51]

This and similar appeals—along with hard behind-the-scenes explorations of the implications of the financial situation and schemes to provide money despite reluctance of members—in fact made insufficient impression to alter national policies.

The budgetary device (created and strongly backed by the Secretary-General) of special accounts for peace-keeping expenditures by UNEF and ONUC furnished the pretext for an argument in the General Assembly that ordinary expenses could be distinguished from extraordinary ones. The extraordinary expenses, it was said, were not subject to Article 17 and members could not be assessed for them. This argument eventually led to a request in 1961 for an advisory opinion from the International Court of Justice on whether ONUC and UNEF costs were expenses of the organization within the meaning of Article 17.

The Secretary-General's views were unequivocal. "[T]he only possible conclusion . . . is that Article 17 must apply to the expenses in question," Hammarskjöld said. "[M]y conclusion would not in any way prejudge or restrict the right of . . . the General Assembly to apportion the expenses as it considers appropriate and equitable." [52] Although the Secretary-General or his representative did not appear before the Court, his view was presented to it in documents which covered the discussions in the General Assembly. His opinion coincided with that of the United States, the principal backer of the reference to the Court and of the view that Article 17 applied. The bare majority of the Court agreed with this view, and it was later accepted without enthusiasm by the General Assembly.[53]

The political implications of the position taken by the Secretary-General were far-reaching, but they were never completely spelled out by him in a public meeting. One of these, however, explored by the United States and its supporters, was that if Article 17 of the Charter applied to the UNEF and ONUC accounts, then so did Article 19. The Soviet Union, France, and several other states would then be liable to lose their votes in the General Assembly. The impasse which grew out of this reasoning made a nullity of the 1964 General Assembly and threatened to wreck the organization. This eventuality probably would have come about had the United States not altered its position before the 1965 General Assembly.

A principal outcome of what Thant called "a policy of drift, of improvisation, of *ad hoc* solutions, of reliance on the generosity of the few rather than the collective responsibility of all" [54] was a still deeper involvement of the Secretary-General in the financing process. Aside from his pleas for financing, the search for expedients impelled the Secretary-General to influence the General Assembly and the members. One of these expedients was authorization to borrow from accounts earmarked for other purposes, such as pension funds and the United Nations Special Fund.

A more striking and original expedient, resulting from Thant's initiative, was a $200 million bond issue. In December, 1961, soon after he had warned that "the United Nations will be facing imminent bankruptcy," he proposed in a memorandum to the five permanent members of the Security Council that the United Nations offer 25-year, two percent bonds for sale to national Treasuries and national banks. Before making the formal proposal he had also discusssed the scheme with several other governments.[55] Eight small countries then proposed the issuance of bonds as projected by the Secretary-General. The United States declared itself ready to seek authorization for the purchase of up to $100 million worth, depending on how much was sold to other governments. The Soviet Union sharply attacked the scheme as illegal and many strong reservations by small nations were made known. The plan was adopted by the General Assembly on December 20, 1961, by a vote of 58 in favor, 13 against, and 24 abstentions.[56] The bond issue brought in more than $145 million.

After approving the bond issue and thus buying some time before a bankruptcy made seemingly inevitable by continuing the Congo operation with no sure financing, the General Assembly became involved in procedures that were rococo in their elaborateness. A Working Group set up in December, 1962 failed to produce a useful report and the United Nations headed into 1963 with a fat budget and an empty treasury. A special session of the General Assembly to deal with financing was decided upon for the late spring of 1963, and in preparation the Working Group returned to its task. It failed again to bring in an agreed report.

Preparations for the special session involved the Secretary-General more deeply in the financial process, and resulted in the formal assignment of new duties to him. He was requested to work out arrangements with member governments for paying up their arrears and also to consult with them on the desirability of establishing a Peace Fund to which governments and individuals could give voluntary contributions. This Peace Fund eventually became one of the bases for relaxing the crisis.

The voluntary principle of the Peace Fund was in fact applied during the financial crisis to provide for the expenses of the peace-keeping forces employed in New Guinea, Yemen, and Cyprus. In all three cases, no obligatory assessment was attempted. In the first two, the parties to the dispute covered the costs of United Nations peace-keeping organization or observers. In the latter case, the United Kingdom and the United States made large voluntary contributions and other states smaller ones for the maintenance of an international force that had from time to time to employ arms. In each case, the time span during which the force was to be maintained was strictly limited, and the Secretary-General made a point of insisting that without financing the entire effort would be abandoned.

The Secretary-General had an important share in estimating the expenses for the three operations, and in drafting precise agreements to cover finances. Since the parties to the disputes were willing or anxious to have United Nations assistance, the Secretary-General had considerable leverage in negotiating, and at the same time was under no compulsion to persuade a recalcitrant Assembly to meet legal obligations. Thant could not, however, regard the experience with voluntary financing as satisfactory, since, unlike the situation which would obtain with a permanent Peace Fund, only short-term planning was possible and the peace-keeping missions in fact had only a hand-to-mouth existence.

After the end of the Katanga secession early in 1963, Thant planned a rapid dismantling of ONUC, in part because of the budgetary difficulties and in spite of acknowledged needs for further United Nations policing in the Congo. His budgets (which were adopted) signified the limiting effect that the financial crisis had on the Secretary-General's capacity to conduct long-term planning and to complete the work he had begun.

The financial crisis demonstrated that the General Assembly could not finance peace-keeping ventures through obligatory assessments on its members. In effect, it abandoned this practice for future ventures when it favored a voluntary peace-keeping fund and encouraged the Secretary-General to work out voluntary financing of specific peacekeeping ventures. At the same time, it weathered the constitutional crisis resulting from the attempt to apply Article 17 of the Charter by failing to act on its implications. Whether the Secretary-General would have favored a decision by the General Assembly to deprive a member of its vote on the basis of Article 19 is not known, but it is clear that Thant actively joined in work to avoid such a necessity. In any case, the Secretary-General now is more involved than ever in the delicate matter of securing finances for the organization. He necessarily must attempt to assert his influence on treasury policies followed by member states if the United Nations is to get on with its work at all. He has sometimes sought technical solutions and other times publicly deplored and denounced the lack of financial support given the United Nations. Had the members accepted Hammarskjöld's scheme, the Secretary-General would have been less a suppliant and influence-wielder in the fiscal field. The Hammarskjöld financial plan became a nullity and the legal implications found in it have not been applied. Nevertheless, the Secretary-General has been forced to test his influence in an unexpected area.

Influence and Routine Functions

As head of the Secretariat, the Secretary-General dominates the internal administrative functions of the United Nations and profits to some extent from the information and consultations arising from routine functions. In appointing and instructing secretaries to deliberative bodies and receiving their reports, he has a constant channel by which to receive information on political activities and through which he can sometimes exert influence.

His position of authority in the Secretariat may have its costs in terms of influence on matters of peace and security, for it can make him a target of attacks that decrease his effectiveness on policy issues. Such attacks can be based on the political sensitiveness of personnel appointments and dismissals, the treatment of influential top-ranking officials, the question of loyalty, and the formulation and execution of the budget.

Lie took the first effective steps toward equipping himself with a staff that would be responsive and politically useful in matters of peace and security when he protected the right of the Secretary-General to distribute work within the Secretariat and to make final decisions on Secretariat policies, no matter what backing top officials might have. Hammarskjöld and Thant also defended and strengthened this position, and in doing so managed to strip the troika challenge of most of its menace.

With the establishment of and experience with the principle that the Secretary-General alone was responsible for the work of the Secretariat, its top level required reorganization to arm the chief administrative officer with more flexible means of control and employment of his staff. Hammarskjöld achieved that reorganization, and during his tenure the Executive Office of the Secretary-General became the center of all important work on political matters. This role accords with a concept of the office of Secretary-General as a consistent and ready influence in international politics. But it does not necessarily lead to the development of political competence and the preservation of political experience in the regular departments of the Secretariat.

No Secretary-General can be adroit enough to deal with the geographical distribution question so as to produce universal satisfaction. The Secretariat is simply too small to take in everyone, and too specialized to take in just anyone. If geographical distribution can at the very least poison relations between the Secretary-General and the members and can consume his time, loyalty issues constitute the plague itself. It is a tribute to the steadfastness of the Secretary-General, and especially to Hammarskjöld, that no worse damage was done to the Secretariat. Yet dealing with issues of geographical distribution and loyalty with a fair degree of success does not give a high return in prestige and influence. It merely avoids trouble.

The Secretary-General has been able to formulate budgets and shepherd them through a complex examination system. His budgets in matters of peace and security have been attacked, not tellingly for any mistakes or unreasonableness but for the policies they reflect. Once a member, especially a powerful one, determines to challenge the policies of the United Nations at all costs, it can always find a means of doing so in parts of the budget. If the policies in question are strongly supported by the Secretary-General, the challenge extends to his conduct of the office as well.

To assemble a sufficient majority to adopt a budget is less difficult than to provide means to pay for expenses. For the Secretary-General, finance is a delicate matter which touches on sensitive points within national governments and policies. Every government guards its financial independence. The Secretary-General has nevertheless had to attempt to exert influence on the members and to some extent may have succeeded, especially in technical arrangements. New financial arrangements for peace-keeping have been worked out with his help, and these may broaden the scope of his influence. But it will scarcely become very heavy if large new expenditures are required or a substantial, well-to-do minority opposes the policies which necessitate spending.

CHAPTER VI

THE SECRETARY-GENERAL AS UN REPRESENTATIVE

Both the San Francisco Conference and the Preparatory Commission in varying degrees anticipated that the Secretary-General would have an important representational role in the United Nations. But there was no general understanding of how much scope and importance it might assume. The Preparatory Commission reported that the chairmen of the deliberative organs would no doubt represent the latter before the peoples of the world. "But the Secretary-General, more than anyone else," said the Commission, "will stand for the United Nations as a whole. In the eyes of the world, no less than in the eyes of his own staff, he must embody the principles and ideals of the Charter." [1] Representational duties were linked to the need for "active and steadfast" public understanding and therefore implied active educative and interpretative tasks. They went beyond those assigned to the Secretary-General of the League, who rarely essayed to stand for his organization as a whole, even though he directed a sizable public information apparatus.

As the channel of communication within the organization, among the organs, and with the Specialized Agencies, the Secretary-General has official functions of a formal and well understood nature. They are representational in the sense that the Secretary-General acts as the authorized spokesman and delegate for one official body before another. Outside the organization, the Secretary-General personifies the United Nations. If he is to be effective in this sphere, he must be more than a displaced foreign minister. His role becomes less formal, less tied to specific tasks, and more general in the material dealt with.

It is therefore possible to divide the representational tasks of the Secretary-General into those of an official representative and those of a representative to publics in an unofficial sense. These two categories of functions are not mutually exclusive, but serve to emphasize that at least two different approaches may be made to the representational role and that each of them has its own characteristics.

Official Representational Functions

The official representational functions of the Secretary-General, in which he undertakes to act on behalf of the organization in a limited way without specific instructions, include numerous rather routine duties and a number of ceremonial activities. He serves as the channel for communications, directs protocol and performs the conventional courtesies of diplomacy, has the responsibility for appearances by the United Nations in courts, and conducts legal transactions.

Because the Secretary-General formally represents the United Nations to governments, he must have a place in the diplomatic hierarchy. His office has always received the treatment due an honored and prestigious rank. Protocol, though often the butt of humor, has its uses to the Secretary-General. From the way in which courtesies are offered him by governments he may sometimes understand how his policies are viewed. Participation in ceremonies which go along with high diplomatic rank manufactures political publicity. Moving with very important persons, the Secretary-General appears to know those who determine the world's destiny. This alone may open the way to serious discussions and may enhance his ability to carry out an independent policy.

The Secretary-General acts as host when heads of state and of governments visit the United Nations headquarters, where they are treated with modest but unmistakable ceremony. He matches this faint shadow of royal pomp with the practice of dispatching telegrams and letters of greeting, congratulations, and condolence to high-ranking governmental personalities. In addition, he makes statements commemorating important anniversaries and sends messages of greeting and interest to private organizations whose work affects the United Nations. Such activities have some effect on various publics, and stand as reminders that the Secretary-General expects treatment consistent with his place as chief officer of the most important international organization.

In the sphere of legal transactions, the Secretary-General brings the United Nations into numerous contractual relationships and is responsible for its representation before courts. His representatives have appeared regularly before the International Court of Justice, where they have expanded earlier practice by presenting a definite point of view, not merely background facts, in matters involving the Secretariat. The Court agreed with his argument—in the hearings preceding the Advisory Opinion on Reparation for Injuries Suffered in the Service of the United Nations—that he represented an international person. His right to appear before the Court in advisory opinions has gone unchallenged, and suggests that if the business of the Court increases in quantity and deepens in substance, the Secretary-General may have further opportunities to present his views.[2]

Most legal transactions arising out of routine business relationships have little bearing either on the prestige of the Secretary-General or his influence on peace and security. But occasionally such contracts as those for clearing the Suez Canal give him an exceptional opportunity to make influential decisions and to undertake negotiations.[3]

Public Representational Functions

Most of the official work of the United Nations and of the Secretary-General takes place in public or is discussed in open meetings. Whatever editors consider "newsworthy" streams out immediately as mass communication, and the rest may be found later in the official record. What comes to the attention of the many publics not directly connected with the United Nations depends on a complex of factors such as subject matter, timing, events taking place elsewhere, ideological settings, and personal initiatives.

The public effect of normal operations can often be seen as a byproduct of other work. If, for example, a speech made in the General Assembly by the Secretary-General on financing the Congo operation is widely disseminated, it is not necessarily because he wanted it to be set before the eyes of millions of persons but because the subject matter and other aspects of it attract attention. In such a situation, the Secretary-General is regarded by most audiences as the representative of the organization.

The Secretary-General can also act directly to attract attention to his actions and words. He can deliberately design them for public consumption. He can ensure that mass communication media have full access to his work. He can use the machinery of the Secretariat to help him represent the organization before large numbers of people or before selected smaller publics among them. These public representational activities can sometimes have a direct and vital bearing on the Secretary-General's influence on the maintenance of peace, and sometimes become integral to the maintenance of peace.

The Annual Report *of the Secretary-General.*[4] The duty, imposed on him by Article 98 of the United Nations Charter, to report each year on the work of the organization has been employed by each Secretary-General as an opportunity to make known his views on matters of peace and security. Thus, he has turned what might have been only a routine report into an instrument of public relations.

The idea that the Secretary-General would report on the state of the organization was familiar to the delegates at the San Francisco Conference from the practice of the League's Secretary-General. The Charter text establishes the *Annual Report* as a basis for the general debate, as had been the case in the League Assembly.[5]

From the beginning, the United Nations Secretary-General has gone beyond a simple narration and summary of the actions of the organization. In some instances he has used the report to indicate his intention of making specific proposals of political importance, e.g., the creation of a United Nations guard force.[6] This use of the report represents a conscious maneuver to bring his views and ideas to bear on the General Assembly, from where mass media and diplomatic missions give them wide dissemination. His right to make such a use of his *Annual Report* has gone unchallenged, and may be counted as a permanent function of the office of Secretary-General.

The clearly designated *Introduction* to the *Annual Report*, signed and often drafted personally by the Secretary-General, contains his own views on the work of the organization. The rest of the report is a dry, condensed account of the year's activities. The maintenance of peace and security is covered in a chapter. An especially important matter, such as the Congo in 1960, may be singled out for a special chapter. The chapters are drafted by the department concerned and edited in the Executive Office of the Secretary-General. The *Introduction* usually appears separately, close to the time of the convening of the General Assembly session, so that the Secretary-General may comment on recent events and so that his remarks will have an impact.

Although the report is listed high on the agenda of the General Assembly, it has not in fact constituted a principal focus for the debates. Rather, it has provided a common background and a point of reference. Because the main body recites known facts and is cautiously worded to avoid giving offense, speakers rarely discuss it as such. But each session hears many references to the *Introduction* to the report.

What precise effect such references and the views espoused in the report have on the debate is impossible to estimate.[7] The speeches during the debate, after all, represent official governmental policies, and mentions of the Secretary-General's opinions usually are cited in order to support an existing national policy. Furthermore, because the Secretary-General usually does not make specific suggestions in the *Annual Report,* representatives who oppose his general opinions reply with silence. Both the form and content of the *Introductions* have varied considerably. In part this reflects the approaches of different personalities, and in part it results from a changing set of events and situations engaging the attention of the organization.

Lie and Hammarskjöld drafted the *Introductions* to their first reports with some caution and employed guarded language. In their later reports they commented in a more straightforward manner and referred directly to such delicate matters as Chinese representation, the effect of the Cold War, the employment of the organization in the face of an ideological conflict, the need to draft peace treaties for Germany, universality of membership, and the liquidation of colonial empires. Both of them implicitly or explicitly defended the conduct of their office. Thant, from the beginning, has been frank and direct.

All the occupants of the office of Secretary-General courageously put their personal views before the organization. Lie submitted *Introductions* which had a subjective undertone and were much more personal than those of his successors. They contained both specific comments and wide, vague appreciations of the state of the world and prospects of peace and war. They were closely tied to the year's developments and gave relatively little attention to statements of underlying principles.

Hammarskjöld, in contrast, customarily reasoned from principles. Although he was writing public documents, what he set down gives the impression of having been directed mainly to his diplomatic peers. He frequently emphasized only one set of problems and couched it in terms of principles. His comments gradually contributed to a doctrine for the operations of the organization. He also employed legal concepts to an extent which Lie never did. As a result, Hammarskjöld's remarks, read *seriatim,* show a developing appreciation of the role of the United Nations in world politics. Lie's more closely resemble the commentaries of serious journalism.

Thant's *Introductions* could in their specific content be more easily likened to the reports of Lie than of Hammarskjöld. But like both of them, Thant has not fled from the chance to make his own opinions known. His *Introductions* have been clearly written and straightforward, personal and not at all flamboyant. There is little discussion of principles along the lines marked out by Hammarskjöld.

Travel, Speeches, and Messages. The Secretary-General frequently receives invitations from both private and official sources to visit various parts of the world, to make speeches, to send messages of greeting or of more substance, and to take part in various discussions, ranging from fraternal to scientific. His willingness to accept such invitations relates both to the manner in which he carries out his work at headquarters and to the impression he wishes to make on possibly influential groups. Few invitations have an imperative character, although those from certain governments might promise such desirable opportunities for conversations that to refuse would be difficult. Thus, the Secretary-General may choose opportunities to make public appearances and attempt to find platforms and other meeting grounds which will produce the maximum effects on public opinion. Furthermore, the device of inspiring an invitation to visit or to make a speech at a time which appears propitious is open to the Secretary-General and has been used.

As the chief administrative officer, the Secretary-General has the right to attend the many meetings of United Nations bodies away from headquarters. Meetings of the Economic and Social Council in Geneva, where the United Nations maintains its important European office, have frequently been addressed by the Secretary-General. He has also opened meetings of the Economic Commission for Latin America and the Economic Commission for Africa. He has addressed numerous *ad hoc* bodies, such as the Advisory Committee of the International Conference on the Peaceful Uses of Atomic Energy, which met at Paris and Geneva during 1955.

These official travels and those for vacations or home leave almost always employ the airways. The Secretary-General then may land at one or another capital at will. He usually has invitations to confer with high officials and members of governments. Thus, he meets a great number of national representatives in attending conferences or traveling and takes part in official or quasi-official discussions in which he represents the United Nations. On these occasions, too, he can often speak to public audiences who might otherwise have little chance to hear him.

Official visits to member countries have a different character. The Secretary-General receives many invitations for such trips, and may inspire others so that he can tour several adjacent countries. These tours consist mainly of elaborate courtesy calls, but may be as informal as Hammarskjöld's rowboat ride with Khrushchev in 1958 during a visit to the Soviet Union. Time is usually reserved for high-level conversations and even negotiation on specific problems, but there is not always enough for thorough talks of lasting importance. They have a public representational purpose quite as much as a diplomatic aim. They provide the beginning or continuation of personal acquaintanceships which have utility later. Or they may be intended to indicate to the people and officials of a particular area that the Secretary-General is interested in their problems and that he expects reciprocal attention to his organization.

Some trips, of course, have specific diplomatic purposes. Those to Peking or to Egypt by Hammarskjöld are examples. They must be considered as part of a political initiative or administrative assignment for which the Secretary-General is responsible.

Both Lie and Hammarskjöld traveled frequently, although, paradoxically for a Secretary-General who claimed to shun the public view, the second Secretary-General visited far more of the globe than did his predecessor. Lie often appeared in the Western European capitals, usually on his way to and from Norway. He also traveled to the Soviet Union and Eastern Europe, southern Europe and the eastern Mediterranean, and Latin America. He never went to South or East Asia or to Africa. In contrast, Hammarskjöld at one time or another traveled to all of the principal regions and touched on a majority of the member countries of the United Nations.

While still Acting Secretary-General, Thant embarked on an ambitious schedule of official voyages. He made the ritual trip to the Soviet Union in August, 1962. He later visited Washington and has made calls in Western Europe, Latin America, and Asia. Since then, his pace of travels perhaps has been even more rapid than that of Hammarskjöld.

Lie, who had full experience with the platform and its political uses, made fewer public addresses than Hammarskjöld, who came into office amid expectations that he would pay little attention to the public world. In general, Lie's most important speeches were delivered to nongovernmental organizations, while Hammarskjöld favored university audiences. Thant probably will have made more public speaking appearances than Lie. Like Hammarskjöld, he favors university audiences, although he has spoken before other nongovernmental groups.

In retrospect, Lie's speeches appear as separate works, each tailored with professional assistance for particular occasions. Only rarely do they deal with sophisticated material or aim at persons used to intellectual approaches to political problems. Some of them contained frank emotional appeals. Hammarskjöld's speeches, in contrast, had a high degree of intellectualization. Like his *Introductions* to the *Annual Report,* they represent a body of doctrine built around his work and initiatives in the office of the Secretary-General. They rarely had much emotional content and frequently contain precise examples. They do not reveal much about the specific operation of the office of Secretary-General, although they disclose a great deal about Hammarskjöld's approach to it. Thant's remarks have a simplicity and directness which recall Lie's speeches, although they differ considerably in substance.

In many instances the Secretary-General issues written public statements. They may be prepared for official meetings of United Nations organs and deal with the substance of the work, or they may be drafted simply as a courtesy toward unofficial organizations.

The messages directed to private organizations have a lesser stature than formal speeches; they tend more to the commonplace and the cliché, and frequently are worded so as to pay compliments but to avoid taking any stand whatever that might give offense.

By sending a message, the Secretary-General can lend his prestige to a gathering without engaging himself or his office beyond the minimum. The recipients of messages frequently reprint them in their own publications and thus bring the ideas of the Secretary-General before a considerable audience. Nevertheless, such statements cannot be considered a major means of carrying out the public representational function.

Press Conferences. From the beginning, most journalists writing about the United Nations have been from the United States, as might be expected from the fact that the headquarters is in the United States and the Charter was written there. Their training and experience caused them to expect that the Secretary-General would be accessible and would meet often with them, as the President of the United States does with the Washington press corps. The Secretary-General's public relations advisers, many of them with United States training or nationality, have supported the idea of regular sessions with the press. Lie and his assistants began early to give periodic press conferences; this tradition, and the procedural pattern of the conferences, have remained unbroken. The Secretary-General calls on his aides for specific information when he desires, but only rarely do they intercede in the proceedings.

In some respects the Secretary-General's press conference, usually held once a month or a fortnight when the General Assembly is not meeting, serves the same purposes as that of the President of the United States. He tries to inform the part of the world that might be listening of his policies, to spread information and to exert some influence on policy formation. But the Secretary-General does not make news simply with routine comments, for he is no chief of a great state whose slightest indication of an attitude may foreshadow far-reaching decisions. The Secretary-General's press conferences get public attention only when he has some extraordinary step under consideration or has an unusual announcement.

Lie usually opened his press conference with one or several substantive announcements, sometimes speaking at some length. From there on he answered questions directly and shortly. When his reply was genuinely responsive, it was usually in specific terms. Not all questions received answers, of course, and whenever Lie considered that a reply might be indiscreet—for example when it would betray information given him on a confidential basis—he turned aside the questioner with a "no comment" that sometimes sounded rather brusque. He generally suffered the reporters' pressure with good will. The most striking characteristic of his press conferences was their directness and specific content. They may not have made the biggest headlines each week, but they did give condensed and accurate, although not necessarily complete, answers to the reporters' queries.

Hammarskjöld at first was dissatisfied with the press conference as developed by his predecessor, and tried other forms, including extended statements of his views and off-the-record discussions. He then returned to the original form but changed its content very considerably. He displayed reticence in giving direct comments, and on the whole did not use his press conferences as vehicles for announcing his actions. He did speak of his travel plans and similar instrumental or procedural activities. His replies were heavily nuanced and frequently not quite to the point raised by the question. Hammarskjöld never lost his coolness and just managed to avoid appearing schoolmasterish. His comments were most responsive when they resulted from a reporter's wish for an explanation of something the Secretary-General had said or done elsewhere. Such explanations gave Hammarskjöld a chance to make theoretical and abstract statements about his work and his office. He generally was quick to endorse a recommendation made by another United Nations organ.

Thant's style in press conferences leans more toward the precise, responsive reaction of Lie than the discursive approach and calculated diversion of Hammarskjöld. Although most of his press conferences have, of course, not made major news, a few of them have included material of great interest. Much of the detail, for example, concerning his efforts to intercede in the Viet Nam conflict was elicited by reporters during press conferences. It was also during a press conference that he indicated his willingness to stay on temporarily in his office until the end of the 1966 General Assembly. He has clearly established a good rapport with a sympathetic press corps and appears to enjoy his encounters with it.

The experience of twenty years of press conferences seems to demonstrate that they have only limited effectiveness as a public representational influence. And reliance on the press conference to inform governmental policymakers of the intentions and interpretations of the Secretary-General would in many instances seem superfluous or futile when more direct channels are available and when no prospect of a popular response offers itself. In exceptional times, as during the negotiations which followed the United States blockade of Cuba in late October, 1962, the Secretary-General has news to put before the world. But even then he typically would not do so in a press conference but rather in a prepared statement which might be explained and expounded later—perhaps much later—in answers to reporters' questions.

Aside from such occasional and unpredictable moments, the Secretary-General's press conference would seem to have two main uses. It permits him to build up a background of understanding among the permanent press corps. It also helps to involve the newsmen in policy processes in the United Nations. If the press conference of the Secretary-General does not equal that of the United States President as a source of news and wide attention, it nevertheless has been of some assistance in the performance of the Secretary-General's public representational function.

The Office of Public Information. In attempting to make a public impression, the Secretary-General has at his service the Office of Public Information, which employs more than 200 professionals in one of the largest single administrative apparatuses in the Secretariat.

The OPI's task is based on the proposition that the success of the United Nations depends on the public understanding it receives.[8] The OPI fosters this understanding by relying on existing information channels, supplementing them wherever they cannot perform adequately. This work is never to be tinged with propaganda.

The OPI has burgeoned over the years. It hires radio broadcast facilities for programs written by its own officials, prepares television and sound recordings, publishes periodicals and pamphlets, maintains public liaison offices and libraries, and helps researchers and free-lance writers to find material. It deals with both the mass communications media and with specialists whose work would help to form the opinions of various publics, especially the better educated and learned groups.

The OPI often strives to enhance and broaden the audience for the Secretary-General's words and activities. It can moreover provide the Secretary-General with advice on public representational matters and with information from the member countries. To a certain extent it supplies him with channels of communication independent of any national government, thus offering a potential for reaching publics when national governments will not provide access to media.

The OPI conceives its duty as that of linking the United Nations with the peoples of the world. Nothing serves this purpose better than the personification of United Nations policy in a single man, and the image of the Secretary-General furnishes such a symbol. In reproducing, interpreting, and extending his words, the OPI emphasizes, willy-nilly, the role of his office in the United Nations scheme. His view will likely be taken for the authoritative interpretation, particularly for audiences too unsophisticated or too impatient to follow an exegesis of policy.

The rather high rate of activity in the OPI could easily give an unwary or vain Secretary-General the impression that he has a major implement of propaganda at his beck and call. It is likely that the professionals in the OPI would try to guard him against such a misimpression, but the office nevertheless has its own dynamic, which includes a constant use of the Secretary-General as a symbol. An active Secretary-General makes a better symbol than a retiring one. It is thus conceivable that the OPI and the Secretary-General might mislead each other in planning and supporting the public representational role of the chief administrative officer.

No amount of public information facilities, however, will ensure that the Secretary-General will in fact be looked to as the authoritative representative of the United Nations. He can ensure this only by the quality of his actions and decisions, his speeches, and his public appearances. If he is determined to make news and to make an impression on a broad public, as Lie was in promoting his twenty-year peace plan, the facilities can help him reach a large number of people but they cannot substitute for the substance of his action.

The OPI has not been able to carry out its program without a good deal of sniping from the General Assembly. This has taken the form primarily of attempts to cut the budget. The attack became so severe in 1958 that Hammarskjöld had to appear in the Fifth Committee to defend the OPI and to warn that a proposed advisory committee would interfere with his exclusive authority over the operation of the Secretariat. From the point of view of the OPI the result was a happy one, for although it was put under some additional restraint in expanding its budget it also received an instruction to enlarge its network of Information Centers.[9]

The establishment of Information Centers increases the usefulness of the OPI to a Secretary-General. Its field offices, now in over forty countries, cover much of the membership of the United Nations and are a source of information about political developments. When they are headed by senior officers, as an increasing number are, they take on a representative quality. This quality may be enhanced when the Information Center is in the charge of an official with political experience or of a Resident Representative of the Technical Assistance Board, who is likely to know important local leaders and governmental processes.

Despite its impressive output, the effect of the OPI should not be overestimated. While it consumes a sizable part of the annual appropriation for the Secretariat, it remains utterly unable to fill in all or many of the gaps in the distribution of public information about the United Nations. Its resources are distinctly limited by the unwillingness of United Nations members to pay any more than absolutely necessary. The use of resources is limited by the sensitivity of governments to "propaganda." Nor will any government tolerate sustained criticism of its policies from international civil servants.

Significance of the Representational Functions

The official and public representational functions of the Secretary-General provide support for his more consequential activities. They enhance his direct influence by keeping alive a consciousness of the United Nations and the office of Secretary-General in the minds of policy-makers and influential publics. However, it is possible to state only generally the degree to which his influence is thus enhanced.

Most official representational functions, and some public ones, may bear specific relationships to the conduct of negotiations by the Secretary-General and the exercise of other aspects of his "special right" deriving from Article 99 of the Charter. The Secretary-General and his staff must keep informed about political disputes and activities of the member countries as they are manifested in the United Nations. This information makes it possible for the Secretary-General to discuss with the concerned members the form of their reference to the United Nations and to shape the manner in which the dispute or other political matter is considered by a deliberative organ.

The performance of official representational duties by the Secretary-General helps to give standing to his office as an existing feature of international politics. Because he may appear before such a formal body as the International Court of Justice and may make a state visit to member countries, because he moves among the leaders of the most important governments, he is associated to some degree with the main decision-makers in high politics. This association facilitates the use of the office of the Secretary-General in matters of peace or security. Its occupant becomes an appropriate third party in negotiations and a center of information in situations in which governments whose policies have developed a great deal of friction may talk to each other.

In addition, the Secretary-General's public representational functions, backed by the United Nations' public information apparatus, can foster and preserve a public view of his office as neutral, disengaged, and available for political work. In such an atmosphere the Secretary-General, well-informed about the United Nations processes and involved in general international politics because of his prestige, can become a most desirable intermediary in resolving international disagreements. Such activities tend at the same time to increase his prestige within the councils of the organization, so that he becomes a potent influence on the political processes within it.

The representational functions of the Secretary-General do not give him the means to promote a policy which goes counter to the wishes of the member countries. Should he attempt such a course, he would soon face severe limitations. His representational functions might well give him great public stature, but this is different from either power of decision or leadership of groups which can influence and control decision-makers. An independent course which encounters objections from the member governments would no doubt have support from some of the members of the United Nations, but this would not necessarily force an unwilling member to give way or induce it to give special honor to the Secretary-General.

Nor can the Secretary-General appeal over the head of a government to the people and expect a positive response for very long. He may influence the opinions of some publics and slowly educate others, but he cannot count on building mass support to produce impressive changes in the policy of a particular government.

The Secretary-General's public representational functions can serve him as instruments of his official functions in the field of peace and security. They can give his office an appearance of strength and prestige which might aid in his administration of United Nations programs. But they do not turn him into a global leader or teacher, and they seem unlikely to do so in a pluralistic world of nation states.

PART THREE

Political Functions

CHAPTER VII

THE SECRETARY-GENERAL AND HIS "SPECIAL RIGHT"

The constant possibility of war and the threat of nuclear destruction, and the ingrained habits of statesmen, dictate close attention to the actions of the Secretary-General in connection with maintaining the peace. This scrutiny bears heaviest on the Secretary-General's power under Article 99 of the United Nations Charter to put before the Security Council any matter which in his opinion involves a menace to peace. For the Secretary-General, this is a grave responsibility indeed, for it is "a special right which goes beyond any power previously accorded to the head of an international organization." [1]

How this special right has been used and its effect on the office of Secretary-General would have been particularly difficult to predict from the language of the Charter and the debates and interpretations which preceded Lie's tenure. Yet initiatives by the Secretary-General in the security field have been undertaken, most notably in the Congo and in Korea. They have proved strikingly dramatic, delicate, and difficult to bring to a successful conclusion.

Article 99: Its Use and Significance

The seemingly simple language of Article 99 becomes complex when it must serve as a guide to action, for to invoke the article means that the Secretary-General on his own responsibility has made a judgment on what is certain to be an involved political situation. The article was designed precisely for such situations, as an alternative to a complaint by a member government to the Security Council. Its language is permissive and somewhat different from that relating to a complaint by a member government. Article 99 speaks of "any matter," not exclusively of a "dispute or situation."

This could be interpreted as having a broader scope than the language setting conditions under which a member might bring a question to the Council. But the variance in language has produced no important practical results, for governments have felt free to bring to the Council affairs which have little direct relation to the idea of a "dispute or situation" affecting international peace.

The Security Council is the only body that figures in Article 99. The Secretary-General's right to bring matters of peace and war before the Council "is largely explicable by the founders' expectation that it would be that organ which would handle the life and death matters of U.N. business." [2] Article 99 exists primarily for use in a crisis. To decide to use it represents an initiative, not the execution of a plan approved by another organ. In parliamentary terms, the Secretary-General in this situation acts as a minister, not as a civil servant. If the Secretary-General is to use his power with maximum effectiveness, he must make a convincing case or present prima facie evidence that the matter to which he is calling attention has sufficient serious content to engage so solemn an organ as the Security Council. He must be highly informed in order to do so.

His information could come from another United Nations body—a field commission, for example—or from his own subordinates or from a member government. With the information at hand, the Secretary-General must try to weigh the several theoretical ramifications of seizing the Security Council of a particular matter. The Secretary-General is expected to act if no member is willing to do so. At the same time, he is not expected to replace the members as the source of judgment of what is important.

Furthermore, he must protect the prestige of his office if his interventions are to have any weight. If he acts, the matter must indeed be important. Nor may he decline to act if peace is threatened, for to do so would be to fail in his duty and to lessen his influence. He must try to move in such a way as not to arouse the enmity of any of the members and especially the great powers. To do so would reduce the standing of his office and his range of possible or useful actions. Nevertheless, in some situations any initiative would incur the opposition of a leading member.

The use of Article 99 begins, but does not determine the outcome of, a possibly highly involved political process.[3] It could lead either to the determination that there has been a breach of the peace under Article 39 of the Charter and to provisional measures, or to enforcement action under Chapter VII. Or it might lead to conciliatory steps under Chapter VI, or to nowhere at all. Because of the possibility of a determination that a breach of the peace has occurred, the direct interests of the great powers are automatically engaged. Whatever the estimates of the Secretary-General may be, the permanent members of the Security Council have the ultimate burden of responding to his initiative.

A prudent and politically-minded Secretary-General might avoid invoking Article 99 whenever possible, thus staying clear of responsibility for putting the Council into a deadlocked position; or else he might consult carefully with the members of the Council to get their reactions to the invocation of Article 99. A confident and bold Secretary-General might make his own estimate of the Council's response and deliberately use Article 99 as the first step in leading the members to a policy. Thus, whatever his decisions in regard to Article 99, the Secretary-General faces a difficult and delicate set of political problems.

Overt Invocation of Article 99—a Unique Example

The Secretary-General has invoked Article 99 of the Charter explicitly and deliberately only once. This occurred at the beginning of the Congo case in July, 1960, when Hammarskjöld took the initiative after receiving two cables addressed to him from the government of the Republic of the Congo.

Hammarskjöld had been receiving a steady stream of information on events in the Congo. Earlier that year he had made a trip to Africa to gain some political background. His original intention was to visit the Congo as part of a trip to South Africa in connection with the Security Council's resolution in reaction to the Sharpeville massacres. The Secretary-General reinforced his display of interest in African affairs by sending Under-Secretary Ralph Bunche to the Congo as his personal representative at the independence ceremonies of June 30, 1960. Bunche's mission involved making arrangements for technical assistance to the Congo, and he therefore had started to acquire knowledge of the situation within the Congolese government. His cables after the independence ceremonies began to warn of ominous possibilities. On July 11, it was reported, Premier Patrice Lumumba asked Bunche to arrange for the dispatch of military experts to help with the reorganization of the Congolese army. Bunche replied that as much aid as the Charter would permit would be forthcoming.[4]

The first of the two cablegrams from President Joseph Kasavubu and Lumumba, dated July 12, asked for the urgent dispatch of military aid to the Congo because of aggression by Belgian troops, sent into action after the revolt of the Armée Nationale Congolaise (ANC). The second cablegram came the next day. It clarified the first, making the point that aid was requested not to restore internal order but rather to protect Congolese territory against Belgian aggression. The military forces requested were to come only from neutral states, not from the United States or other great powers.[5]

Although these cablegrams were addressed to Hammarskjöld, they did not require him to invoke Article 99. He might simply have circulated them to the members of the Security Council as he had with communications in the Laos case. Or he might have consulted the members, as indeed he did, but left the matter for them to decide. One or another member of the Council or of the United Nations might then have acted to bring the complaint to the Security Council under either Chapter VI or Chapter VII of the Charter. Or he might have asked Bunche to consult with the Congolese government in the hope of getting it to make a direct appeal to the Council.

In effect, Hammarskjöld rejected all of these possible approaches in favor of direct initiative on his own responsibility. During the afternoon of July 13, he told the permanent representatives of the members of the Security Council, representatives of African states, and the President of the Security Council, of his intention to invoke Article 99.

Hammarskjöld requested the urgent summoning of the Council, which met that same evening. Its provisional agenda included the following item: "Letter dated 13 July 1960 from the Secretary-General addressed to the President of the Security Council." This item, as drafted by Hammarskjöld, referred to an action of the Secretary-General rather than the substance of the issue. It had a neutral tone and in no sense indicated what action was anticipated from the Council or under what constitutional provisions it might be expected to act. It would be up to Hammarskjöld to explain his intentions. No member state, thus far, had any official part in seizing the Council of the situation in the Congo.[6]

Sobolev, then Soviet representative, noted that the agenda failed to indicate that the demand for United Nations action "emanates from the Congolese government" [7] and proposed adding a mention of the telegrams. Hammarskjöld defended the wording on the ground that the Congolese cables were addressed to him and included no mention of the Security Council, which could of course decide to list the cablegrams as documents of reference. He explained:

I made a distinction between what is proper for the Secretary-General to do and what is proper for the Security Council to do. I should follow the indication given the Governments which addressed me. They have not themselves made it a Security Council issue and their documents Security Council documents. Under such circumstances I felt that I should not do it. I wanted to point out that it is obviously a matter for the Council.[8]

Hammarskjöld's argument at bottom was simply a claim that as Secretary-General he had acted in the way that seemed best to him. Since the documents had been circulated, the substance of the issue to come before the Council was perfectly well and formally known. His argument rested on formal and verbal considerations which had been undermined by the cables themselves. Since the rules of procedure require the Secretary-General to bring to the attention of the Council communications from states concerning "any matter for the consideration of the Security Council in accordance with the provisions of the Charter," [9] and since a question of aggression and of the provision of a United Nations force had been raised, the cables themselves might have become the basis of the Council meeting, rather than Article 99 of the Charter. Sobolev did not, however, press his argument so far as to cause a paralyzing quarrel, and the original agenda item was adopted.

Hammarskjöld's subsequent statement made it clear that he had looked beyond the mere summoning of the Security Council. In a solemn tautology, he said that the difficulties in the Congo, connected with the maintenance of law and order, "have an important international bearing as they are of a nature that cannot be disregarded by other countries." He referred to a request for technical assistance in the field of international security, which he said was within his competence and on which actions had been taken. But he remarked, some time was needed to get results and he would not pronounce himself on the earlier arrangements for the continued presence of Belgian troops. He continued:

I must conclude from the communications received from the Government of the Congo that the presence of these troops is a source of internal, and potentially also of international, tension. In these circumstances, the presence of the Belgian troops cannot be accepted as a satisfactory stopgap arrangement pending the reestablishment of order through the national security force.[10]

Even though he did not deal directly with the charge of aggression, which would have made necessary a determination by the Security Council under Chapter VII of the Charter, Hammarskjöld did not regard enforcement action as necessary. In effect, he rejected the Congolese government's appreciation of its own situation.

Then the Secretary-General urged a specific program, strongly recommending that he be authorized to provide the government of the Congo, with whom he would consult, with military assistance until United Nations technical assistance had the effect of helping the national security forces of the republic to deal with their tasks. "It would be understood," he continued, "that were the United Nations to act as proposed, the Belgian government would see its way to a withdrawal."[11] The United Nations forces, he made clear, would have the right to fight only in self-defense, would stay out of internal conflicts and would be made up of troops from neutral states, including Africa. Troops from the permanent members of the Council would be excluded. In short, he would rely on the experience of Suez.

Hammarskjöld's approach to the Council and the program he laid before it had a number of distinctive and imaginative features. By disregarding the Congolese charges of aggression and by relying on a precedent, he attempted to make it unnecessary for the Council to determine whether the peace had been broken. Enforcement action need not be undertaken. Nor were the messages from Leopoldville to be regarded as bringing a dispute before the Council under

Chapter VI. The Security Council in fact was to be asked only to assign duties to the Secretary-General, who would execute a program it would decide upon. The Council might do this under Article 98 of the Charter; it might also do so in view of its own precedents in the Lebanon case. If the great powers had no desire for a showdown in the Security Council on the issue, or if they wished to keep a flexible position, to assign the leading role to the Secretary-General was an attractive course. Finally, the Secretary-General himself suggested the instructions he wanted. This implied that once the Council acted to give him the powers he desired—it did so during the early hours of July 14—his task could be regarded as primarily administrative. And then indeed any initiatives he took would result from an approach that differed from that of Article 99.

Article 99—Two Uses by Implication

In two other noteworthy instances, the Secretary-General has acted in such a way as to call attention to his powers under Article 99. These were when the Security Council met to consider the North Korean attack on South Korea, and during the Suez Canal controversy when Israel, Great Britain, and France attacked Egypt. Neither of these instances, however, involved such a direct and explicit initiative by the Secretary-General as the Congo case did.

The first news to reach United Nations headquarters of the outbreak of fighting in Korea in late June, 1950, came from the United States. The somnolent United Nations Commission on Korea had no concrete information upon which to base an expectation of an attack. Although Lie indicated a willingness to summon the Council, the United States decided to request an emergency meeting. Only after this decision was made did the Commission on Korea respond to a cable from the Secretary-General, who had asked for information. In effect, the Commission confirmed the reports of the United States and suggested that the Secretary-General bring the matter to the attention of the Council.[12]

When the Security Council convened during the afternoon of June 25, 1950, little more than half a day after the first news of the attack in Korea had been received at New York, the provisional agenda used the language of the United States note. The item relating to Korea read, "Aggression upon the Republic of Korea." The President of the Security Council, Sir Benegal N. Rau of India, suggested that it be amended to "Complaint of Aggression . . ."; evidently, in the haste of convening the Council in its first emergency session, he had not had time enough to give his approval to the Secretary-General's formulation. His proposal was accepted without demur. By previous arrangement, he invited Lie to speak first.[13]

This invitation would have been logical, even if Article 99 never existed. As the official memory of the organization, the Secretary-General could always be called upon to supply background information. Furthermore, a cable had been received from the United Nations Commission on Korea (UNCOK), the only United Nations body in a position to report directly on events in Korea. Much of Lie's intervention had a ministerial quality, since it recited the origin of the UNCOK cable, and recalled in neutral tones the earlier actions of the General Assembly and other commissions in Korea.

But Lie's own estimates, which followed the factual part of his statement, had anything but a neutral tone. He said that military actions undertaken by North Korean forces were a violation of a General Assembly resolution and of the principles of the Charter. He made his recommendation in the following words:

> The present situation is a serious one and is a threat to international peace. The Security Council is, in my opinion, the competent organ to deal with it.
>
> I consider it the clear duty of the Security Council to take steps necessary to reestablish peace in [Korea].[14]

Lie's appreciation of what was happening in Korea clearly accorded with the spirit of Article 99, but it can scarcely be regarded as the exercise of his powers as they had been foreseen at San Francisco and by the Preparatory Commission. Only later, and then before the General Assembly, did he claim that his intervention on July 25, 1950 had constituted the exercise of the powers of the Secretary-General under Article 99.

Whatever its precise legal status, the main importance of his intervention at the time lay in associating the office of Secretary-General with the forthcoming effort by the United Nations.[15] By the same token, the intervention produced results which endangered the office. The statement itself, nevertheless, was very limited in both legal and political scope. The Secretary-General proposed no program and probably could not have done so, as his successor was to do ten years later. Nor were subsequent actions by the Security Council to give Lie a great deal of influence on the policy toward Korea.

On one other occasion, Lie by implication cited Article 99. This was during the Greek frontier case dispute, when he claimed for the Secretary-General the right "to make such inquiries or investigations as he may think necessary in order to determine whether or not he should consider bringing any aspect of this matter to the attention of the Council under the provisions of the Charter." [16] His declaration remained unchallenged, but it was never followed through then or on another occasion. It received positive support only from the Soviet Union, whose representative said that the Secretary-General was correct in calling attention to his rights under the Charter. At that time the Soviet government supported a wide measure of authority for the Secretary-General. Later the Council established a commission of investigation without indicating that Lie's claim had had any influence in its decision.[17]

During the dangerous crisis which followed the Israeli attack on Egypt, the second Secretary-General found himself in a position reminiscent of Lie's after the Korean attack. Hammarskjöld's reaction in many respects resembled that of his predecessor.

The Israeli invasion of the Sinai Peninsula on October 29, 1956 came after a long period of friction between Israel and its Arab neighbors. Since 1947 the entire eastern end of the Mediterranean had been continuously under United Nations scrutiny, as had Korea from about the same time. No great power was directly involved in the Palestine dispute at the beginning, but the power alignments began to resemble those that prevailed in Korea when the Soviet Union after the death of Stalin began to take a keen interest in the area and became a firm supporter of Nasser's revolution. In both regions the United Nations had observation functions, but those carried out by the United Nations Truce Supervision Organization (UNTSO) far surpassed in quality and experience anything attempted in Korea. Moreover, the Secretary-General had personally worked at the intractable Palestine problem and had taken an important part in the Suez Canal negotiations with Egypt, both in

New York and in Cairo. The ultimatum delivered on October 30, 1956 by France and the United Kingdom to Egypt and Israel, demanding a cease-fire within twelve hours and withdrawal to ten miles from the Suez Canal, marked the direct involvement of two permanent members of the Security Council in the conflict.

The Secretary-General, as in the Korean case, had no need to seize the Security Council of the events in Egypt. As earlier, the United States decided to bring the matter to the Council; Hammarskjöld is reported to have told the United States representatives, as Lie did six years before, that he would have acted had a member of the Council not done so.[18] In this instance the Secretary-General was not the first speaker on the matter, for the Council actually had begun to consider the Israeli attack when the Anglo-French ultimatum was delivered. Hammarskjöld able to tell the Council that UNTSO had pointed out that the attack contravened the Palestine Armistice Agreements. He asked for a cease-fire and withdrawal of Israeli troops from Sinai.

Only after the Anglo-French military action had begun did Hammarskjöld make clear his personal view of the situation. Without mentioning Article 99 or formally invoking it, he used it to underline his view that the Charter had been violated. But his pressure for an expression of confidence went beyond anything Lie attempted in June, 1950. On the one hand, Hammarskjöld was preparing the ground for a strong personal role in the response to the situation; on the other hand, he was warning the members of the United Nations that he would not be content—and might well resign—if he did not have such a role. He did this, however, without making a specific suggestion, as he later would in the Congo case, of what his part should be in subsequent procedures.

Hammarskjöld's intervention in Suez, like Lie's in 1950, can scarcely be listed as the direct use of Article 99. But the existence of the article heightened the significance of his intervention. Unlike Lie, the second Secretary-General was able to prevent the intervention from endangering his office. Expressions of confidence from the Council members helped accomplish this. Hammarskjöld thus demonstrated how Article 99 could be employed in at least this situation to build future credit for the use of the office of Secretary-General. This credit, strengthened and expanded by the success of his later efforts in the Suez case, was used by him when he invoked Article 99 in the Congo conflict in such a way as to lead the Council toward drafting administrative instructions agreeable to him.

Procedural Arrangements and Initiative

As the examination of the use of Article 99 shows, the Secretary-General has been able to speak in the Security Council as if he were a governmental representative. His ability to do so depends on specific rules of procedure, adopted by the deliberative organs. These rules can usefully be examined here to determine their political ramifications and their relevance to the influence of the Secretary-General.

The rules of procedure of the Security Council are paralleled by privileges for the Secretary-General in other organs. Even though Article 99 does not apply to the work of other organs, the Secretary-General has been provided with possibilities for influence analogous to those he has in the Security Council. The need for these privileges could be taken as consistent with the broad political role implied by Article 99.

The Preparatory Commission agreed on provisional rules which were to be adopted by each organ and changed later as necessary. Although there is no clear indication of the precise sources, the secretariat of the Preparatory Commission based its drafts on such precedents as the League of Nations, UNRRA, the newly established Food and Agriculture Organization, and the European Central Inland Transit Organization.[19]

The present rules of procedure in the Security Council provide that "the Secretary-General, or his deputy acting on his behalf, may make either oral or written statements . . . concerning any question under consideration."[20] This represents an expansion of the privileges granted in the provisional rules, which had simply repeated the language of Article 99.[21] The widening of the rules was connected with one of the first efforts by Lie to establish the political competence and prestige of his office.

Lie interceded in a legal and procedural question growing out of the status on the Security Council agenda of the Iranian complaint against the presence of the Soviet Army in Iran in 1946 in violation of treaty commitments. The complaint, the first to come before the Security Council, had been discussed through several meetings despite the opposition and subsequent departure of the Soviet representative, when the Iranian delegate suddenly announced he was retracting it. Other members of the Council insisted on keeping the item on the agenda.[22] Lie's intervention in such a situation had a logical basis, since the Secretary-General had some influence under the rules on the drafting of the agenda and since an early case offered a good opportunity for creating a precedent.

The Secretary-General put before a surprised Council President a legal memorandum on the question of whether the Council might keep on its agenda a complaint after the parties involved had requested its withdrawal. Lie argued that unless the Council took specific action to remain seized of the matter, it should automatically be dropped. This intervention, aside from the substance of the argument, received a lukewarm reception, and Quo Tai-chi, President of the Council, emphasized the administrative character of the office of Secretary-General, pointing out that decisions remained in the hands of the Council. The Polish and Soviet delegates underlined the obligation of the Secretary-General to give his advice.[23]

Lie's unsolicited counsel made some clarification of the rules of procedure necessary. In the Committee of Experts the Assistant Secretary-General for Security Council Affairs, Arkady A. Sobolev, raised the question of whether the Secretary-General could take the floor on his own initiative or only at the pleasure of the President. Referring to Lie's "embarrassment" because of the imprecision of the rules, he proposed a text which would permit the Secretary-General to speak "at the invitation of the President." The General Assembly rules included this phrase, which had been accepted in the Preparatory Commission as giving the Secretary-General the right to speak out; the invitation of the President merely represented the reality that the Secretary-General would first inform the President. But Lie recalls that Spaak as President of the first session of the General Assembly had failed to give him the floor in the General Committee.[24] Perhaps for this reason Sobolev based his text on the provisional rules of the Economic and Social Council, where no question of the Secretary-General's right of intervention was likely to be raised.

Sobolev found himself in a middle position, with the United States pressing for a narrower definition of the rights of the Secretary-General to intervene than the virtually unlimited one sought by the Soviet Union and Poland. Australia supported this position, and the British delegate later came around to it. At this point the remaining members of the Council agreed, and Sobolev formulated the present text.

Lie had good reason to be satisfied with the outcome of what has been described as a "bitter fight."[25] He received a broader rule than he had requested, and his right to intervene in the Iranian case was more than vindicated. The right of the Secretary-General to intercede in the Security Council has rarely been questioned since then. Where there was such an intervention, the substance of what was said became the primary subject of any criticism.

Hammarskjöld broke new ground in the application of the rules of procedure, and in extending the implications of Article 99, when he reported to the Security Council on his dealings with the government of Laos in 1959. He had referred to them in his *Introduction* to the *Annual Report* of 1958–1959, and then decided to report to the Security Council after the Royal Laotian government requested the dispatch of an emergency force. A meeting of the Council was convened by the President on the request of the Secretary-General. Called on to speak first, Hammarskjöld declared that he had based his action on the practice according to which "the Secretary-General when he requests it, is granted the floor in the Council in order to make such statements on subjects within the range of responsibility of the Council as he considers called for under the terms of his own responsibility." But he was not going beyond a report and formally introduced nothing on the agenda. He continued:

> It should . . . be clear that the request is not based on the explicit rights granted to the Secretary-General under Article 99 of the Charter. If it had been so based, the Council, under Rule 3 of the Provisional Rules of Procedure, would not have been free to refuse the Secretary-General to address it—as it is now free to do—and it would have meant the inscription by the Secretary-General of a substantive issue on the agenda.[26]

Hammarskjöld was attempting a novel tactic, and its significance was not lost on Sobolev, who was serving as Soviet representative.

Sobolev immediately called attention to the "irregularities" involved in hearing a report from the Secretary-General which he said did not fall into the usual categories of items for the provisional agenda and which concerned a matter which was not under consideration by the Council. Hammarskjöld replied that he had the right under the rules of procedure to communicate with the Council. Cordier, the knowledgable former Executive Assistant to the Secretary-General, writes that this intervention, which he lists with those of less controversial character and those during the Suez crisis, had "top significance." [27] The Soviet objection received no support in the Council, which adopted an agenda including an item for a report by the Secretary-General, and went on to hear Hammarskjöld.[28]

Hammarskjöld employed the right to intervene more frequently than did his predecessor. Lie reserved it for extraordinary occasions, exercising it in the Korean case and for the submission of legal memoranda concerning Palestine, Berlin, the representation of China, and the appointment of a governor of Trieste.[29] Hammarskjöld's mandates from the Security Council required the reporting of administrative activities. He thus spoke frequently in the Council on the execution of his instructions to negotiate with Israel and the Arab states to quiet the situation in the Middle East in 1956, in the Suez case in 1956, in the Lebanon case, and especially during the consideration of the Congo question. Whether such interventions might have been possible without a specific, permissive rule of procedure raises a question which cannot be answered. It seems likely that if such practices as the submission of legal memoranda or reporting on an administrative assignment had become usual, an informal rule would have established itself. But the existence of a rule alone, as Drummond's reluctance to use the permissive arrangements of the League shows, does not guarantee that the Secretary-General will actively employ it.

Because Article 99 of the Charter was an innovation, the rules of procedure of the Security Council with regard to intervention by the Secretary-General had an aura of novelty. Those of the General Assembly rested more firmly on practice in the League of Nations and other international organizations. In these a secretariat furnished expert knowledge and, at times, counsel on problems that were on the whole unconnected with matters of peace and security. Moreover, in technical questions the participation of a secretariat official was necessary, for without it the delegates, less expert than the staff on most questions, would lack guidance.

The General Assembly, however, has the capacity to study and advise on political issues of every shade. The eagerness of the small powers at San Francisco to build up its role indicated that it might well be used to reduce the influence of the Security Council. The Charter itself contained a provision [30] to restrict the General Assembly from dealing with the most crucial questions of peace and security. Thus, a certain tension existed from the beginning between the General Assembly and the Security Council.

This tension was reflected at the Preparatory Commission stage in some of the discussion of the rules of procedure of the General Assembly. A draft of the rules by the Secretariat set off a debate in which, on the one hand, a group of delegates argued that because Article 99 mentioned only the Security Council, the Secretary-General had no implied powers in the General Assembly. Therefore he needed no privilege of intervention. On the other hand, a group of representatives favoring a strong General Assembly insisted that the San Francisco Conference intended he should have at least the powers of the League's Secretary-General to intervene, that he would need such powers in order to coordinate the work of the various organs, and that since he would have to limit his interventions to questions under consideration, he would be acting under the Charter, which gave the General Assembly a wide scope. This latter point contained the crucial issue, for the representatives opposing wide powers of intervention for the Secretary-General wanted in reality to limit his ability to become involved in political matters. The issue was settled by writing a rule which was as broad as the competence of the General Assembly.[31]

The rule as it was drafted won the endorsement of the General Assembly. It still needed some interpretation in practice, as Lie's recollection of his difficulty in speaking at the first session of the General Assembly indicates. This interpretation came very rapidly after the impact of the Security Council's adoption of a rule which gave the Secretary-General virtual carte blanche in addressing it. Without difficulty, the General Assembly agreed to delete the provision that the Secretary-General must be invited by the President to address the Assembly; in effect, he now could make his own invitation. Similar rights to speak were accorded him in the subsidiary bodies of the General Assembly. On the basis of this rule, the Secretary-General has frequently made statements on his own initiative at the end of or during the General Debate, he has defended the conduct of his office, and he has made general and specific suggestions of policies.[32]

The Secretary-General, His Representatives, and Preventive Diplomacy

Hammarskjöld's doctrinal elaboration of Article 99 included those initiatives by the Secretary-General which are covered by his term, "preventive diplomacy." It refers to action to fill vacuums in politics so that contending parties are discouraged from behaving so as to induce counteraction and has special relevance to situations in which the great powers could become engaged. Although the specific content of preventive diplomacy differs from case to case, Hammarskjöld said they all have a common element: "[T]emporarily, and pending the filling of a vacuum by normal means, the United Nations enters the picture on the basis of its non-commitment to any power bloc, so as to provide to the extent possible a guarantee in relation to all parties against initiatives from others." [33]

A series of specific developments, beginning in 1958, furnished the basis for Hammarskjöld's theory of preventive diplomacy. The Secretary-General's activities preceded any legal or theoretical justification of them as authorized under his "special right." They began when Thailand and Cambodia asked him to help settle a dispute involving the ownership of the temple of Preah Vihear. Then Laos apprised the Secretary-General of what it considered were threats to its security from incursions of troops from North Vietnam.

In the first case, Hammarskjöld discussed the dispute separately with representatives of the two governments and consulted members of the Security Council. He was then invited, no doubt in part at least on his own suggestion, to send a representative to help them with conciliation. He named Ambassador Johan Beck-Friis of Sweden as his Special Representative. The latter was eventually successful in easing the tension between the two governments, to the extent that they resumed diplomatic relations.[34]

The title of Special or Personal Representative of the Secretary-General was no novelty, for Lie had frequently used it for members of his staff on important missions. After the outbreak of the conflict in Korea, for example, he appointed Alfred Katzin of his office as Personal Representative and assigned him duties which brought him into negotiations on relief matters with General Douglas MacArthur and other officials of the American Far East Command. Earlier, in Korea, Victor Hoo had been named Personal Representative and head of the secretariat of the Temporary Commission on Korea.[35] But in these cases Lie acted within a policy framework determined by a deliberative organ. In the Beck-Friis appointment, Hammarskjöld himself determined the terms of reference for his representative, and sent him on a mission involving not direction of the work of the Secretariat but a dispute between governments.

The Secretary-General's relations with Laos went on after the Beck-Friis mission had ended. In the Thailand-Cambodia case, unlike that in Laos, there was no special examination by any deliberative organ of the United Nations.[36] In the Laos case, the Secretary-General used his report as an opportunity to elaborate the idea of "preventive diplomacy" through the dispatch on his initiative of Personal Representatives. This and related aspects, Hammarskjöld held, were within the intentions of Article 99.

Hammarskjöld's report to the Security Council on his dealing with Laos preceded the appointment of his Personal Representative and also was followed by some rather precise explanations of his intentions in the diplomatic realm. The Security Council reacted to the Laotian request for an emergency force by conducting a tortuous debate and sending a subcommittee, bitterly opposed by the Soviet Union, to the field to collect information. Its report did not support Laotian claims and was rather inconclusive.[37]

Immediately after this report was made public, the Secretary-General let it be known that he had been considering a visit to Laos. Earlier, Hammarskjöld had said that if he had to take the initiative without authorization from another organ, he would have to act most conservatively and without legal ambiguity. Apparently, he meant that although he was empowered to act, he would have to do so without crossing the lines established by another organ. When on November 8, 1959 he decided to accept an invitation from the Laotian government, he said that he wanted to obtain "independent and full personal knowledge of the problem of which the United Nations had become seized." [38] The inference could be drawn that he was acting under Article 99, but the precise nature of his duties was unclear. There was no explanation of why it was necessary to gather yet more information immediately after a subcommittee of the Security Council (the secretary of which, incidentally, was a member of the Secretariat) had just made its report.

The Soviet Union, meanwhile, continued to oppose any United Nations involvement in Laos. The Soviet representative wrote to Hammarskjöld in less violent tones than had been used in the Council to the effect that the trip would be a further complication. The Secretary-General nevertheless decided to go ahead, taking a "carefully calculated political risk." [39]

Some further glimmerings of the course Hammarskjöld would follow appeared during his visit to Laos. He summoned Sakari S. Tuomioja, Executive Secretary of the United Nations Economic Commission for Europe, to Vientiane for discussions on the economic situation and to make a report within a month on the "role of economic and technical assistance rendered by the United Nations for the furtherance of economic growth and stability." The Special Representative recommended a series of coordinated developmental actions by the United Nations and the Specialized Agencies, and urged that a senior official be kept on in Laos to coordinate this work. Tuomioja's work was followed by a visit from Roberto M. Heurtematte, the Secretariat's Commissioner for Technical Assistance, who did some specific planning of a program of economic and social assistance. Finally, Hammarskjöld appointed Dr. Edouard Zellweger, a Swiss jurist and member of parliament, as his Special Consultant and posted him to Vientiane.[40]

Zellweger, whose "background strongly suggested that he would primarily be a political adviser and, secondarily, an economic adviser," [41] stayed on through 1960. Very little information was made available on his activities, and despite the continued political discord and some striking changes in the Laotian government during his stay, his work was ignored by the press.

The three United Nations representatives in Vientiane must have been informing the Secretary-General of events there, carrying his own views to the government, and managing an increasing program of United Nations aid which could not fail to have some effect and perhaps influence on the government. But this influence could scarcely depend on the expenditures of great sums to aid the Royal Government of Laos. By the end of 1959, the Laotians had asked for some $1,000,000 a year in assistance, but were to be given less than a fifth of that during 1960 and not more than a half of that sum in each of the two succeeding years. The Secretary-General's diplomacy then was based less on gold than it was on the maintenance of a prestigious official. While spokesmen for the Soviet bloc claimed that the mission in Vientiane was excessively large, it consisted in fact of the Special Consultant, Zellweger, a principal secretary, an administrative officer, three secretaries, and three field service men, plus local recruits for technical and service functions.[42]

Another Soviet line of criticism charged that posting a high-ranking representative of the Secretary-General in Laos was in itself an illegal action. Hammarskjöld's reply to this accusation exposed the logic by which the Secretary-General had connected Article 99 to fact-finding missions and the expansion of technical assistance. He insisted that in acting under Article 99 he was not compelled to take second-hand information but had to "find out for himself," even traveling personally as he did to Laos. To deny him the right of direct fact-finding was to erase Article 99 from the Charter, he declared. Furthermore, because the mission of the Personal Representative of the Secretary-General was arranged at the request of the government of Laos to work in the economic and social field and had been approved by successive governments, the Soviet criticism, Hammarskjöld insisted, meant that he could only respond to such a request after action by one of the deliberative organs. "It is not because we want to interfere," he remarked, "that we take on ourselves the burden to help a government at its request. . . . We do it, and I have done it, because I believe that this is part of the duties of the Organization."[43]

By this time, Laos was not the only instance of the use of a Personal Representative to deal with economic assistance in a touchy political environment. Adrian Pelt had been assigned to Guinea as a

Personal Representative to carry out similar high-level tasks, but there had been no prior reference in this case to any possibility of a breach of international peace.[44] Hammarskjöld included Guinea in his defense of the use of personal representatives. He explained that technical assistance missions might be divided into two sorts, the first kind which had little political impact but a second kind which involved advisers in central planning. The second variety, he said,

> . . . may be of political significance but in a way entirely under the control of the government. Various governments have in the past sought such more qualified technical assistance and various governments have received it. Is that also to be considered illegal? And is it to be considered illegal if the Resident Representative in a regular technical assistance mission frequently is called in by the Cabinet for discussions and, maybe, has direct access also to the Chief of State? But if that is not the case, what is then the difference between a technical assistance mission and a special representative of the kind against which objections are now raised and of which you find examples in Laos and Guinea?
>
> Or is the present line of criticism based on the view that governments should not ask for, receive and accept technical assistance which is more than marginal and which may strengthen their hand so as to make them more independent of bilateral arrangements from whatever source and for whatever reasons they may be offered? [45]

Hammarskjöld then capped his argument by referring to his remarks in the *Introduction* to his *Annual Report* for 1959, where he first spelled out his conception of diplomatic action by his office. He claimed the right to carry on diplomatic activities in order to inform himself. Article 99 might then be used with a background of full information. The United Nations could also assist member governments as far as possible to carry out internal programs of economic and social developments. At the same time, he juxtaposed the two lines of action and made it difficult to separate one from the other.

Some Consequences of the "Special Right"

The "special right" of the Secretary-General has evolved far beyond original expectations for it as an alternative means for engaging the Security Council in consideration of an international dispute or a situation which could become serious. It has been built up so that now the chief executive officer has an opportunity to attempt to influence almost any action involving the maintenance of peace and security. Its elaboration and the rationalizations to explain its expansion have furnished a firm base for activities by the Secretary-General.

The legal underpinnings of the "special right" in its evolved form are impressive. The Secretary-General may speak personally and may report to any United Nations organ. He has exercised his privileges under the rules of procedure of the Security Council and the General Assembly in delicate situations. No challenge to his right to speak has ever been sustained. The procedural questions discussed in the Council when Hammarskjöld reported on his work in Laos make it clear that the Secretary-General may use his right to speak in order to attempt to involve the deliberative organ in consideration of a complaint, without his having invoked Article 99.

As Hammarskjöld suggested, the expansion of the "special right" did not stem from any directed or planned development. Rather it resulted from the constant attention to political affairs which characterized the tenure of the first two Secretaries-General. This attention, unchanged during the incumbency of Thant, has taken several forms. One of them resulted in the early creation of legal rules which allowed the Secretary-General to make known his views in the deliberative organs. Yet another form encouraged the development of preventive diplomacy, which Hammarskjöld claimed was explained by the fact that the "Organization has begun to gain a certain independent position, and that this tendency has led to the acceptance of an independent political and diplomatic activity on the part of the Secretary-General as the 'neutral' representative of the Organization." [46]

If indeed the organization did grow to some independence, it scarcely resulted from the direct exercise of the powers of the Secretary-General under Article 99 narrowly construed only as an alternative means of seizing the attention of the Security Council. The powers delimited by narrow interpretation were used but once, and in circumstances which suggest that the Security Council would have in any case soon been engaged. And in the Korea and Suez cases, mention of Article 99 by the Secretary-General was used as a means of underlining the seriousness of the situation and the strength of his views rather than as a beginning of a process of debate and decision. The main use of Article 99, then, was not to activate the Security Council. Rather, the establishment of its implications through a broad interpretation became important. It thus became a means of encouraging the growth of the general political functions of the office of Secretary-General and supporting his diplomatic role.

The chief officers always tried to take advantage of opportunities to enlarge the scope of their activities. All made recommendations, took part in negotiations, and insisted that the United Nations was important. They acted as if the organization had an independent life. Their doing so represented personal choices in the role they attempted to fill. Increasingly, the United Nations institutionalized earlier practices and the member states accepted the practices; not the least of these was the high degree of political activity of the Secretary-General.

As is perhaps inevitable in political situations, the dramatic innovations proved the most dangerous to the innovator. Intervention by the Secretary-General in a Korea or a Congo discussion—notwithstanding Article 99 and its implications—could lead to specific embarrassment and unexpected difficulty. His intervention could be tolerated when a temple in the Thai jungle was at stake; the level of tolerance was much lower when even a small amount of assistance or the involvement of another organization might prevent the success of an effort to alter the regime in Laos.

Although the new face of Article 99 has been introduced and generally accepted, it can only be displayed with discretion. The use of novel techniques, which contrast so greatly with the guarded conversations of the League days, can not only fail to affect the substance of a problem for which they were employed; they may also threaten the very office of Secretary-General. The political acumen of the Secretary-General must be great to guard him against untoward reactions from the use of Article 99 and its implications. Such a reaction caused attacks by the Soviet Union on the office of Secretary-General. But the source of these attacks was in a sense only accidental; no immutable compulsion ensures that the Secretary-General will act only against the perceived interests of the Soviet Union. Another time it could equally well be the United States, or India, or all of Africa.

CHAPTER VIII

NEGOTIATION AND MEDIATION

Consultations which necessarily arise from the "special right" and from his general administrative activities provide the Secretary-General with options and opportunities to undertake diplomatic activity, the results of which may influence governmental and United Nations policy.

Consultative activity and the consequent opportunities for diplomatic initiatives have been broadened and deepened by the growth of a corps of more than 100 permanent representatives at the United Nations headquarters. Lie and his associates took for granted that many, if not most, of the members would maintain permanent missions at the headquarters city. Establishment of a permanent mission in New York became normal for each new member as it was admitted to the organization. Moreover, nonmember states often posted observers to the United Nations. All this was not the case with the League.

By 1959 Hammarskjöld was calling the establishment of permanent missions a "development of special significance" which tended to give deliberative organs "greater real weight in present-day diplomacy." [1] This "standing diplomatic conference," he said, comprised

> . . . to a decisive extent pioneers in the development of international co-operation within the United Nations, giving to the work of the major organs a perspective which is not less valuable for being less publicized. The permanent representation at Headquarters of all Member nations, and the growing diplomatic contribution of the permanent delegations outside the public meetings—often in close contact also with the Secretariat—may well come to be regarded as the most important "common law" development which has taken place so far within the constitutional framework of the Charter.[2]

From the earliest days of the organization, the Secretary-General has kept contact with a large number of delegates. At a minimum, these conversations carry to the Secretary-General a flood of information, comment, and counsel. He can better time any formal intervention of his own in the deliberative organs and can more effectively execute their instructions. He can initiate further discussions with delegates specifically aimed at the settlement of disputes or the elimination of friction. Some of these efforts have resulted in the easing of difficult situations, or in clear success in settling disputes. Others have been near misses, and many have left little impression.

Hammarskjöld believed that the use of the diplomatic functions of the Secretary-General was an innovation not to be measured superficially in terms of success or failure but rather by "whether the governments co-operating within the United Nations have felt the need of such new techniques—and use them." The implication is that, in any case, the presence of the Secretary-General in negotiations, itself not a "direct or planned development," serves to further the growth of an effective alternative to customary diplomatic practice.[3]

Diplomatic activities carried on by the Secretary-General may be divided into two broad classes, the first of which includes his exercise of negotiating and mediating functions. The second class comprises the execution by the Secretary-General of politico-administrative tasks assigned by a deliberative organ under Article 98 of the Charter, as in the Suez or Congo conflicts, to be discussed in later chapters.

Negotiating and mediating functions can, in turn, be classified into two types. The first includes diplomatic consultation connected with maintenance of the peace in which the Secretary-General on his own initiative makes substantive suggestions for easing friction or conflict among member states. He functions as a mediator without necessarily having a formal appointment for the task. He acts in accordance with general political powers which can be seen as connected with Article 99 as well as on the basis of other instructions.

The second type of mediation (which may also be connected with Article 99) includes suggestions which the Secretary-General makes on his own initiative to the parties to a conflict regarding means of reaching a settlement of their difficulties. Such suggestions emphasize not the content of an agreement but rather steps toward it. In making such suggestions he may offer his good offices, which, if accepted, may result in the assignment of tasks under Article 98. But at other times his talks may result in the parties' choosing a means of negotiation which will take the dispute entirely out of his hands and leave him without responsibility.

The Secretary-General's exercise of negotiatory and mediatory functions on his own initiative depends exclusively on his willingness to intercede in political situations and on his diplomatic skill. Assigned functions require no less adroitness, but the responsibility for defining the issue and for deciding on the terms of reference under which he acts formally lies outside of his office.

Once undertaken, negotiatory initiatives by the Secretary-General employ techniques no different from those of assigned functions. Consultations and diplomatic actions are undertaken. New administrative machinery is not necessarily required, but a positive and receptive attitude toward diplomatic ventures is necessary. Such an attitude has been characteristic of all the Secretaries-General and has helped to expand their influence in matters of peace and security.

Lie—Palestine, Berlin, and the Peace Plan

Two of Lie's most important diplomatic efforts fell into the category of suggestions regarding procedures. Both occurred in 1948.

In that year he conducted intense, private discussions aimed at ending the fighting in Palestine. He employed members of his immediate staff as a foreign minister uses his ambassadors, asking them to seek information and to make suggestions.[4] They carried his ideas to London and Washington in person. Lie had numerous talks in New York, and conferred with the United States Secretary of State. His intervention included a personal appeal to the great powers on the Security Council, and a legal opinion that it had the competence to carry out the partition plan approved by the General Assembly. It cannot, however, be said that these efforts resulted in any resounding success. Indeed, a legal memorandum on the powers of the Security Council in the Palestine affair caused so much controversy that Lie disavowed it.

A similar involvement in the negotiations over the Berlin blockade came rather closer to a solution, and served to show that the involvement of the office of Secretary-General could be very practical.[5] Lie had kept informed of the crisis which began developing in the summer of 1948 and came to the Security Council in the autumn. He did not enter the negotiations actively, however, until the Security Council failed to agree on a course to be followed in Berlin. Again, he employed members of his staff to negotiate and to draw up suggestions. One of real promise foresaw the replacement of the currency used in West Berlin, occupied by France, Great Britain, and the United States, with that of surrounding Russian-occupied East Germany, in return for lifting the blockade; it set off serious negotiations among the parties. Eventually, Lie's activities, supposedly strictly secret, leaked to the press (through British channels, he recalls).

Soon afterward Lie joined Herbert Evatt, the Australian Foreign Minister, who was then President of the General Assembly, in a public appeal to the great powers that they be guided to cooperation by a resolution just adopted by the General Assembly. They urged a meeting of heads of governments and a determined effort, including the use of the Secretary-General's studies of the currency question, to reach a settlement of the blockade. The furor that followed ended any chance that the Secretary-General might be effective in the dispute. Eventually a settlement was reached without his influence in talks between Philip C. Jessup, the United States Ambassador-at-large, and Yakov A. Malik, the Soviet Deputy Foreign Minister.

By far the most spectacular of Lie's diplomatic initiatives included suggestions of both substance and procedure. It took place during the spring of 1950, when he publicly sought to encourage negotiations among the great powers on specific problems listed in a twenty-year peace plan, which he drafted himself.[6] The first mention of the idea came in a speech in Washington in March, 1950, before a meeting of a Jewish fraternal organization. As it gained altitude, this barely floating trial balloon expanded into a ten-point memorandum which Lie personally presented to the United States President and the Soviet, British, and French Premiers, and to important governmental figures of Switzerland, the Netherlands, and Nationalist China. He traveled to Washington, London, Paris, Prague, and Moscow, in a flare of public interest which he found gratifying.

While his *démarche* was courteously received everywhere (except in Czechoslovakia, where his discussion dealt with the question of the return of Greek children captured during the civil war), it once more produced few concrete results. The nature of his memorandum militated against any remarkable reaction, because for the most part it called only for, as he told Stalin, "new efforts at finding some area of common ground" on broad controversies among the great powers. Its ten points dealt with the following: (1) Inauguration of periodic, high-level meetings of the Security Council and further use of United Nations machinery for peaceful settlement; (2) a new attempt to achieve an international control system for nuclear energy; (3) a new approach to arms control; (4) renewal of efforts to place an armed force at the disposal of the Security Council; (5) universality of United Nations membership; (6) technical assistance for economic development and encouragement of capital investment; (7) more vigorous use of United Nations Specialized Agencies; (8) vigorous, continued United Nations work on human rights; (9) use of the United Nations to promote the peaceful advancement of dependent peoples to equality; (10) efforts through the United Nations to develop international law toward enforceable world law.

After sounding out the opinions of the governmental leaders, and warding off the questions of the press, Lie communicated his ten points to all United Nations members, listed his peace plan on the agenda of the General Assembly, and discussed it at a plenary meeting. But three weeks after making his memorandum public, North Korean troops began the attack which opened the Korean conflict.

Lie's efforts to restore diplomatic exchange among the Soviet Union, then led by an ever more secretive Stalin, and the distrustful Western powers, had some practical basis in that he could at that time communicate with both sides in the Cold War. Normal diplomatic contacts had disappeared in the growing tension which followed the Berlin blockade and preceded the Korean conflict. But the program the Secretary-General designed had only one really concrete proposal. This was the first point, calling for periodic meetings of the Security Council under Article 28 of the Charter. At least it had the advantage of never having been tried, but it more closely related to procedure than to anything substantive. Of all his points, it aroused the most positive, but still mixed, response.

The other parts of the twenty-year peace program all pointed to matters which had long been under discussion in the United Nations. Lie merely suggested new attention to them as the substantive sources of international friction. It was not surprising that he could go no farther, since the Cold War had quite thoroughly blocked the kind of detailed discussion and trading of specific ideas in which the technical skills of the diplomat can flourish. He could only seek, in a manner reminiscent of his joint letter with Evatt during the Berlin crisis, talks leading to peace.

From the point of view of the office of Secretary-General, Lie's twenty-year peace plan provided some evidence that the chief officer of the United Nations could engage in high-level discussions and could be taken seriously. It showed that he might sometime serve as an intermediary in blocked diplomatic channels. But it cast doubt on his ability as an individual, even with a considerable body of vocal public opinion behind him, to deal with the fundamental conflicts which caused the disuse of United Nations machinery.

Lie's three major *démarches* did have boldness and sincerity. But whether they were wise in the political context of the moment was a question with a less attractive answer. Their effect on the office of Secretary-General was not to heighten its prestige, even though it contributed to precedents for future claims on information and discussion regarding international security matters.

Hammarskjöld—the Suez Canal

Hammarskjöld needed no precedent by the time he attempted to intercede in a major political affair with a view to making suggestions to settle it. His most important diplomatic initiative of this sort came during the long tension which followed the seizure of the Suez Canal by Egypt. He had already been negotiating with the governments of Israel and its neighbors, especially Egypt, in regard to the Palestine truce agreements, which were imperiled early in 1956 by repeated raid and reprisal.[7] When the Suez matter was finally brought to the Security Council by the French and British governments,[8] Hammarskjöld's knowledge of the eastern Mediterranean made him a natural participant in the behind-the-scenes discussions.

Hammarskjöld's entire intervention on the Canal seizure question developed within the framework of the Security Council, rather than parallel to it as Lie's attempt to solve the Berlin blockade problem had. In a speech on October 5 in the Security Council, British Foreign Secretary Selwyn Lloyd made a suggestion which was the initial step toward Hammarskjöld's intervention:

> It seems to me that, after there has been a chance for those who wish to state their views in public session, it might be a good thing for this Council to move into private session. . . . That would give us the opportunity to consider the next step in a less formal atmosphere. . . . We of the United Kingdom have come here earnestly seeking a peaceful solution and we wish to explore the possibilities for a peaceful solution as rapidly as possible. That is why I throw out the suggestion of a private meeting early next week.[9]

Such a private session would of course include the Secretary-General, since it would be an official gathering.

On October 9, the first private meeting was scheduled.[10] It is possible to reconstruct enough of the private meetings to conclude that Hammarskjöld moved ahead quickly to put before the delegates statements which were intended to help solve the Suez Canal problem. Like Lie during the Berlin blockade, he sought both to encourage negotiations and to provide a basis for them.

After the first of the private meetings, Lloyd, Pineau, and Mahmoud Fawzi, the Egyptian representative, came together in the Secretary-General's private quarters for a series of conversations. While the Secretary-General apparently claimed to be taking a minor role, he evidently used the discussion as a basis for drafts written on his initiative. These were subjected to close examination. When the three Foreign Ministers agreed in the course of six meetings on the Secretary-General's draft, it was presented to a closed session of the Security Council.[11]

For a public meeting of the Security Council on October 13, the British and French governments introduced a new draft resolution, which incorporated the language proposed by the Secretary-General. This language contained the "requirements," as they were termed, for dealing peacefully with the Suez Canal problem. The requirements provided for free and open transit through the Canal, respect for Egyptian sovereignty, insulation of the Canal from any country's politics, fixing of tolls and charges by agreement between Egypt and the users, allotment of a fair proportion of dues to development and arbitration of unresolved matters between the Suez

Canal Company and Egypt. This part of the resolution won unanimous approval. But Egypt, sitting at the Council table without a vote, opposed a second part of the resolution, in the drafting of which Hammarskjöld had apparently had no part. Fawzi was joined in opposition by the Yugoslav and Soviet representatives. The latter's veto left only the first part of the resolution standing.[12]

Thus far, Hammarskjöld had seen his formulation survive the test of a vote and he had the basis for continuing discussion. The fact that each member of the Council had pointedly praised his efforts made further discussion even more inviting.

During the next six days, Hammarskjöld talked several times with Fawzi, achieving what he thought were "significant further developments." He went further than his earlier "requirements," now seeking "arrangements" to fill out the principles approved by the Council. He kept the United Kingdom and France informed and even raised the question of further talks. Because he had had no replies, Hammarskjöld told Fawzi, he was transmitting his ideas in a letter. But he declared (in a perfect example of his negotiating technique), he was not trying to "put out any proposals of my own," nor of Fawzi or others.

Just as I did at the end of the private talks in New York, I just wish, in my own words, to try and spell out what are my conclusions from the—entirely-non-committal—observations made in the course of the private talks, adding to some points in the light of my interpretation of the sense of the talks where they did not fully cover the ground.[13]

Since, of course, the disagreements must have come in great part at the places "where the talks did not fully cover the ground," while Hammarskjöld seemed to be saying that he was not proposing anything, he was doing exactly that. (It was during this exchange of views, which perhaps might have had high promise, since Fawzi agreed with almost all of the Secretary-General's proposals, that the British and French were secretly planning their attack on Egypt.)

Hammarskjöld seems to have come far closer to success in this intervention than Lie had with diplomatic initiatives in the Palestine and Berlin cases. At least, the Security Council adopted the principles which the second Secretary-General had negotiated and drafted. Moreover, even had Hammarskjöld's efforts been rebuffed early in the consideration of the Suez case, he could scarcely have suffered a major loss in influence, for he had in fact committed little of the prestige of his office. He always tried to claim that he was merely assisting the delegates to see their own somewhat obscured agreements. But if the words of the delegates to the Security Council may be taken as evidence, he did a great deal more without ever putting intolerable pressure on the governments or turning his intervention into a public matter. Surprisingly little of the details of his conversations have ever been published. Lie, on the other hand, had difficulty in keeping his interventions from leaking into the press, which proceeded to give them a dramatic quality.

Lie's interventions in the Palestine affair and his effort to open broad talks through his twenty-year peace plan both fell to pieces when the general political situation underwent a sharp change. Hammarskjöld, too, encountered such a lightning change when the Israelis, British, and French attacked Egypt. It cannot be said flatly that the interventions were useless. But it is hardly contestable that neither Lie nor Hammarskjöld succeeded in bringing to a brilliant end their diplomatic initiatives intended to deal with the substance of international disputes.

Hammarskjöld—Bizerte

Because the Secretary-General and his staff have continuous experience with the process of making decisions and recommendations in the United Nations and are therefore likely to be better acquainted with the rules and practices than any individual delegates, they are consulted constantly with regard to the possible engagement of United Nations organs on problems of international politics.

It is a slight step from acting as a consultant on procedures to intervening with a suggestion about possible approaches to the substance of a political problem. The Secretary-General makes this sort of suggestion constantly in private conversations. Indeed, it is precisely the sort of political activity which member governments expect from him, for such initiatives often have a great deal of utility to parties to a political conflict.

Hammarskjöld used his consultations with delegates in a creative fashion, and may be given credit for having a strong voice in the development of all attempts at peaceful settlement of international disputes within the United Nations context during his term of office. It is probable that he suggested the use of his own office to deal with the approaching crisis of Laos. He clearly had views regarding the proper procedure and the use of United Nations organs in the Lebanon case. He had offered his services to the parties to the Palestine armistice agreement during his first year in office. In general, he urged that the normal course of diplomacy would be served if the position of the United Nations were safeguarded by keeping the organization "in the picture" even when conferences were arranged outside its framework.[14] He insisted that he was not eager to manage all negotiations:

> [I]f governments are seized of a matter, if there is no deadlock, if discussions are going on and if contacts have been established, those facts in themselves represent reasons, as I see it, why the Secretary-General,—no matter how concerned he may be—should keep back. Basically, in that sense, his activity should be supplementary. He has no reason to jump on the stage and take over the part of any responsible government.[15]

This certainly meant that Hammarskjöld had a policy of watching for opportunities to discuss approaches to settlement of particular political problems.

How he seized such chances was sharply demonstrated during the brief, bloody crisis between France and Tunisia over the naval base at Bizerte during the summer of 1961. An attempt by President Habib Bourguiba's armed forces to invest the Bizerte base, which was to be evacuated by France at a yet unagreed date, brought a sharp response with modern weapons. Hundreds of Tunisians apparently were killed, and a hitherto cooperative relationship between France and its former colony vanished.

At Tunisia's request for an emergency meeting, the Security Council convened on July 21. Mongi Slim presented the Tunisian complaint of acts of aggression. Armand Bérard replied for France with a denial of aggression, a recital of the history of the affair, and an offer of cooperation. On the following day Hammarskjöld interceded in the debate to appeal for "an intermediary decision" for a cease-fire, pending further consideration. He said it would not prejudge further action by the Council and that he made his appeal "in view of the obligations of the Secretary-General under Article 99 of the Charter." [16] Two resolutions had been submitted by this time, but Liberia, the cosponsor of one, proposed tabling another draft along the lines suggested by the Secretary-General.

During a recess, when Hammarskjöld surely discussed the resolution with the delegates, a new draft was worked out which merely called for an immediate cease-fire and continuation of the debate. It can be surmised, moreover, that the Liberian representative had been informed in advance of the intention of the Secretary-General to speak and of the gist of his remarks. The Council adopted the simple cease-fire resolution by ten favorable votes, with France not participating. During the afternoon of the same day, Bérard told the Council that the French troops had been ordered out of action and pointed out that the French government would not favor resolutions telling it to do what it had all along wanted to do.[17]

Three days after his intervention in the Security Council, Hammarskjöld received an invitation from Bourguiba, with whose representatives he had been in constant consultation in New York, to come to Tunisia for "a direct and personal exchange of views," which he said was necessary and urgent.[18] This move grew out of a conversation in which Hammarskjöld and Tunisian representatives took part. As soon as the idea of his going to Tunisia was broached, Hammarskjöld developed it and began to lay plans for seeing responsible French officials as well. Hammarskjöld's reply to Bourguiba was affirmative, but it hedged on the subjects they would discuss:

> Such a request on your part imposes upon me the clear duty to place myself at your disposal for such a personal exchange of views, which, I hope, might help to lead towards peace. I would point out, however, that the problem is still before the Security Council, which has decided to continue its discussion of the matter, and that, that being so, the substance of the problem is outside my personal competence.[19]

He departed immediately for Tunis, stating that he had made the trip on a matter of urgency. But little of the substance of his conversation leaked out.

The French, too, apparently were brought into the conversations at headquarters, where they were informed of the Secretary-General's hope to go to Paris on his way back from Tunisia. Because Franco-Tunisian diplomatic relations had been severed, Hammarskjöld might have been thought the possessor of useful information.

The Secretary-General knew both Maurice Couve de Murville, the French Foreign Minister, and Charles de Gaulle, and evidently estimated that they would certainly want to talk with him under the circumstances. He now had reached the limit of his consultations, for the French refused to have him in Paris. Moreover, the French military authorities searched his car in Tunis when he crossed the lines in a fruitless attempt to carry on discussions.

Although he knew that he would not be welcome at Paris, Hammarskjöld wrote to Couve de Murville, voicing his serious concern that more than two days after the Security Council's resolution there had been no progress toward a withdrawal of troops and asking that he be sent information. He explained the basis of his request in these words:

> In view of the responsibilities incumbent upon the Secretary-General for the execution of this resolution, as of any other decision of the Security Council or the General Assembly, I consider it my duty to explore the possibilities of improving this disturbing situation by making an effort, at least, to establish immediately the necessary contact between the two parties, the basis for which must be strict compliance with the terms of the resolution and respect for Tunisian sovereignty.[20]

Hammarskjöld was offering his good offices in the hope of reopening negotiations.

The French government, which had been displaying hostility to the United Nations as a result of the insistence by the General Assembly on discussing Algeria, replied coldly that Hammarskjöld seemed to be taking the Tunisian position, and simply sent him a communiqué.

Later in the Security Council, at the suggestion of Nathan Barnes of Liberia, Hammarskjöld was invited to make a statement. The Secretary-General's remarks had obviously been carefully prepared, and for the most part they precisely restated his earlier comments. But he added that he had personally observed French military units around Bizerte, in the city and on the road to Tunis and that they "exercised functions for the maintenance of law and order in the city which normally belong to organs of the sovereign Government."[21] He did not remark that they searched automobiles. He also intimated that he had testimony showing that the French had violated the cease-fire. He declined to enter the substance of the still-continuing dispute, but noted that he could not present the French view.

By this time the French had officially declined to take further part in the debate, and only a second-rank representative sat, silently, with the Council. It failed, however, to agree on a resolution, and President Barnes announced that his and other delegations would seek a special session of the General Assembly.[22] In that session, the last gasps of Hammarskjöld's incomplete intervention were echoed in the speeches of some of the members who deplored the French snub to the Secretary-General.[23] Hammarskjöld was not again directly involved with the negotiations.

In many ways the Tunisian episode is a revealing one. It showed how the Secretary-General could use consultations to prepare for action in open meetings of the Security Council which might have considerable effect. There can be little doubt that Hammarskjöld had carefully opened the way for the calm reception his call for a cease-fire enjoyed. It demonstrated that he could use private discussions and conversations to stimulate requests for his further involvement in a Security Council action. From one of those conversations came the idea that he should go to Tunis. But the French refusal to invite him to Paris indicated that the Secretary-General cannot depend on receiving information and conducting conversations as an immutable right, nor can he persuade or press each member to discuss its actions with him, even within a limited framework.

Thant—West New Guinea and Cuba

The Secretary-General, taking the initiative against the background of Article 99 without explicitly invoking it, can sometimes suggest or induce consultations and conciliatory procedures. His own role may be limited only to a good offices procedure, in which he tries to bring the parties to a dispute together for negotiation inside or outside the United Nations framework. Or it may bring him personally into a mediatory procedure. Two remarkable examples of diplomatic initiative—one concerning the future status of West New Guinea and the other during the Cuban missile crisis—illustrate how the Secretary-General has helped with the choice of means toward the settlement of disputes.

The West New Guinea case grew out of friction between the Netherlands and Indonesia over that territory, which had remained under Dutch administration after the independence of the former Dutch East Indies. Indonesia pressed its legal claim simultaneously with a buildup of arms, pressure against the Netherlands, and finally infiltration and armed raids. The Netherlands claimed full title, insisted it would defend the territory and would entertain no proposal for transferring sovereignty unless the Papuans inhabiting the islands were protected. But by 1961 the Dutch attitude became flexible to the point of proposing what amounted to a United Nations trusteeship for the territory.

After armed skirmishes between Dutch and Indonesian forces, Thant suggested that the permanent representatives to the United Nations of the two governments consult with him, and that the governments refrain from precipitate action.[24] Both governments assented (which probably indicates advance consultations), and discussions were undertaken. Meanwhile, in the background the United States applied some pressure on the Dutch government to come to a settlement. A retired United States ambassador, Ellsworth Bunker, was appointed representative of the Secretary-General to carry on the discussions.

Although negotiations were anything but smooth and Thant had several times to intercede to urge the governments to resume talking, Bunker was able to pass from merely trying to open negotiations to mediatory functions. But the Secretary-General's own communications to the parties continued to deal with approaches rather than with substance. On August 15, 1962, the two governments reached an agreement to end Dutch control and turn the administration over to the United Nations for a temporary period before Indonesia took control and eventually held a plebiscite on the future of the territory. (This United Nations administration will be discussed below in connection with peace-keeping.) It was only then that the negotiations and their results were referred to a deliberative body of the United Nations. Until the General Assembly endorsed the agreement in its 1962 sessions, the Secretary-General had acted entirely on his own responsibility in relation to maintaining the peace and had had an influential but not decisive role in bringing about agreement.

Thant's initiative in the Cuban missile crisis,[25] in which the United States and the Soviet Union came so close to a direct military clash, had elements in common with the Secretary-General's action in the Suez case, for the Security Council had begun dealing with the matter without his intervening. But the quality of his initiative makes it more akin to the good-offices and mediatory functions that the Secretary-General attempted in the Tunisian and West New Guinea examples.

Following President Kennedy's announcement that Soviet missiles had been emplaced in Cuba and that the United States was imposing a naval quarantine on the island until they were withdrawn, the Security Council took up the dispute at the request of the Soviet Union, the United States, and Cuba. A United States draft resolution foresaw a role for the Secretary-General as the organizer of an observer corps to assure compliance with a demand that the missiles be withdrawn. But Thant did not immediately respond to the crisis or the resolution, waiting a day until he had been consulted by delegates speaking for some fifty member states.[26]

Thant's initial suggestion, made in letters to Kennedy and Khrushchev, aimed primarily at getting negotiations into motion. In order to do this he pleaded for time, which was to be obtained by a voluntary suspension for several weeks of arms shipments to Cuba and of United States quarantine measures. Thant also called attention to Hammarskjöld's doctrine that the Secretary-General must be guided by the Charter, not by measures of expediency.

This initiative drew a rather favorable response from the Soviet Union and the United States, both of which had been engaged in intense diplomatic maneuvering and military preparations without any connection with the United Nations. Kennedy said that Stevenson was prepared to discuss arrangements for preliminary talks, while Khrushchev agreed in principle to the proposal. On October 28, the fifth day of the crisis, pressure on the Soviet Union resulted in a change in that country's policy, and Khrushchev agreed to the return of the missiles under United Nations supervision.

The proposal for United Nations supervision and inspection of the withdrawal of the missiles, suggested from the first by the United States, involved the Secretary-General. When Castro's government proved reluctant to permit it, Thant went to Havana for discussions.

Although the outcome was negative, the Secretary-General nevertheless maintained a neutral channel of communication with the Cuban government that perhaps had some value in reducing the tension. The formal end of the crisis came in January, 1963, when the United States and the Soviet Union jointly expressed appreciation to the Secretary-General for his assistance and said that the matter need no longer occupy the Security Council.

During the entire crisis, Thant consulted with representatives of the United States, the Soviet Union, Cuba, and other members of the organization. His initiatives were taken seriously and employed as items for negotiation. But it is still not clear whether the Secretary-General's role was more than minor and incidental. Thant himself says only that the United Nations aided in averting a conflagration and provided an opportunity for dialogues between the disputants.[27] The United States Assistant Secretary of State for International Organization Affairs credits the Secretary-General with serving "as a middleman in crucial parts of the dialogue between President Kennedy and Chairman Khrushchev which led to a peaceful solution." [28] Yet it is obvious that the most important negotiations were carried on by the United States President and the Soviet Chairman, quite outside of the purview of the Secretary-General.

Thant—Viet Nam

Thant has attempted since 1963 to aid in opening negotiations among the parties to the Viet Nam dispute.[28a] His efforts have for the most part been secret, employing diplomatic channels, private conversations, and his network of acquaintances. Although they have been based on the theory that Thant as Secretary-General can be separated from Thant as an individual who perhaps could help, it is his official position and the political role connected with Article 99 of the Charter which gives his activities their standing. Yet he does not envisage action by the Security Council as a means to a settlement. The United Nations, if it is involved at all, would enter at a later stage.

Although Thant has often discussed the Viet Nam conflict with statesmen, the fact that he had made concrete efforts to bring Washington and Hanoi into contact did not become public knowledge until after Adlai Stevenson's death in 1965. Before then, he had publicly deplored the violence which month by month mounted in Viet Nam and had appealed to national leaders to seek peace through diplomatic and political means. During 1965, he secured an agreement from Ho Chi Minh to send an emissary to secret talks with a United States representative in Burma, but the United States government declined to make use of this possibility.

Early in 1966 the Secretary-General began to speak more freely, later making it plain that his disappointment with the lack of progress was a factor in his reluctance to serve another term.

Thant said that his efforts in 1963 aimed at creating stability in South Viet Nam. During the next year he sought informal private dialogues among the concerned parties, and followed this in 1965 with attempts to achieve cessation of hostilities and informal conferences among the big powers, including Peking. Two firm beliefs conditioned his initiatives. One of them, on a moral plane, was that human life was sacred and that the people of Viet Nam should be spared further suffering after a quarter century of violent conflict. The second was political, for he foresaw that continued fighting in Viet Nam would bring further escalation and eventually a general war.

To bring peace to Viet Nam, Thant proposed three steps: the cessation of bombing of North Viet Nam; scaling down of all military operations by all parties; and the willingness of all parties to enter into discussions with all who are actually fighting. This program ran the obvious risk of offending the United States, which had systematically increased bombing in North Viet Nam, had stepped up the level of the conflict, and for many months professed unwillingness to have any contact with the National Liberation Front of South Viet Nam.

In one sense Thant's efforts have succeeded, for the United States, while generally maintaining its earlier position, has labored long to indicate its willingness to cooperate with the Secretary-General. Within three weeks after his reappointment, and perhaps as a result of the discussions which preceded it, the Secretary-General was asked by United States Representative Arthur Goldberg to take whatever measures he thought necessary to reach a cease-fire in Viet Nam. One of Thant's responses was to ask the United States, which he said had the strength to afford it, to take the initiative in ceasing bombing without conditions. Thant left no doubt that he would go on with his probing for a basis on which peace could be brought to Viet Nam. Yet it can hardly be said that his influence thus far has gone beyond the earliest stage of facilitating contact among the warring parties.

Diplomatic initiative by the Secretary-General has become quite ordinary and even predictable in international disputes which threaten to disturb the peace. The record suggests that successful outcomes probably depend more on special political conditions than on the powers of the office or the skills of the incumbent. It is striking that so few of the substantive interventions which the Secretary-General himself initiated have been brought to complete success. Even the West New Guinea settlement saw the Secretary-General acting in a largely facilitative manner. Hammarskjöld perhaps came closest with his work in the Suez case, for at least the Security Council accepted his six principles.

The scope of the office of the Secretary-General is limited in such activity, because he can do little to alter the terms of the situation with which he is working: He can move no armies, impose or lift no economic restrictions, instruct no administrators who can direct the actions of a civil population. He has only his diplomatic skills and political acumen and the good will of the parties to depend upon. The former are not infallible, and in the case of a situation as aggravated as Berlin or Suez, the latter is likely to be absent. Thus, a great deal depends on the conclusions reached by the Secretary-General himself regarding the nature of the conflicts. If he can persuade the disputants to accept his intervention or if he correctly estimates that his intervention will be matched by receptivity, he can be successful. But to make such an estimate after, perhaps, a dozen disciplined foreign offices have been working for months on the same problem is at best difficult and at worst impossible. The chances that the Secretary-General may fail in a direct intervention into the substance of an international conflict must always be high.

Proposing possible procedures to the parties to a conflict seems much more likely to be fruitful. Such a course also engages the office of the Secretary-General to a much lesser degree. A suggestion might simply involve a new approach by a United Nations deliberative body, with the Secretary-General stating his readiness to help. Urging parties to negotiate has become part of the routine consultations conducted by the Secretary-General in carrying out other duties. The opportunity to make a procedural suggestion or to offer "good offices" is readily available. The member states may so easily refuse or accept, that such moves need not become public issues.

Hammarskjöld—China and the United States Airmen

Hammarskjöld's success with the first of his assigned tasks, which took him to Peking to secure the release of eleven United States airmen held by the Chinese Communists, established the confidence in his abilities and the potentialities of his office necessary for the major broadening of its functions in subsequent years.

How to deal with prisoners of war became an issue which long impeded the signing of an armistice in Korea. Most of the prisoners were Chinese or Koreans, but a number came from the 16 nations that assisted the Republic of Korea after the Security Council's request in June 1950.[29] Among these were United States airmen on whom no information could be obtained. It was thought that some of them were prisoners of the Chinese.

At the height of the tension over Quemoy and Matsu during 1954, the Chinese Communists announced with considerable publicity that 11 United States airmen, prisoners since January, 1953, had been tried and sentenced to long prison terms. The announcement from Peking caused a sharp reaction in the United States, and powerful interest groups began a public campaign to free the airmen.

It is not clear precisely why the United States decided to employ the United Nations to press its claim for the return of the airmen and certain civilian personnel who had fallen into Chinese Communist hands. A number of reasons for the United States decision might be adduced. There was no real, continuing contact between the United States and Communist China; the United Nations might have seemed a possible avenue of communication. Hammarskjöld himself was a fresh figure in the rather stale Korean conflict and had not advertised a set of views on the Chinese representation issue. Little could be lost, from the United States point of view, by trying his services. If he succeeded, the Eisenhower administration might pride itself on resourcefulness in liquidating many of the remaining points of difficulty in Korea. If he failed, another demonstration would have been made of the uncooperativeness of the Peking regime, and the existing United States policy of boycotting the Communist Chinese would have additional support.

In any case, the State Department consulted with the other fifteen governments which had sent troops to Korea, and Ambassador Henry Cabot Lodge then submitted a joint resolution to the General Assembly in an effort to effect the release of the detained airmen. A principal feature of the resolution asked the Secretary-General, in the name of the United Nations, to seek the release of the United Nations Command personnel still held in violation of the Korean armistice agreement. The resolution requested the Secretary-General "to make, by the means most appropriate in his judgment, continuing and unremitting efforts to this end." [30]

To request the Secretary-General to deal with such a delicate and emotionally-weighted political issue was at that time almost without precedent. A situation of some similarity had occurred when Lie was requested to take part, along with the International Red Cross, in talks to free Greek children who had been captured during the Greek frontier conflicts and transported to Communist countries in Eastern Europe. But the issue of the imprisoned airmen was more serious because of the tension between the United States and China and the implications for the Cold War, the generally sour aftertaste in the United States of the Korean conflict, and because Communist China had been at odds with the United Nations.

The debate in the General Assembly disclosed open opposition from the Soviet group to the entire resolution. This could only be expected, because the resolution explicitly declared the actions of the Chinese a violation of the armistice agreements and condemned the trial of the prisoners. Other speakers generally supported the resolution. The Asian and African states abstained on the ground that they objected to the condemnatory passages of the resolution, but at least one representative from their number supported the mission for the Secretary-General. Sweden exhibited misgivings about the entire resolution, its representative declaring that the General Assembly was no place for the United States complaint while the machinery in Korea was open; but his delegation voted for the resolution.[31]

Presumably Hammarskjöld had been consulted by the sponsors of the resolution and was found willing to attempt the negotiations.[32] Lodge did not, however, spell out the actions the Secretary-General might be expected to take. Most other speakers simply echoed the implication of the resolution that the organization had confidence in its Secretary-General. The British and French representatives went somewhat beyond general terms. Anthony Nutting declared for the United Kingdom that the General Assembly should not lay down the methods by which the Secretary-General proceeded, but made the point that it was proper to ask him to report. The implication was that the Secretary-General had to bear in mind that he was a civil servant. The statement by Henri Hoppenot, the French representative, praised Hammarskjöld's personal qualities lavishly and said that all knew "that he will aim, not to secure the victory of public defeat of a legal position for purposes of propaganda, but to secure the release of these men." How he would go about it was his responsibility; he was the "sole judge." [33] The request for a report by the end of 1954, according to Hoppenot, was a concession to public opinion, not a time limit to which the Chinese government had to conform. Hoppenot implied that the Secretary-General would proceed in secret on the basis of complete confidence from the members of the General Assembly.

Hammarskjöld emphasized that in carrying out the General Assembly's resolution, adopted by 47 votes to five with seven abstentions, he would rely on his own judgment. His brief statement resembled Hoppenot's and mentioned specifically the French delegate's point about the date of the first report. He thus kept a free hand for himself. In private consultations [34] he tried to square the contradictions of a resolution which sought negotiations with the very government it condemned. In fact, a reconciliation of the terms of the resolution could not be accomplished, and Hammarskjöld had to disregard its moral strictures in order to work toward the main end.

The Secretary-General moved ahead in two stages. First he had to establish contact with the Peking government. Then he had to get negotiations under way. Immediately after the adoption of the resolution on December 10, 1954, Hammarskjöld cabled Prime Minister Chou En-lai, expressing the desire to meet with him in Peking for direct talks on the subject of the prisoners. Chou cabled back that "he would be prepared to receive the Secretary-General in Peking to discuss pertinent questions with him." [35] The first stage of negotiations was opened, but not on the basis of the resolution, which Hammarskjöld did not forward. The Peking government in a second cablegram specifically denounced the resolution, thus giving notice that it did not intend to proceed with talks on the basis of the General Assembly's opinion of its actions. The trial of the prisoners, said Chou, was an internal affair and nothing more.[36]

During the remainder of December Hammarskjöld completed what he told Chou were the necessary "practical arrangements." The Secretary-General flew to Stockholm for talks with the Chinese Ambassador there. "This discussion," Hammarskjöld reported in his guarded fashion, "served to clarify some of the pertinent arrangements." [37] On December 30 he left New York on what he called a "too spectacular" [38] journey to China. He was accompanied by Ahmed Bokhari, his Under-Secretary for Public Information, Humphrey Waldock, Professor of International Law from Oxford University, who was a special adviser, and a small technical staff.

In the Chinese capital the Secretary-General and his party were received with ceremony and honor. He had discussions with Chou lasting more than thirteen hours. Hammarskjöld's personal reaction was that he had never encountered such skillful negotiators.[39] As Hammarskjöld later reported to the General Assembly, he sought

> to establish a direct contact with the Central Peoples Government of the People's Republic of China, since this Government was not represented in any organs of the United Nations. The visit, aimed primarily at clarifying the substantive and legal aspects of the matter, established direct contact on a personal basis. It thus provided possibilities to pursue the discussion concerning the problem raised by the detention of the United Nations personnel referred to in the General Assembly resolution.[40]

Precisely how the negotiations proceeded and what lines of policy were projected and discarded remains unknown. The official reports of the mission, which was the subject of only an interim report within the original time scheme, were sparse and formal. But after the first report, contact continued with Chou. It proved fruitful.

Sweden became the contact point, and late in May, 1955, Chou announced that four of the detained fliers would be released. On August 1, Chou told Hammarskjöld of his government's decision to release eleven others. One point remained. Chou expressed the desire to continue the contact, and Hammarskjöld agreed with him. But since that time China seems to have discontinued its interest in close personal relations with the Secretary-General.

Even without the details of the negotiation in Peking, it is easy to see that Hammarskjöld's first special mandate from the General Assembly produced important results. The substance of what the General Assembly wanted done was indeed accomplished. The success of such a mission tends to increase the use of the office of Secretary-General in political situations, because there is hope that a further assignment will produce a similar favorable outcome.

Moreover, the performance of the mandate set important precedents. What Hammarskjöld did was to treat the resolution of the General Assembly as something less than a literal instruction which had to be fulfilled in every regard. He did not, for example, seek to carry out his talks in Peking in an atmosphere of moral stricture. In fact, he dealt only with the problem "referred to in the General Assembly resolution." [41] What he did take literally was the possibility of using his own judgment. He shifted the basis of negotiation from that of an agent of the General Assembly to that of the Secretary-General acting personally on the basis of whatever prestige his office gave him. He cannot be said to have acted in the first instance on his own initiative or to have relied on powers implied by Article 99.

Hammarskjöld, in his ingenious and somewhat devious way, created a formula which would permit him simultaneously to satisfy the General Assembly and not humiliate his opposite number in negotiations. It would be idle to pretend that Hammarskjöld was acting as a citizen of the world to smooth out a family difficulty. He was, of course, acting as Secretary-General. The formula simply permitted him to shunt aside the aspects of his instructions which would prove least acceptable to the Chinese. Once this was done, the Chinese government proved willing to go farther. In any case, the Peking regime must have been prepared for and interested in the possibility of releasing the United States airmen in its prisons.

Hammarskjöld's cable and his presence in Peking under the formula that he was acting in a personal capacity offered a neutral and useful avenue to Chou. At the same time, the talks in Peking were only talks and not agreements. Only later were the airmen set free, as a demonstration that the Chinese Communists made their own decisions about whom they should keep in jail and whom they should release.

The Peking formula provides great flexibility to a Secretary-General with an assignment to negotiate. Permitting him to reduce the moral temperature of resolutions by other United Nations organs, it may sometimes encourage agreement from a usually recalcitrant government. But it is no universal instrument. The General Assembly or the Security Council could always take their moral strictures more seriously than the goal of negotiations; in such a case, the Secretary-General would scarcely act in a personal capacity. The lack of contact with such a government as that in Peking could produce such a depth of misunderstanding that no possibility of negotiations could be found. A high degree of political acumen and great diplomatic skill and ingenuity must be part of the Secretary-General's equipment if he attempts the employment of the Peking formula.

Hammarskjöld—Israel and the Arab States

Unlike the case of the United States prisoners in China, relations between Israel and her neighbors represented anything but a novel subject for the United Nations. Since the first special session of the General Assembly in 1947, continuous attention had been given to problems connected with the former British-administered League of Nations mandate. The bitter war between the organized Jews of Palestine and the forces of the surrounding Arab states ended during the first part of 1949 with the signing by four governments, under the supervision and encouragement of the Security Council, of four separate but simultaneous Armistice Agreements.

The Security Council has been active in connection with the Armistice Agreements. An endless series of incidents came before the Council, involving Israeli irrigation works on the Jordan River; the passage of Israeli ships through the Suez Canal; and a series of sharp conflicts and reprisal raids at Qibya and Nahhalin in Jordan in 1953, Gaza, Patish, and Nahal Oz in the Egyptian sector in 1955, and on Lake Tiberias on the Syrian border in the same year. Before the Security Council dealt with these disputes, they had been considered in the Mixed Armistice Commissions and had been observed and investigated by UNTSO. Officers from UNTSO acted as impartial chairmen of the Mixed Armistice Commissions, which assigned responsibility for border incidents.

The presence of the United Nations in the area constituted one of the three main quieting elements in a shifting and confused political situation. The Tripartite Declaration of Britain, France, and the United States, which since 1950 tended to reduce the flow of armaments to the Middle East, and the rather indifferent attitude of the Soviet Union toward events in the area, permitting the Western powers to follow a reasonably consistent line, served as two other quieting factors. So long as these influences operated, some means were available to limit the scope and intensity of conflict.

Beneath the relative calm, the perennial turmoil of Middle Eastern politics provided the United Nations little ground on which to build a permanent settlement, let alone suppress all disturbances of the peace. The constant friction and border incidents, along with the military inefficiency of the Arab countries, encouraged Israel to attempt sharp reprisals for minor outbreaks. During 1955, and especially after the return of the redoubtable David Ben Gurion to the Prime Minister's office, the Israelis renewed border area raids, killing a considerable number of people. A sharp attack on the somnolent Egyptian forces in Gaza in April woke up a relatively static sector. Nasser soon began to seek arms with which to reply to what he saw as a threat to his prestige. The Soviet Union, not engaged by the Tripartite Declaration, offered him the supplies he sought and thus ended its indifference to the Middle East. At the same time, the Israeli reprisal raids and a hardening refusal to deal with the Mixed Armistice Commissions were destroying the remaining efficacy of the United Nations machinery in the area. Two of the three quieting elements thus were eroded by the early months of 1956.

The Secretary-General's active negotiations to bring about the renewed effectiveness of the Palestine Armistice Agreements really began with his first trip to the Middle East in January, 1956. While he had already had to deal with problems growing out of that area and had even protested Israel's policy of barring the El Auja region to UNTSO observers,[42] he had not met the principal political leaders.

The Israeli attack on Syrian regulars in the Lake Tiberias area on December 11, 1955 provided a somber background for his visit. It was one of the strongest reprisal raids thus far mounted. It brought not only bitter protests from Syria but also a stiffening attitude in the Security Council, which unanimously condemned the Israeli action as a violation of the Armistice Agreements and of the Charter. The Council added the threat that, if Israel did not comply with the Armistice Agreements, it would consider what further measures would be required to maintain peace and security.[43]

Because the Israeli violations of the Armistice Agreements resulted from a governmental policy of reprisals, compliance would require a major shift of attitude. And because Israel regarded the *fedayeen* raids from Egypt and the violations by that country of the demilitarized zone in the Gaza strip as intolerably provocative, the principal policies of the most dynamic government in the area also would have to be altered.[44]

Hammarskjöld held major consultations in Israel and Egypt. In both countries, his long talks with the heads of government centered on the El Auja attack and the situation generally in the Gaza strip.[45] Both Ben Gurion and Nasser insisted that their positions resulted from provocation and actions with military significance on the part of the other's government. The Israeli Prime Minister told Hammarskjöld that he could not depend on the United Nations to protect the El Auja area and had acted accordingly. Nasser had a long list of complaints about Israeli behavior, including the charge that Ben Gurion's government disguised its military forces in the demilitarized zone under the cover of police and kibbutz personnel.

The Secretary-General summed up his experience in an extremely general but not meaningless statement on his return. He declared that his discussions were full and frank and gave him "a deeper understanding of the many and great difficulties with which the situation is fraught. These were not minimized." [46] In a press conference he remarked that he now had a "map of the problem." [47] He did not comment on the configuration of the map and avoided any specific suggestions, except to say that he and General E.L.M. Burns, the UNTSO commander, had agreed that the number of observers ought to be expanded. But he noted that new decisions would be required to bring in outside personnel.

Despite his caution, the Secretary-General conveyed the impression that there was a future course which could be read from the map of the problem. He avoided any idea of opening up the entire Palestine dispute again, but he indicated that some progress might be expected in keeping the Middle East quiet by means of the guidance inherent in the armistice agreements.[48] Whether or not the determination to bring about peaceful settlements was as strong in the hearts of Ben Gurion and Nasser as it was in Hammarskjöld, the Secretary-General thought that his personal contacts had broadened his chances of making realistic judgments. He could make proposals, "when there is a need for proposals," with a fuller recognition of the problems facing the statesmen of the Middle East.[49] There was little chance, however, for him to develop his possible proposals before he was again on his way to the Middle East.

The United States proposed in the Security Council in March, 1956 that Hammarskjöld return to the Middle East, for the first time under instructions. The lead offered by the United States has certain remarkable facets. Hammarskjöld had made public no clearly defined idea of a program for stabilizing the border incidents in Palestine and bringing peace to the eastern Mediterranean. He did, however, show himself to be willing to do his personal best. He also discussed his consultations on his own authority with Secretary of State John Foster Dulles. It can be inferred that Hammarskjöld and Dulles talked about the possibility of Security Council action, for soon afterward the United States caused that body to convene.

That the United States adopted a policy which did not have the open sponsorship of France and the United Kingdom was in itself a break from the practice which had been given formal expression in the Tripartite Declaration on the Middle East. The United States *démarche* had a deliberately moderate tone and sought the condemnation of no government or specific action. And the language of the draft resolution presented by Lodge echoed Hammarskjöld's comment to the effect that progress could be made along the lines of the Armistice Agreements.[50]

Despite the implication of close collaboration between the Secretary-General and the United States, it is not at all certain that Hammarskjöld actively desired the intervention of the Security Council. He is reported, in any case, to have been strongly opposed to a tripartite attempt to secure more peaceful relations in the Palestine area, on the grounds that this would draw opposition and an eventual veto from the Soviet Union. If this indeed was Hammarskjöld's view, he perhaps influenced the United States, Britain, and France enough to prevent a tripartite call on the Security Council for action, although he did not prevent a formal consideration of a mandate for the Secretary-General.[51]

The debate in the Security Council was unusually even-tempered and relevant to the resolution at hand. It produced, through a process of question and statement, quite a clear idea of the limits which were to apply to the consultations that Hammarskjöld was directed to undertake. Lodge explained that the United States proposed that the Secretary-General conduct a personal investigation of the problems which stood in the way of peace in the area. It would be based on the Armistice Agreements and the three previous Security Council resolutions. In addition to a survey, the Secretary-General, according to Lodge, would undertake discussions with the parties and with General Burns. But, said Lodge:

> The draft resolution . . . is not intended in any way to derogate from the overall responsibility of the Security Council in this question. . . . We have therefore proposed in the draft resolution that the Secretary-General should report to the Security Council not later than one month from the date of the adoption of the resolution, at which time the Council would consider what further steps might be necessary or desirable for it to take.[52]

Thus Lodge made it clear that Hammarskjöld's duties would be limited in scope, primarily exploratory and administrative, and that the Security Council would continue to maintain political direction.

A further definition of Hammarskjöld's duties was included in the statement which Hervé Alphand made on behalf of France. Alphand, in phrases recalling those used before Hammarskjöld's mission to Peking, warned that the Secretary-General might not be able to do much to reduce existing tensions along the demarcation lines. He cautioned against building up too great expectations in world opinion, and declared that the Council could not expect, despite the wide terms of reference, more than "a full and faithful account of the situation in Palestine, accompanied by any suggestions which he may consider useful." But the Council, he said, would have to make the decisions dependent on the report and "to assume the responsibilities incumbent upon it and upon no one else while it continues to perform its duties." [53]

Without exception the parties involved in the Armistice Agreements spoke of their confidence in Hammarskjöld. But the Arab states wanted reassurance that the whole question of Palestine was not to be reopened. They wanted to know what sort of suggestions might be made, and in the end the Soviet Union attempted to secure amendment of the United States resolution in order to underline the necessity for the agreement of the parties. Lodge offered explanations and assurances, while rejecting the proposed Soviet amendments, to the effect that Hammarskjöld should make suggestions only within the framework of the armistice agreement and after consultations with the parties and the chief of staff of UNTSO. Any additional arrangements would require the agreement of the parties directly concerned.[54] Lodge remarked that:

> . . . it would not be a service to the Secretary-General or the parties directly concerned to enumerate further the problems or the measures with which, together, they might wish to deal, or those with which he should not deal. We feel that with the clear understanding that the mission of the Secretary-General is governed by the Security Council resolutions, and the armistice agreements, such a spelling out is not necessary nor, indeed, desirable. The kind of task which we are asking the Secretary-General to undertake becomes quite clear when seen in this context. Let me point out . . . further that the Secretary-General naturally cannot amend or set aside the undertakings of the general armistice agreements. . . . [T]he Security Council is, of course, not relinquishing its primary responsibility for maintaining international peace and security.[55]

Since Sobolev had already declared that the Soviet Union would not stand in the way of a plan which had the agreement of the parties, there seemed little danger of a veto if the Soviet amendments were rejected, as in fact they were. The Council adopted the United States resolution unanimously.[56]

Only then did Hammarskjöld openly intercede in the debate. He had been consulting behind the scenes, and the favorable comments made about him in the course of the discussion indicated that his taking on an exploratory mission to the Middle East had general and enthusiastic approval. Yet the discussion showed that the mission was conceived of as closely limited. Hammarskjöld said that he had no hesitance in taking on the responsibility, and noted that his exploration of ways to reduce the tension along the demarcation lines would depend on the willingness of all the parties to cooperate in an effort to inspire mutual confidence. In effect, the Secretary-General was requesting a continuation of the kind of conversations from which he had just returned. But this time he had the added prestige of a resolution by the Security Council, even if perhaps he was dubious of its necessity.

In one unusual respect, however, Hammarskjöld indicated a strong view of his own. He matched Lodge's insistence that the Security Council had the sole responsibility for managing the Armistice Agreements with an equally stout insistence that the Secretary-General had his own authority. Speaking of the resolution, he said:

> The scope of the Security Council's request is well indicated and it has been clarified further in the course of the debate. The specific responsibility which this request puts on the Secretary-General is entirely in line with the character and obligations of his office. It is obvious that this request neither detracts from nor adds to the authority of the Secretary-General under the Charter.[57]

Hammarskjöld in this way clearly indicated that he would act on the basis of a reserve of power to which the Security Council had not alluded. He explained to the press the day after the Security Council's action that aside from his instructions he had the regular right to bring up points he thought worth considering in his conversations with governments. And to Joseph Lash he remarked that his right in this regard was unlimited, and that his statement gave him both flexibility and the opportunity to slip around a subsequent Soviet veto in order to continue negotiations.[58] Hammarskjöld's views remained unchallenged at the time, even though they seemed to contradict the sense of the careful definition of his duties in the Council and certainly flew in the face of the expectations voiced by Alphand in regard to what the Secretary-General would do.

Three days after the Security Council gave him his mandate, Hammarskjöld was on his way to the Middle East. He had already conferred in New York with the permanent representatives of the governments he would visit, and had had the news of another outbreak of violence at Gaza. He claimed that the new attack heightened the importance of his mission. On his way to the Middle East he conferred with British Foreign Secretary Selwyn Lloyd and stopped off in Rome to visit the Pope. By this time the small team of experienced officials he put together to collaborate with him was hard at work. It included Henri Vigier, a veteran of the League of Nations who had assisted with the armistice negotiations in 1948 and 1949; George Ivan Smith, an experienced public relations specialist; and Leo Malania, a Canadian who had served for many years in the Secretary-General's executive office. Henry Labouisse, the Director of UNRWA, and General Burns also gave their advice and collaboration.[59] With these officials Hammarskjöld shuttled from one capital to another during the next month. He negotiated with Nasser in Cairo and Ben Gurion in Jerusalem. He committed the results of his complex negotiations to letters, telegrams, and reports. At the same time he helped to deal with the latest outbreak in Gaza.

His return to New York early in May was greeted by popular applause for a job well done and by diplomatic admiration. "Mr. Hammarskjöld's stature," said Alphand in the Security Council, "has been increased by the trial to which we have subjected him, and the same is true of the prestige—which I know to be dearer to him than his own—of his office." [60]

It was the fresh conflict in Gaza which served as an entering wedge for renewed negotiation.[61] The complaint by Egypt of an Israeli attack and the counter-complaint of raids by irregulars deep into Israeli territory illustrated precisely the sort of violations of the Armistice Agreements which had caused the Security Council to warn Israel of possible enforcement measures and to dispatch the Secretary-General to the Middle East.

Even before he arrived on the scene, Hammarskjöld began his negotiations. From Rome he addressed letters to Nasser and Ben Gurion, seeking compliance with the Armistice Agreements between Egypt and Israel. Burns had opened the door for the Secretary-General's persuasive efforts by reporting to him that Ben Gurion wanted an unconditional undertaking from Egypt that it would comply with the part of the Armistice Agreements which prohibits warlike acts or violation of the demarcation line by military or para-military forces. Burns requested this of Egypt, and Hammarskjöld endorsed the request.

Hammarskjöld secured formal undertakings from both Israel and Egypt to comply fully with the prohibition of warlike acts and violations of the demarcation line. But the pledge to comply was not entirely without reserve, for Israel noted that if Egypt continued warlike acts it would regard itself as free to defend itself. The Secretary-General used this reservation to put on record his understanding that self-defense was to be interpreted in conformity with Article II, paragraph II, the relevant part of the Armistice Agreements, and with the United Nations Charter.[62]

This initial exchange of undertakings at the behest of the Secretary-General fitted precisely with the hints he had given about future discussions he might seek on the basis of his January trip to the Middle East. It moreover put the negotiations squarely within the framework of the Armistice Agreements, as the Security Council had desired. The basis of the initial discussions was thus limited. Hammarskjöld was clearly using every opportunity to begin work on specific problems and avoid broad and general conversations which would immediately open up the entire problem of relations between Israel and Egypt.

While the initial undertakings were being negotiated and the diplomatic notes regarding them were entering final drafts, Israel complained of yet another border incident. Once again, Hammarskjöld used what might otherwise have been a very serious disruption of the progress he had begun to achieve in order to seek reaffirmation of the armistice system. The new incident occurred just after Israel had agreed to keep its patrols back from the demarcation line in order to assist Hammarskjöld's efforts. Egypt also notified the Secretary-General of a similar undertaking on its side of the line. Hammarskjöld promptly began pressing both governments to issue orders—or at least to assure him that they would do so—to keep patrols away from the demarcation lines. It also developed that Hammarskjöld intended openly by that time to extend the undertaking regarding Article II, paragraph II of the Armistice Agreement into promises to comply generally with the entire agreement. By the time this stage had been reached, Hammarskjöld had had long and full talks with Nasser and with Egypt's Foreign Minister, Mahmoud Fawzi, and was ready to continue similar work in Israel, where Ben Gurion had already favored face-to-face talks with the United Nations official.[63]

The negotiations with Ben Gurion, whose government was inclined to skepticism, took place during the middle of April on the basis which Hammarskjöld had built in his Cairo talks. His limited success in getting commitments from Nassar by itself tended to bring pressure on the Israeli government, for it had been in communication with Hammarskjöld during the entire discussion.

In addition, both the United States and the Soviet Union used their influence to gain a viable cease-fire. While Hammarskjöld was in Cairo, it became known that the United States was pressing Egypt to agree on steps to end the border violations. Soon afterward President Dwight D. Eisenhower sent a personal plea on the same subject to Prime Minister Ben Gurion. The Soviet Union followed up with an offer of support for the United Nations in gaining a settlement in the Middle East.

While the two superpowers may have had different aims and methods in mind, their combined but coincidental pressure aided the Secretary-General. By April 20, both Israel and Egypt had agreed to the same terms, proposed by Hammarskjöld, for respecting the Armistice Agreement. The Secretary-General rounded out the month by consulting and getting the agreement of the governments of Lebanon, Syria, and Jordan. From that point on, the discussions went beyond the Armistice Agreements into the Israeli-Arab dispute generally, and such controversial matters as the Jordan River irrigation project came on the agenda.[64]

In two comprehensive reports on his negotiations, the Secretary-General insisted that he had confined himself to talks on the basis of the Armistice Agreements. But with typical appreciation of the broader implications of his mandate from the Security Council, Hammarskjöld strove both to adjust the view held by the Middle Eastern governments of the Armistice Agreements and to put before the Security Council his own assessment of the possibilities for further progress.[65]

Hammarskjöld did not regard his work merely as adding another signature on an already existing pact. Rather, he viewed the result of the negotiations as lifting the entire level of the agreements:

> I wish to draw attention to the difference in character between previous cease-fires, which have been established locally, or between military commanders, and a cease-fire of the character envisaged in my negotiations. The cease-fire I have aimed at under my mandate from the Security Council is one governed by a reaffirmation by the Governments, given to the United Nations, to comply unconditionally with the fundamental clause of the various armistice agreements and establishes anew the legal situation on which the armistice regime was to be founded. It furthermore expresses a recognition in this particular situation of the obligation to observe a fundamental principle of the United Nations Charter.[66]

Rather than tinker with the existing machinery at the operating level, the Secretary-General had pulled the Armistice Agreements up to the Arab-Israeli summit.

Two principal difficulties had led to the weakening of the Armistice Agreements, according to Hammarskjöld. One was that the incursions of irregulars had led to well-founded suspicions that they had the support of the government from whose territory they operated. This resulted in reprisals and an increasing disrespect for the Armistice Agreements. In addition, "each party considers its compliance with the stipulations of an armistice agreement as conditioned by compliance of the other party to the agreement," Hammarskjöld declared. This would lead to a situation in which one infringement of the agreement by one party could lead to the nullification of the entire pact. In referring to the doctrine of reciprocity in its extremest form, which he did not say was the view of either Egypt or Israel, Hammarskjöld drove to the heart of the policy of guerrilla raiding and reprisal. He argued that the logic of the agreements did not permit violation of the cease-fire clauses simply because another section of the pact had been breached.

The Secretary-General soon got accord on two points relating to these difficulties. The first was that the agreements in their entirety must be complied with. The second saw the acceptance of the cease-fire articles of the agreements "as establishing independent obligations within the framework of the various agreements." This laid a basis for "a balanced return" to the execution of other clauses, and then to the best means for continuing compliance. In addition, the Secretary-General prepared for specific steps by redefining the status of the UNTSO observers. He made it clear that he did not consider them merely appendages of the Mixed Armistice Commissions but an agency with its own powers. This led him to demand freedom of movement and action for UNTSO, as intended by the Security Council.

Hammarskjöld excluded from the report any discussion of the question of the use of the Suez Canal by Israel. Despite the demand by the Security Council that the Canal should not be barred by Egypt to Israeli ships, it was effectively closed to them. Nor did he comment on the Jordan River irrigation project, which Israel had planned and then suspended; the Israel government displayed much impatience with the delay in the project caused by the objections of Jordan, Lebanon, and Syria. But Hammarskjöld did not refuse to talk about these matters with the four governments. He hinted in his report that he had spent considerable time on them. The implication was that they were the sort of questions which belonged to the Secretary-General's jurisdiction under the general powers of his office, which remained intact even though he had a mandate from the Council.

Although he turned away from a chance to report on these two points, which he considered outside his mandate, Hammarskjöld did comment on the broader issues raised by his mission. He flatly stated that to leave aside fundamental issues did not meet the needs of the situation in the Middle East. His mission, he remarked, could be regarded as a first stage in dealing with the basic problems. The next steps would depend on the good will of the governments directly concerned. He added to this obvious remark a more subtle reference to the need for support from other governments, which would, of course, include Britain, France, the United States, and the Soviet Union, whose policies would necessarily have much bearing on what the Middle East governments permitted themselves.

As a whole, the reports made by Hammarskjöld disclose a considerable success in negotiating. To some extent, this success can be attributed to a brilliant technical approach. By lifting the level of negotiations to the Arab-Israeli summit, Hammarskjöld effectively brought the prestige of his office and of the Security Council's momentary unanimity to bear on the Middle East governments. He also pushed aside the dreary record of discord in the Mixed Armistice Commissions and in connection with the work of UNTSO, all the while preserving these bodies for the execution of specific steps to prevent further violence. By redefining the role of UNTSO, he strengthened his own instrument in the area and opened the way to influence not only at the top but at the field level as well.

Hammarskjöld's remarks on the broader problems of the Middle East, those which fell outside his mandate, seemed calculated to open every possible avenue of approach to any government which had the intention of creating more stability in the area. At the same time, he attempted to limit the discussion in the Security Council to the specific results of the narrower talks under the terms of his mandate. If he was successful in this effort, he could have an important part in any future negotiations on such questions as the right of passage through the Suez Canal and the long-standing Jordan River diversion plan. And he could use his influence in the Middle East generally to find partial solutions, perhaps applying the pattern of negotiations which had proved so rewarding during the early part of 1956. But his challenge to the good will of the governments directly concerned and to the other members of the United Nations indicate that he looked ahead with less than perfect confidence to a quick end to the constant turmoil of the eastern Mediterranean area.

The Secretary-General followed his technical success with a round of negotiations in New York. He began with the members of the Security Council, to sound out the extent to which it could be relied upon to take the next step toward firmer agreements in the Middle East. In this way, a meeting of the Security Council was being prepared and the discussions became more intense and purposeful as the month went on. At the same time, the tension which pervaded the Middle East since the Soviet Union had taken a stronger role there scarcely abated but had at least leveled off. For one thing, the great powers at this time did not seem intent on stepping up tension in the Middle East, and Khrushchev and Bulganin during a visit to London set limits to the Soviet Union's involvement in the area.[67] The situation seemed far from hopeless.

From the time the Security Council assigned Hammarskjöld to his mission until the end of May, when his report came under public discussion, no war had broken out in the Middle East. During the month of consultations in New York, the Secretary-General had gathered opinions and indicated his own views. To what extent these were embodied in a resolution presented by the United Kingdom is not clear, but the division in the Council until a compromise on several issues could be reached disclosed that the British formula had not been totally agreed upon beforehand. The part of the formula which most closely affected the future role of the Secretary-General, however, passed through the discussions without alteration in principle.[68]

The Soviet delegate specifically noted that the consultations before the Security Council meetings had not been sufficient. The attitude of the Arab states—Egypt, Lebanon, Jordan, and Syria—whose delegates had joined the debate, had Soviet support. This may have indicated a suspicion on the part of the Moscow government that the earlier tripartite arrangements to control conflict in the Middle East underlay the British resolution. Such suspicion accorded with the Arab repugnance for any agreed solution to the problem of border troubles with Israel if Israel was to be one of the parties to an agreement. The Arab argument was that the General Assembly had already decided how the eastern end of the Mediterranean should be divided, and that Israel's present existence violated that plan. Therefore, the preambular paragraph in the British resolution, which expressed consciousness of "the need to create conditions in which a peaceful settlement on a mutually acceptable basis . . . can be made," drew particularly strong opposition from the Arab states. The majority of the Council supported this paragraph but in the end gave way to the Soviet and Arab pressure and to an Iranian draft threatening to delete the offending language. A vague and milder paragraph was inserted in the resolution, which then was adopted unanimously.[69]

The rest of the British formula, which had strong support from France and the United States and lukewarm acquiescence from Nationalist China, recalled the history of the Council's concern with the Palestine border troubles, commended the Secretary-General, urged putting into effect the agreements which Hammarskjöld had made, and endorsed his view that the cease-fire was a stage which had to be passed in order to make further progress possible. The role of UNTSO was underlined, and the parties to the Armistice Agreement were asked to take steps to carry out the resolution. Council support for the concern of the Secretary-General with the Palestine problem was reiterated.

The new instruction to Hammarskjöld, as Omar Loutfi, the Egyptian delegate, remarked, had required explanation. The text of the resolution merely requested the Secretary-General to continue "his good offices" with the parties, and to "report to the Security Council as appropriate." Such language, it can be surmised, had the approval of Hammarskjöld, who usually sought not to be tied down to specific tasks and who had during his recently completed negotiations ventured beyond the limits of a closely interpreted version of his mandate. But Loutfi and the other Arab delegates were anxious to know whether this was a new mission, whether it was intended to replace the United Nations Conciliation Commission for Palestine, and whether it was connected with the irritating idea that a general agreement with Israel should be sought on the basis of consent of all parties.

Sir Pierson Dixon denied that a new mandate was to be given to Hammarskjöld. The Secretary-General would simply be available to the parties to help with progress toward full compliance with the armistice agreement—"and no doubt he would, if he thought it desirable, make suggestions to that end." Dixon's idea urged leaving it to the Secretary-General to decide precisely what to do, expressing confidence that he would seize every opportunity to move toward full compliance. As the result of Arab and Soviet criticism and of consultations so extended that they delayed the opening of a Security Council meeting, Dixon made the instructions to the Secretary-General more elaborate. Hammarskjöld now was to carry on his good offices in order to secure the execution of the resolution which had sent him to the Middle East in the first place, and to bring about compliance with the Armistice Agreements.

The discussion of the instructions to Hammarskjöld signified that he did not have general backing for a broad-scale, frontal assault on the problem of Arab-Israeli relations. Rather he would continue to be limited, when acting under instructions from the Security Council, to the framework of the Armistice Agreements. Hammarskjöld did not intervene in the debate, and only at the end of it did he indicate his willingness to go on. But he pointed out that in undertaking his new work he would be guided by his report on his earlier mission. Since that report grew out of instructions which he had said neither added to nor detracted from his own powers, and since he had openly stated that his negotiations had not gone beyond his mandate, he could still attempt to step over the limits which the Arab and Soviet positions seemed to place on his use of good offices. At least a chance to employ the "Peking formula" remained open.

At the same time, the Secretary-General could not minimize the difficulties ahead. These had been exposed in the explanations which delegates gave of their votes in the Security Council. Generally, the representatives either based their positions on the expression of some vital national interest or on the wish to help the Council to act. Dixon minimized the effect of the changes in his draft resolution, and the Arab delegates emphasized the importance of taking their view into account. Abba Eban, the Israeli representative, showed that his government was anything but sanguine about the chances of negotiations against the background of so much discord. For the Secretary-General, the point was that the first stage toward peace in the Middle East was far from the final one.

In fact, Hammarskjöld was unable to push his earlier success in getting accords pointing to the reapplication of technical provisions of the Armistice Agreements very far in the direction of a second stage. His success remained only technical when the Suez crisis boiled up during the summer of 1956, after the United States refused to participate any longer in the project to build the Aswan high dam and Egypt seized the Suez Canal in retaliation. Now a larger problem of world politics overshadowed any chance of further talks on the Armistice Agreements, for Israel followed up the conclusions to which Eban had referred with violent measures to maintain its threatened national security.

Thant—Kashmir

A difficult negotiating assignment was given to the Secretary-General as a result of the renewal of fighting between India and Pakistan in Kashmir in August and September, 1965. The conflict reached the highest levels since 1948, from which time the United Nations had kept a cease-fire line under continuous observation.

Thant interceded in the new flareup on his own initiative, and kept a high degree of influence throughout subsequent efforts by the Security Council to deal with the conflict. The Secretary-General appealed twice to the parties to respect the cease-fire agreement before the Security Council began discussions early in September.[70] He proposed sending Bunche as Personal Representative and thought of issuing a public statement, but the response from India and Pakistan convinced him that these steps would not produce favorable results. He did ask Lieutenant-General Robert H. Nimmo, head of the United Nations Military Observer Group in India and Pakistan (UNMOGIP), to consult with him at headquarters.

Reports by the Secretary-General to the Security Council furnished a focal point for all of its debates. Thant's first mandate was to report on the implementation of a call for an immediate cease-fire and withdrawal by the Indian and Pakistani forces.[71] He reported on September 6 that he had had no official response, but that the fighting had worsened. His mandate was broadened on the same day in a resolution which asked him to exert every possible effort to give effect to a renewed call for a cease-fire and withdrawal, and to strengthen UNMOGIP. The debate in the Council left no doubt that his efforts were welcome and that he had strong support.

Thant immediately told the Council that he would go to India and Pakistan. He spent nine days there in discussions with governmental leaders, and his written report disclosed that while both governments favored a cease-fire, they had attached conditions that made it impossible.[72] His oral report to the Council on September 17 comprised a set of bold suggestions looking toward the possible application of Chapter VII of the Charter, beginning with the use of provisional measures and going on to a determination of a breach of the peace if necessary. This implied enforcement measures in case of continued violation.

Thant also suggested the possibility of a meeting of the heads of the Indian and Pakistani governments, and assistance in ensuring the observance of a cease-fire and in withdrawing armed personnel. His declaration of his own availability strongly implied an important role for the Secretary-General. In their discussion Council members made frequent references to his reports and warmly praised his efforts.

The Secretary-General's suggestions anticipated all of the subsequent actions taken by the Security Council and the parties themselves that led eventually to deflation of the conflict. The Security Council, moving in the direction of more forceful measures, replaced the mild "calls upon" with the stronger "demands" in its resolutions seeking a cease-fire.[73] By mid-September both India and Pakistan had agreed to halt military action, although the United Nations observers reported a continuous stream of complaints and violations until the end of the year.

Thant was also asked to provide assistance for supervision of the cease-fire and the withdrawal of forces. As chief administrative officer, he obviously would have a leading role in making these arrangements. Nevertheless, one of his actions resulted in a strong objection from the Soviet Union, which claimed that he acted without authority in organizing a United Nations India-Pakistan Observation Mission (UNIPOM) to supervise the cease-fire and withdrawals outside the area where UNMOGIP operated.[74] He consulted with governments to arrange for provision of the additional observers, and coordinated their work closely with UNMOGIP. He also later appointed a senior military officer to help draw up a plan for the withdrawal of troops.

The eventual end of the crisis, which had been diluted by the military exhaustion of both sides, came in a meeting of Lal Bahadur Shastri, the Indian Prime Minister, and General Ayub Khan, the Pakistani head of state, at Tashkent in January, 1966. Such a meeting had figured in Thant's early suggestions, although there is no clear evidence that he contributed to the eventual use of Soviet good offices, which had been offered as early as September. Nevertheless, the Secretary-General played an influential and effective part in setting United Nations policy, in carrying out negotiations with the parties, and in creating conditions which contributed to the settlement.

The Potentials of Mediation

When the Secretary-General has attempted to initiate mediation without prior action by a deliberative body, the results have been mixed. He has clearly been more influential in suggesting means for dealing with conflicts than in putting forward the terms of settlement. In some respects, his interventions in the Berlin case and the Cuban missile crisis had the flavor of desperate attempts to act in perilous situations. It is hardly surprising that these situations proved more intractable than localized conflicts. But on the whole the office of Secretary-General lost so little from its unsuccessful diplomatic initiative, and perhaps gained so much in experience, that such methods may well be regarded as having some promise for selected use in the future.

The assignment of negotiating tasks to the Secretary-General has on at least three occasions proved rather profitable as a means of making some progress toward solution. In both his Peking and Middle East missions, Hammarskjöld brought the prestige of his office with him, and returned with it even higher. Thant played a leading part in dealing with the Kashmir crisis of 1965. In all of these missions, the Secretary-General benefited from the strong backing of a major political organ of the United Nations and a consensus of its members. Such a consensus is the prerequisite, both legally and politically, for the assignment of such a mission.

In some respects, the negotiatory functions assigned the Secretary-General recall the practice of the Council of the League of Nations in using rapporteurs on political problems. Such a rapporteur was a representative on the Council. He took in hand the political problem with the understanding that he would examine it carefully, discuss it thoroughly with the parties, seek a settlement outside the Council, and report the results of the negotiations. The rapporteur had, as Hammarskjöld did, the benefit of working in connection with a major political organ. And he soon acquired intimate knowledge of the principal statesmen and their views, as Hammarskjöld had before his trip to the Middle East.

The difference between the Secretary-General's assignments and those of League rapporteurs silhouette both the advantages and limits of the latter device, so far little used in the United Nations. As an international civil servant, the Secretary-General can build up a reputation for impartiality and ingenuity, as Hammarskjöld did in the Peking case. This can make his ministrations even less suspect than those of a neutral rapporteur, who after all may still receive instructions from his government. The Secretary-General of course receives no instructions from a single government. He has, moreover, an independent office which carries influence no matter who occupies it.

The mandates given to Hammarskjöld, furthermore, provided not only for explorations but carried with them the positive desire of influential governments that some progress be made along at least partly defined lines. In the case of the United States fliers, the approach was less well understood than in the Arab-Israeli case, but even in the former the United Nations had acted often enough in connection with the Korean conflict so that some guidelines existed. These policy guides tend both to give the Secretary-General's mission the strength that comes from clarity and the limits that derive from precision.

The assignment to the Secretary-General of such negotiatory tasks contrasts sharply with the earlier practice of using international commissions. Such bodies showed certain operational defects which disappear with the employment of a single person. No matter how carefully instructions to a multinational commission are framed, they are inevitably filtered through as many foreign offices as there are members on the commission. If the commission is made up of persons chosen for their qualifications, each of them is likely to see his instructions in a particular light. Commissions must either reach unanimous decisions or be suspected of partiality or weakness. Because of their multiple memberships, they demonstrate an inherent cumbersomeness and lack of suppleness in negotiating, for each step must be considered and made subject to the agreement of members. This need for agreement may result in reference by representatives to their foreign offices and further delays and reinterpretations. Finally, representatives to such commissions may change frequently, destroying the continuity of thought and the experience that a rapporteur or Secretary-General may provide.

The special status of the Secretary-General's office limits as well as gives advantages in negotiations. Although the chief administrative officer may be regarded as both impartial and clever, he must nevertheless design policy suggestions which will not create prejudices against his office for future work and operations in other fields. The need to answer to so many governments, any of which may become critical and perhaps embarrassingly so, checks his freedom of initiative and operation.

To a considerable degree, the Secretary-General can influence the instructions given to him. He not only can follow consultations leading to the drafting of instructions but can also take part in the public discussions if he wishes. Although in both the Peking and Middle East missions the Secretary-General took little part in the debate itself, he was active in consultations outside the General Assembly and the Security Council. His reports become the basis of further discussion and decision in the deliberative organs. He thus can heavily influence his followup instructions, as he did in the Middle East mission.

While the mandate he is given and the nature of his office set certain limits to his "other functions," the Peking formula provides a way around some of them. In the Peking mission, his mandate from the General Assembly was used as little more than an instruction to try; the basis of negotiations was the implied powers of the office of Secretary-General. Hammarskjöld made it explicit in the Middle East negotiations that he would use what he considered the powers of his office despite the limited nature of his mandate. Because both negotiating ventures proved quite successful, his doctrinal expansion of the scope of his office tends to be taken as acceptable for future negotiations.

In the hands of an adroit Secretary-General, the "other functions" which could be assigned him would provide a useful avenue by which the United Nations might approach severe political conflicts. At the same time, the influence of the Secretary-General on the policy of the organization has been expanded by the negotiations in which he has taken part. If more negotiatory functions are assigned to him, the influence of the Secretary-General quite likely can continue to grow. This is not to pretend that his role in matters of peace and security would become ever more important; but with careful prior consultations and a talented official in the office of Secretary-General, the negotiatory functions promise more than their use so far can demonstrate.

CHAPTER IX

INVESTIGATION AND OBSERVATION

The first two major mandates to test the capacity of the Secretary-General to investigate and observe international conflicts emerged during storms caused by Middle Eastern politics. The first of these tasks developed during the Hungarian revolution in the autumn of 1956, in the midst of the Suez crisis and the creation of UNEF. The second assignment concerned disorders in Lebanon in 1958, and were linked to the events two years earlier in Egypt by reason of the dynamic qualities of Nasserism, the symbol of social revolution and modernization of the Arab world.

One of the two subsequent investigation and observation tasks also had part of its roots in the United Arab Republic; it concerned the aftermath of a revolution against the traditional regime in Yemen. The next case to be considered here related to the future of Sarawak and British North Borneo and whether they were to become part of the forming Malaysian Federation. The last one to be discussed is an outcome of the insurrection and subsequent United States intervention in the Dominican Republic in 1965.

Investigation and Observation in Hungary

The active stage of the Hungarian revolution, in which a determined, quickly organized popular movement forced changes in an oppressive regime and then had to bow to the superior power of the Soviet Army, endured little more than a fortnight. Its suppression profoundly shocked Communists and non-Communists alike and its victims attracted widespread sympathy. Its aftermath included some 200,000 refugees, most of them fleeing to Austria. During this fortnight, at the end of October, 1956, first the Security Council and then an emergency special session of the General Assembly tried to deal with the revolt as an international problem.

The Security Council was seized of the situation in Hungary by the United Kingdom, France, and the United States, who asserted that the rights of the Hungarian people, guaranteed under the peace treaty signed in 1947, had been violated by foreign military forces. They sought consideration under Article 34 of the Charter, which points toward an investigation. On October 28, while the Security Council was discussing the matter despite Soviet objection, Imre Nagy's government, the "softer" regime which had taken control only days before, broadcast that it was negotiating with the Soviet Union. Three days later Nagy informed the Secretary-General that Soviet forces were entering Hungary, and on November 2 he asked the Security Council to instruct the two governments to negotiate. Discussions ensued without Security Council action, but on November 4 the final onslaught of the Soviet Army began and Nagy soon was forcibly replaced by Janos Kadar.[1]

The Secretary-General did not speak publicly on the issue until after the decisive Soviet attack. The United States had proposed instructing him to explore urgently, in consultation with the Specialized Agencies, the need of the Hungarian people for relief, and to report back. Linked with this instruction was a demand that the Soviet Union end its intervention. A Soviet veto blocked the adoption of the proposal at a dramatic meeting which opened at 3 a.m. on November 4, but could not prevent the summoning of the General Assembly. At this point Hammarskjöld intervened to declare that his statement of October 31, in which he warned that he could not follow a policy of expediency or serve on any other assumption than that the members would observe the Charter, also applied in the Hungarian case. In reading into the record of the Hungarian case his declaration and implied threat to resign if he did not have the confidence of the members, Hammarskjöld gave no concrete indication of his further intentions.[2]

Hammarskjöld's first official instructions came from the Second Emergency Special Session of the General Assembly, which fitted its meetings into the chinks left by those on Suez between November 4 and November 9, 1956. His declaration to the Security Council may have given some encouragement to the United States, which presented the first draft resolution on Hungary to the newly convened General Assembly to engage the Secretary-General in the Hungarian problem. Hammarskjöld received his mandate in a resolution supported by a majority of the General Assembly, but 15 members abstained and eight voted against. The 50 supporting states included all the North Atlantic Treaty powers and those linked to United States policy in the Pacific. The neutralist Afro-Asian states showed slight enthusiasm for any condemnatory action on Hungary. Some of their delegates explained later that they had lacked instructions, and while indicating revulsion at the repression in Hungary they did not endorse the strong words of the majority-supported resolutions from which the Secretary-General received his mandate.[3]

As in the resolution which the Security Council had considered, the General Assembly instructed the Secretary-General to attempt to mobilize the support of the Specialized Agencies for relief purposes. The novel element came in a request to the Secretary-General

> . . . to investigate the situation caused by foreign intervention in Hungary, to observe the situation directly through representatives named by him, and to report thereon to the General Assembly at the earliest possible moment, and as soon as possible to suggest methods to bring an end to the foreign intervention in Hungary in accordance with the principles of the Charter of the United Nations.[4]

Hungary and the Soviet Union were called upon to permit the Secretary-General's observers to go into Hungary, travel freely, and report back; and the other members were asked for their cooperation.

Whatever influence the Secretary-General had on the formation of his mandate was exercised primarily in private consultations. Beyond his intervention in the Security Council, he did not in a public session clarify his views of his own role in the Hungarian crisis, although at a later stage he began to intervene more actively. Even his private consultations at this time must have been rather limited with respect to the number of persons consulted and the amount of time spent, because he was simultaneously putting UNEF together. In view of this strength-sapping assignment, it is an indication of Hammarskjöld's talents, ambitions, and willingness to serve that he played as important a role as he did in the Hungarian crisis.

Primarily a product of the United States, Hammarskjöld's instructions to observe in Hungary had not been exposed to systematic debate in the General Assembly. Nor did the United States representatives explain precisely how they supposed the Secretary-General would carry out his assignment. Hammarskjöld was expected to fill out the general terms of the resolutions by administrative means, but it was impossible to do so without very considerable interpretation. Any policy except premature relinquishment of the mandate would have some bearing on Soviet plans, while failure to act would certainly bring objections from the United States and the other 49 governments which had voted for the mandate.

The task of observation would involve the presence of the Secretary-General or his representatives—perhaps both simultaneously for at least short periods—in Hungary and no doubt in neighboring countries as well. The observers could scarcely force their way in. Thus, negotiations to secure permission for entry would be required. Moreover, the Secretary-General would have to have some plan for the scope of observation and for administration. The nature of the observation, too, would require decisions. It might deal only with political events at the highest level at the capital, or it might include military and administrative affairs down to the village level, or anything in between. Again, negotiations would be required. Furthermore, the General Assembly had told Hammarskjöld to suggest methods for bringing the "foreign intervention" to an end. The investigation and observation would be linked to the possibility of further action impinging on the policies of a government which objected categorically to the resolution under which Hammarskjöld would act. His mission, if it could be performed at all, would therefore be extremely delicate.

Hammarskjöld proceeded carefully, but directly into the political heart of the matter, as his mandate warranted. In touch with the Hungarian government while the emergency special session of the General Assembly was still considering his assignment, he wrote an *aide-mémoire* indicating his wish to have approval of the principle of investigation and observation of the Soviet intervention, which the Soviet Union had insistently declared a matter outside the United Nations purview. The Hungarian government flatly refused to regard the events in its territory as anything but a matter of domestic jurisdiction. Its central contention was that the Soviet Union had been invited to send troops only when a democratic movement had been seized by "organized fascist elements"; after order had been restored, a withdrawal of Soviet troops would be negotiated. "[T]he sending of representatives to be appointed by the Secretary-General of the United Nations is not warranted," said Foreign Minister Istvan Stebes.

Hammarskjöld replied that he would not discuss the decision under which he was acting, but asked that the Hungarian government "reconsider this judgment in the light of the opposite view, so widely expressed by Member Governments in the General Assembly and reflected in the vote, and as a Member of the United Nations, to cooperate with the great majority in the clarification of a situation which has given rise to such concern in the General Assembly." Concurrently, Hammarskjöld asked for aid from the Soviet government in fulfilling his mandate "to the extent that this is within its authority." The reply was that the affair was within the jurisdiction of the Budapest government.[5]

Some indication of the means by which Hammarskjöld would have proceeded in a more favorable climate was given by his announced intention to organize two groups of eminent political figures to execute his mandate. One of these groups was to investigate the situation caused by foreign intervention. The other was to observe the current conditions in Hungary. But in the face of Hungarian opposition, strengthened by Soviet backing, the Secretary-General abandoned the plan for the latter group. All that remained was a group to investigate the situation caused by the foreign intervention. This would have as its members Dr. Alberto Lleras Camargo, a Colombian who was former Secretary-General of the Organization of American States and was to become President of his country; Arthur Lall, permanent representative of India to the United Nations; and Justice Oscar Gunderson, a Norwegian jurist.[6]

At first, the issues of investigation and observation were kept separate from the humanitarian effort to succor the refugees and the buffeted population of Hungary. The government then indicated its gratitude for the General Assembly's resolutions proposing assistance, and indicated to Hammarskjöld that it was anxious to discuss a relief program. The Secretary-General expressed his thanks at hearing of this attitude, and later offered to go to Budapest himself. This offer was made in a personal interview with the Hungarian Foreign Minister in New York; it can be surmised that the import of all of the resolutions on Hungary was discussed in detail. Hammarskjöld declared that he wanted a broader basis of personal contact for his discussions, and for this reason he declined to meet Hungarian representatives in Rome, pressing for a visit to Budapest. Furthermore, said the Secretary-General, it appeared that wider discussions than those touching only on relief might be undertaken.

Meanwhile, the General Assembly kept up its pressure on Hungary to open the door to observers, to cooperate with the Secretary-General, and to permit the organization of relief programs. Hammarskjöld reported formally on November 30 that his aim was to expand the invitation to discuss relief matters into general pourparlers covering his mandate, and to gain permission for observers to enter. The group of three had begun working on information available at headquarters and had found it insufficient for a report. The Secretary-General took the position that it was natural to begin with an investigation. He concluded that he and his representatives had to journey to Hungary and move freely to secure information; a relief effort organized from the outside would be insufficient. The farthest the Hungarians would go in the face of this pressure was to offer Hammarskjöld a chance to talk about relief matters in Rome or New York, and to come to Budapest at a later date convenient to both parties. In effect, Hungary was insisting on controlling the movements of the Secretary-General within and to the country.[7]

Subsequent pressure by the General Assembly and the Secretary-General failed to change the Hungarian position. The General Assembly adopted additional resolutions, and noted the Secretary-General's latest information that he had met the Hungarian Foreign Minister and proposed definite dates for a visit. Hungary finally declared the dates mentioned by the Secretary-General as inappropriate. By the end of December, the Secretary-General was unable to report any progress whatever in getting observers and investigators into Hungary, and the record contained nothing but flat refusals from the government of the country. Meanwhile, Hammarskjöld's mandate had grown to include the dispatch of observers to other countries and any initiative he thought desirable in conformity with the principles of the Charter. Thus, his inability to cut into the wall of refusal presented by Hungary and the Soviet Union resulted in yet broader instructions. But the discussions in the General Assembly had in fact done little to define the mandate, beyond stating that he was to use his own judgment.[8]

The Secretary-General used the report of his committee as the basis of suggestions to the General Assembly for further action. He judged that hearing recent refugees might provide necessary first-hand information on events in Hungary. He urged the Assembly in effect to relieve him of his duties to investigate and observe by setting up a special committee to conduct such hearings. It might go to Austria, the only country receiving refugees which offered to open the way to observers.

Hammarskjöld's lead was accepted by the Assembly, which acted to set up a special committee and thus to revert to a more common organizational form. But the Secretary-General still retained the responsibility "to take any initiative that he deems helpful in relation to the Hungarian problem, in conformity with the principles of the Charter of the United Nations and resolutions of the General Assembly." For the next eight years, the Hungarian issue was in the hands first of the special committee set up by the General Assembly and later of Sir Leslie Munro, former permanent representative of New Zealand and President of the General Assembly. The main task of the Secretary-General in connection with this work was the furnishing of Secretariat assistance, which can be presumed to have been influential.[9]

The willingness of the Secretary-General to take on the responsibility for organizing and conducting an investigation in Hungary was a great deal more striking than his success. The problem for the Secretary-General in the Hungarian case was that of getting the operation underway. His responsibilities were assigned in an atmosphere which handicapped him from the start.

The Secretary-General's mandate, which was extended in successive resolutions, was given him by a General Assembly in which a significantly large group of states refused to take responsibility and in which the debates failed to define his role. In that context, almost any step would be bound to be branded as objectionable by the Soviet and Hungarian governments. What the Secretary-General did in these circumstances was to ask for permission to enter Hungary while refusing to disclose specifically what he intended to do until he could begin to do it. The Hungarian government gave him no chance to start, and told him that the resolution was inacceptable.

The inability of the Secretary-General to carry out his mandate in the Hungarian issue was traceable to unswerving opposition from the parties concerned. They could, moreover, enforce their opposition by refusing him admittance to Hungary and refusing to deal with him on any but their own terms. In addition, he was exceedingly pressed for time because of the concurrent crisis in the Middle East. His ultimate conclusion was that he could neither effectively carry out his mandate nor provide the most appropriate ways of keeping the situation under surveillance. He therefore proposed to the Assembly that it accept the return of his mandate while he accepted for the time being the limitation on his actions.

Observation and a Broadened Mandate in Lebanon

The involvement of the Secretary-General in Lebanon grew out of preelection turmoil in the summer of 1958. A part of the population had taken up arms, or at least produced severe disorders, after it became known that President Camille Chamoun had plans to run for office again in spite of an understanding that he would leave. The disorders danced in cadence to the propaganda from Cairo radio, and the Lebanese government eventually decided that the United Nations should be asked for help in keeping arms from entering over the frontier from Syria, then part of the United Arab Republic.

The situation differed sharply from that of Hungary. No great power was directly involved at the beginning. The first stage, which saw the development of an observation function under the direction of the Secretary-General, was soon succeeded by a second in which the United States and the United Kingdom landed troops in the Middle East, while the Western-oriented conservative government of Iraq was erased in favor of a radical nationalist regime. The final stage saw the return of calmer relationships among the countries of the area and the withdrawal of the British and United States troops.

The Secretary-General's eventual assignment to observe in Lebanon originated in a complaint that armed bands were infiltrating from Syria, that nationals of the United Arab Republic were involved in a rebellion within Lebanon, and that numerous provocative acts had occurred. The Security Council responded to a Lebanese request for a meeting, but it developed that the Arab League was considering the matter. It was not until June 6, more than a fortnight later, that Lebanon could explain before the Council its claim that massive intervention in its affairs had taken place. The reply of the representative of the United Arab Republic was that the Lebanese President sought to stay in office illegally and that the whole affair was strictly domestic. The Soviet Union took a similar position.

Lebanon complained two days later that the situation was growing more serious. Only then did the Council receive a draft resolution, proposed by Sweden. It projected the urgent dispatch of an "observer group to proceed to Lebanon so as to ensure that there is no illegal infiltration" of men or arms across the Lebanese border. It authorized the Secretary-General "to take the necessary steps to that end," and requested the observation group to keep the Council informed through the Secretary-General. A majority of the Council, led by the United States and the Iraqi representative, Mohammed Fadil al Jamali, supported the draft. The Soviet Union abstained in the eventual vote, which was ten to none with one abstention, on the grounds that neither the United Arab Republic nor Lebanon objected to the resolution. But Arkady Sobolev blamed the United States and the United Kingdom for the disorders, insisting that they were preparing to intervene by shipping jet aircraft.[10]

The discussion of the Swedish resolution cast little light either on what Lebanon anticipated from the Security Council or on precisely what the Council expected from Hammarskjöld. The Lebanese complaint did not specifically or by implication envisage any particular action, although if the Council were presumed to be acting under Article 39 of the Charter, enforcement measures might be possible. But no determination of a breach of the peace was made; nor were the provisions for peaceful settlement specifically invoked in the draft resolution.

Perhaps the nearest thing to a discussion of the Secretary-General's duties came from C. A. A. Ritchie of Canada, who thought that Hammarskjöld would have an opportunity and the flexibility to contribute to the solution of the problem. Henry Cabot Lodge, who had strongly supported the resolution on behalf of the United States, was confident that the Secretary-General would act with his accustomed speed to have someone in Lebanon in 24 hours. During the debate, Hammarskjöld himself guarded his silence, intervening only after the vote.

The resolution itself was no model of clarity. It referred to the charges and countercharges made by Lebanon and the United Arab Republic. It provided for dispatch of an observation group. It did not explicitly establish the group or make clear what sort of membership it was to have. The group's task was to ensure that no men or matériel were brought across the border. But an observation group would scarcely seem to be the appropriate instrument to ensure anything except that information would be gathered and perhaps interpreted. To ensure against infiltration a police or military force would be needed. The Secretary-General was authorized to take the necessary steps, but it was not certain whether this meant to organize observation or to ensure against infiltration. If it were the former, he would have the implied power to appoint observers, but it was not clear whether he was to direct their work.

This obscure draftsmanship received little comment in the debate, even from the Soviet representative. The result was that Hammarskjöld had to make something specific of the resoultion. It seems unlikely that he was not consulted about its terms before it was presented. He personally always had close relations with the Swedish delegation. Moreover, courtesy alone would demand that he be informed, if not asked for comment, on any resolution which projected a role for his office.

The night which intervened between the introduction of the resolution and its adoption on June 11, 1958, gave Hammarskjöld a chance to do some specific planning. It is likely that he consulted with the members of the Council on his ideas, and these talks may even have helped to ease the adoption of the resolution. He remarked to the Council that his advance preparations might make it possible to live up to Lodge's hopes of speedy action. He spoke of two levels of organization. One of them would be an Observation Group (which now appeared with capital letters), and the other would include actual observer personnel which might be brought from UNTSO in Jerusalem. The second category might be on duty the next day, while the superior group would take longer to organize. Beyond this, there was no further comment, except the expectation expressed by the President of the Council that it would receive constant information.

The advance preparations were highly effective. On the day following the action of the Security Council, the first five observers arrived in Beirut from UNTSO. By the second day they had begun reconnaissance, while additional observers came to Beirut. Within the first five days of work they had pushed to the limits of government-held territory in the direction of the border, but soon began to encounter difficulties in extending their range into rebel territory.

Meanwhile, Hammarskjöld was also busy with the organization of the supervisory body to direct the observers. On June 14 he appointed Galo Plaza, former President of Ecuador; Rajeshwar Dayal, an Indian diplomat who later was to have an important role in the Congo; and Major General Odd Bull of the Norwegian Air Force, as members of the United Nations Observation Group in Lebanon (UNOGIL). These three senior officers were to have the responsibility of reporting to the Security Council through Hammarskjöld, but would organize themselves and determine their own procedures. To help them the Secretary-General named as secretary David Blickenstaff, who had been in the Executive Office of the Secretary-General during Lie's tenure and was then Director of the United Nations Information Center at Paris. General Bull was to have special responsibilities for the military observers, who would constitute one part of the mission. UNOGIL would constitute another part, while the United Nations Secretariat would be a third part. Lebanon was to deal with UNOGIL through a specially appointed minister and a five-member commission.[11]

The Secretary-General, reporting to the Security Council, left little doubt that at first he would keep the entire Lebanon case firmly in his own hands. He decided that the situation was so urgent that the members of UNOGIL (with one exception) should go directly to Beirut. "In view of all the circumstances, and the character of the task of the Observation Group," he said, "I have decided that I should give assistance to the Group by being present when the three members assemble in Beirut and attending the Group's first meeting there." [12] He took advantage of his stay in Beirut to speak not only with his own staff members who would be serving the UNOGIL and with the members of the commission, but also with the President Chamoun and Prime Minister Sami es-Solh. The first meeting of UNOGIL was opened by the Secretary-General in the President's chair. Galo Plaza later was elected President. Hammarskjöld remained in close touch with UNOGIL during his five-day stay in Lebanon. He subsequently went on to Amman, Jerusalem, Gaza, and Cairo, gathering information which would serve later.[13]

Hammarskjöld's initial steps gave a good deal of specific content to the Security Council's resolution. His idea of a three-member observer group of high-ranking officials resembled the international commissions of the past, and especially his initial arrangements for observation in Hungary. The resemblance was the more striking when the Secretary-General explicitly told the Security Council that UNOGIL would have the responsibility for its own organization. The actual observation functions would be carried out by military observers, as they had been in Greece, Kashmir, and Korea.

UNOGIL would presumably clarify its conception of its mandate, which would then be reported to the Security Council. But here the pattern differed sharply from the past, for the Secretary-General appeared to have a direct opportunity to comment on the report. He would be in a position to influence the commission because of the fact that he had appointed it—no doubt taking care to select persons whose views were congruent with his own—and through a strong Secretariat. Not only could he add his views to the reports, but he also could apparently join fully in the Council discussions.

UNOGIL directed a rapid building up of an observer corps, and by the end of June white jeeps carrying teams made up of nearly 100 military officers from eleven countries were beginning to roll into the frontier areas. The task of the observers had been defined, mainly by Hammarskjöld,[14] in a conservative fashion. UNOGIL interested itself primarily in collecting information. Action to prevent infiltration was limited to stationing observers in the frontier areas. The observers found substantial movements of armed men, but reported: "It has not been possible to establish from where these arms were acquired. Nor was it possible to establish if any of the armed men observed had infiltrated from outside; there is little doubt, however, that the vast majority was in any case composed of Lebanese."[15] Even after UNOGIL had been at work for another month and had doubled the number of observers, it was still unable to report that a mass infiltration had taken place.[16]

Despite Hammarskjöld's preparatory consultations in Beirut, neither UNOGIL's approach to its task nor its reports satisfied the government of Lebanon. It called the first UNOGIL report "obviously misleading." The nervousness of the Lebanese government grew more intense than ever when Abdel Karim Kassem and his revolutionary group seized power in Iraq in the middle of August. Now Lebanon appealed for armed assistance from the United States. Within hours, Lodge told the Security Council that United States troops would be landed to help stabilize the situation until the United Nations could act. United States forces were instructed to cooperate with UNOGIL, even though its work was termed only a limited success.[17]

The United States, which for weeks had kept its Sixth Fleet prepared for action in Lebanon, had taken its decision as political alignments in the Middle East altered rapidly. From the United States standpoint, Lebanon was precariously safe with its Western-oriented government, but Iraq now had moved in a direction which was still unclear. The hardly-tried federation of Iraq and Jordan had fallen apart. Moreover, the Jordanian government believed itself threatened now on three sides by Nasserism, and the King was extremely apprehensive, toying with the idea of invading Iraq to succor his friends. He invited the protection of British troops, which began landing on July 17, as Jordan complained to the Security Council of interference by the United Arab Republic in its internal affairs. Thus, shortly after the United States had put its Marines ashore to produce an entirely different set of political facts in Lebanon, events in Jordan and Iraq and the presence of British troops also became part of the Middle Eastern question facing the Security Council.

Hammarskjöld strongly defended his interpretation of the unhappily worded resolution which had led to the creation of UNOGIL. The heart of his argument was that UNOGIL had the task of observing. He said that the Security Council defined not only the character of the operation but also its scope "by linking the observation to illegal traffic in arms and infiltration." "[I have had] a free hand as to the structure and organization of the operation but have considered myself as barred from an interpretation of the authority granted which would have implied that I changed the policy, laid down by the Council, by my decisions on the scope of the operation and the authority of the observers." [18]

The point of this declaration was that Hammarskjöld refused to change "the observation operation into some kind of police operation." To do so would have required action under Chapter VII of the Charter. The observation operation would be made as large as necessary and would be uninfluenced by any other efforts the Secretary-General might make. In any case his actions, he insisted, "have had no relation to developments which must be considered as the internal affairs of Lebanon." He obviously referred here to the presidential election and to the landing of United States troops.

But Hammarskjöld acknowledged that he had been busy in the diplomatic sphere beyond merely making arrangements for the observers to work, which was done in consultation with the members of the Security Council and the Lebanese representative. He declined to explain his diplomatic approaches, which he said were based on his authority under the Charter but were within the terms of the resolution: "[T]he Secretary-General in this situation obviously is neither an arbiter nor a mediator." He hinted, however, that he was attempting to use diplomatic consultations as a means of stopping arms trafficking and infiltration. This would seem to admit at least part of the Lebanese case that arms were arriving from abroad and imply important talks with the United Arab Republic.

In view of the United States landing, Hammarskjöld's comments could be taken as opposed to the policy of that country. They equally opposed the insistence of Lebanon that more than a corps of observers had been intended by the Security Council. But neither United States nor Lebanon was willing simply to have the Council abandon the use of observers.

When the UNOGIL report was presented just after the United States landing, Lodge introduced a resolution that he claimed would support and strengthen the initial observation operations. At that moment UNOGIL first reported that it had achieved access to the entire border. The United States urged the Security Council to give the Secretary-General authority to undertake additional arrangements, including the use of a force to protect the territorial integrity of Lebanon. Hammarskjöld did not reply directly but indicated that the Council should not act until a further report had been submitted.

The alignment of the members of the Council appeared to have changed little so far, with one significant exception. Sweden, which had sponsored the original resolution leading to creation of UNOGIL, now believed that it had no appropriate place in the altered situation in Lebanon. Gunnar Jarring said for Sweden that the United States landings could not be justified under Article 51 of the Charter because no armed attack had occurred, and that the proper course would be the suspension of observation. Hammarskjöld, however, supported the proposals of UNOGIL to expand and strengthen observation.[19]

Meanwhile, the Jordanian complaint had been joined to that of Lebanon. But the Council could not reach agreement even though the United States draft resolution received a majority vote, as did a later Japanese compromise. The Japanese draft used broad language in asking the Secretary-General to take appropriate actions to carry out the original resolution of June 11. The Soviet Union blocked the adoption of both of them. Its own resolution was overwhelmingly defeated, as was a Swedish proposal to discontinue observation. The United States and the Soviet Union then separately proposed an emergency special session of the General Assembly.[20]

Although the Security Council was unable to take any new action in the Lebanon-Jordan situation, the Secretary-General intervened to recall his earlier remark that he had a duty to avoid mere expediency and to take such action as practical circumstances permitted. He intended "to use all opportunities offered to the Secretary-General within the limits set by the Charter and towards developing the United Nations effort so as to help to prevent a further deterioration of the situation in the Middle East and to assist in finding a road away from the dangerous point at which we now found ourselves." Regarding UNOGIL as still acceptable, he intended, without spelling out precisely what he meant, to develop it as far as possible. This, he said, "will be recognized by you as being in the best interests of the Organization, and, therefore, of the cause of peace. . . .

Were you to disapprove of the way these intentions were to be translated by me into practical steps, I would of course accept the consequences of your judgement." [21] That Hammarskjöld could count on considerable good will from the members had been demonstrated during the debate. A further evidence was the surprise, but eventually futile, proposal by the Soviet Union for a summit conference within the United Nations framework, at which the Secretary-General would be a participant.[22]

During the discussions in the Security Council, the Secretary-General could at least employ one influence which he derived from a plan to assign functions to him. He had to be consulted and could join informal talks. Moreover, once UNOGIL was established, he had the additional influence which derived from the operations of a field organization. Although his policy did not prevail, as the presence of United States troops in Lebanon and British soldiers in Jordan attested, his efficient and swift organization of UNOGIL made it possible for him to step from direction of observation to influence on more general policy. That was the burden of his peroration in the Security Council.

In the emergency special session of the General Assembly, Hammarskjöld never was distant from the heart of the substantive discussions. Even the unusual appearance of the President of the United States, who made a number of substantive proposals, failed to overshadow the Secretary-General in the fortnight of General Assembly meetings. From the beginning, he was favored by some elements in the Middle Eastern situation.

UNOGIL's observations had failed to coincide with the claim of the Chamoun government, strongly backed by the United States, that there was massive infiltration. They fitted with the views of Nasser, who could be the central figure in a *détente*. Hammarskjöld's endorsement of UNOGIL's findings seemed to make him an ally of the nationalistic governments of the new states. For this reason he had considerable support in the General Assembly. Furthermore, in Lebanon the results of the election at the end of July were known before the General Assembly met, and UNOGIL reported a quieter countryside.[23] General Khalad Chehab had been elected Prime Minister, and he favored the withdrawal of troops. This view also could give fiber to the Secretary-General's policies based on

UNOGIL's reports. The Soviet proposal for a summit conference had made some impact on the United States and the United Kingdom, and the possibility that the Secretary-General would attend gave his words extra weight in Washington, London, and Moscow.

Hammarskjöld quickly made the most of his advantages. His speech to the General Assembly, most of it hardly specific, was nevertheless a program. Declaring that he was outlining some basic needs of the Middle East which required action, he referred to UNEF, the Truce Supervision Organization, and UNOGIL. The latter had rendered useful service but was related to conditions which might soon change. Hammarskjöld recommended some form of United Nations representation as "a desirable expression of the continued concern of the Organization for the independence and integrity of Lebanon." In any case, the organization should be represented in the region. He also indicated in vague terms that some representation should be established in Jordan. He emphasized the need to gain the consent of the countries involved, and suggested the use of the Arab League as a means of cooperation in the region and a channel for help in the economic sphere. He also pleaded for recognition by the rest of the world of the special problems of the Middle East, which included that of the refugees from Palestine.[24]

Every specific proposal drafted for consideration of the General Assembly projected a role for the Secretary-General in accordance with suggestions in his address. This was perhaps only logical, since the speech covered much ground, but the fact to be emphasized is that the participation of the Secretary-General in any further action was never excluded.

Eisenhower's speech claimed that the central question in Lebanon and Jordan was "indirect aggression," but also supported economic development in the Middle East and offered extensive help to an Arab development institution which would be formed with the aid of the Secretary-General. Gromyko took precisely the opposite view of the crisis, and demanded the immediate withdrawal of foreign troops. But the Soviet Foreign Minister introduced a draft resolution to instruct the Secretary-General to strengthen UNOGIL in accordance with its second report, already endorsed by Hammarskjöld; to extend observation to Jordan; and to observe the withdrawal of foreign troops. Mahmoud Fawzi, the Foreign Minister of the United

Arab Republic, thought this resolution "clear and extremely moderate." A number of other speakers urged the creation of a United Nations police force for use in the Middle East in line with another suggestion by President Eisenhower. Creation of such a force, even over his objections, would certainly entail important functions for the Secretary-General.

In private consultations, the first draft resolution with a serious chance of adoption was drawn up. Hans Engen, the Norwegian representative, together with the delegations of Canada, Colombia, Denmark, Liberia, Panama, and Paraguay, managed the talks. Hammarskjöld frequently gave his advice. The draft tried to satisfy the demands for troop withdrawals by noting the United States declaration of its intentions in Lebanon, and a similar statement by the United Kingdom. It met the United States concern over "indirect aggression" with a reaffirmation that all nations should refrain from stirring up directly or indirectly any movements tending to disturb the internal tranquillity of other states, and called upon all the members to act in accordance with their obligations in this regard.

The rest of the draft was less hortatory and involved the Secretary-General in "other functions." The first of these was "to make such practical arrangements" as he and the governments concerned would find useful in upholding the principles and practices of the Charter. This was almost as broad a mandate as that given him in the latter stages of his work on the Hungarian question. It noted that he had a study in progress of the possibilities of a stand-by United Nations peace force, which was to be based on the experience of UNEF, and invited him to continue his studies of an Arab Development Institution. This instruction would satisfy more than a few members of the General Assembly, including the United States. All members were asked to cooperate in carrying out the resolution, and the Secretary-General was asked to report by September 30, 1958.[25]

Because of Hammarskjöld's close association with the drafting of the seven-power resolution, Engen's speech introducing it to the General Assembly has special relevance to the role of the Secretary-General. The resolution itself contained no instructions regarding observation, although UNOGIL continued in existence under the Security Council resolution. Its only overtly political provision for execution by the Secretary-General was vague and broad. Engen said that through negotiations, not only a formula to win the approval of the General Assembly had been sought but also one which entrusted the Secretary General

> . . . with a task which it is within the realm of reality and possibility for him to accomplish. . . . [T]he Assembly must take great care in formulating the instructions which it wants the Secretary-General to carry out in order not to put him into untenable positions. . . . [S]peaking in practical terms, the Secretary-General should never be instructed to act from extreme positions. His field of operation is the middle ground, the ground of mutual accommodations, the ground of conciliation and of mutual sacrifice.[26]

Engen declared that consultations had disclosed that all parties wanted a situation in which the peoples of the Middle East could shape their own lives without disturbance, and that the United Nations should take the approach of enabling its chief executive officer to assist members toward this goal. In fact, the subsequent debate did not disclose enthusiastic support for the new draft, but it did stimulate negotiations which led to an acceptable text, further political activity by the Secretary-General, and finally the disengagement of the United Nations in Lebanon and a subdued role for it in Jordan.

A new draft, presented and adopted on August 21, two days after Engen's speech, was backed by all the Arab states, including Lebanon and Jordan. Foreign Minister Mohamed Ahmen Mahgoub of Sudan introduced the resolution and disclosed that Hammarskjöld and Sir Leslie Munro, the Assembly President, had contributed "wise guidance" in developing its terms. The resolution asked the Secretary-General to bear in mind the Arab League arrangements and "to make forthwith in consultation with the Government concerned and in accordance with the Charter . . . such practical arrangements as would adequately help in upholding the purposes and principles of the Charter in relation to Lebanon and Jordan in the present circumstances, and thereby facilitate the early withdrawal of the foreign troops from the two countries." The draft also picked up the language of Engen's resolution regarding an Arab development institution and the Secretary-General's studies of a police force. The text received unanimous approval, and Hammarskjöld had a new and wider mandate which afforded him every opportunity to take action, as he had promised the Security Council he would.

The decision of the General Assembly received enthusiastic public praise from Hammarskjöld, who said at a press conference that it had made an "invaluable contribution" to international politics. His own action was hardly less enthusiastic, for he started immediately on a round of visits to the capitals of Jordan, the United Arab Republic, Iraq, and Lebanon. There he collected views on what was meant by practical arrangements, and held his counsel regarding specific lines of action. He also informed himself on the "good neighbor" policy, which he thought the first part of the General Assembly resolution projected. All of this and his subsequent actions he related in a report to the General Assembly. This report marked the end of the crisis and the gradual liquidation of his observer role, as well as the height of his diplomatic effectiveness in the area.[27]

As an account of the performance of his "other functions," Hammarskjöld's report discloses remarkable accomplishments but omits many specific details. The language of the report exemplifies the involved, turgid style with which Hammarskjöld liked to intrigue the General Assembly. This time he outdid himself, and one can only marvel that so obscure an instruction could have resulted in so involved a set of hypotheses. With the blessing of hindsight, a reader of this report can discern that the Secretary-General interpreted his instructions to mean that practical arrangements looking toward troop withdrawals excluded mediation on a grand scale but included assistance to any government which wished to negotiate or develop good relations with its neighbors in the Middle East. As he put it,

> . . . the resolution does not give the Secretary-General a mandate to negotiate with the Arab states regarding additional or more specific assurances with regard to their policies. This, obviously, does not exclude any action which may properly be his under the Charter, or that, in consultations with the Governments concerned, he would seek all the clarification, regarding their intentions with respect to the implementation of the good-neighbor policy, which he would consider necessary as a background for decisions on practical arrangements. A clear distinction should, however, be made between such clarifications and any further assurances regarding intentions formally given by one Government to another.[28]

The qualifications and nuances of the report leave the impression that Hammarskjöld sought the best of all worlds by acting as a leading diplomat and at the same time claiming that he was not doing so in the sense of developing general policies.

From the point of view of his office and of the organization, such a tactic had a brilliant quality, for if the negotiations succeeded he could both let the parties enjoy their success and keep his influence on the subsequent developments through his practical arrangements. If no framework for practical arrangements in fact developed, the Secretary-General could not be blamed and would have whatever recognition an earnest effort deserved. At the same time, Hammarskjöld left unnoticed Engen's comments about the need to instruct the Secretary-General precisely and realistically. What he seemed to be saying was that although he could act under the orders of the General Assembly, he could act beyond them under the authority of his own office. This was a doctrine which he had enunciated during the dual crisis of 1956 and again in his second "inaugural address."

On the basis of his consultations and the coincidences of national policies in an easing situation, Hammarskjöld built up a set of modest "practical arrangements" which do not match the elaborate rhetoric with which he described them. One sort of arrangement was observation—"means for the United Nations to keep the implementation of [the good neighbor policy] continuously within its purview"—and efficiently functioning machinery for this existed already in UNOGIL. This could be a public function. Beside it, yet separate, would be arrangements for diplomatic action in case of departure from the good neighbor policy. This would be strictly private. The products of the parallel sets of machinery would funnel into the Secretary-General's Office and he would "decide on the political and diplomatic action to be taken through the means created for that purpose." [29]

This theoretical description fitted UNOGIL, which was to be continued as a "purview" mechanism, with another creation of the Secretary-General. This was the United Nations representative—the United Nations "presence"—in Jordan. The Secretary-General and the government of Lebanon found that UNOGIL's present functions did not have to be expanded. If there were violations of the "good neighbor" policy, they could be brought directly to the attention of the Secretary-General, without specifically indicating by whom. No doubt UNOGIL might do so in a private report, although strictly speaking Hammarskjöld's theory of separate observation and diplomatic functions in the field forbade this.

No difficulty in principle attended the stationing of a high-ranking representative of the United Nations in Amman. Hammarskjöld named P. P. Spinelli, Under-Secretary in Charge of the European Office of the United Nations at Geneva, as his delegate in Jordan. In this case Hammarskjöld seemed to be openly assigning both "purview" and diplomatic functions to the same official, apparently in contradiction of the announced separation of channels leading back to the Secretary-General. It had been the intention to organize a network of representation and diplomatic communication in the capitals of surrounding countries, but in the end Hammarskjöld decided that high-ranking officials would have too little to do in such jobs.

In effect, this meant that relations with Lebanon and Jordan would be handled primarily through field represenatatives, while discussions with Nasser and Kassem would be within Hammarskjöld's personal province. The representative in Jordan found the situation less grave than had first been imagined, and within six months could recommend the abolition of his mission, although it was nevertheless continued at the suggestion of the Jordanian government.

Spinelli was armed with little else than the ability to persuade and report. But he had a favorable situation in which to do so, for King Hussein and the Jordanian government, protected by British troops, perceived that Iraq was at that moment no threat. Britain's action in sending troops and the United States battalions in Lebanon effectively countered any great territorial ambitions which might be attributed to Nasser. Acting largely autonomously as a diplomatic adviser to the Jordanian government, Spinelli sought mainly to reduce misunderstanding, press for moderation, and remind the local government of the broader context of international politics outside of the Middle East. The long continuation of the mission, now inactive but always available to a Secretary-General hoping to influence events in the area, testifies to its acceptability and usefulness.

While the broad assignment given the Secretary-General by the General Assembly and the doctrine he expounded in his report to the General Assembly are intriguing developments, the most practical arrangement worked out by Hammarskjöld apparently was his own diplomatic discussions in the Middle East. Lebanon, Jordan, the United States, and the United Kingdom all were informed of his "conclusions" and about the arrangements planned. Whether discussions between the Arab governments and their more powerful associates ensued because of Hammarskjöld's efforts or because of the general easing of the situation cannot be accurately discerned, but it is a fact that after his visit both Britain and the United States opened talks looking forward to the withdrawal of their troops. Both governments provided Hammarskjöld with memoranda, which he placed before the General Assembly, informing him of definite plans for withdrawal of their forces in accordance with the "good neighbor" clause of the resolution under which Hammarskjöld acted.

It seems likely that Hammarskjöld's consultations, together with the very simple practical arrangements, permitted the four governments directly involved in the troop withdrawal question to make the fullest use of the agreement reached among the Arab countries during the emergency General Assembly session. By the middle of November the situation had improved enough in Lebanon so that UNOGIL could report no further evidence of illegal infiltration. Lebanon had resumed friendly relations with the United Arab Republic. All that remained to be done there was to withdraw UNOGIL, for the United States forces had departed at the end of the previous month. Hammarskjöld reported a plan for abolishing UNOGIL to the Security Council, and on November 25, acting on the request of Lebanon, the Council deleted the original complaint from its agenda. In Jordan, too, the troops were withdrawn, the Secretary-General having helped with getting air clearance for the British planes which flew over neighboring territory to Cyprus.[30]

Yemen and Malaysia

If the Secretary-General's observational assignments in Hungary and Lebanon are regarded as experimental, the field work in Yemen and simultaneously in North Borneo and Sarawak during 1963 appears firmly based in experience and practice. In both of the latter cases, quite clear definitions of the Secretary-General's functions preceded operations. But this definition was achieved by the Secretary-General himself in negotiations with the parties. Unlike the earlier cases, no action was taken by deliberative organs to initiate the missions, and whatever resolutions were adopted later reflected the views of the Secretary-General. He kept his influence throughout the operations. He maintained full responsibility for managing the missions and had the unequivocal consent of the parties.

The mission in Yemen grew out of Thant's close attention to the aftermath of a revolution and had remarkably little guidance, compared with the assignments in Hungary and Lebanon, from deliberative organs. The task in Yemen, carried out from mid-1963 to September, 1964, consisted only of observation of the execution of an agreement between the United Arab Republic and Saudi Arabia to disengage their interventions in Yemen.

Soon after the traditional imamate of Yemen was overthrown by republican modernizers late in 1962, Thant began consulting with the representatives of Yemen and its neighbors about the effects of the civil war which had ensued. As in Lebanon, Nasserism was an important factor in the disturbances, and the United Arab Republic gave strong material and military manpower support to the Arab Republic of Yemen. Saudi Arabia intervened on behalf of the Royalists. The civil war, therefore, began to unsettle much of the Middle East.

Thant soon offered the assistance of his office to the parties, and sent Bunche to San'a at the end of February, 1963 to investigate the situation. Separately, the United States sent Ellsworth Bunker, who had worked closely with Thant on the West New Guinea issue, to the area. Their reports indicated that the three governments would accept a program of disengagement and withdrawal of foreign forces and the establishment of a 20-kilometer demilitarized zone on either side of the Saudi Arabian border. Impartial observers would be needed to check on the execution of the disengagement plan. Those observers, in Thant's view, should be furnished by the United Nations.

After getting the consent of the parties, the Secretary-General called on the head of UNTSO, General C. C. von Horn, to consult on the role of the United Nations and the assignment of observers. In the financial crisis then affecting the United Nations, Thant avoided budgetary problems by arranging that any expenses must be borne by the disengaging parties. Some 200 observers for a period not exceeding four months would be needed.[31]

All of these negotiations were initiated and brought to final stages without either authorization or discussion in a deliberative organ. The genesis of the entire plan for observers was Thant's responsibility, and presumably (although this was never discussed) it was permissible under the implications of Article 99 of the Charter. Perhaps in part because no strong public positions had been taken by the great powers and none of them, except the United Kingdom in a minor way, was involved in the dispute, the Secretary-General had been able to get a close definition of the role and scope of any United Nations operation in Yemen.

The Security Council had three reports in its hands before it held its only discussion of what became the United Nations Yemen Observation Mission (UNYOM). The last of these contained Thant's announcement that two months of observation had been agreed upon, and that financing was available from the parties. At the request of the Soviet Union, the Council met on June 10 and 11, 1964, to hear the Secretary-General urge speedy action.[32] The main purpose of the meetings apparently was to give the Soviet Union a chance to insist again that since peacekeeping was involved in the Yemen mission, the Security Council, not the Secretary-General alone, must act to authorize it. The resolution adopted by the Council, with the Soviet Union abstaining because of its reluctance to see any expansion of the Secretary-General's role, gave Thant an instruction to proceed with the work he had been doing and with the operation he had defined. UNYOM began operating on July 4, somewhat more than six months after Thant had begun to lay the basis for it and less than a month after the Security Council acted.

During the subsequent fourteen months, Thant demonstrated a high degree of influence and control over UNYOM, and expanded its role to include greater political content through a civilian presence in the area. Nevertheless, the precarious financing and the short-term authorization of the mission restricted the possibilities of bringing the fighting in Yemen finally to an end.

The original agreement to finance UNYOM for two months was eventually renegotiated so that observations could be carried on for fourteen months. Thant merely communicated to the Security Council the agreement of the parties to continue the mission for two to four months at a time.[33] At the end of the second two-month period in October, 1963, UNYOM nearly had to be withdrawn because of the reluctance of Saudi Arabia to continue financing it in the absence of a time schedule for the evacuation of United Arab Republic troops.

Thant's effort to strengthen the political content of UNYOM's work came in part as a result of his dissatisfaction with the results of observation. His reports noted repeatedly that despite rough terrain it was possible to carry out reasonable observations. But he remarked that the mandate limited UNYOM too closely to observation to play a positive role in encouraging disengagement. He therefore appointed Spinelli as his Special Representative for Yemen and head of UNYOM. At the same time, the observer corps, which originally had been manned by Yugoslavs borrowed from UNEF, was reorganized and reduced in size. When the parties declined to finance UNYOM any longer, it had to be abandoned even though Yemen was still not entirely peaceful. Thant called the UNYOM mandate, which he had helped to develop and to elaborate, weak and inadequate. Presumably he would have strengthened its conciliatory potential if the parties had been willing. Nevertheless, he did think that it contributed to the reduction of tension in the area and kept the door open to the high-level United Arab Republic-Saudi Arabia conference he thought should be the next step.[34]

While the Secretary-General was seeing UNYOM through its first two-month period, he was asked to take up observational duties in connection with the formation of a broader Malaysian Federation, with which he apparently had had no previous connection. The governments of the Malaysian Federation, Indonesia, and the Philippines, meeting in Manila on the controversial proposition to incorporate further territories with Malaya and Singapore in a Federation of Malaysia, cabled him to ask aid in determining the wishes of the populations in Sarawak and North Borneo. There is no evidence that Thant stimulated the request, but the Resident Representative of the Technical Assistance Board in Manila was consulted before the cable was sent, and therefore some exchange may have taken place. The request included a reference to the General Assembly's resolution on the integration of non–self-governing territories.[35]

Thant's reply set conditions on his acceptance. He insisted on the consent of the United Kingdom, still the governing authority, and wanted to appoint a representative to carry out the observation. His representative would be assisted by two teams, one for each territory, who would make on-the-spot investigations of whether the people wished to join Malaysia, and whether in this regard the recently held elections had any significance and were fairly conducted. The Secretary-General also set as a condition that he alone would supervise the investigation and would receive the reports from it. He would then report to the governments concerned. What this meant was that the Secretary-General would have a chance to interpret the results of observation and to consult governments on them, and would also safeguard the independence of the investigation. The governments would pay for the costs of the mission.

When these conditions were met, the mission, headed by L. V. Michelmore of the Secretariat, was dispatched to consult citizens and groups in order to make the "fresh approach" demanded in the original request. On the basis of the report from his investigating mission, Thant told the governments that the majority of people in Sarawak and North Borneo wanted to bring their dependence to an end and to associate freely in the Federation of Malaysia. He reminded the three governments that they had supported the foundation of the Federation, provided the people backed it and provided that the conditions which had been set for integration by the General Assembly were fulfilled, as they were in this case.

The report had little effect. The announcement that the Federation would be officially formed was made before the report was issued on September 14, 1963. Only two days later the Federation came into being, to the great resentment of Indonesia and to a lesser extent of the Philippines. Thant remarked that this resentment might have been avoided had the announcement been delayed until his own report had been made.[36]

At no time during the investigation had a deliberative organ of the United Nations issued instructions to the Secretary-General or given him an authorization to proceed. Nor did he request any authorization, but rather went ahead to meet the request of the three governments. He had no great preparation in the way of consultations or involvement with the substance of the problem. Recourse to him may have been suggested by his successful part in the settlement of the West New Guinea dispute in the same area.

The technique used by the investigating teams was not entirely similar to the procedures employed in Hungary, Lebanon, or Yemen. In the first, the Secretary-General accomplished little but suggested the formation of an international commission to continue investigations. In the second two, military observers were posted to the field. The Secretary-General did exert some influence on his terms of reference in Malaysia, but in fact the principal questions were posed well before he participated in consultations. Negotiations on the terms of reference, and the selection and organization of the mission, proceeded smoothly and rapidly. But the formation of the Federation of Malaysia nevertheless went ahead as if the Secretary-General had not carried out the investigation.

The Dominican Republic

The mandate given the Secretary-General to conduct observations during the upheaval in the Dominican Republic beginning in the spring of 1965 differed in important respects from earlier incidents. In the formative stage, Thant kept his consultations far in the background and offered no public suggestions. This extreme discretion can be attributed to the unrelenting opposition of the United States to a role for the United Nations in a dispute within the inter-American system. Consequently, Thant intervened in the Security Council [37] during a long series of meetings only to answer questions or to provide technical information. His comments were always exceedingly brief.

The precise mechanism designed for observation fitted with the restricted role given the United Nations and with the need for only very discreet initiatives by the Secretary-General in view of the United States attitude. The Security Council requested, despite an unenthusiastic United States attitude, that the Secretary-General send an observer to the Dominican Republic. His duty was to report on the situation. Thant appointed José Antonio Mayobre, a Venezuelan who was serving as Executive Secretary of the United Nations Economic Commission for Latin America. He had a staff of fewer than ten officers, including General I. J. Rikhye, to carry out his duties. His reports provided an important focus for an involved debate in the Security Council, where United States resistance to the expansion of the United Nations role was challenged by the Soviet Union in a harsh manner, and with less vituperation by France, Uruguay, and Jordan.

On several occasions, Thant was given the opportunity by proposals in the Security Council to support enlargement of the Mayobre mission or expansion of its mandate. But he never did so, no doubt because of the confused political situation both in the Dominican Republic and in the Council. Nor did Thant assume the lead in directing Mayobre's work or interpreting its results. Instead, his presentation of reports from the Dominican Republic was limited to rather colorless compilations. The impression left by the Secretary-General's tactics was that he neither wished a greater influence on events in the Dominican Republic in the existing circumstances nor sought any personal involvement in the field operations.

Despite the limited nature of Mayobre's mandate, he occasionally found it possible to step beyond the boundaries of observation to exert a direct influence. Thant credits him with a major role in bringing about a cease-fire between contending Dominican forces soon after his arrival in mid-May. His reports also indicate that he kept in close contact with political developments in the country.

As the cease-fire became increasingly effective and the Dominican political maneuvering finally pointed toward an election, Mayobre himself left the island and visited only occasionally, leaving behind his staff to carry on the work. He was present during the election in mid-1966, and his reports that it was calm and orderly were placed before the Security Council.[38]

Observation, Investigation, and Influence

Investigation and observation seem to imply further action. In some circumstances, as in Hungary, they can have a threatening tone. In Lebanon and Yemen the Secretary-General was asked to set up observation machinery as part of an effort to prevent further disorders. In the Lebanon case the Beirut government hoped for some stronger action and assumed that observation might lead to it. In the latter case, Hammarskjöld himself moved to extend his functions from observation to broader consultation and mediation. In Malaysia, the task of the Secretary-General was so limited that no new further action seemed indicated on his part. In the Dominican Republic, the strongest supporters of United Nations involvement hoped to employ a reluctant Secretary-General in moving from observation to mediation or other means of peaceful settlement not within the inter-American system.

The disturbances in Hungary, Lebanon, Yemen, and the Dominican Republic had reached acute stages when the Secretary-General began observation. It is hard to see how such a procedure alone, no matter how successful, could have led to an alteration of the fundamental causes of the crises, but certainly some influence on them was intended. Yet the opposition of the great power that dominated the respective area severely limited the Secretary-General's effectiveness in Hungary and the Dominican Republic. He had less than decisive influence in Lebanon and Yemen. In Malaysia, despite the efficient mounting of the mission, events moved more quickly than the Secretary-General could, and he was powerless to influence their course.

In any case, observation and investigation involve the Secretary-General in delicate situations. His staff must enter the territory of the states involved. Such entry requires consent and therefore negotiations and interpretation of any mandate from a deliberative organ, so that proper conditions for effective work can be established. Investigation or observation eventuates in some conclusion or statement of facts. This requires interpretation and can easily arouse hostility, as was demonstrated in Lebanon. Or the findings can cause the Secretary-General to proceed only with great caution, as in the Dominican Republic. Moreover, establishment of machinery for observation or investigation may require a very considerable effort. The form and personnel employed can easily irritate sensitive political nerves.

The Yemen and Malaysia incidents demonstrate that in special circumstances the Secretary-General can embark on observation and investigation missions without the authorization or explicit support of either the General Assembly or the Security Council. In such a case, his mission may become even more delicate, for while he attempts to aid the parties his first responsibility is still to his organization. His successes in observation must be susceptible of treatment as United Nations achievements. His errors or the results of unexpected developments can bring him under severe criticism.

In Hungary and Lebanon, the deliberative organs, with the consent and (at least in Lebanon) encouragement of the Secretary-General, broadened his mandate to one resembling general concern with the substance of the crisis, for in each case he was instructed to proceed as seemed best to him in the circumstances. And if, as in Lebanon, the mandate could be interpreted narrowly, the Secretary-General may attempt simply to extend his action beyond it by virtue of the innate powers of the office to foster the interests of the organization. In Yemen, the Secretary-General also broadened the scope of his concern by offering political assistance from a high-ranking representative. In the Dominican Republic, however, he offered little encouragement to an extension of his mandate and initiated nothing in that direction.

This suggests that observation during a crisis cannot be undertaken by the Secretary-General without the possibility that he may have to enter deeply into substantive discussions of the situation he is surveying. He is likely to have to move toward mediation, conciliation, and a very active diplomatic role. To prevent such a development, it would be necessary either to entrust observation to an international commission of the kind employed earlier, or else to begin observation only when the general terms of a political settlement are to be maintained.

In both Hungary and Lebanon, the functioning observational machinery came to resemble the international commission form. After trying to work through committees organized by himself, Hammarskjöld recommended, and the General Assembly approved, the establishment of an international commission to assemble whatever might be learned about the Hungarian revolt. In Lebanon, he organized under his own authority a three-member commission of senior officials. This body functioned autonomously after a few weeks, and its reports were its own. Hammarskjöld commented on them but did not take responsibility for them. It seems likely that the international commission form sometimes has advantages when highly controversial investigations must be undertaken in the face of opposition of the parties or during the acute phase of a crisis, when the Secretary-General may have a great deal of negotiation to carry on.

Because machinery for observation and investigation must be put together and managed, the Secretary-General will always have an intense influence on decisions to begin such work. In the cases where he has been instructed to carry out observation functions, he has been deeply involved in consultations leading to the successful presentation of a resolution to the General Assembly or to the Security Council. This seems indispensable, for if the Secretary-General should judge himself incapable or declare himself unwilling to carry out observation functions, the project would either be dropped or assigned to an international commission. In those instances where the Secretary-General proceeds without prior specific authorization his ability to define his own task is concomitantly higher. Furthermore, the necessity to negotiate with the governments affected by the actual observation process gives the Secretary-General a large measure of influence on field bodies and operations.

CHAPTER X

PEACE-KEEPING—POLITICS AND POLICIES OF FORCES

The duties of the Secretary-General in helping to create and manage peace-keeping forces have broadened his share in determining the policies of the United Nations in maintaining peace and security. Formally belonging in the category of "other functions" under Article 98 of the United Nations Charter, these duties have required the use of every means of influence at his command.

Peace-keeping forces have been established in four separate instances. The first of these forces, growing out of the Anglo-French and Israeli attack on Egypt during the Suez crisis, laid down the initial and, in many ways, lasting definition of such operations. The second, set up in order to control the disturbance resulting from the breakdown of the newly formed Congolese Republic in 1960, became by far the largest peace-keeping operation ever undertaken by the United Nations. The third peace-keeping force served in less sensitive conditions in West New Guinea during the brief United Nations administration of that territory. More recently, a force has undertaken dangerous and trying duties during and after communal disorders on Cyprus.[1]

In several ways, these forces contrasted with those employed in Korea. They neither had nor used large amounts of heavy military equipment and were, compared with the armies in Korea, minuscule. They had no duties related to checking aggression but only to ensuring, as far as eschewing the use of force permitted, that no further fighting took place. They were, unlike the force in Korea, under the direction of the Secretary-General.

Yet the new peace-keeping forces were organized on a military basis and bore arms. Their personnel was almost entirely drawn from military forces of member governments. They served in the field in atmospheres of violence. And as in Korea, their creation and operation was sanctioned by a deliberative organ of the United Nations. Nevertheless, the fundamental distinction between the new peace-keeping forces and the counter-aggression force in Korea remains unaltered.

Each peace-keeping force was established only after violence had been employed. In the Suez case, heavy military units had attacked Egypt from two different directions. In the West New Guinea case, naval forces of the Netherlands and Indonesia had skirmished and Indonesian infiltrators had landed in the territory. In the Congo and in Cyprus, civil disorders and the use of foreign troops to deal with them preceded the involvement of the United Nations.

Military forces of permanent members of the Security Council were directly involved in the Suez and Cyprus cases. But in none of the peace-keeping enterprises was one of the superpowers directly engaged. Indirectly, the Soviet Union was affected by the attack on Egypt, to which it had been giving considerable assistance. In Suez, the Congo, West New Guinea, and Cyprus, close allies of the United States mounted military actions.

In each peace-keeping operation, the Secretary-General had the task of executing a mandate from a deliberative organ. The Security Council authorized the Secretary-General to act initially in the Congo and Cyprus cases. But the General Assembly bore the responsibility for assigning him "other functions" in the Suez and West New Guinea cases. The General Assembly was also involved at various stages of the Congo operation.

The military capacities of the peace-keeping forces differed sharply. If the force in Korea be taken as the measure of a heavy military establishment under United Nations auspices, the UNEF set up for Suez and the United Nations Temporary Executive Authority (UNTEA) force in West New Guinea rank as very light. The forces set up for the Congo and Cyprus must be placed somewhere between these two extremes. The former had a great deal more capacity than the latter.

The missions of the forces varied greatly in duration. UNEF has been in existence since 1956, but the UNTEA forces served for only a few months. The Congo force was in the field for three and a half years; the Cyprus force has been on duty for more than two.

The Development of Mandates

Because each peace-keeping enterprise involved an assignment for the Secretary-General, his tasks had to be delineated in formal instructions or a mandate. The initial mandate in each peace-keeping mission had crucial importance. It set into motion the recruitment and deployment of a force whose early momentum strongly influenced its future development.

Under no circumstances can the Secretary-General, acting on his own authority, dispatch a peace-keeping force. No standing force is in existence. Nor is one likely to be formed by the Secretary-General without the authorization of a deliberative organ. The formation of any such peace-keeping group raises difficult legal questions, for it can be argued that only the Security Council may employ a military force and then only under the specific organizational framework laid out by Article 43 of the United Nations Charter. In general, the Secretary-General has taken the position that the instructions of the General Assembly in regard to peace-keeping have validity and can be accepted as easily as those of the Security Council.

The Secretary-General has usually had an early and continuous influence in the development of his mandate. His consultations with permanent representatives and with governmental leaders often have given him timely insights into the building up of conflicts. Deliberative organs representing the United Nations as a whole have also acted on, or become conversant with, matters of conflict before the actual outbreak of violence or the creation of peace-keeping forces. Palestine had been a matter of continuous concern for the United Nations from 1947 on, and both the General Assembly and the Security Council had acted to maintain peace in that area. The West New Guinea issue remained after the Dutch decision—in which the Security Council had an important part—to give independence to the Netherlands East Indies. The Indonesian complaint about the status of West New Guinea had frequently been heard in the General Assembly. At least some information had been placed before the General Assembly on the Belgian Congo, and its future had been part of the Assembly's consideration of non-self-governing territories. Greece had raised the question of the future of the British-administered Cyprus as early as 1954, and the General Assembly had discussed it and acted twice before the Cypriot state was created and admitted to the United Nations.

As a result of his own appreciation of political potentialities, Hammarskjöld explicitly gave priority to his concern with Suez and the Congo. In the first instance, this priority was based on the development of tension and the progressive decline of the effectiveness of the 1948 Armistice Agreements. It was supported by his negotiatory assignment in the Middle East. In the second instance, Hammarskjöld reacted to a trip to Africa by publicly discussing the importance of that area in the development of world politics and by stressing the needs of the new Congolese state forming there in the immediate post-independence period.[2] A concrete manifestation of his deep interest in the Congo was the presence of Bunche at the independence ceremonies and in the crucial days immediately afterward.

Thant's expression of concern with West New Guinea and Cyprus remained less explicit before the issues approached the crisis stage. But he did carry on conversations with the Netherlands and Indonesian governments months before open warfare threatened, and was assisted in his talks by the Dutch government's decision in 1961 to offer to put West New Guinea under United Nations administration. In the Cyprus case, Thant did not act openly until he received a request from the government in Nicosia to send observers to watch a peace-keeping operation mounted by British troops late in 1963. He then responded quickly. He sent Lieutenant-General P.S. Gyani to Cyprus as his Personal Representative to report on the possible use of observers, and also had his Deputy Executive Assistant confer with the Cypriot Foreign Minister.[3]

As the crises which led to each of the four peace-keeping ventures intensified and matured, the Secretary-General played a more energetic role. This consisted in part of more intense consultations and in part of making precise suggestions. His activity had foundations both in the increasingly broad conception of the office which had been developing since Hammarskjöld's successful mission to Peking, and in the interpretation of his authority under Article 99.

Yet his enterprise took somewhat different forms in all four of the cases because of the obvious difference in circumstances. West New

Guinea is no Suez Canal; nor did upheavals in the vast expanses of the Congo present the same problems as Turk fighting Greek in the confines of Cyprus. The cases may be distinguished further by the openness and directness with which the Secretary-General assumed leadership in the Suez and Congo and the wary negotiations of the other two cases.

Hammarskjöld made it plain, in a striking public gesture, that he would resist the Anglo-French adventure in the eastern Mediterranean. As a Secretary-General who witnessed two permanent members of the Security Council join Israel in an attack on a fourth United Nations member, Hammarskjöld had every justification for a strong response. It comprised his hint in the Security Council that he would resign if he could not have the support of members in applying the Charter.

The Secretary-General's intervention in the Security Council added to the general pressure, especially strong from the United States and the Soviet Union, that built up against France, the United Kingdom, and Israel in the subsequent emergency special session of the General Assembly convened on November 2, 1956.[4] That meeting approved a United States draft which instructed the Secretary-General to observe and report promptly on the observance of the General Assembly's call for a cease-fire. But this instruction merely was the forerunner of a novel role for the Secretary-General which began to emerge from an intervention by Lester B. Pearson, then Canadian Secretary of State for External Affairs.

Pearson suggested that the Secretary-General be authorized to put together a United Nations force to hold the line while a political settlement was in the making. The Canadian government, he declared, would be glad to recommend participation in such a force. United States Secretary of State Dulles immediately endorsed Pearson's suggestions, about which he had been informed in advance.[5]

The earlier stream of speakers in the General Assembly discussion had not come close to such a thought, although Sir Pierson Dixon's careful statement on behalf of the United Kingdom alluded more than once to the lack of a suitable international force as a justification for the Anglo-French "police action" in the Suez area.[6] The Canadian suggestion set off a spate of consultations among delegations and with Hammarskjöld.

The Secretary-General, at first doubtful, began to endorse the suggestion and within another day, further consultations with him and among governments resulted in the formation of a group in the General Assembly to back a resolution which Pearson would present on November 3. Moreover, Hammarskjöld and Cordier began to outline the principles which would guide such a force. This planning had the benefit of a flow of information from his own staff members, serving in UNTSO, the Cairo office of OPI, and a technical assistance mission. Thus, at the earliest stages of the formation of UNEF, the Secretary-General was intimately involved with the policies he would later administer.

When Pearson formally put his suggestion before the General Assembly on November 3, it did not take the shape of a complete scheme but rather of an instruction to Hammarskjöld to advance the planning for a force. The Canadian Secretary of State for External Affairs proposed that Hammarskjöld be given 48 hours in which to work up a plan. The discussion made it clear that the projected force would be based on the principle of voluntary contributions. There was no pretension that the United Nations force would do more than stand between the Egyptians and Israeli troops. None of the supporters of the Canadian resolution had any doubt that the British and French forces should stop their action and leave as soon as possible. The resolution was adopted by 57 favorable votes with 19 abstentions. Britain, France, Egypt, and Israel numbered among the abstainers. So did the Soviet Union and its allies.

The indications at this point were that Hammarskjöld had a wide-open chance to make useful suggestions, but that some delegations, including all but one direct participant in the conflict, still needed to be convinced and were reserving their views until they had a specific focus for further discussion.[7]

Within hours, the already excellent collaboration with leading delegations increased in intensity. Hammarskjöld received commitments from the representatives of Canada, Colombia, India, and Norway that their governments would furnish troops. Foreign Minister Pearson, Colombia's Ambassador Francisco Urrutia, Ambassador Lall, and Foreign Minister Engen joined Hammarskjöld, Cordier, and Bunche to make the sketchy preliminary proposals more complete. The Secretary-General had spent some time after the

General Assembly meeting, which lasted almost to dawn on November 3, in formulating proposals for discussion with his informal advisory group. Within less than a quarter of the time given him by the General Assembly, Hammarskjöld had a plan ready.[8]

What the Secretary-General reported to the General Assembly seemed simplicity itself. The nucleus of a force was already available. General Burns, head of UNTSO, was near the battle zone. He would be named chief of the new command and could use his observers as the officer cadre. Hammarskjöld wanted authorization to obtain more troops, determining through negotiations which countries had them immediately available and which might later.[9]

The report, in fact, did not spell out a mission for the force, beyond the general statement in echo of the Assembly resolution that it was to secure and supervise the cessation of hostilities. The shadow of the political background fell over the report, which on the whole was in antiseptic, diplomatic language. In recruiting either for immediate service or at a later time, said Hammarskjöld, "I would endeavour to develop a plan where, as a matter of principle, troops should not be drawn from countries which are permanent members of the Security Council." This provision had two effects. It denied to France and the United Kingdom the possibility they had suggested of employing their troops under United Nations auspices; it forestalled direct entry of the forces of the Soviet Union or the United States. The first effect would help to calm anti-imperialist sentiments and violent governmental policies in the Middle East after a cease-fire; the second would reduce the likelihood that the conflict would become a major one in the Cold War context.

The first report of the Secretary-General on UNEF was quickly adopted by the General Assembly. The resolution presented by Engen on behalf of his government, Canada, and Colombia merely established a United Nations command for an emergency force to secure and supervise the cessation of hostilities, and appointed Burns to head it. The Secretary-General got the authority he wished and was invited "to take such administrative measures as may be necessary for the prompt execution of the actions envisaged." The determination of how the force would be organized and what it would do remained for the future and for decision by the Secretary-General.

The vote on the resolution was no different from that which asked the Secretary-General to work out a plan. France and the United Kingdom took no position, because their delegates had had no time to consult with their capitals. The Israeli spokesman displayed some perhaps justified pique at not having been consulted. The United States strongly supported the report, while the Soviet delegate moved somewhat closer to a position by claiming that if the attacking forces obeyed the cease-fire call, no emergency force would be necessary since the whole world could see that fighting was over.[10]

Since the General Assembly had given Hammarskjöld an initial broad mandate that reflected his views, his further actions to fill in the details fell even more under his influence. Along with his planning of UNEF, the Secretary-General was attempting to arrange a cease-fire. In the negotiations, Hammarskjöld was put in a pivotal position by Israel, which demanded confirmation from him that Egypt would accept a cease-fire. France and the United Kingdom, responding to heavy diplomatic pressure and the weight of domestic public opinion, also indicated willingness to call off their action if the United Nations could organize a successful emergency force. This put the Secretary-General equidistant between the parties to the dispute, whose demands amounted to saying that cease-fire depended on the creation of a force, which depended on a cease-fire.[11]

In a second and final report on UNEF, Hammarskjöld both gave further definition to his mandate and broke the circle described by the cease-fire negotiations. By insisting on the principle that permanent members of the Security Council were excluded from UNEF, he turned aside any proposal that an effective force had to include British and French troops. UNEF had closely limited purposes. "[T]here is no intent in the establishment of the force to influence the military balance in the present conflict and, thereby, the political balance," the Secretary-General reported.[12] This responded to Israeli demands and indicated that UNEF was to be an instrument useful in confirming Egyptian acceptance of a cease-fire. His mandate, as he interpreted it, permitted no military aims. UNEF would help maintain quiet after the withdrawal of non-Egyptian troops; it would be more than an observer group, but would not control the territory on which it was stationed. This ensured that UNEF would not be the instrument of further defeat for Egypt. Nor could UNEF be converted to use in enforcement without additional action by the Security Council. As a creation of the General Assembly, UNEF could not be imposed on any government but had to have consent before entering any territory.

Hammarskjöld avoided giving the details of the size, organization, and recruitment of the force, preferring to keep that under his own jurisdiction. "Time has so far not permitted the necessary technical studies,"[13] was his understatement of the situation. He did note it would be wise to accept only units of battalion size which could support themselves. Although some troop offers had been made, including possibly embarrassing ones from Czechoslovakia and Romania, the Secretary-General guarded his authority to negotiate them into satisfactory form.

The reactions of the British, French, and Israeli, as well as Egyptian, delegates in the General Assembly indicated that the Secretary-General had found a formula in which they could acquiesce without utterly contradicting their earlier positions. Hammarskjöld's report also left room for negotiation on the many vague and fragmentary points. By preserving the possibility of a role for the Security Council, the Secretary-General also avoided the anathema of the Soviet bloc.

Despite the way Hammarskjöld's report worked into the interstices of opposed policies, he did not escape from some telling questioning by V.K. Krishna Menon, the Indian representative. Noting that India had had some painful experience in Korea and Indochina, Krishna Menon wanted to know how the military balance could remain uninfluenced. Was it not intended, he asked, that the occupation troops would withdraw? Hammarskjöld replied that he meant to convey that the General Assembly resolutions would "constitute the fundamental law of this whole operation."[14] In fact, Menon had put his finger on one of the potential weak points in the entire scheme, for it was inconceivable that the military and political balance in the area could remain uninfluenced if the international organization and its Secretary-General were propelled into negotiating, organizing, and policing tasks by a combination of Anglo-French-Israeli attack, United States and Soviet pressure, and the support of the entire General Assembly.

That support was expressed in the adoption, by 64 votes to none with 12 abstentions, of a resolution approving the report and authorizing the Secretary-General to go ahead with the organization of what became UNEF. This authorization resulted as much as anything else from the persuasiveness of ideas formulated by the Secretary-General. It meant, as Gabriella Rosner remarks, that

> . . . the General Assembly was delegating a remarkable degree of power to its chief administrative officer. . . . Hammarskjöld and his staff were clearly . . . to be not only the major architects of the emergency force, but the chief administrative and executive officers as well.[15]

The Secretary-General took an unmistakable position of leadership in developing a mandate for the peace-keeping mission in the Congo. He built this position out of his use of Article 99 and the experience of UNEF.

In the Congo case, Hammarskjöld assumed the practicality of assembling a force and began planning it before obtaining the instructions he sought from the Security Council. He expressly employed the lessons of UNEF as the basis of his planning.

As in the Suez case, he regarded the foreign troops in the Congo —sent by a Belgian government intent on protecting its nationals from what was believed to be a violent threat to their personal safety—as unacceptable "as a stopgap arrangement pending the reestablishment of order through the national security force." Hammarskjöld told the Security Council, entirely on his own initiative:

> I strongly recommend to the Council to authorize the Secretary-General to take the necessary steps, in consultation with the Government of the Congo, to provide the Government with military assistance during the period which may have to pass before, through the efforts of the Government with technical assistance of the United Nations, the national security forces are able to fully meet their task. It would be understood that were the United Nations to act as proposed, the Belgian Government would see its way to a withdrawal.[16]

The Secretary-General intended to base his actions, if the Council approved military assistance, on his summary of the UNEF experiences.[17] It followed, he said, that the new force would not be authorized to act beyond self-defense, would not take part in internal conflicts, and would comprise personnel whose nationalities caused no complications; forces of the great powers would be barred, while the first call would go to African states. He wanted consultations and then additional meetings formally to elaborate his mandate.

As in the Suez crisis, Hammarskjöld had had numerous consultations and direct information from his own staff in the field. Bunche's talks with the Congolese government on technical assistance had developed a request for help in reorganizing the ANC. Hammarskjöld had favored the scheme. The Congolese government soon followed this request with one addressed to the United States for the dispatch of troops to maintain order. Hammarskjöld was informed of this new request.[18]

At the same time, the Secretary-General had begun conversations at headquarters with the representatives of nine African states. Tunisia, represented by Mongi Slim, assumed the task in the Council of managing the introduction and adoption of a resolution. With the other eight consultants, he reached an agreement with Hammarskjöld about the nature of technical assistance for military reorganization in the Congo, but the problem there changed radically after the Congolese telegrams of July 12, 1960, demanding aid to eject the Belgian troops. Yet the consultations were an admirable preparation for the later decisions of the Security Council, for at the time that Hammarskjöld urged it to instruct him to organize a force he already knew that Tunisia, Ghana, Guinea, and Morocco were willing to furnish troops.[19] Presumably the other members of the Council also knew of this willingness when Hammarskjöld began his initiative.

In many ways the discussion in the Security Council resembled that in the General Assembly when it was working out the initial instructions leading to the formation of UNEF. Although the Soviet Union and the United States clearly were alert to the possibility that they could become fully involved in the dispute, neither sought a direct hand. The United States delegate welcomed the initiative of the Secretary-General, while his Soviet colleague played for more time and tried to prevent a decision supporting Hammarskjöld. The British and French representatives took the position, not inconsistent with their views in 1956, that the United Nations force, which they favored, would have only the limited duty of taking over from the Belgian troops, whose intervention they did not at all disfavor in the circumstances. The discussion, which was generally of a high quality, made it clear that the force would be temporary, and only paramilitary, just as Hammarskjöld had suggested. Belgium accepted the proposals of the Secretary-General to "ensure security" in the Congo, where for the moment this job could be done only by the Belgian forces.[20] At the same time, Walter Loridan, representative of Belgium, told the Council that his country would withdraw those of its troops sent to the Congo from the metropolitan bases as soon as the United Nations force could take over. He did not mention those left in the Congo under the independence agreement.

The actual instruction to Hammarskjöld was contained in a draft resolution presented by Slim. It called for a Belgian withdrawal and echoed the words of the Secretary-General authorizing the provision to the Republic of the Congo, after consultation with it, of military assistance until in its opinion the national security forces could perform their task. This resolution[21] was adopted, by eight votes to none, after the Council refused Soviet amendments intended to put Belgium in the worst possible light. China, France, and the United Kingdom abstained, the last two explaining that they opposed the call for immediate withdrawal of Belgian troops or anything which might be interpreted as a condemnation.

The influence of the Secretary-General in developing the new mandate surpassed that of the Suez case in 1956. He involved himself earlier in the planning and more openly sought the lead in defining the mandate. Despite the differences between the Congo and the Sinai Peninsula and between the Security Council and the General Assembly, his ideas provided the main content of his mandate. The Security Council reached enough agreement in principle so that the way was open for inventive, executive action. And this time, the hand of the administrator was more practiced in turning a broad mandate into a peace-keeping force.

The Secretary-General's leadership and influence in developing the mandate for the peace-keeping forces employed in West New Guinea differed in several ways from his situation in the Suez and Congo cases. Although he had information and some relationship to the unfolding of events in the West New Guinea and Cyprus cases, existing conflicts intensified while Thant was engaged in consultations on their substance. His actions therefore did not appear to emerge suddenly, but rather seemed directly connected with the evolution of the conflicts.

Thant's involvement with both the West New Guinea and Cyprus cases was for the most part confined to the diplomatic background and was not the subject of intense public proceedings. He neither intervened forcefully in the deliberative organs to initiate organization of the forces nor, as in the UNEF and ONUC experiences, had he to improvise entirely new forms of action. In neither case, moreover, did he on his own initiative seek mandates from deliberative organs.

In the West New Guinea case,[22] Thant's mandate with regard to peace-keeping evolved entirely from discussions between the Netherlands and Indonesia, and from Ellsworth Bunker's mediation. Unlike the Suez and Congo cases, where the control of fighting was the principal aim of the peace-keeping forces, the West New Guinea negotiations centered on the future sovereignty of the territory. Any peace-keeping force would be incidental to a political settlement. The mandate for the force, therefore, posed fewer difficulties than it had in the earlier two cases.

When the text was presented to the General Assembly in 1962, in accordance with the agreement, the Secretary-General's mandate to create a United Nations Special Force (UNSF) received little attention in a debate which overwhelmingly favored what had been done. The main rationale for UNSF could be found in the vacuum which would be left by the withdrawal of Dutch troops in favor of the interim United Nations administration. The parties therefore agreed that UNSF should be set up, leaving it to the Secretary-General to operate it to maintain law and order. Since the cease-fire which was also part of the agreement became effective immediately, few reminders of violence remained by the time advance units of UNSF arrived.

The mandate of the United Nations Force in Cyprus (UNFICYP) grew out of diplomatic consultations that in their privacy resembled those in the West New Guinea case. But public discussion of the merits of the dispute among Cyprus, Turkey, Greece, and the United Kingdom went on at length in the Security Council.[23] The mission given UNFICYP, for all its vagueness, had more in common with UNEF and ONUC than with UNSF.

Thant had been consulting continuously with members of the Security Council during March, 1964, while the Security Council discussed the complaints and counter-complaints growing out of communal disorders and the presence by treaty right of three foreign forces on the island. He had the benefit of Gyani's explorations of the situation. Only after consultations on the role of UNFICYP had reached the point of agreement did the Council take it up. The Soviet and French representatives criticized a resolution presented by small powers to establish UNFICYP "in the interest of preserving international peace and security, to use its best efforts to prevent a recurrence of fighting and, as necessary, to contribute to the maintenance and restoration of law and order and a return to normal conditions."[24] They objected to the delegation of so much authority to the Secretary-General.

Thant's statement hardly spelled out UNFICYP's mandate any further, although it made clear that he welcomed the backing of the Security Council. The new force, the Secretary-General declared, would have duties substantially similar to those of earlier groups.

The most striking aspect of this mandate is its vagueness. Whatever specific meaning it had was to be elucidated later by the Secretary-General himself in working out conditions for its operations. But he was later to complain that UNFICYP operated under handicaps because of the "inadequacy and lack of clarity" in its mandate.[25]

Initiating Operations

Whatever the faults or merits of a peace-keeping mandate given the Secretary-General, his immediate response has to be the formation of a force. In many respects, his efforts to assemble forces have a technical, administrative character. The determination of which proffered troops have suitable qualifications, or the arrangements for transportation and marshaling camps, for example, must rest largely on technical grounds. Such decisions are left almost entirely to the Secretary-General.

Political questions arise in putting a force together. They require the Secretary-General to act in his familiar role of persuader, consultant, and source of ideas.

Because of the nature of the conflicts requiring peace-keeping, not all troop offers can be taken up. British and French troops, for example, hardly would have been permissible as part of UNEF; the

Secretary-General ruled them out, as he did Belgian troops in the Congo. Moreover, the motives for offering troops have some weight in the decision concerning their acceptance. The Soviet Union, for example, offered three times to put soldiers into the Suez area; this willingness had more behind it than a desire to heighten United Nations prestige. Neutral Sweden proposed giving troops for both UNEF and ONUC as part of a policy of participating in exceptional United Nations ventures. The national policies which dictate such offers become part of the setting in which the Secretary-General puts together a force.

In each case, consultations and negotiations relating to the mandate gave the Secretary-General some indications of which governments would offer troops. After the authorization of the peace-keeping forces, other governments either volunteered contributions or could be persuaded by the Secretary-General to take part. Because he always had a nucleus of offers around which to assemble the force, the Secretary-General could accept some units and reject others on ostensibly technical grounds. Such choices permitted him to achieve such political aims as impartiality and acceptability to the host government.

From a technical and administrative point of view, the recruitment and deployment of UNEF and ONUC had a number of similarities. Above all, they represented triumphs of improvisation and unprecedented speed.

In the case of UNEF the Secretary-General suggested that Burns be appointed to head the new force, and in the ONUC case the choice of a commander was left to him. He was given responsibility in both instances to search for troops. "I would try to determine," said Hammarskjöld with regard to UNEF, "from which countries the necessary troops might be drawn without delay, as well as from which countries recruitment may be possible for a somewhat later stage." [26] Aside from the great powers, further exclusions from the forces would be made on the judgment of the Secretary-General.

It was not long before a flood of offers of troops for UNEF came in. Hammarskjöld insisted that self-contained units would be needed and that a panel broad enough to make choices of units would be necessary, but he did not commit himself on either the size or the organization of the force. The choice of units would to a considerable degree hinge on the size and task of the force, matters reserved for the decision of the Secretary-General. The Secretary-General had an authorization to issue regulations and instructions to the force.

UNEF was put together with extreme rapidity and at the price of sleepless nights and nerve-wracking work by the Secretary-General and a very small staff. The nucleus of the group which worked on UNEF consisted of Hammarskjöld, Cordier, and Bunche. They had not even the assistance of a military adviser at the beginning. Countries which contributed to the force lent military attachés from their embassies in Washington. The United Nations Field Service, that vestige of Lie's hope for a standing guard force that had become the principal service agency for field missions, provided experience and open channels to the world outside of headquarters. As offers of troops came in and were negotiated into definite form, United States logistical assistance provided invaluable help in bringing the men to the staging area which had been improvised near Naples.

From there, the soldiers went on to Egypt as soon as the conditions for their entry had been negotiated by the Secretary-General. On November 15, to Burns' frank amazement at the speed with which they had been gathered, the blue-helmeted men of UNEF landed for duty in Egypt.[27] Eventually, UNEF numbered some 6,000 men from ten countries.

Once the Security Council instructed the Secretary-General to go ahead with the organization of ONUC, scenes which recalled the hectic days of the formation of UNEF were enacted at United Nations headquarters. Following the Security Council meeting which gave Hammarskjöld his instructions, he and his close associates, including Cordier, worked through the early morning of July 14, 1960, to get troops moving. By dawn all the arrangements had been made. Kano, in Nigeria, was to serve, thanks to British cooperation, as the staging area. Telephonic and cabled requests for assistance went out to additional governments, and the contributions offered initially were confirmed. Bunche was consulted and kept advised by telephone in Leopoldville.[28]

Within 48 hours the first Tunisian units disembarked from their transport planes, furnished again by the United States, at an airport near Leopoldville. Within four days 3,500 troops had arrived. By

July 20, Hammarskjöld reported to the Security Council that 12 African and two European battalions had come to the Congo to take over from the Belgians. Again, UNTSO furnished the commander, General von Horn, a Swede, whose country had temporarily contributed its battalion serving with UNEF. The Secretary-General also stated that he was seeking further contributions and had planned a second phase in which more European troops, with an Asian and a Latin American group, would take part. At the same time 27 governments had been asked for food and other nonmilitary contributions, which were beginning to come in by United States, British, Canadian, Soviet, and Swiss aircraft.

The improvisation of UNEF was a tour de force. It was repeated and, if anything, carried out more efficiently in the case of ONUC, where the time required for the actual landing of men was only half that needed in the Sinai Peninsula. In part, these remarkable performances resulted from the concentration of executive power in the hands of the Secretary-General. In part, his own energy and imagination produced success. And for the rest, the happy coincidence of policies of middle and small powers with troops available contributed much. Some of these circumstances, Hammarskjöld remarked of UNEF, "are of such a nature that it could not reasonably be expected that they would often be duplicated elsewhere." [29]

The recruitment of forces for West New Guinea and Cyprus broke sharply away from the UNEF and ONUC pattern in important respects. One of the most important of these was the injection of the question of finance at the beginning.

Both UNEF and ONUC existed before any extended consideration was given to their financing, which the Secretary-General regarded as a necessary charge on the United Nations membership. The resulting financial crisis made it impossible for the Secretary-General to proceed with the establishment of UNSF or UNFICYP until funds were available. Because Thant entered the West New Guinea and Cyprus negotiations at early stages, he could give attention to novel financial understandings. In the first case, a simple arrangement that the parties to the dispute would pay for the expenses of the United Nations overcame financial obstacles.

Cyprus proved complex. The parties there agreed that the governments providing contingents would meet their costs and that voluntary contributions might be received. Since the British government was asked to make its troops on Cyprus part of the force, a nucleus existed. Canada, Ireland, and Sweden, the middle-rank powers which had so strongly supported peace-keeping forces in Suez and the Congo, were willing to provide contingents. The Secretary-General also approached Austria, Brazil, and Finland in an effort to build a force totaling 7,000 men. The United States and the United Kingdom agreed to make substantial cash contributions. On the basis of individual agreements with contributors on financing and the number of troops to be furnished, Thant was able to put together UNFICYP. He appointed the military commander.

UNSF had a much more unified quality, since it consisted entirely of Pakistani troops. The Secretary-General apparently dealt with the Pakistan government directly, and, it can be surmised, with the support of the United States and the parties to the dispute. This approach resulted in an agreement that Pakistan would furnish some 1,500 men under the command of their own general. In addition, the Secretary-General obtained vital aircraft and crews from the United States and Canada.

UNFICYP was improvised rapidly and in a crisis atmosphere, although the conflict on Cyprus had been anticipated, as that in the Sinai Peninsula could not have been. Yet more time was available for UNSF, which was markedly smaller than the other forces. No aura of novelty surrounded the idea of peace-keeping forces, and the negotiating role of the Secretary-General, familiar from UNEF and ONUC, caused no surprise. In fact, the earlier efforts probably made it easier to reach more precision regarding the kind and numbers of troops which were to be made available for West New Guinea and Cyprus.

Conditions for Operations

The establishment and employment of peace-keeping forces brings the Secretary-General into close and influential relationships not only with those countries furnishing troops but even more importantly with those governments on whose territory they are to be employed. He may also have to deal with governments whose troops are to be withdrawn in favor of the peace-keeping forces.

In the UNEF case, the novelty of the Secretary-General's assignment had necessarily to bring to light unanticipated problems and to set precedents for future operations. More than the subsequent cases, too, the use of UNEF met with hesitant responses from the host government, which sought to define new kinds of relationships that affected its interests. In later cases, the UNEF experience offered fixed standards which could be applied. To some extent, this may explain why in the Congo, West New Guinea, and Cyprus cases, the initial entry of the United Nations force was accomplished with little difficulty despite the vagueness of some of the mandates.

Hammarskjöld himself took the lead in defining the conditions under which UNEF would enter Egypt and operate there. Immediately after the Anglo-French-Israeli attack, the main aim of the Cairo government had to be a cease-fire. This led it easily to accept the establishment of UNEF, since the General Assembly had linked UNEF with the end of fighting.

Hammarskjöld consulted Egyptian representatives throughout the process of forming UNEF. Whatever the weakness of the Egyptian position, Nasser had no intention of accepting whatever the Secretary-General proposed. He went beyond the Secretary-General's original principle that the great powers would be excluded from the force, by trying to refuse the participation of any member of NATO. The Egyptian leader then issued a call for volunteers to help Egypt, soon after Soviet statements had suggested that the Soviet Union might be a willing source.[30] These developments, which suggested the possibility of the involvement of another great power in a way that would be extremely difficult to deal with, made it impossible to ignore Egyptian claims, even if there had been a desire to do so.

The Secretary-General, interpreting the principle that UNEF would neither have enforcement duties nor take any action to affect internal conflicts, concluded that Egypt's consent would be required before UNEF could operate. This ensured that further negotiations would follow and necessarily meant that Hammarskjöld would have an influence on decisions. It also meant that his influence would be great only in proportion to the Egyptian desire to see the force employed. Two points apparently affected Nasser's policy. His government wanted UNEF kept away from the Suez Canal and involved only with the armistice demarcation lines, and also objected to the inclusion of Canadian troops in the new force. Enough progress was made so that advance units of UNEF were permitted to land at Abu Sueir on November 16.

The Secretary-General took over the negotiations with Nasser when permission was granted for the first UNEF men to land in Egypt.[31] In two days of personal diplomacy, Hammarskjöld worked out with the Egyptian government a formula which permitted the full development of UNEF and its deployment. It was agreed that it would assume no duties around the Canal or in Port Said unless a prior agreement was negotiated. Nor would UNEF be used as an "instrument of enforcement directed against the Egyptian government," [32] but would rather occupy agreed-upon areas at the armistice demarcation lines. Furthermore, the Secretary-General would negotiate with Egypt over any additional contributions to the force. Meanwhile, the problem of the Canadian troops appeared solved when General Burns asked External Affairs Minister Pearson for air transport and administrative elements as the most useful contribution that could be made by Canada.

Hammarskjöld reported the results of his negotiations to the General Assembly in a very guarded statement, to which he attached an *aide-mémoire* embodying the legal results of his talks. This *aide-mémoire* was built around a formula in which both Egypt and the United Nations agreed to be "guided, in good faith" by the resolutions adopted by the General Assembly. Concrete problems of staging and operations of UNEF would be the subject of further negotiations, which in fact were largely matters that could be dealt with in the field.[33]

The "good faith" formula, new to United Nations practice and of unknown content, on the whole served very well. It was expanded into further agreements later. The Secretary-General later summed up the experience with the comment that the formula offered an adequate solution to the problem of the presence of an international force that could possibly take detrimental unilateral action in relation to a host government. The declarations by the United Nations and Egypt meant, according to Hammarskjöld, that if the United Nations decided on withdrawal or if Egypt asked the force to leave, "an exchange of views would be called for towards harmonizing the positions" if either party believed the "good faith" formula had been violated. The Secretary-General saw in the formula a pattern for the future:

> It is unlikely that any Government in the future would be willing to go beyond the declaration of the Government of Egypt with regard to UNEF. Nor, in my view, should the United Nations commit itself beyond the point established for UNEF in relation to the Government of Egypt. In these circumstances, I consider it reasonable to regard the formula . . . as a valid basis for future arrangements of a similar kind.[34]

The formula as interpreted and used by Hammarskjöld was anything but a cut-and-dried set of legal rules. It was rather a clear recognition of a balanced and rather precarious political relationship in which a number of interests—those of Egypt, the United Nations as represented by the Secretary-General, the governments sending troops, and other United Nations members—were involved.

The very existence of the UNEF formula and its general success may have led to its rather facile acceptance as the guide for ONUC's relations with a Congolese government eager for assistance and by a Security Council that looked to the Secretary-General as leader. Hammarskjöld deduced the guidelines of the new force from the UNEF experience. It would not be authorized to take any action beyond self-defense. It would not be a party to internal conflicts. Its components would be selected so as to avoid objections by the host government. These guidelines were elaborated later but not fundamentally changed from those used in Egypt. The Secretary-General would make the final decisions on which contributions to ONUC would be accepted. He would be the sole source of orders for national units, and would exclude the host and the contributing governments from directing the force. ONUC would also have freedom of movement within the Congo, the whole of which made up the site of the conflict.

The marked difference in the situation ONUC was entering from that of UNEF was perhaps not immediately perceived, or perhaps it was thought better to begin at once under dubious guidelines than wait until the crisis had deepened. The proximate cause of the Congolese complaint to Hammarskjöld was the use of Belgian troops, and could be likened to the attack on Egypt in the sense that a military blow was struck against the Congo. But Belgian troops were employed because of a breakdown in discipline in the Congolese army and a weakening of the entire fabric of government. The situation in Egypt in 1956 was quite different.

While Belgium accepted without hesitation the call of the Security Council to withdraw its troops in favor of an international force, ONUC would have no determined cease-fire line to oversee. Nor would it be able to deal with a government that controlled most of its territory. Rather, an incapacity to govern lay behind the crisis in the Congo.

ONUC was welcome in the Congo, and its entry required no extended negotiations. But its welcome had a different reason from that in the UNEF case. Nasser wanted a cease-fire and accepted a force to police it in order to prevent further losses. He naturally tried to set limiting conditions. The Congolese government, insofar as it could be clear about its policies, wanted both to restore its own control in the land and to get rid of the Belgian force. Because the UNEF pattern of relationships was proposed by Hammarskjöld for ONUC, the new force necessarily had more relevance to the second task than to the first.

In West New Guinea and Cyprus, the conditions under which the United Nations forces entered resembled those of the Congo in one important way. The governments concerned positively desired the employment of a force under the direction of the Secretary-General.

Such policies did not mean, however, that the terms of the invitations to the United Nations forces were increasingly explicit. In fact, in West New Guinea and Cyprus, the conditions under which the forces took up their duties received only a minimum of public discussion. The terms of reference were worked out, if at all, in private discussion before the deliberative organs gave their broad and vague mandates to the Secretary-General.

After the force in Cyprus had begun functioning and became the subject of controversy, Thant reluctantly disclosed some details of his instructions to it. He had already agreed with Cyprus on the application of the "good faith" formula familiar from UNEF. UNFICYP would avoid actions influencing the political situation, would employ its arms only in self-defense, and would be responsible only to the Secretary-General and the commander appointed by him.[35] No similar announcement appears to have been made with regard to UNSF.

The lack of explicitness and action by deliberative bodies on the conditions of entry for UNSF and UNFICYP both increased the influence of the Secretary-General and made his administrative task more difficult. Because he had responsibility for the functioning of the force, his interpretations of his mandate had great importance in the absence of highly defined guidelines. But precisely because such interpretations had little basis in discussion in deliberative organs, the Secretary-General had to act with extreme discretion and sureness to avoid creating new controversies with the host governments. The precedents of UNEF and ONUC also had a persuasive bearing on the work of the Secretary-General, for they provided some firm background to which he could refer.

PART FOUR

Political Administration

CHAPTER XI

PEACE-KEEPING—OPERATIONS AND ADAPTATIONS

Once a mandate and conditions for entering the territory of its concern are set for a peace-keeping force, the Secretary-General begins a second stage of his work. He must actually start operations and then adapt his policies to meet new problems as they develop. The existence of the force gives him a certain automatic influence, for it represents a considerable degree of commitment on the part of important members of the United Nations and of the host country. But its operations, not its instructions, create effects on governmental policies.

These effects mean that local conditions change. So may the policies of the host governments, the contributing governments, and the governments with troops to withdraw. In order successfully to execute his mandate, the Secretary-General therefore must also seek to adapt his policies to changing conditions.

Because peace-keeping forces operate in very sensitive situations, the Secretary-General must have both advice and the means by which to make his instructions to the field effective. He must decide how great his personal involvement will be and what administrative machinery will be required. This machinery can contribute counsel to him, but additional, more political, arrangements could also prove useful. Several different mechanisms have been put together for directing peace-keeping operations.

Operations and Politics

The Secretary-General's first major operating task in regard to a peace-keeping force is to get it into place, either behind evacuating troops or between fighting units. In Suez and the Congo, the peace-keeping forces began operating by taking over military positions to be vacated by troops from outside the country. In West New Guinea the UNSF was to deal with the maintenance of law and order until the Dutch forces could withdraw, and then was to hand over authority to the Indonesian forces. In Cyprus the mission was less well defined, and became one of intervening where it was moderately safe to do so in order to keep opposed military entities apart.

In order to move his force into place, the Secretary-General must reach an understanding regarding the withdrawal of occupying troops. This necessarily involves sensitive negotiations, for the Secretary-General in a sense symbolizes foreign opposition to a national policy, even though he acts on behalf of the United Nations and not of individual governments. Since he does not dispose of the means of pressure available to governments, he depends in the first instance on the commitment of the governments backing the policy he is to carry out. He can persuade most easily when powerful governments join his efforts.

Britain, France, and Israel. When UNEF's first units were prepared for deployment, Britain and France avoided obstructive actions and agreed without undue difficulties with Hammarskjöld's plans and suggestions. Withdrawal of their troops proceeded quite smoothly. Securing the withdrawal of Israeli troops proved much more difficult.

Hammarskjöld experienced little obstruction in securing, as a first step, British and French agreement on a cease-fire. By November 6, 1956, both governments had made clear their intention to order their troops to halt. But they nevertheless made their cease-fire orders contingent on the Secretary-General's assurance that Israel and Egypt had given similar orders.[1] Britain and France did not immediately begin withdrawing their men. Rather, they maintained their right to decide for themselves whether the effective United Nations force on which they had conditioned their withdrawal really existed.

As November drew to an end, the Anglo-French forces were in contact with UNEF and received the first units in a friendly fashion. After the British and French governments conferred, they agreed early in December to carry through a complete withdrawal. This decision followed Foreign Secretary Selwyn Lloyd's return to London from extensive discussions with the Secretary-General.[2]

The main line of continuous contact between the United Nations and the British and French then shifted to Egypt, where the problem of transferring control from the invading troops to UNEF had to be faced. Almost from the moment that he was appointed to head UNEF, General Burns had been in touch with General Sir Charles Keightley, commander of the Anglo-French forces. Early in December, Keightley was given formal instructions to agree with Burns on a timetable for withdrawal. Burns meanwhile carried on conversations with the Anglo-French staff and with the Egyptian authorities, all of whom received him in a cooperative spirit. Hammarskjöld had come to Cairo during November, and Burns concerted his policy with that of his chief. The series of discussions produced a mutually acceptable *aide-mémoire*, which defined the manner in which UNEF would take over from the Anglo-French forces. Thus the formal orders by the British and French governments could be executed quickly.[3]

The Secretary-General had brought all the pressure he could on the British and French governments and augmented his persuasiveness with reports to the General Assembly. He guided the technical field negotiations to some extent, but left them largely to the experienced Burns. UNEF units verified that the withdrawal was in fact accomplished by December 22, slightly later than Hammarskjöld and Burns had hoped for. UNEF was then free to give its full attention to the withdrawal of Israeli forces to the armistice lines.[4]

The Ben Gurion government did not quickly give up its determination to revise the Palestine armistice system. Fighting by the Israeli forces ceased on November 5, leaving them in possession of much of the Sinai Peninsula, the Gaza Strip, and the strategic points which controlled the Gulf of Aqaba. Meanwhile, the General Assembly discussed and quickly passed a resolution which called on Israel to withdraw to the 1949 armistice lines, and asked the Secretary-General to report on compliance.[5]

By November 24 the Israeli army had retreated across the Sinai Peninsula, and UNEF filled the gap. The withdrawal continued slowly until UNEF reached the international frontier on January 22,

1957, but Israeli troops still controlled the Gaza Strip, with its overflowing refugee camps, and the Gulf of Aqaba positions. Israel wanted strong commitments that *fedayeen* raids from Egypt would be stopped, and refused to release its occupation of the Gaza Strip except to create a demilitarized zone. As for the Gulf of Aqaba, Israel would withdraw provided UNEF would guarantee free navigation. Hammarskjöld insisted that Israel had to back up until positions were exactly as they had been when fighting began.[6]

Hammarskjöld himself and the General Assembly, following his lead, increased the pressure on Israel. The Secretary-General typically used legal language to declare that "the United Nations cannot condone a change of the *status juris* resulting from military action contrary to the provisions of the Charter."[7] "Our view is simple," Abba Eban, the Israeli representative, replied. "In the three outstanding issues—the Suez Canal, the Gulf of Aqaba and the Gaza Strip—our duty is not to re-establish but to prevent the re-establishment of the previous situation, for in each case the situation on 28 October 1956 was one of illegality and not of law."[8] The Israelis also challenged Hammarskjöld's conception of UNEF's work on the grounds that if it took over in the Gaza Strip, as the Secretary-General envisaged, Egyptian consent to its remaining there could be withdrawn.

The General Assembly followed the line laid down by the Secretary-General. It adopted resolutions deploring the failure of Israel to withdraw and supporting the stationing of UNEF on the demarcation line, along with other measures proposed by Hammarskjöld. The Israeli government rejected the demands of the General Assembly. Serious discussion of the possibilities of sanctions now began, and the United States reduced its financial aid. After a week-long consultation, Hammarskjöld reported reaching an impasse. He suggested that the General Assembly now had to instruct him regarding further steps to carry out its wishes, but cautioned in a veiled way against the employment of sanctions which might simply introduce new conflict.[9]

Hammarskjöld did his best to capitalize on the intense pressure on Israel. He continued his negotiations with Egypt in order to clarify as far as possible the position in the Gaza Strip. The Egyptians naturally were anxious to get the Israeli civil government out of the strip, which along with the Gulf of Aqaba points was all that was left of the Israeli occupation of territory defined in the Armistice Agreements as administered by Egypt. Hammarskjöld was able to report personally to the General Assembly that Egypt wanted UNEF in the first instance to take over civilian control from Israel. The Secretary-General's statement indicated that UNEF and other United Nations agencies, especially the Relief and Works Agency for Palestine Refugees, would be prepared to govern the strip for a considerable but undefined period. In any case, according to the Secretary-General's statement, Israel would not have to give way to Egyptian administrators and could also expect United Nations agencies to put "a definite end to all incursions and raids across the border from either side." [10] Hammarskjöld seemingly had devised a formula which went some way in meeting Israeli needs for security without interfering with the principle that UNEF entered Egypt with the permission of the government.

While Hammarskjöld negotiated with Egypt and Israel, the latter government was also carrying on conversations outside the United Nations framework. Israel finally gave way at the beginning of March, after United States pressure, plus the numerous consultations involving Egypt, Israel, and other states, had taken full effect. Foreign Minister Golda Meir told the General Assembly that Israel would remove its forces from the Gulf of Aqaba and Straits of Tiran region and from the Gaza Strip area so that UNEF could enter. Lodge spoke immediately afterward to give the Israeli statement the full support of the United States. In the field, Burns met with Israel's General Yigael Dayan and soon worked out an agreement. By March 8, UNEF had taken over from the Israeli forces and was in position in the Gaza Strip and in Sharm el Sheikh.[11]

Hammarskjöld had served as the center of delicate and difficult parleys and at every stage had given them a tone and flavor, even if some critics thought them excessively legalistic and ambiguous.[12] In the process, the persuasive force of the Secretary-General had been used to its limit.

The continued stubbornness of the Israeli government—its suspicions were not unreasonable, as the subsequent Egyptian take-over in Gaza was to testify—gave way not so much before the ingenuity of Hammarskjöld's diplomacy or the demands of the majority of the

General Assembly as under the pressure of the United States. The work done by Hammarskjöld and his agents in the field may have helped Israel to accommodate its policies to the program of the General Assembly, for the Egyptian position was subsumed under a United Nations plan; thus, the Ben Gurion government did not seem merely to be bowing to the wishes of the power it had just defeated in battle.

Nevertheless, there was little divergence between Hammarskjöld's position, based on an interpretation of the resolutions of the General Assembly, and Nasser's demands. The Israeli government scarcely misunderstood the situation, and its behavior soon left the Secretary-General with the unpleasant alternatives of relying on diplomatic skill alone; calling for positive actions, such as sanctions, from the General Assembly or the Security Council; or combining his work with the pressure that could be built up elsewhere in the diplomatic landscape. He chose the last alternative and exploited it with adroitness. And in doing so, he demonstrated that the resources at the command of the office of Secretary-General in peace-keeping operations are severely limited when it becomes necessary to deal with a convinced and determined government.

Belgium. The task assigned the Secretary-General with regard to the Belgian withdrawal, on which ONUC's operations hinged, was in principle not different from that given him in the Suez crisis. The immediate response from Belgium to demands from the Security Council that its troops give way to ONUC was at least as favorable as the Anglo-French reaction to the similar request in the Suez area. In fact, even before the Security Council adopted its formal call to Belgium to withdraw, its representative pledged that "[w]hen the United Nations forces have, as the Belgian government hopes, moved into position and are able to ensure the effective maintenance of order and the security of persons in the Congo, my Government will proceed to withdraw its intervening metropolitan forces, which are at present alone capable of ensuring the accomplishment of these ends." [13]

The speed with which ONUC was formed and deployed made it possible for Belgium to begin withdrawal from the Leopoldville area within less than a week after the Security Council first acted. By

July 23, according to an agreement signed with the Belgian commander, all troops in the Leopoldville area were to have been withdrawn and the first units left a week before that. Nevertheless, the Congolese government exhibited high dissatisfaction with this progress. The Security Council again called on Belgium to withdraw, despite an emotional speech by Foreign Minister Pierre Wigny, who had come to New York, where he maintained the position that his government's troops would be sent out of the Congo as soon as ONUC could provide for law and order. He even declared that Belgium, having faith in the judgment of the Secretary-General, would take no arbitrary position on when law and order had been restored. The clear implication was that Hammarskjöld would have a great deal to do with timing of the Belgian withdrawal.[14]

It is hard to believe that initially the Belgian government had intended anything more than the protection of its nationals in the face of a threat which, hindsight tells us, was exaggerated. Even if there had been a hope in some hearts that the colony could be retrieved, the grave and virtually unanimous demands abroad that Belgium withdraw would have been a persuasive counter-argument. Nor is there evidence of a plan to stay on for an extended time. In the Security Council, Belgium, which its representatives rather sadly described more than once as only a small country, came under the degree of pressure which Israel, France, and the United Kingdom had not been able to withstand during the Suez conflict. Moreover, the highly satisfactory speed with which ONUC appeared on the scene soon provided the conditions for withdrawal which Belgium itself had proposed.

The promise of cooperative relations with the Belgian government soon became doubtful as the result of the efforts by the provincial government of Katanga, led by Moïse Tshombé, to secede and set up an independent state. In several important ways, Hammarskjöld and the Belgian government reacted identically. Both regarded Katanga as a matter of Congolese internal politics, which could not be settled from the outside. Neither showed any intention of using direct force for the benefit of either the Tshombé or Lumumba governments. Both professed the desirability of the withdrawal of the 1,700 Belgian troops as quickly as possible. And both implicitly or explicitly put the responsibility for deciding when the conditions for a withdrawal had been met directly and personally on the Secretary-General.

Yet a note of reserve was soon sounded. As early as August 2, Wigny said that his government was obliged to "face facts," asserting that in Katanga, unlike elsewhere in the Congo, law and order prevailed and work went on. The implication was that the continued presence of Belgian troops guaranteed future law and order. But Belgium continued to take the position that it would offer no resistance to United Nations troops. "No Belgian officer will take part in any such operation," Wigny declared to the Security Council.[15]

Meanwhile, Hammarskjöld had instructed Bunche to take ONUC to Katanga and received the latter's discouraging report on the prospect of doing so without violence. The Secretary-General consequently came back to the Security Council for further instructions. The presence in fact of Belgian troops in Katanga, he asserted, "now is the main cause of continued danger," [16] although it was Belgian policy to remove them as soon as possible. He interpreted the Belgian position as giving ONUC little help though not opposing its entry. Because it was necessary for the withdrawal of the Belgians to be followed immediately, if not preceded by, the entry of ONUC into Katanga, where the provincial government stood in the way, a circular situation (similar to that at the beginning of UNEF) had developed.

Hammarskjöld's approach had a subtlety that matched the nuances in the position of the Belgian government. By pointing out the reinforcing effect of Belgian troops on the Katangese regime, he avoided accusing Brussels of any misdeeds. But his stand also provided him with leverage against the Katanga regime while not directly supporting the unifying aims of the Lumumba government. Furthermore, it helped to keep together the coalition in the Security Council which strongly objected to the initial Belgian action. The Secretary-General did not surrender his own opinion that the Belgian evacuation must take place very soon. At the same time he avoided having to admit either that Katanga would be unsafe for Europeans unless the Belgian forces were there, or that the United Nations had to await the pleasure of Brussels in entering Elisabethville.

The reaction in the Security Council strongly favored Hammarskjöld's position. Only France and Italy, whose delegates abstained, failed to give positive support to a draft which confirmed the authority of the Secretary-General to secure the withdrawal of Belgian troops and called upon the Brussels government to get its soldiers out of Katanga immediately "under speedy modalities determined by the Secretary-General." [17]

The adoption of the "speedy modalities" resolution early in August marked a considerable success for Hammarskjöld in keeping heavy international pressure on the Belgian government. The Eyskens government maintained its pledge to withdraw as soon as the Secretary-General could inform it that Belgian citizens would be safe. The responsibility implied by this policy was readily assumed by Hammarskjöld. But Foreign Minister Wigny did not accept the new resolution without registering objections to the pressure which the Secretary-General had helped to organize.

Hammarskjöld personally and with considerable daring arranged the entry of United Nations troops into Elisabethville by the middle of August, 1960. By August 21 the Secretary-General was able to report that almost all Belgian soldiers had left. Some non-combat personnel would be retained, he said, so that the problem of Congolese dependence on employment at the Kamina and Kitona bases could be dealt with, but the United Nations should ensure that the remaining personnel would have no political influence. Hammarskjöld even spoke of the evacuation of the Belgian forces as entitling the Council to the expectation that the threat to international peace and security had been ended.[18] Some delays were encountered, apparently as much because of technical reasons as any others, and by the beginning of September Hammarskjöld and the Belgian government were still exchanging explanations about the need for speed and the reasons for lack of it in evacuating the last remaining soldiers. Hammarskjöld increased the pressure and exhibited some impatience with the repeated delays when his representative discovered some 650 combat soldiers in the Congo five days after the Belgian deadline.[19]

In fact, the organized Belgian military forces under the direct command of the Belgian defense establishment did leave the Congo and Katanga with reasonable speed, considering the reasons which impelled them to come in the first place. As far as the first operational stage of ONUC was concerned, Hammarskjöld, backed by the Security Council, had proved influential and effective. The proof was the presence of ONUC detachments throughout the country.

Netherlands. Setting the peace-keeping force for West New Guinea to its task proved far less difficult than in any other instance. Above all, the simplicity of the operation depended on the absence of a large-scale confrontation between Dutch and Indonesian forces. Moreover, the Dutch government was anxious to withdraw its forces under an agreement that provided more precise and comprehensive arrangements than other peace-keeping situations permitted.

The withdrawal of Dutch forces was planned in detail, with participation by the Secretary-General's representatives, before the first UNSF units began arriving. A cease-fire was in effect and Indonesian units had been concentrated under the eyes of United Nations observers. José Rolz-Bennett of the Secretary-General's personal office worked out detailed arrangements for receiving the UNSF. After advance units landed in October, 1962, final plans were made for phasing out the Dutch military forces, and the UNSF took up its positions without incident.[20] Thus, in a largely technical operation, the policies of the Secretary-General necessarily dominated and were free of interference from the tension which characterized the UNEF and ONUC operations.

Cyprus. The relative simplicity of the West New Guinea operation contrasted sharply with the complexity in which UNFICYP was interposed. On a crowded and mountainous island, three separate armed forces had taken up positions and had clashed with enough vigor to create an international crisis. UNFICYP's assignment was not to take over as invading troops withdrew, but rather to try to prevent further violence.

UNFICYP was assembled with notably less dispatch than UNEF and ONUC forces. But once its advance units were ready, they entered Cyprus with little difficulty. They were joined by the British forces, which were placed under United Nations command. Thus, UNFICYP came into possession of some strategic spots immediately.

UNFICYP had to take positions and to intervene between clashing troops without using force. To do so, it had to engage in a large number of *ad hoc* negotiations on the spot. This procedure differed markedly from the more regulated patterns in early instances. It also required close limits on the UNFICYP command.

"The plain fact . . . is," Thant reported after the first six months of operations, "that the United Nations Force in Cyprus is in the most delicate position that any United Nations mission has ever experienced, for it is not only in the midst of a bitter civil war, but it is dangerously interposed between the two sides of that war." [21]

Adapting to Changing Conditions

From the time a peace-keeping force takes up its positions, the Secretary-General must adapt its work to changes in its political and military environment. Such changes have created great difficulties for the Secretary-General and even extreme diminution of his influence. They also have offered opportunities for exerting influence.

The presence of a peace-keeping force induces changes. No matter how nonpartisan its instructions may be, it has an immediate military effect, for it reduces or halts any fighting and leaves clashing armies suspended in their positions. In some cases, as in Suez, the employment of a United Nations force results in the withdrawal of invaders from prized territory. Each emergency force has had instructions to avoid taking sides in local politics. Yet in such a situation as the Congo, the presence of a peace-keeping force must necessarily affect internal political trends if in no other way than by protecting politicians who might otherwise be assassinated or imprisoned.

Other changes are imposed on the peace-keeping forces. The host government may alter policies which originally favored active employment of the peace-keeping force. It may revoke its welcome. It may obstruct the operation of a force or violate its cease-fire undertakings. Or it may seek to undermine the Secretary-General's influence in deliberative organs. Or, as in the Congo, contributing governments may unilaterally withdraw their soldiers because of disagreements with policies or dissatisfaction over developments in the host country.

Changes can also be induced by shifts in other national policies. An influential government, responding to stimuli from its own people or to a new perception of its interests, can impede the work of United Nations deliberative organs. The resulting situation can seriously reduce the ability of the Secretary-General to act with reliable backing, and can block formal alteration of his mandate to deal with new situations faced by peace-keeping forces.

Finally, changes in peace-keeping situations can be induced by the settlement of the underlying causes of conflict. Such a settlement obviates the need for the force. In such a case, the Secretary-General would usually call for the end of his peace-keeping mandate.

The Secretary-General may respond to changing conditions in several ways, depending on the situation and his estimate of it. He may seek new—or reaffirmation of—previous instructions from the deliberative organ which is responsible for the peace-keeping force, or he may ask for guidance from another organ. He may develop new interpretations of his mandate, either on his own responsibility or after discussions with interested governments or with any consultative organs which may have been established. He may seek additional material support from governments. Or he may urge that his mandate be ended and take actions to support such a step.

Much of the record of the Secretary-General's management of peace-keeping forces consists of attempts to adapt missions to new conditions, which differ vastly in character and cause. It is therefore impossible to give a comprehensive account here. Rather, illustrations of various attempts to adapt to changing conditions will be employed in the following discussions. Many of the major examples will come from ONUC, which demanded unparalleled efforts from the Secretary-General. Other peace-keeping forces have also provided at least some instances of challenge as a result of new conditions.

Reference to Deliberative Organs. The Secretary-General or any member of the United Nations may take the initiative in opening a discussion in the Security Council or General Assembly, as appropriate, of the instruction given with regard to a peace-keeping force. Such a discussion can either enhance or reduce the influence of the Secretary-General. It can give him more specific instructions or leave untouched or weakened a mandate which imperfectly covers a changed situation.

The Secretary-General, if he has rather secure support for the policies his peace-keeping force is following, may propose reference to a deliberative organ as a means of applying pressure to a reluctant government. Hammarskjöld employed this tactic in attempting to speed the withdrawal of Israeli troops from the Gaza Strip and the Gulf of Aqaba. In this case, he probably augmented his ability to persuade the Israeli government.

In the early stages of the Katanga secession, Hammarskjöld intensified his pressure on Belgium to make way for ONUC in Elisabethville by asking the Security Council for clarification of his mandate. He sought explicit authority to make the necessary arrangements with Belgium to take over the task of maintaining law and order in Katanga, thus satisfying Belgian objections to early withdrawal of remaining troops. A favorable Security Council commended his earlier work and gave him the backing he wanted. When Bunche reported his inability to secure the entry of ONUC into Elisabethville, the Secretary-General once again successfully went to the Security Council for further backing. [22]

The Katanga problem, an outstanding example of an internal development which required adaptation on the part of the Secretary-General, led to a breakdown of relations between the Secretary-General and the Congolese Premier. Hammarskjöld saw the cause of the quarrel in the question of the use to which ONUC should be put. Lumumba insisted that the force should primarily serve the aims of the Central Government, leading Hammarskjöld to put his opposed view before the Security Council.

The Congolese Premier became violently angry when Hammarskjöld led ONUC troops into Katanga without bringing units of the Armée Nationale Congolaise (ANC) along. "[T]he Government and people of the Congo," Lumumba declared, "have lost their confidence in the Secretary-General of the United Nations," and in effect proposed his replacement by a committee of African states.[23]

By this time, developments in the policy of the Soviet Union added to the changing situation in which ONUC was finding itself. Opposed to Hammarskjöld's cautious policy toward internal Congolese affairs, the Soviet Union gave Lumumba aircraft and other support. The Soviet Union and Poland severely criticized ONUC policies, which Hammarskjöld stoutly defended. Although several members of the Council supported the Secretary-General, the discussion did not encourage the adoption of a resolution. On this occasion, then, the Secretary-General failed to get an explicit reaffirmation of his mandate and formal support for his interpretation of it.[24]

From this time on, the confusion of Congolese politics and the opportunistic policies followed by an influential handful of United Nations members imposed on ONUC and the Secretary-General the necessity to adapt frantically to situations increasingly built up of contradictory elements. Hammarskjöld's abilities to influence the Security Council and the General Assembly waned and waxed rapidly and without predictability.

The Security Council, for example, reflected the widening disparity of views between Lumumba and the Soviet Union on the one hand and the Secretary-General and the majority on the other. It was unable to act in September, 1960, after Cordier, then serving as the Secretary-General's representative in Leopoldville, closed all airports and radio stations in the Congo amid a governmental crisis caused by the issue of Soviet aid and the dismissal of Lumumba by President Joseph Kasavubu. The *coup d'état* produced soon afterward by Colonel Joseph Mobutu and the army did little to clarify the situation. Hammarskjöld made a long and spirited statement in which he in effect demanded that the Security Council request that all aid to the Congo be channeled through the United Nations, a policy he had attempted to apply from the beginning.[25] The Council could agree on nothing, and summoned the General Assembly into an emergency special session, immediately preceding the regular session.

The emergency special session in effect was a triumph for Hammarskjöld's policies. He received a specific recommendation to continue the execution of the mandate given him by the Security Council.[26] Members were asked not to provide military aid to the Congo, except through the ONUC channel. Hammarskjöld had every right to point up the fact of his policy leadership by noting the "correspondence between the attitude reflected in the resolution and that of the Secretariat as presented most recently." [27]

Yet a scant three months later the General Assembly could not respond to the Secretary-General's pleas for additional support and instructions in dealing with an even more confused Congo. Some of his African supporters were beginning to withdraw their troops.

Financing was becoming a crucial matter. The very office of Secretary-General was under severe attack. The unfortunate Lumumba was under arrest and thus the immediate cause of a crisis. The Security Council—to which Hammarskjöld declared that "the United Nations Force, the United Nations Command, is the only body that can today rescue the Congo from the situation into which it has fallen" [28]—could adopt no resolution. And when the debates were repeated in the General Assembly, it could do no more than state that previously adopted resolutions were still in effect.[29]

Hammarskjöld nevertheless made the best of his resources. In a long letter to Kasavubu, he not only pointed out that his previous instructions remained in effect but also argued that a large enough number of governments had indicated support for the draft resolution before the General Assembly so that Kasavubu would do well to pay attention to them. The United States and the United Kingdom had sponsored a resolution which failed by only one vote, Hammarskjöld noted, pointing out that there was serious determination to have him help keep law and order and to help in the reconvening of parliament. The Secretary-General insisted that the votes for the resolutions demonstrated a firm intention not to dissociate the United Nations from Congolese affairs. He warned again that if a civil war developed, ONUC would be withdrawn, producing exactly the kind of consequences which the majority was anxious to avoid.[30]

The deliberative organs themselves can take the initiative in revising the Secretary-General's mandate. To a considerable degree this occurred after the murder of Lumumba while in the custody of the Katanga authorities in February, 1961. Since the beginning of that month, Hammarskjöld had been taking part in Security Council debates,[31] with little visible success, in an effort to get an explicit statement that his mandate included the reorganization of the ANC to get it out of political life. The storm of indignation that followed the killing of Lumumba cast up the broadest mandate yet given to the Secretary-General and ONUC.

The members of the Council (with France and the Soviet Union abstaining) decided that the United Nations should take measures to prevent civil war, using force if necessary.[32] The Secretary-General had never directly requested the right to use force, although he had at times remarked that no part of his mandate entitled him to do so. The resolution also urged the departure of Belgian and other foreign paramilitary personnel, the reconvening of the Congolese parliament, and the retraining of the ANC. These last two provisions accorded precisely with Hammarskjöld's ideas. He nevertheless did not get everything he expressly hoped for in the revised mandate, for he still could not control the import of arms or funds into the Congo.

Thant has not referred to deliberative organs for new or revised instructions for peace-keeping forces as frequently or positively as Hammarskjöld did. The Security Council nevertheless discussed the Katanga problem in November, 1961, and strengthened the mandate of the then Acting Secretary-General.[33]

This attempt to adapt the role of ONUC to a new situation came soon after the failure of Operation Morthor, ordered by Conor Cruise O'Brien in a controversial attempt to end the Katanga secession; the death of Hammarskjöld; and the appointment of Thant as Acting Secretary-General. Thant does not appear to have arranged the summoning of the Security Council in November, 1961, after nine months of inactivity on the Congo problem. But the all-African trio of governments—Ethiopia, Nigeria, and the Sudan—which called for the meetings had always been in close touch with ONUC and had contributed troops to it.

After a debate centering on the activities of Belgian nationals and mercenaries who supported the Katanga regime, the Security Council (with France and the United Kingdom abstaining) adopted a strong resolution which authorized the Secretary-General to take vigorous action, including the use of force, to bring to trial or deportation foreign military personnel and political advisers not under the United Nations command. This broadened and reinterpreted the Secretary-General's mandate, giving him added authority to deal with the hardening Katanga problem.

Thant, who undoubtedly was completely informed and consulted on this resolution, intervened only after it had been adopted. By denouncing the activities of the Katanga mercenaries as intolerable, he showed himself fully in accord with the intentions of the Council. He promised to discharge his mandate with "determination and vigor" and offered to redouble peaceful efforts to end the secession.

For all of Thant's positive reaction, he had nevertheless kept his influence on the Security Council in the background and, unlike Hammarskjöld, had not taken up a position of open leadership. This became the new Secretary-General's usual practice.

In the case of Cyprus, however, the Secretary-General took the responsibility for leading the Security Council to a renewal of UNFICYP's mandate as a response to conditions on the island. After UNFICYP's first three months, the period of authority specified when it was organized, Thant secured the support of the parties for an additional three-month period. The Council reacted favorably, and during the next two years, at his suggestion, repeatedly extended the life of the mission. The Secretary-General put written reports before the Council, explaining UNFICYP's operations and the need for its continued existence, but he did not demand a clarification of its mandate. The main adaptation he sought was the lengthening of UNFICYP's life so that mediation might be undertaken and brought to some conclusion.[34]

Interpreting Instructions. As the official responsible for peace-keeping forces, the Secretary-General responds quickly and directly to new situations and emergencies by interpreting his formal instructions. Such interpretations take the form of directives to the forces or of pronouncements of policies within which field commanders may operate, and are the usual and most frequent reaction to changing conditions. The influence of the Secretary-General dominates in interpreting his formal instructions, and as a result he has deeply affected the policies and activities of member governments.

In the UNEF operation, the Secretary-General worked closely with the General Assembly in spelling out his mandate and getting specific approval of his policies. Once UNEF took up its positions, it encountered relatively few challenges and had only minor adaptations to make. Therefore, his directives and policies in that instance were less striking than those for ONUC, whose record from beginning to end abounds with cases in which the Secretary-General had to interpret his instructions.

A remarkable early instance was the closing of the airports and radio stations by ONUC troops under Cordier's direction. This action, aimed at checking a threat to the maintenance of law and order from agitation by Lumumba acting with Soviet support, was taken without a direct order from Hammarskjöld. But he strongly supported it in statements immediately afterward, arguing that it was consistent with his mandate.[35] It had the effect, whether or not it was intended, of weakening Lumumba's political position and of worsening ONUC's relations with his supporters.

Thant's use of ONUC's military capacity in Katanga on two occasions under interpretation of his mandate constitute milestones in the United Nations involvement with the Congo. In both instances, in December, 1961 and a year later, the Secretary-General was responding to threats and violence which might have ended his and ONUC's influence in Katanga.

When Katangese forces installed roadblocks in December, 1961 which threatened the eventual encirclement and immobilization of ONUC in Elisabethville, the result demonstrated that Thant had decided on a policy of less reserve in the use of force. This decision applied the mandate he had been given a month earlier by the Security Council and the agreement with the Congolese government that ONUC should have freedom of movement. The Secretary-General directed ONUC to restore order in Elisabethville. The continued harassment of ONUC by mercenaries led George Ivan Smith and Brian Urquhart, the senior United Nations officials in Elisabethville, to the conclusion that the Katangese planned to attack. The ONUC force received instructions to move against them. That these orders had the approval of the Acting Secretary-General was underlined by his message of praise for ONUC's restraint up to that time.[36]

The power of the ONUC force implied the near certainty that the Katanga regime would disappear if the fighting continued. Another result of the fighting could be seen in intense diplomatic consultations in Washington, London, and Paris. In all three capitals, a strong segment of opinion opposed the use of force and some favored the Katanga regime.[37] The fact that the Acting Secretary-General was applying force with increasing success, put him in a position of exceptional influence on Katanga and turned him into a central figure in the diplomatic efforts directed toward achieving a cease-fire.

Thant refused to stop ONUC's campaign short of a favorable outcome, even though he was feeling strong pressure from Britain and France. ONUC officials in Leopoldville and Elisabethville so thoroughly distrusted Tshombé that they balked at anything in the nature of a phased cease-fire. The United States clearly supported ONUC. The United Kingdom formally demanded a cease-fire. The Soviet position exhibited little agreement in principle, either with that of the Secretary-General or the United States. By pressing for a quick end to the Katangese secession through the use of force, however, the Soviet Union in fact was interfering far less with the Secretary-General's policy than were the British and French governments. Most African states either acquiesced or gave Thant their backing.[38]

The multifaceted pressure on Katanga which built up as a result of the ONUC force's action helped make successful Thant's suggestion that Congolese Premier Cyrille Adoula and Tshombé meet at the Kitona base under ONUC protection. The Acting Secretary-General made it clear that the ONUC forces would resume their action if the Kitona talks were obstructed. An agreement was in fact reached.[39]

The final use of the ONUC force in Katanga in December, 1962 followed the failure by Tshombé to permit the application of the Kitona agreement. United Nations officials exercised endless but futile ingenuity in trying to bring Tshombé and Adoula to a new agreement.[40]

Thant interpreted this situation as requiring new and strong efforts. He embarked on extensive consultations, many of which were carried out in Europe, and obtained close collaboration from Belgium, the United Kingdom, and the United States.[41] The Secretary-General then developed an extraordinarily far-reaching plan for dealing with Katanga within his mandate as he interpreted it.

The new plan consisted of a number of provisions which had to be accepted in their entirety; if they were not, the Secretary-General intended to organize a series of economic and diplomatic sanctions to force the Tshombé government to integrate with Leopoldville. The Acting Secretary-General's initiative had taken a concrete form as early as mid-August, when the details of a "Plan of National Conciliation" were decided upon and transmitted to Robert Gardiner, the head of ONUC, for further action.[42] The plan itself read like an agenda of the main political disagreements dividing the Tshombé and Adoula governments. It proposed a federal constitution; sharing of the tax revenues between provincial and national governments; unification of the currency, the armed forces, and the channels through which foreign governments would be dealt with; a general amnesty; and a revised pattern of representation for political groups in the Central Government. ONUC would have an important share in working out the details of the plan and would provide expert advice on a new constitution. In return, it would receive the full cooperation of all parties.

The Thant plan was set before the Tshombé and Adoula governments by August 24, and the Katanga authorities had ten days within which to accept or reject it as a whole. Both Tshombé and Adoula approved the plan by September 3, and for the moment Thant had no reason to order the application of further pressure. But by the middle of November, Gardiner reported from Leopoldville that "it was becoming ever more obvious that the reintegration of Katanga, under the Secretary-General's plan or otherwise was far removed from the minds of the Secessionist leaders." [43] He had plenty of evidence on which to base his claim. Not only had the negotiations come to nothing, but also an increasingly formidable Katangese *gendarmerie* had been harassing the ONUC forces continually since September.

The ONUC head, who certainly had the approval of the Secretary-General, told Tshombé on December 10 that the full gamut of pressures sketched in Thant's plan would now be applied. He referred to the readiness of the ONUC force to take defensive measures.

The growing pressure on Tshombé, who was playing out the last negotiating hand, reached the breaking point on Christmas Eve, when a considerable amount of firing began in Elisabethville. The ONUC forces restrained themselves and in the following days came under increasing Katangese fire. Tshombé laid down the final challenge on December 29 in a statement demanding the end of ONUC roadblocks under the threat of a scorched earth policy. The United Nations force replied with military action "to restore the security of ONUC troops . . . and their freedom of movement." [44]

Wherever the ONUC force encountered it, the *gendarmerie*

melted away. The ONUC force not only established order again in the Katangese capital but spread out into the surrounding countryside and went on to Kamina, Kipushi, and finally on January 4 to Jadotville, where the mercenaries furnished the sole example of earth-scorching of which Tshombé had warned. In fact, the advance took place so rapidly toward Jadotville along a mined road and over the wrecked bridge that Leopoldville and the Secretary-General's office in New York lost control of the movements of the ONUC force.

Tshombé had fled at the beginning of the battle in Elisabethville. At Kolwezi on January 13, he proclaimed the end of the Katangese secession. The declaration became final for all practical purposes on January 21, when ONUC moved into Kolwezi in the presence of Tshombé and his ministers. Joseph Iléo, representing Premier Cyrille Adoula, met with the Katangese cabinet to take over the functions of government before the end of January.

As the Katangese fuse sputtered out, the Secretary-General reached the height of his influence in the Congo. It was built in considerable part on the military action which he ordered as a means of carrying out his mandate in the face of new conditions. It produced direct effects on the Katanga government, whose forces were in fact defeated. It also evoked great political activity on the part of member governments. The political outcome within Congolese borders was the reunification of the country and the elimination of the threat of Katangese secession. The Secretary-General certainly was one of the main, if not the dominant, influences in this development.

The West New Guinea and Cyprus peace-keeping assignments also include examples of interpretation of his mandate by the Secretary-General to meet changing situations. These examples do not have the forceful character that the use of ONUC's military arm had. But they illustrate the usual technique by which the Secretary-General adapts to change without consulting the deliberative organ from which his mandate comes.

Soon after the evacuation of Dutch troops from West New Guinea, Indonesia began to urge the Secretary-General to end United Nations administration of the area and withdraw the UNSF before the earliest scheduled date. Indonesia was to take over the administration some time after May 1, 1963.

Thant responded to Indonesian pressure in two ways. He stated publicly that he could not alter the minimum period of United Nations administration without the agreement of both parties and action by the General Assembly. At the same time, he scheduled the turnover of authority for the earliest possible date. He thus went as far as possible within his mandate to meet Indonesian demands. But he limited the effect of Indonesian pressure on the plans for the West New Guinea mission.[45]

In Cyprus, UNFICYP made at least some progress in stabilizing the situation, but the host government in effect continued to impede its work by a disinclination to reduce the number of armed personnel on the island.[46] Thant therefore sought a more fundamental approach to the conflict than the stationing of a peace-keeping force.

Acting within the terms of his mandate as he interpreted it, Thant appointed a Mediator to attempt to harmonize the policies of the governments of Cyprus, Turkey, and Greece.[47] The Secretary-General attempted to seize the initiative before the uneasy truce in Cyprus broke irreparably and to stimulate talks among the governments. He formulated a program of action to that end but in no respect attempted to use it as a means of intense pressure as he did with his plan for Katanga. These moves broadened the scope of the Secretary-General's involvement in Cyprus and probably contributed considerably to the maintenance of peace.

Completing Missions. Only two of the four peace-keeping assignments have resulted in the withdrawal of the forces under the Secretary-General's direction. UNEF and UNFICYP remain at their stations long after original expectations.

The Secretary-General can have a great influence on bringing a mission to an end, for his reports to the deliberative organs can persuasively plead that this mandate has been carried out and that force is no longer needed. Even without referring to a deliberative organ, the Secretary-General can usually release some of the national components of a force, reducing its military capacity. Or he can narrow the scope of its operations in response to favorable local conditions.

The termination of the UNSF in West New Guinea fitted into the limits set by preliminary plans. The UNSF was simply withdrawn in favor of the Indonesian armed force which was to occupy the area from the end of the United Nations administration until the outcome of a plebiscite scheduled for 1969. After Thant decided to turn the area over to Indonesian administration on May 1, 1963, the earliest possible date under his instructions, it was a foregone conclusion that the UNSF would not be needed after that time. It was phased out as Indonesian forces entered the area and Thant was able to report that his mission was completed.

Little in the entire life of ONUC went according to plan, and certainly the termination of the Secretary-General's peace-keeping assignment did not. Two main factors bore on the withdrawal of the ONUC force by mid-1964. The first of these was the integration of Katanga with the rest of the Congo and the second was the severe financial crisis.

The collapse of Tshombé's power in Katanga meant that the Secretary-General could report to the Security Council that four main aspects of his mandate had been largely fulfilled.[48] The threat to the territorial integrity and political independence of the Congo was at an end, civil war had been prevented, foreign military and paramilitary personnel had been removed, and vast improvements had been made in maintaining law and order. On his own initiative, Thant began planning a substantial reduction in the ONUC force.

This reduction could be questioned on political grounds. The Adoula government was by no means anxious to reduce ONUC's pacifying effects. The situation in the Congo, moreover, had not yet achieved any genuine stability, as the Secretary-General acknowledged, and the withdrawal of peace-keeping forces could conceivably cause another breakdown.

Yet at the height of the financial crisis, the Secretary-General had little alternative but to reduce the forces sharply. It was doubtful at the time that enough support to pay past bills, let alone future expenditures, would be forthcoming. The reduction of the ONUC force on the ground that the mandate had largely been fulfilled was an attractive rationale for a Secretary-General who had to face the somber financial outlook of early 1963.

The decisions relating to the phasing out of the ONUC force were hardly clear-cut. Part of the ONUC mandate—assistance for the retraining of the ANC—had not been fulfilled, but in view of the financial crisis alone it was unlikely that the Secretary-General could do much about it. Thant therefore encouraged planning, led by the United States, to provide bilateral aid channeled through the United

Nations. But when the Adoula government announced that it was seeking direct bilateral aid in modernizing the ANC, Thant refused to give his support in view of the policy that all assistance should be channeled through the United Nations.[49]

The Adoula government nevertheless sought a prolongation of the ONUC force to help deal with persistent turbulence in the Congo. The force had already been reduced, and Thant objected in September, 1963 that Adoula's request for some 3,000 officers and men would provide too little to be of practical value.[50] The Secretary-General showed anything but a warm desire to extend the life of the force.

The General Assembly responded half-heartedly to the Congolese appeal for continued aid, and closely to the Secretary-General's views on the importance of maintaining a reasonable level of troops, if any at all were to be present, and also of dissolving the ONUC force.[51] It decided to continue a financial account for ONUC only until June 30, 1964, at which time military aid from the United Nations would be ended. The last ONUC troops, who numbered 5,474 officers and men at the end of 1963, left the Congo on June 30, 1964.

The Secretary-General had been one of the dominant, if not the outstanding, influences in the decision to close down ONUC's military side. He not only helped determine the conditions which made a withdrawal of forces possible, but he also took the initiative in reducing them. His reports and negotiations shaped the views of members.

In general, the Secretary-General will have a great influence on deciding when a peace-keeping mission is to be ended if there is general agreement that much of his mandate has been fulfilled. If there is no such agreement, it is unlikely that he would suggest dissolving a peace-keeping force since to do so would tend to aggravate existing conflicts. Thus, success in employing a peace-keeping force increases the influence of the Secretary-General on the decision to withdraw it and terminate his mandate.

Commanders and Representatives

Because peace-keeping operations necessarily take place away from United Nations headquarters, the Secretary-General depends on a field staff for the execution of his directives and for information and advice about new developments and future plans. As is the case with his top-level officials at headquarters, the field personnel can increase or make more effective his influence on policy issues, and can be selected so as to meet political exigencies. The principal field officers have included the commanders of peace-keeping forces and the representatives of the Secretary-General who have direct charge of operations.

The Secretary-General has been the single most important factor in the appointment of commanders for field forces. In the Congo, West New Guinea, and Cyprus cases he had the responsibility for appointing the commanders. In the case of UNEF, the General Assembly appoints the commanders, but in fact they are nominated only by the Secretary-General.

The Secretary-General is the source of general directives for the force commanders. His ability to exercise close supervision has varied from case to case and with the press of other urgent matters. Only in the Congo case, especially in Operation Morthor of August and September, 1961 and in the rapid advance of the ONUC force in Katanga at the end of 1962, is there evidence of an important breakdown in control from headquarters. Nevertheless, the appointment of a Military Adviser in the Secretary-General's office after the establishment of ONUC points to the existence of difficulties in translating policies into action in the field.

Fundamental qualifications for the commanders of peace-keeping forces have included nationalities which caused no immediate objection from concerned governments, wide experience, and senior rank. Thus, Irish, Ethiopian, and Swedish generals have commanded ONUC, and Indians headed UNEF and UNFICYP. Because the UNSF in West New Guinea was almost entirely from Pakistan, a senior officer of that country headed it.

Several of the most important appointments tapped earlier experience with the United Nations. General Burns, suggested by Hammarskjöld to the General Assembly as commander for UNEF, was in charge of UNTSO and had represented Canada in the General Assembly. General von Horn also was commanding UNTSO when he was made first commander of ONUC forces. General P.S. Gyani was shifted from command of UNEF to UNFICYP.

The Secretary-General took a leading role in working out the arrangement for the entry, deployment, and advance of UNEF. He personally negotiated many details of UNEF's military mission with the Egyptian and Israeli governments. His instructions went directly to Burns without any intervening level of officialdom. In other peace-keeping assignments, the Secretary-General appointed a civilian official to take charge of the field mission and to a greater or lesser degree left immediate management of the force and political and diplomatic tasks to him.

Hammarskjöld tended to involve himself personally more frequently in the detailed direction of UNEF and ONUC than Thant did with them and with succeeding missions. Hammarskjöld made two important trips to the Congo for the purpose of negotiating directly with the Leopoldville and Elisabethville governments. His death occurred on the second of these trips. Thant has not visited peace-keeping missions, and has tended to emphasize the importance of his subordinates in the field.

Both Hammarskjöld and Thant have employed special staffs in their own office to supervise the activities of the peace-keeping missions. In the case of UNEF, Bunche and Cordier were the key officials. They served in equally important roles in the "Congo Club," which included a few more top officials than the UNEF effort. Bunche has continued to have an important function in other peace-keeping enterprises. The Military Adviser to the Secretary-General also has assisted.

All of the chief civilian officers of the peace-keeping missions had important experience in the service of the United Nations. Bunche first had charge of the Congo enterprise. Cordier succeeded him. He was followed by Rajeshwar Dayal, who was one of the three members of the Observer Group in Lebanon. Mekki Abbas, Executive Secretary of the United Nations Economic Commission for Africa, took over and was followed by Sture Linner, who headed the technical and civil assistance activities in the Congo. He was then succeeded by Robert Gardiner, who had carried out important political negotiations with the Congolese government.

In West New Guinea, the Secretary-General appointed Djalal Abdoh of Iran as United Nations Administrator. Abdoh had been United Nations Plebiscite Administrator in the British Cameroons in 1959 and 1960.

The arrangements in Cyprus were more complex. Thant was instructed by the Security Council to appoint a Mediator to deal with the fundamental issues in the conflict. He first sought to appoint Rolz-Bennett, whom Turkey would not accept, and then selected Sakari S. Tuomioja of Finland, who had represented the Secretary-General in Laos, to consult with the governments of Cyprus, Turkey, Greece, and the United Kingdom in an effort to work out a long-term solution. In addition, Thant appointed Galo Plaza of Ecuador, who also had been one of the Observer Group in Lebanon, as his Special Representative in Cyprus, with an administrative and negotiating assignment separate from that of the Mediator. The Special Representative's function was akin to that of the officer-in-charge of ONUC. After Tuomioja's death, Galo Plaza took his place.

The chief officers of the field missions served both as administrative aides for the Secretary-General and as sources of advice and information. Gardiner, for example, had much to do with the development of Thant's plan for dealing with Katanga. These officers could be a source of strength or of difficulty for the Secretary-General, and sometimes had substantial influence on the host governments. Two examples from ONUC's experience illustrate these effects.

Dayal's tenure in the Congo proved controversial, and his relations with the Leopoldville government became unpleasant and unprofitable. His reports had a remarkably frank and cogent quality. In the face of the Congolese constitutional crisis of September, 1960, for example, Dayal remarked that "almost every significant measure taken by ONUC . . . has been interpreted by one faction or another as being directed against itself by the United Nations." [52] Dayal insisted that he had to deal with whomever he could find in authority, and left no doubt that General Mobutu's improvised government had no legal standing and no more effectiveness than the ANC gave it. This and other independent opinions and actions proved highly irritating to Kasavubu, who demanded Dayal's recall.[53] After the Congolese President accused Dayal of dereliction of duty, the Secretary-General responded that "Ambassador Dayal is not a diplomatic representative accredited to . . . the Congo and he can therefore not be subject to a declaration that he is *persona non grata,*" [54] and also put the matter to the Security Council. In the end, Dayal had to be replaced so that ONUC could carry on its work in a more favorable atmosphere.

After Dayal's replacement by Abbas, who was welcomed with a brass band, the Secretary-General augmented the political staff in Leopoldville with two more Africans, Gardiner, and Francis Nwokedi. They conducted careful negotiations with the Leopoldville government on the basis of the Security Council's resolution of February 21, 1961, and finally on April 17 reached an agreement aimed at the replacement of foreign personnel in the service of the government and the reorganization of the ANC. This understanding inaugurated a new spirit of cooperation, which was fed with another agreement early in June to provide the Congo with $10 million in immediate funds.[55]

From the base of the April 17 agreement, the ONUC officials began working toward the reconvening of parliament, an end which the Security Council had endorsed and which the Congolese constitutional conference at Coquilhatville also favored. The representatives of the Secretary-General in Leopoldville were deeply involved in the discussions of arrangements for the parliament. It met at Lovanium University on July 22, behind a tight security ring. ONUC forces guaranteed the safety of the members of parliament.[56]

Inside the security ring, Gardiner and Mahmoud Khiari, a principal political adviser in ONUC, pressed for the selection of Cyrille Adoula as head of a new government. The Congolese parliament overwhelmingly approved the nomination of Adoula and the government chosen by him, and explicitly expressed gratitude to the United Nations. Adoula openly sought assistance from the United Nations when he informed Hammarskjöld of the end of the constitutional crisis. Hammarskjöld declared that he would deal with Adoula's government as the constitutional regime and that it would be the exclusive recipient of United Nations aid in the Congo. This statement signaled the renewal of the Secretary-General's strong influence in Leopoldville.

Advisory Comittees

On occasion, the Secretary-General has been provided with or has made use of advisory bodies composed of representatives of national governments. These advisory bodies can help to acquaint governments with the problems of peace-keeping and build a basis of support and legitimacy for changes and adjustments of his mandates. They can also usefully inform the Secretary-General of opinion in the General Assembly.

In the negotiations leading to the reconvening of the Congolese parliament, the Secretary-General had the support and counsel of an Advisory Committee on the Congo, made up of representatives of governments contributing to ONUC. This device for providing advice first appeared in the Suez case, when, as in the Congo, the Secretary-General needed every possible channel of close liaison with deliberative organs and member countries.[57] The use of advisory committees in peace-keeping assignments has attracted much favorable comment from observers. Hammarskjöld stated that the UNEF Committee performed "indispensable services" and that such bodies would be of value in future politico-military assignments and "represent a desirable development." [58]

Hammarskjöld himself suggested that the General Assembly appoint a small committee to take up those questions which his hurried planning for UNEF had not yet dealt with. In addition, he remarked that the body "might serve as an advisory committee to the Secretary-General for questions relating to the operations." [59] The General Assembly accepted and elaborated the concept of the advisory committee, reflecting sophisticated consideration that owes much to Hammarskjöld's own thought.

The Advisory Committee, according to the General Assembly resolution, had four specific functions. It had to develop planning for UNEF where the General Assembly had not acted and it was not the task of the commander to do so. It was to consult with the Secretary-General before essential regulations and instructions for UNEF were issued. It would then continue to assist the Secretary-General in undefined ways. Finally, it could request the convening of the General Assembly whenever it thought it important to do so. The Advisory Committee had the Secretary-General as its chairman, and its membership consisted of one representative each from Brazil, Canada, Ceylon, Colombia, India, Norway, and Pakistan.

Despite Hammarskjöld's later compliments for the work of the committee, it does not appear that it was a constant and crucial element in setting policy for UNEF. The Advisory Committee was composed of states that had expressed themselves in favor of the UNEF operations. Most of them had supplied troops. They could, therefore, have exercised considerable influence on the operation should it have begun to proceed in a manner contrary to their expectation. The membership of the Advisory Committee could from the start have been expected to favor the Hammarskjöld policies unless drastic mistakes or unexpected disasters developed. It is known, however, that the Secretary-General did consult the UNEF Advisory Committee from time to time, and it is probable that it met most frequently during the period of difficulty in securing the withdrawal of Israel from the Sinai Peninsula.

Because the committee advised the Secretary-General, who was its chairman, it could scarcely intercede entirely on its own initiative to attempt to influence or determine policy. As chairman, the Secretary-General controlled or at least greatly influenced its agenda and the frequency of its meetings. Although he would no doubt have reacted sensitively to complaints from its members, the smoothness which the operations of UNEF developed and the firm control over the negotiations with Israel and Egypt which Hammarskjöld maintained, seem to support an inference that the Advisory Committee served primarily to verify the existence of a consensus favoring the pattern he set for UNEF.

To the extent that the Advisory Committee served as a sounding board and a means for clarifying ideas and proposals,[60] it offered the Secretary-General a channel for maintaining and increasing his influence with the General Assembly, Egypt, Israel, and the contributing countries. The Advisory Committee appears never to have done anything to reduce that influence and certainly it never had to consider the possibility of summoning the General Assembly.

The Secretary-General did not immediately suggest to the Security Council that an Advisory Committee be established for ONUC. This omission is striking when the Secretary-General's comments on the relevance of the lessons of Suez to ONUC are recalled.

One possible explanation lies in the fact that action was taken initially by the Security Council. Since it comprises a rather intimate group as compared with the General Assembly and is always prepared to meet, Hammarskjöld may have thought it superfluous to create additional liaison channels. Yet such a view lacks logical consistency, for ONUC excluded the great powers, and the contributors to the force were not necessarily members of the organ. They could send representatives to debates which concerned them, but the influx of eight or ten temporary representatives tended to destroy intimacy.

Another possible explanation depends on the presence in New York of permanent missions from all of the donor countries. They could be consulted by the Secretary-General at any time, and furnished the normal channel of communication with the member governments. But similar delegations could have served in the UNEF operation, for which the Secretary-General found an advisory committee so valuable. In any case, the omission never was explained and ONUC began its work and reached impressive strength before such a body was suggested.

The first public suggestion of an advisory body for ONUC came from Premier Lumumba, who tried to get the Security Council to set up a group of observers on Congolese territory. The Soviet delegate immediately expressed his support, remarking that the observers might "facilitate the Secretary-General's task of implementing the Security Council's decisions,"[61] by which he meant an immediate and, if necessary, forcible entry into Katanga. Hammarskjöld took a noncommittal attitude, pointing out that high-ranking staff officers had already been furnished to ONUC by India, Morocco, Ethiopia, and Ghana. "I wonder," said Hammarskjöld, "in those circumstances if observers from those same countries, perhaps with an addition or two, could make a useful contribution."[62]

During the explosion in relations between Hammarskjöld and Lumumba, the Secretary-General attempted to transmute the Congolese suggestion of observers into a form that would accord with his own views and needs. He welcomed "a more formal and regular arrangement for the current and highly useful consultations which I have with the countries contributing units to the United Nations Force. If that would not meet any objection from the Council, it would therefore be my intention to invite the representatives of those countries to serve as members of an advisory committee to the Secretary-General personally, following the pattern established by the Advisory Committee functioning for UNEF."[63] By putting forward this suggestion, the Secretary-General made a tactical move to prevent the creation of a layer of obstructions in the direct relationship with his field representatives. The Soviet Union subsequently withdrew from the Security Council a draft resolution to establish a committee of observers, thus permitting Hammarskjöld's plan to prevail.

While no member of the Security Council, including the Soviet Union, explicitly objected to the Secretary-General's forming an Advisory Committee, it did not have the support of an authoritative vote in the Council. "[N]o Advisory Committee on the Congo officially exists," [64] the Soviet representative was able to claim later, correctly pointing out that the body formed by Hammarskjöld grew out of his own initiative.

Hammarskjöld built his committee around the representatives of the governments contributing troops to ONUC. It met with him before the end of August, 1960, to hear his report of the latest military and economic developments in the Congo. From that time on, it met frequently, although apparently without any set schedule. The occasional nature of its meetings indicated that the Secretary-General remained faithful to his intention that the body should advise him, not serve as another control on his policies.

It appears that both Hammarskjöld and Thant brought the ONUC Advisory Committee into most of their important decisions. It was consulted several times on the development of a policy toward Katanga and toward the Central Government. Such principals in the negotiations as Dayal, Rikhye, and Gardiner personally supplemented the reports of the Secretary-General. Thant appears to have employed the committee more fully than his predecessor, perhaps because of his style of diplomacy, or perhaps for no other reason than his adoption of policies with wide political ramifications, as in the case of his Katanga plan. In addition, he consulted the ONUC Advisory Committee on the attitude of the governments of the Rhodesian Federation and Portugal when the possibility of controls on arms and soldiers crossing the Congolese border was under consideration.[65]

Thant called the services of his Advisory Committee "invaluable," as Hammarskjöld had in the case of the UNEF group. The Congo body offered the Secretary-General a chance to "test proposed lines of actions," discuss national policies with regard to the ONUC operation, and receive "sound guidance." [66] The precise degree to which the Advisory Committee participated in the development of the Secretary-General's policy remains difficult to estimate in the absence of fuller information. But his policies, once discussed in the Advisory Committee, had necessarily a more persuasive ring. This persuasiveness and advance indication of approval by members contributed to the influence of the Secretary-General when the General Assembly and the Security Council examined the Congo operation.

On one outstanding occasion, the Advisory Committee on ONUC was treated by the General Assembly as a corporate body and as capable, despite some doubts about its legal character, of organizing a subsidiary with important political duties. This was the Conciliation Commission for the Congo.

Suggestions for a Conciliation Commission were first broached in the Security Council in September, 1960, following the *coup d'état* by Colonel Mobutu. Some explicit and interested support came from influential delegates but not enough to win Security Council approval. But several representatives urged the Secretary-General to take up the idea with the Advisory Committee.[67]

The idea of a Conciliation Commission emerged full-blown in the subsequent emergency special session of the General Assembly. It can be assumed that conversations with the Secretary-General had been held, for the chief administrative officer would necessarily be heavily involved in the new venture. The establishment of the commission was not made mandatory but permissible if other efforts to bring the Congolese leaders together failed. As the representative of Ghana explained it, the resolution adopted by the General Assembly foresaw the selection of a conciliation group by the Advisory Committee, in consultation with the Secretary-General, from the entire Asian-African membership of the organization, not just those contributing troops and therefore serving on the Advisory Committee. Other representatives made it clear that the commission would be established only if the Congolese government wanted its assistance.[68]

The conciliation group did not escape without challenge from the Communist bloc. The Soviet representative, Valerian Zorin, raised doubts about the legal existence of the Advisory Committee. He warned against giving the impression that consultations were to be imposed in violation of Congolese independence. His arguments, stated in an unusually reasonable manner for a debate on the Congo problem, received no real answer. Alex Quaison-Sackey of Ghana simply appealed to Zorin to respect the results of long consultations among the African and Asian delegations. Zorin heeded the plea and withdrew amendments he had offered.[69]

One of the few really clear points in the resolution [70] emphasized that the Secretary-General was not to be excluded from influence on the new committee. In selecting its membership, the Advisory Committee had to consult with the Secretary-General. He remained chairman of the Advisory Committee and would retain the influence emanating from that position. Yet even this source of influence might have waned, for the provisions of the General Assembly resolution implied that the Advisory Committee would act corporately in naming the members of the Conciliation Commission.

Before the actual appointment of the new body, the Secretary-General had ample time to consult with the members of the Advisory Committee. The consultations presumably ranged over the entire mandate of the commission. The Advisory Committee appointed the Conciliation Commission on November 5, 1960, and soon thereafter it took the initiative in going to the Congo. The membership of the commission consisted of the 15 Afro-Asian members of the Advisory Committee; only Canada, Ireland, and Sweden of the contributors to ONUC were excluded. Guinea, Indonesia, Mali, and the United Arab Republic soon withdrew, as was consistent with the repatriation of their troops from the Congo. The commission elected the vigorous and influential Nigerian Foreign Minister, Jaja Wachuku, as its chairman.[71]

The Congolese government submitted no request whatever for the services of the Conciliation Commission. Nevertheless, the Advisory Committee, which was chaired by Hammarskjöld, developed a broad mandate for its offspring. It can be presumed that the Secretary-General at least influenced and probably approved of the mandate. The actual text of the commission's terms of reference instructed it not to interfere in internal Congolese affairs. The aim of this noninterference, however, was to assist in restoring parliamentary institutions as a specific measure to maintain the territorial integrity and political independence of the Congo. Since the nature of a future regime in the Congo underlay the deep and confused dispute among the several factions and between the Central Government and Katanga, the commission appears to have gotten instructions to interfere without doing so and without being asked to do so!

The Advisory Committee no doubt hoped by late November, after the coup by Mobutu, that it could play a real role in Congolese affairs by dispatching its Conciliation Commission. The commission was asked to leave for the Congo during the week beginning November 21, 1960. But Kasavubu, who had reacted with silence to the availability of the commission, managed to delay its arrival until the beginning of the new year. Before that, however, the Advisory Committee had forced his hand by sending Wachuku, two other officers of the commission, and a staff to Leopoldville to make arrangements for full operations. Because movement of personnel was involved in these maneuvers, it can be assumed that the Secretary-General not only took part in the discussion but may have suggested tactics.

Once the advance party had agreed with Kasavubu on a date for the arrival of the full commission, the Congolese President demonstrated a durable reluctance to deal enthusiastically with it. He unsuccessfully demanded that its composition should be changed. It was during the commission's stay in the Congo that Lumumba was put into the hands of the Katanga regime, out of the reach of the visitors.

The members of the commission did travel widely through the country and managed to speak to many of the leading political figures, in jail and out. Some could not be reached, and others, such as Antoine Gizenga and Tshombé, treated the commission rather contemptuously. The commission had extensive discussions with United Nations officials in the Congo. The directors of ONUC no doubt gave freely of their knowledge and experience in the country. But even they did not simply welcome the work of the commission. As Wachuku stated in individual observations attached to the final report, the responsible ONUC officers suggested that the commission "had no right to comment on the activities of the ONUC or make comments on the operations" [72] in the Congo.

Before leaving the Congo in mid-February, 1961, the commission transmitted its main conclusions to the Advisory Committee. These conclusions, circulated at the height of the excitement which reached its climax with the murder of Lumumba and the adoption of a new mandate for the Secretary-General, contained recommendations which could hardly be viewed as contrary to Hammarskjöld's policies. Some of its ideas were later applied, to the accompaniment of a great deal of encouragement from the Secretary-General's representatives. These included broadening of the political base of the government; reorganization of the ANC; a summit meeting of Congolese political leaders under ONUC's protection; reconvening of parliament under ONUC protection; and enforcement of the appeals by the Security Council and the General Assembly to member countries to cease sending military aid to the Congo except through the United Nations.

The work of the Conciliation Commission may have contributed to strengthening the influence of the Secretary-General at the stage of negotiations which brought about the resumption of meetings of parliament. But it is hard to deny the justice of Quaison-Sackey's comment that the whole report had been overtaken by the events of mid-February.[73]

With the submission of its report, the Conciliation Commission went out of existence. The Advisory Committee never again operated a field body, and its meetings resumed the customary unspectacular course. It seems likely that the Secretary-General and his representatives, including the Principal Secretary of the commission,[74] must have had much influence in shaping the conclusions reached in Leopoldville and Geneva. In any case, the outcome of the Conciliation Commission's work can hardly be viewed as reducing the Secretary-General's influence over the Advisory Committee or in the deliberative organs. Because the suggestions made by the Conciliation Commission lost their novelty by the time Gardiner and Nwokedi sought a reconciliation between ONUC and the government, they may have added to the Secretary-General's ability to present acceptable proposals. To this extent, the Conciliation Commission may have increased the influence of the Secretary-General on the Central Government of the Congo.

CHAPTER XII

PEACE-KEEPING—CIVIL RAMIFICATIONS

United Nations peace-keeping forces operate where the civilian population has been upset by military action. Simply to halt fighting with no regard to the welfare of the affected people would deny plain humanitarian concern as well as the exigencies of high politics. The Secretary-General has therefore been given tasks involving administration, relief, and rehabilitation ancillary to the employment of peace-keeping forces.

Civil assistance has been a partner of peace-keeping operations in Suez and the Congo. In two other instances, welfare programs of wide scope were directed or influenced by the Secretary-General. The United Nations actually administered West New Guinea. In Korea, along with the attempt to repel aggression, the United Nations attempted a massive rehabilitation program.

Each of these cases differed rather markedly from the other. But in all of them, the Secretary-General had considerable importance, for he had to develop close working arrangements with national governments. The programs for which the Secretary-General was responsible projected him into sensitive situations bearing directly on the lives of the people in the affected territories.

UNTEA

In West New Guinea the United Nations had the widest authority. The peace-keeping role given to the UNSF formed one part of a larger assignment. The Secretary-General was instructed to establish a United Nations Temporary Executive Authority (UNTEA), which for all practical purposes constituted the government from October 1, 1962, until May 1, 1963. It was the first time that an international organization had ever been given the exclusive administration of a territory.

The Secretary-General did not involve himself directly in the administration. José Rolz-Bennett, his deputy *chef de cabinet,* temporarily took charge of UNTEA from its beginning stages until Djalal Abdoh was appointed administrator and arrived on the scene. C. V. Narasimhan, the Secretary-General's *chef de cabinet,* visited Indonesia and New Guinea in February, 1963, and represented the Secretary-General when UNTEA was terminated in May. It can be inferred that the Secretary-General's office maintained a close watch over UNTEA and that his views were constantly influential.

UNTEA had as its principal tasks the maintenance of law and order and the continuation of economic and social services.[1] It seems to have accomplished on a minimum basis what it set out to do. No civil disturbances occurred, and despite the extremely rapid dismantling of the Dutch administration, a handful of UNTEA officials managed to keep the wheels of government turning.

Nevertheless, the period of administration was far too short to permit UNTEA to undertake long-term plans or leave a permanent imprint on the area. This outcome was made certain by the Secretary-General's willingness to shorten UNTEA's tenure under the Netherlands-Indonesian agreement.

It seems doubtful that a more positive influence from UNTEA would have been possible under the circumstances. The Netherlands had made the principal concession of giving up sovereignty and UNTEA represented a face-saving device. UNTEA depended increasingly on Indonesian good-will. Moreover, the United Nations had no independent source of finance for a long-term program.

The influence of the Secretary-General then was exercised primarily to ensure a smooth transfer of sovereignty. In that sense, it was an important influence.

Reconstruction in Korea

If the Secretary-General had a great deal of authority with few means of using it to the fullest in West New Guinea, he had insufficient authority in Korea to use all the means available for relief and rehabilitation.

The major military operations in Korea took place in the very locales where the population was concentrated. The damage to civilian lives and property was immense, and a stream of refugees flowed into the way of the fighting forces. From a humanitarian or military standpoint, the situation demanded attention by the United Nations to the civilian sector.

Lie had reports from Colonel Alfred Katzin, an experienced relief administrator, whom he had sent to Korea as his Personal Representative.[2] These assessments and consultations at headquarters helped prepare the way for a Security Council resolution in late July, 1950, to give the Secretary-General authority to act both as a channel of communication for offers of help from members and to conduct relief operations. He could exercise influence as the coordinator of assistance and would be in a position to affect decision-making in several deliberative organs.

Some governments had proffered civilian aid in their responses to Lie's initial appeal under earlier Council resolutions. But the Secretary-General did not renew his broadcast appeal. Rather, an agreement was reached with the Unified Command that underlined the role of the Secretary-General as the focal point for requests and offers of aid. He could decide where to channel requests from the command and would be engaged in a continuous process of consulting, refining, and crystallizing.[3] This authority permitted him not only to direct his own staff but also to engage the attention of Specialized Agencies and nongovernmental organizations.

The Secretary-General was to be kept fully informed of developments until the Unified Command accepted offers. He thus had an opportunity to discuss the procurement of assistance and even, to the extent that he and his staff members had knowledge of affairs, the kind of aid sought. Nevertheless, the Secretary-General could not act as an initiator of an aid request but rather had to await action by the Unified Command, which also could reject offers at any stage for whatever reason seemed appropriate.[4]

Within a few weeks, the entire system of requests from the Unified Command and responses from the United Nations system, with the Secretary-General as the pivot, began full operation. It remained in operation until it became part of the new United Nations Korean Reconstruction Agency (UNKRA). By the beginning of July, 1951, the Secretary-General's calls for aid, based on 16 requests from the Unified Command, had netted pledges or contributions worth more than $18 million, while nongovernmental sources contributed another $6 million. More than 101,000 tons of supplies either had been delivered or were in the pipeline during the first year. Furthermore, the United Nations helped to supply sixty specialists from governmental and nongovernmental sources for work in Korea.[5]

Organization and operation of a relief program suited the talents and practices of the United Nations system in many respects. Many of the senior officers had had relevant experience. A program taking advantage of it could be presented as nonpolitical in the sense that it concentrated mainly on humanitarian problems and not specifically on the maintenance of peace. The Secretary-General and his staff might have a considerable influence on such a program without risking the accusation that they were meddling in high politics. And with the Security Council's decision to place the direction of the enforcement effort in Korea in the hands of the United States as the Unified Command, relief activities might be among the most appropriate responsibilities remaining to the Secretary-General.

In fact, the particular arrangements under which Lie had to operate tended to limit his influence. Requests for assistance became to an extent an adjunct of military operations. Although Katzin and his staff in Tokyo had some possibility of influencing requests, they could hardly have initiated them or controlled the use of the resulting supplies. Furthermore, the personnel recruited by the United Nations to serve in the relief field in Korea also worked exclusively under military orders and did not report to the Secretary-General. By the end of 1950, these non-American specialists perhaps gained some greater influence in the immediate direction of their work, for the assistance of the military population was put in the hands of a new United Nations Civil Assistance Command, Korea (UNCACK). Enough civilians from countries other than the United States were included to give it some international flavor, and were essential parts of teams posted to the provinces.[6]

Much of the responsibility for relief operations devolved on Lie's staff. Able and experienced as they may have been, it took more than a handful of hard-working officials to prevail against the weight and inertia of a massive military organization. To the Secretary-General, questions involving military operations and diplomatic negotiation must have seemed more pressing at the time. Yet relief to the Korean people logically became an imperative accompaniment of the military effort; it too required the influence of the Secretary-General. It can be suggested that the full possibilities for influence inherent in coordination of the relief effort were from the beginning not realized in the Korean case.

As the United Nations forces recovered their balance, they soon changed not only the military situation but also that of civilian relief. By the beginning of October, 1960, the 38th parallel was in sight by the United Nations forces and South Korean units, and the unification of Korea by military action appeared to be firm United States policy. It was realized that on the one hand the United Nations would have a role in the civil government of the newly occupied territories; on the other hand, reconstruction would logically replace direct relief. The General Assembly accordingly acted to authorize the United States, acting as the Unified Command, to attempt to carry out its policy of unification and at the same time provided for a major reconstruction effort.[7]

This effort both fitted into Lie's long-term aspirations for the United Nations and reduced his ability to influence actual operations. Before the outbreak in Korea, he had stated that the United Nations had begun to make a contribution to the economic and social well-being of the people of underdeveloped countries. While the outcome in Korea still remained doubtful, he declared that "hundreds of millions of human beings are anxiously awaiting the dawn of a new life. . . . The peoples of Asia and of under-developed areas in other parts of the world as well, are calling for action now." [8] United States proposals for the reconstruction of Korea fitted closely into the Secretary-General's thinking.

The Secretary-General and his staff apparently did not exercise a great deal of leadership or influence when the General Assembly made its first decision on an agency to be charged with the task of rebuilding in Korea. But when it asked the Economic and Social Council to draw up, with the help of the Specialized Agencies, plans for the relief and rehabilitation of Korea and to study long-term economic development for that country, his influence assumed greater importance.

Katzin returned to New York to explain the relief situation in Korea. His remarks disclosed that the Secretary-General hoped that the rehabilitation would be directed by a powerful United Nations commissioner, responsible to him and endowed with authority to decide on the size of a staff. Katzin's statement ran counter to a plan developed by Australia, which had been a member of the United Nations Commission on Korea and would be part of the new Commission for the Unification and Rehabilitation of Korea (UNCURK). The Australian plan clearly subordinated the administrator of Korean relief to UNCURK, which would appoint him, and treated the entire effort as a counterpart to unification of the country.[9]

The United States, retaining the most important capacity to influence the final decision, favored the appointment of a prestigious official, who would have considerable independence of action, to head up a projected Korean Reconstruction Agency. Accordingly, it began a series of private discussions with the Australians to arrive at a formula. The two delegations finally agreed that the Agent-General should be appointed by the Secretary-General after consultation with an Advisory Committee on UNKRA, to be appointed by the General Assembly. The Agent-General was to be responsible to the General Assembly, but UNCURK would advise him on matters related to unification. This formula, eventually adopted by the General Assembly, far from conformed to Katzin's outline of an appropriate organizational scheme.

Meanwhile, the Economic and Social Council had appointed a temporary committee to report on the probable scale of the UNKRA program. In its discussions, Katzin offered further concrete recommendations. He stated that more than $500 million dollars' worth of outside assistance would be needed over several years and suggested that a budget of $250 million for the first year should be a minimum. Somewhat different and larger estimates came from the Unified Command and the Republic of Korea. The Secretary-General's view was later recommended by the Economic and Social Council to the General Assembly. As for long-term development for Korea, the Council asked the Secretary-General to make further information available to a subsequent session, but later developments left little scope for continued work along this line.[10]

The General Assembly set up UNKRA, essentially as "the United

States wanted it to be," [11] after a discussion in which the Secretary-General made only technical suggestions. Lie took little or no part in the negotiations and public discussions. The views presented by Katzin, as his representative, had for the most part failed to determine the important administrative relationships between UNKRA and the Secretary-General. Because the UNKRA Agent-General was to report to the General Assembly, the Secretary-General was given little formal authority over him. Nevertheless, both officials were expected to work in close cooperation while taking into account the recommendations of two other bodies, the Advisory Committee and UNCURK.

Meanwhile, the entry of Chinese Communist forces in the Korean struggle greatly changed the relief and political situations. The expected operation of UNCURK as a policy-making organization in unifying Korea died aborning. Reconstruction projects and the hope of using Korea as a pilot project in economic development had to be put off, at least until the fighting had ended if not until that distant day when all of Korea could receive United Nations help. In this somber atmosphere, UNKRA had to begin its organization and planning work.

Before the UNKRA organizational pattern had become firm, Lie settled on J. Donald Kingsley, then serving as Director-General of the International Refugee Organization, as the leading candidate for Agent-General, who, it was understood, was to be a United States national. Kingsley proved reluctant to accept the new post but reconsidered Lie's offer, and early in February, 1951, took over direction of the new agency.[12]

Lie was less than a free agent in appointing Kingsley. To begin with, he had to clear the appointment with the Advisory Committee on UNKRA. The United States intended to keep the direction of the Korean enterprise as much as possible in its own hands, whether or not a United Nations umbrella provided shelter. Any UNKRA head therefore had to have positive backing from the United States. Kingsley not only was acceptable but had been approached by United States representatives about the post. His reluctance to accept Lie's offer suggests that the first Agent-General undertook his new job with some notions about how he would operate. He had prestige of his own which he was ready to employ.

Although the United States in principle supported early operations by UNKRA, the military situation impeded both planning and determination of the new agency's position. Kingsley thus had to face the same sort of a problem of civilian relations with the military forces in the field that Lie had encountered earlier. At the same time the Agent-General could hardly let UNKRA slip unhindered into the status of an adjunct to the military forces, for the organization was in fact established as an operating body independent of the Unified Command. Kingsley's attempts to establish some working arrangement with the United Nations Command on the one hand and Lie and UNCURK on the other quickly led to friction. The Agent-General responded to pressure by making it clear that "he had to run his own show."

UNKRA's short and rather dismal career, including as it did operations under the sufferance of the United Nations Command and checked by a chronic shortage of funds, remained largely the Agent-General's show. The Secretary-General appears to have had a minimum of influence on UNKRA and its top officials, most of whom were recruited by Kingsley. Relations with UNCURK in Korea continued to be distant. UNKRA operations in New York and elsewhere were autonomous and relatively little affected by the proximity of the United Nations Secretariat.

Kingsley gave up his post after the election of President Eisenhower in 1953, and was replaced by Lieutenant-General John B. Coulter, who had been a deputy chief of staff in Korea. UNKRA operations, already overshadowed completely by United States bilateral aid, increasingly merged with it.

The Secretary-General had never had a leading influence in UNKRA, and if anything it waned with the decline of United States interest in the agency. At the same time, the inspired plan that Korean reconstruction should become a gage block for the economic development of underdeveloped areas vanished in the political uncertainty created by the Chinese intervention and the military armistice agreements which the Eisenhower administration negotiated. Hardly five years after it was created, UNKRA was ripe for the liquidation which soon followed.

Clearing the Suez Canal

The task of civilian reconstruction which accompanied the operations of UNEF contrasted sharply with that in Korea. The main damage caused by the Israeli, British, and French attacks affected either strictly military targets or else was narrowly confined to Port Said and the Canal area. Nasser's response to the invasion was sabotage of the Canal itself. It was on this highly specialized facility, the importance of which spread over many lands but affected relatively few Egyptians directly, that the attention of the Secretary-General became concentrated.

Unlike the situation in Korea, the clearance of the Canal called for no broad-scale reconstruction of a nation's livelihood but rather a specific, if difficult, engineering operation. Only where the refugee camps operated by UNRWA were concerned did the civilian relief task resemble that in Korea. But the resemblance was superficial, for UNRWA already had responsibility for the camps in the Gaza Strip area. Despite the capture of the camps by Israeli forces, their administration was relatively undisturbed.

The Secretary-General received a vague mandate in connection with clearing the Canal before he was instructed to set up UNEF. It was adopted by the General Assembly without debate and with scant attention along with the demand, formulated by the United States and presented by Secretary of State Dulles, for a cease-fire. The resolution spoke of taking steps to reopen the Canal and restoring freedom of navigation after a cease-fire went into effect.[13]

With the energy and imagination that contributed so much to the formation of UNEF, Hammarskjöld and his staff quickly consulted the Danish and Dutch governments, and on their advice got commitments from private companies to make large-scale salvage equipment available.[14] His extensive, earlier consultations with leading governmental personages also worked to his profit. He secured the aid of John J. McCloy, the influential chairman of the board of the Chase Manhattan Bank and former head of the International Bank for Reconstruction and Development, as financial adviser. McCloy's involvement permitted the Secretary-General to make a convincing enough financial statement so that the private companies were willing to work with a resourceless international agency.

McCloy, with the concurrence of General Lucius Clay, whose advice was also asked, urged that the services of Lieutenant-General Raymond A. Wheeler be obtained from the International Bank. Wheeler's experience as chief of the United States Army's Corps of Engineers made him an outstanding possibility to head up the salvage operation. A telephone call by Cordier to Eugene Black, President of the International Bank, made it possible for Wheeler to come to New York, where Katzin had been charged with directing the clearance operations. Within a week, Hammarskjöld's efforts resulted in the creation of a salvage fleet which would efficiently open the Canal to full operation during the succeeding four months.[15]

A series of difficult political questions soon arose. The first of these involved British and French policy. The two governments had little liking for Hammarskjöld's latest improvisation. They hoped that the opening of the Canal would be their job, no doubt because to take on the task would give them political influence and because both countries needed the supplies which normally came through the blocked Canal. They officially offered technical assistance to the United Nations.[16] At the same time, they displayed skepticism about the possible success of a clearing operation handled out of the strained office of the Secretary-General.

Nasser's attitude raised difficult problems. His government refused consent to Hammarskjöld to begin operations before the withdrawal of British and French troops. Presumably that meant no employment whatever of the Anglo-French salvage fleet. But Hammarskjöld made progress in clarifying the Egyptian attitude while visiting Cairo during November, 1956. The Nasser government was induced to make a specific request for aid in clearing the Canal, after, of course, the withdrawal of invading forces. Hammarskjöld accepted this condition which helped him to counter pressure from France and the United Kingdom to employ their ships.

If the Canal was to be cleared rapidly, it was necessary to make firm plans. Hammarskjöld therefore asked the General Assembly to authorize him to make practical arrangements for the job. The members of the General Assembly, with significant exceptions, readily assented to the Secretary-General's program, which was endorsed in a resolution presented by six of the UNEF contributors.[17]

Three main issues were raised in the debate.[18] The first concerned the beginning of the clearance effort, a question on which Hammarskjöld had pronounced himself. The second issue arose from the presence of an Anglo-French salvage fleet in Port Said. Both the British and French representatives in the General Assembly urged that it be used and Selwyn Lloyd said: "We shall do everything in our power to help, and we welcome the assumption of United Nations responsibility." [19] But earlier communications had failed to de-emphasize the fact that the salvage fleet was part of the Anglo-French force [20] and, in any case, Egypt was still highly suspicious of any attempt to use their resources. Finally, Soviet Foreign Minister D. T. Shepilov opposed any United Nations responsibility for clearing the Canal, which he insisted should not be linked with the UNEF assignment. A debate lasting a day and a half sufficed to overcome opposition. It did not, however, do much to answer the complaint of the Philippine delegate, who thought that a great many things had been left out of Hammarskjöld's reports.

Beyond a brief, factual opening statement, Hammarskjöld took no part in the discussion. Immediately afterward, however, he made official the appointments of Wheeler, McCloy, and Katzin. The Smit-Svitzer consortium, organized by the Dutch and Danish firms contacted by the Secretary-General's representatives, was ordered to begin sending equipment to the Canal. Wheeler and a survey team arrived soon afterward and the work began at the end of December. Some 32 vessels took part and by April, 1957, a month ahead of schedule, the Canal was opened. In the end, even the Anglo-French fleet proved useful in the Port Said area and some of the ships, with British and French crews under United Nations orders, even went down the Canal for special work.[21]

The clearance of the Canal had a lesser political charge than UNEF did, and was also susceptible of technical treatment. Hammarskjöld therefore found it possible to stay somewhat more clear of details than he had in directing UNEF. Nevertheless, the directors of the Canal project worked in the Secretary-General's office and were under his immediate control.

The task of clearing the Canal supplemented other policies followed by the Secretary-General. Because the whole world wanted the Canal opened and because the people of Western Europe particularly felt the effects of its closing, Hammarskjöld added to the pressure on Britain and France by his willingness to defer clearance operations until the non-Egyptian troops had departed. He easily gained the support of the General Assembly for his position. By proposing that the United Nations take on the task, he emphasized the independence of UNEF and his office from the policies of the British and French. At the same time, he kept the strong support of the numerous opponents in the General Assembly of the Anglo-French adventure in Suez. Finally, he guaranteed impartial control and efficiency in the salvage operation without impairing Nasser's position of insistence on Egyptian ownership of the Canal.

The Congo

The scope and complexity of the civilian operation undertaken by the United Nations in the Congo exceeded those in Korea and Suez. The principal determinant in the Congo was neither a task of relief and rehabilitation such as had remained after the fighting in Korea, nor that of specific repair of a technical facility as in Suez. Rather, it was the absence of a dependable administrative machine and the evaporation of trained personnel. In this respect, it could be likened to aspects of UNTEA.

As a result of the comprehensiveness of the civilian operation in the Congo, United Nations officials dealt with every ministry, every administrative body, every public corporation. They helped to restore or operate almost every conceivable governmental function. In fact, at times, United Nations officials had to make the decisions normally reserved to government officials. For the Secretary-General, the civil assistance undertaking in the Congo produced responsibilities of a unique character.

Everyone concerned with the government of the Congo after independence knew that it could not simply sever every link to Belgium and strike out boldly on its own administrative and economic course. Belgians had to stay until replacements had been trained. The leading Congolese politicians sought continuing aid and association with Belgium, although some called attention to the adjustments which Belgian personnel would have to make to the situation after independence.[22]

Continuing cooperation in economic, social, and administrative spheres was prepared with as much care as inexperience and a shortage of time in the period immediately before independence permitted. But the disorders immediately after independence destroyed this preliminary work within hours. Almost all of the Belgian technicians and civil servants, some 10,000 in number, fled without notice or leave. Much of the modern economic and social structure disappeared with them. Within six weeks after independence, many of the lucrative export industries approached paralysis, and government, shorn of dependable communications and law and order, scarcely functioned in the Congo.[23]

The United Nations had involved itself in aiding the weak new government of the Congo before its breakdown. With Bunche at the independence ceremonies in Leopoldville was the Director of the United Nations Bureau of Technical Assistance Operations, accompanied by several advisers. Stüre Linner was appointed Resident Representative of the Technical Assistance Board and arrived in Leopoldville during the second week of July.[24] The presence of so many high officials and the speedy establishment of a technical assistance mission indicates that the Secretary-General and his organization were prepared to undertake an aid program which in United Nations terms up to that time would have assumed impressive proportions.

Before the Secretary-General invoked Article 99 to summon the Security Council, he had decided on his own initiative to act positively on any Congolese request for technical assistance to help train the ANC and had begun to seek resources. He linked this approach with his response to the Kasavubu-Lumumba cable demanding help to repel aggression.

"It is a matter of course," he told the Security Council, "that the only sound and lasting solution to the problem which has arisen is that the regular instruments of the Government, in the first place its security administration, are rendered capable of taking care of the situation."[25] The Security Council's response indicated that the military measures were intended to make possible the effective application of technical assistance over a long period, after which the Congolese government could be confident of maintaining law and order.

The particular emphasis which Hammarskjöld and, subsequently, the Security Council gave to technical assistance made it a key operating device. This alone was highly unusual. The implications were even more novel, for given the collapse of the administrative establishment in the Congo, the real role of the United Nations could be regarded as training a colonial people for self-government. If the military arm created to deal with the immediate needs gave the Secretary-General influence both inside and outside the Congo, his position at the head of the technical assistance effort gave him a concomitant means of exerting influence over a long term.

Within a week after Hammarskjöld's statement to the Security Council, the civil assistance aspects of the Congo operation had taken on new breadth and depth. Food and fuel supplies, both dependent on adequate modern transportation, had begun to run out. Some foodstuffs, contributed by United Nations members, had to be airlifted to locales where famine had begun to affect the people. The Congo River, one of the main transportation facilities of the Congo, began to clog from silting, the result of the breakdown of the Belgian-operated dredging program. General Wheeler was recruited by the Secretary-General to organize the resumption of necessary dredging. An even more menacing threat arose from the breakdown of health services. Hammarskjöld appealed to the World Health Organization for a crash program of health assistance.[26] A few days later a refugee problem of sizable proportions was to arise in South Kasai Province, and subsequently in Katanga. In these respects, the civil assistance tasks faced by the United Nations in the Congo resembled in substance if not in size those of Korea.

In another respect, the Security Council acted in a manner reminiscent of the Korean case. It officially invited the Specialized Agencies to render such assistance to the Secretary-General as he might require in dealing with problems in the Congo. Since aid had already begun as a result of Hammarskjöld's initiative, it seems clear that the Secretary-General sought high-level political backing for his efforts and that of the Directors-General of the Specialized Agencies who might otherwise be open to criticism. In a later interpretation of the Council's resolution, the Secretary-General took a rather different position, emphasizing that although the Specialized Agencies as always had to act autonomously, the Security Council's call for assistance was nevertheless mandatory, since it emanated from Chapter VII of the United Nations Charter.[27] This remarkably strong view of the quality of support due from the Specialized Agencies was based on a legal interpretation rather more far-reaching than any other expressed by the Secretary-General on the origin and role of the ONUC force.

The overriding immediate task set for civil assistance in the Congo was that of supporting the military effort. In turn, the military effort was to provide fertile conditions for the long-term outcome of technical assistance. The close linking of the military and civil tasks dictated a special form of administrative organization. It departed from the usual practice in technical aid missions, which were always officially treated as "nonpolitical" and in which the responsible Resident Representative of the Technical Assistance Board had primarily coordinating, rather than directing, duties.

The chief of the United Nations Civilian Operation, according to Hammarskjöld's original plan, received rank and authority equal to that of the commander of the United Nations Force. Through the Personal Representative of the Secretary-General in Leopoldville, both were responsible to Hammarskjöld. This status emphasized the importance which the civilian operation was supposed to have. The civilian operations chief directed two kinds of activities. The first of these involved technical assistance in the usual sense: advisers furnished by the United Nations would work with Congolese counterparts to improve the functioning of governmental services. The other came much closer to the decision-making processes in the Congolese government: it involved "higher administrative responsibility,"[28] including service at senior levels of ministries.

The senior administrative personnel, recruited in large part from the Specialized Agencies, formed a Consultative Group, headed by Linner, as chief of the Civilian Operation. The group covered almost all governmental functions, including agriculture, communications, education, finance, foreign trade, health, military training, labor, magistrature, national resources and industry and public administration. The Specialized Agencies remained in touch with their employees, some of whom were on the ground before the formation of the Consultative Group. Such persons were coopted to the Consultative Group.

Although the Specialized Agencies appointed their advisers for the benefit of the Congolese government, the Secretary-General nevertheless remarked that the agencies could

> . . . profit from the fact that they can act under the security provided by the United Nations force and use the services provided by the United Nations administration and the United Nations communication system and, finally, seek guidance from the head of the whole United Nations operation in the Congo, who has the position of political adviser and personal representative of the Secretary-General; naturally such consultation should take place through the Chief of the Civilian Operation. These advantages obviously add a further reason for the administrative arrangements.[29]

The Secretary-General moreover planned to pay for the services of the Consultative Group and to control the number and nature of appointments to be made, even when the Specialized Agencies were willing to provide financing. The financing of the Consultative Group and the office of the United Nations Civilian Operation were included in the budget for the military force, while other civilian operations, including financial aid for the Congolese government and technical assistance, made up a separate category to be paid for from voluntary contributions to the United Nations Fund for the Congo.

Only after the constitutional crisis in the Congo republic had been resolved could the administrative apparatus for technical aid begin to demonstrate its full effectiveness. Immediately following the dismissal of Lumumba, United Nations advisers scarcely knew with whom they were working. As if the insufficiently trained Congolese administrators and cabinet members were not handicapped enough, the effect of local political confusion, secessionist movements, and tribal conflict produced further elements of irrationality and confusion.

Technical aid also became entangled with the role of Belgium in the Congo. Despite the desperate need for technicians to keep some sort of administrative, economic, and political mechanisms operating, Dayal and his advisers judged that the Belgians who began returning in significant numbers in the autumn of 1960 simply produced one more threatening crosscurrent which interfered with the creation of an efficient United Nations advisory effort.[30] Hammarskjöld agreed with the ONUC view. The Belgian advisers returned Dayal's hostility, with the result that their services often could not be built into the ONUC plan.

ONUC offered Congolese authorities the advantages of a centralized apparatus with direct links to an outside community, which in principle at least was broad enough to match and exceed any resources Belgium or a single government had to offer. The United Nations, after all, was able to release $5 million in foreign exchange to finance imports even during the constitutional crisis, and a grant of $10 million for similar purposes accompanied the reconvening of parliament. Furthermore, even where large grants and other forms of aid were made available from such copious sources as the United States government or the Ford Foundation, the donors clearly designed them so as to fit into the United Nations Civil Operation.

Dayal's remarkably frank reports, the activities of Khiari and Gardiner, both of whom came to the Congo as advisers on public administration, the eventual appointment of Linner as overall chief of ONUC, and the introduction of ONUC personnel at key governmental junctures, all provide evidence to indicate that the Civilian Operation offered a useful and independent channel of communication between the Secretary-General and the Congo government. Hammarskjöld used this channel directly, for example, during his visit to Leopoldville in September, 1961. The discussions he had with Congolese officials and his ONUC staff resulted in a statement of guiding principles for civilian operations. ONUC advisers, the statement indicated, were to have a leading role in planning for economic development and stabilization, the elimination of sheer waste, the Africanization of civil service, redefining relationships among Congolese administrative organizations, and training and provision of teachers.[31] In helping to work out such principles, the Secretary-General lent to the civilian operations some of his own prestige and that of his office and, at the same time, projected a long and continuously influential involvement of his organization in the Congo.

Although Hammarskjöld always spoke and acted with the sharp realization that a large-scale civilian effort would be required in the

Congo, the emergency assumed proportions that no one could have fully anticipated. As the crisis deepened, demand piled on demand until the entire civilian program became the largest ever mounted directly by the United Nations.

Within 120 days, civilian operations were directed along six related lines. These were emergency action, operational assistance, long-range planning, liaison and reporting, training, and recruitment.[32] By the end of 1960, ONUC had 176 officials engaged in these functions. A year after after the civilian program began, more than 300 advisers and technicians were at work. As of the end of 1962, the United Nations Civilian Operation comprised more than 600 consultants, advisers, and staff members. A year later, some 600 advisers of 48 different nationalities were still at work, having faced additional problems in Katanga, in a civilian operation that ONUC claimed had been necessary to prevent a "total collapse of the social, economic and administrative structure of the country." [33]

By the end of 1963, more than $44.5 million had been raised for the United Nations Fund for the Congo from 16 governments. This provided the main support for the Civilian Operation, although the Congolese government added another $11.5 million and the Expanded Program of Technical Assistance and the United Nations Special Fund began taking over some projects. In addition, the Congo received large-scale bilateral assistance from the United States and the Federal Republic of Germany. These generated counterpart funds which also helped support the civilian program.[34]

ONUC's liaison and reporting system provided the Secretary-General with a communication link to provincial authorities and local events. Designed at first to bind together the parts of the civilian operation, the work of the liaison officers in each province soon underwent a metamorphosis, dictated by the confusion and breakdown of civil authority and the presence of ONUC military forces and various fragments of Congolese armies. The liaison officers had to concern themselves with matters of law and order and the protection of foreign technical aid personnel. Their reports contained invaluable political information as well as data on civil affairs matters. As a result, their work soon had a political content. The offices in Elisabethville and Stanleyville, particularly, became primarily political missions.

Despite the size of the Congo civilian operation by United Nations standards, it was not intended as a means of controlling the nonmilitary side of life in the Congo or as a replacement for the fleeing Belgians. Underlying the effort could be found the idea of technical assistance, rather than colonial administration. As in the military function, Hammarskjöld laid down a principle of noninterference. Although the sad lack of preparation by the colonial government meant that the ONUC mission had far more authority and responsibility than is customary in technical aid missions, the Secretary-General and his staff had nothing like the governing capacity held by the Belgian civil servants. Nor did they claim it, for even had they wanted it numerous pressures would have constrained their use of it in the United Nations effort.

In civil assistance as in military affairs, the great powers were to be excluded from direct roles. Yet only the great powers could in fact have provided the necessary finance and materials to guarantee the restoration of economic efficiency and administrative stability. In fact, more than half of the contribution to the United Nations Fund for the Congo came from the United States. Assuming unfailing generosity on the part of the United States, it is hard to see how aid from that country could have been much increased without provoking an even more outraged reaction from the Soviet Union, which had been so unsuccessful with its attempt at bilateral support for Lumumba. Thus, with each stroke of the aid pump for the Congo, the involvement of the great powers, which the Secretary-General wanted to avoid, would come closer.

If a restoration of the efficiency and productivity of Congolese society that prevailed at the moment of independence is set as the short-term goal of the United Nations Civilian Operation, the effort clearly has not succeeded. But the Secretary-General has never declared such a goal to be his. Rather civilian operations were treated only as the beginning of a long-term effort in which military force had an enabling purpose.

In one important respect, the original technical aid program seems completely to have miscarried. The initial request by the Congolese government involved provision of military training for the disintegrating ANC. Novel as it was (and perhaps inappropriate for a peace organization), the idea of aid in training the ANC remained part of ONUC's program from the earliest days until the Adoula government sought bilateral help. Although ONUC appointed provisional advisers, the turmoil in the ANC, the political confusion in the government, and the suspicion of Congolese political and military officials, prevented any progress. Had the retraining of the ANC with ONUC help been successful, the Secretary-General would have had an invaluable channel of communication to some of the most disturbing elements in the Congolese situation.

Peace-Keeping and the Influence of the Secretary-General

The Secretary-General had a great influence in initiating and directing four peace-keeping operations which involved global political interests and quite real dangers to general international peace. In the cases of the Suez Canal, the Congo, West New Guinea, and Cyprus, new kinds of peace-keeping mechanisms—including armed forces and related civilian assistance programs—were built up.

The Security Council and the General Assembly embellished with new precedents their power to assign additional duties to the Secretary-General. He in turn made real his legal authority to carry out functions assigned to him.

The decisions of the deliberative organs and the responses and initiatives of the Secretary-General include gifted improvisation, as in UNEF and the mounting of ONUC; sheer courage, as in the introduction of ONUC soldiers to Katanga; close and sometimes canny bargaining, as when UNEF was introduced to Egypt, and Israel was prevailed upon to withdraw; and unmistakable errors of conception and performance, as in the strained adaptation of ONUC instructions or the relationship of UNKRA with the United Nations Command.

Nothing had more novelty than the role of the Secretary-General in organizing and directing the deployment of armed battalions. In the Congo instance, he even moved from responsibility for a force which was not intended to fight, to the direction of an army in actual battle. The role of the Secretary-General in Suez, the Congo, and Cyprus thus contrasted sharply with his secondary position in the organization and employment of forces in Korea. The same might be said of his role in civilian assistance.

What was even more striking was the leadership that the Secretary-General exerted on the Security Council and the General Assembly in the creation and guidance of the military forces. In this influential role, Hammarskjöld and Thant accomplished what Lie was not permitted in the Korea case. They also had similar roles in the creation of civil assistance agencies and were able to maintain control over them, unlike Lie in relation to UNKRA.

The crises which led to peace-keeping assignments for the Secretary-General took place in a broader political context, which did not obviate his attempts to innovate and lead in policy decisions. In none of the three cases had the superpowers preempted the political field, barring any effective interest by smaller countries. The superpowers appeared eager to prevent the disputes from spreading immediately or from complicating their relations with each other. Moreover, such lesser powers as Canada, Tunisia, Norway, and India, proved willing to take some risks to support what they described as a cause of peace. They uncovered means to support a military force for duty under United Nations colors. They also found in the office of the Secretary-General diplomats with the suppleness and imagination to develop new ideas, expand and elaborate old ones, and create sufficient administrative apparatus and direction to put these ideas into practical use.

In the circumstances of the crises, which required speedy administrative action fully as much as imagination, it was only natural that United Nations members should attempt to cut short the cumbersome procedures of the deliberative organs. In the UNEF case, they did so by asking the Secretary-General himself to elaborate a plan for an emergency force. That he selected and projected practical plans which met with approval only emphasizes the fact that he was aware that the support of United Nations organs goes to the workable, not necessarily to a search for the pure and the just.

In the Congo case, the Secretary-General took a leading role immediately as a result of employing the formal powers of his office to an unprecedented extent. Within a few days of receiving its mandate to act, the office of Secretary-General had acquired greater prestige than ever. It became the pivot around which all politico-administrative work in the Congo turned. It never lost this status despite the death and replacement of Hammarskjöld and the appointment of an intergovernmental Conciliation Commission which could have confounded the Secretary-General's guidance.

Nevertheless, prestige and administrative centrality failed to protect the office of Secretary-General from criticism ranging from friendly to determinedly destructive. As the situation in the Congo gave birth to one crisis after another, affecting not only technical military and civilian operations but also the conceptual foundations of ONUC, the influence of the Secretary-General declined both in the deliberative organs and with the Congo government. The Secretary-General never irretrievably lost all of his leading place in shaping policy for the Congo, but for a time his ability successfully to suggest action became perilously slight when he had to bear the simultaneous effects of querulous and stumbling Congolese authorities, secessionist elements, probing and meddling by member governments, attacks in the Security Council and the General Assembly, and disturbing and provocative behavior by private interests.

In both Suez and the Congo, the military forces created by the Secretary-General at the direction of the deliberative organs served as the core of his continuing influence. The rapidly organized and quickly deployed UNEF became a principal element in maintaining the quiet political atmosphere which succeeded the crisis in Egypt. Because the Force from its inception, if not its original idea, was an arm of the Secretary-General, it provided him with the means for influence on the policies of member governments, the host country, and contributors to the force. The ONUC force had similar effects, although the Secretary-General could depend less on it to generate influence as the task which it faced became confused and its components began to leak away. Yet, in the end, it was the ONUC force which permitted a new Secretary-General to revivify the influence exercised by his predecessor.

In Cyprus, too, the United Nations force has been a main source of the Secretary-General's influence, for its presence on the island has emphasized the international concern with the situation there and at the same time provided a means of damping conflict. The UNSF in West New Guinea had a much less significant value in the ability of the Secretary-General to influence the situation there.

The advisory committees and the civilian assistance programs made secondary contributions to the influence of the Secretary-

General. The advisory committees served primarily to acquaint members committed to the general policies of the United Nations in Suez and the Congo with the projects and detailed policy changes decided on by the Secretary-General. As much as anything else, they had legitimizing functions, permitting the Secretary-General to claim that his programs had support from the most concerned members of his organization. Furthermore, because they comprised diplomats from permanent delegations in New York, the Secretary-General had the collaboration of a rudimentary "client group."

The civilian assistance programs established a parallel rudimentary client relationship with the host governments in Korea, Suez, and the Congo, although in the first instance the Secretary-General soon lost control of the organization because of the overwhelming effect of a military establishment over which he had little influence. But in the latter two cases, civilian aid encouraged constant contact between the Secretary-General and his immediate staff and the host governments. It also provided a direct lever of influence which could be used to some extent to help change governmental policies.

The peace-keeping assignments made by the deliberative organs widened the dimensions of influence wielded by the Secretary-General and associated with his office. In fact, the success of UNEF seemed so great that it was tempting to imagine that the writ of the Secretary-General might run through yet more enterprises with only a minimum of obstacles.

The experience of the Congo (and perhaps also of Cyprus), filled with the unexpected and improbable, indicates that even with the prestige and ramified relationships which depend on the direction of an armed force, the Secretary-General is limited both in the scope of the tasks he may undertake and in the constancy of influence he may exert in forming policies in the deliberative organs and carrying out his mandate. His influence reflects changes in policy by the host government and by influential members of the organization. Since these changes sometimes result from his decisions, the Secretary-General can help to some extent to widen or restrict the limits of his own influence.

CHAPTER XIII

INFLUENCE—EXPANSION AND LIMITATION

The influence of the Secretary-General in matters of peace and security is a fluctuating and rather unpredictable factor in the policy processes of the United Nations. But a factor it is, capable of development and decline, sometimes strong and sometimes weak.

On a few occasions, the influence of the Secretary-General has determined United Nations policy in keeping the peace and has deeply affected the policies of member governments. Usually, it has not been the sole element but rather one of several operative factors in maintaining the peace. It is not possible to offer accurate quantification of how much influence the Secretary-General has exerted and what he will do in the future. But it is hardly arguable that the office of Secretary-General will have to be counted among the factors which determine whether peace will be kept.

No matter how dispassionately or scientifically the office of Secretary-General is studied, it still is occupied by a human being with a will. The human qualities of the Secretary-General contribute to his influence. But to determine precisely how much this influence results from personal charm, sensitivity, intelligence, ideological suppleness, mental limitations, neurosis, individual character, or cultural background would require knowledge and research techniques unavailable for this study. It may be possible for future researchers to use psychological and social research methods that may result in a firmer estimate than can be found here.

Even if every aspect of the office and its holders cannot be confidently dealt with, what is left nevertheless seems firm and plausible: The office of Secretary-General has a formal, legal structure; its functions have expanded, and this expansion took place in defined conditions, in which certain techniques were employed and limits to influence can be discerned.

The office of Secretary-General has but a short institutional history and a few precedents and past successes on which to rely in efforts to exert influence on United Nations policy in the field of peace and security. Only the experience of the League of Nations provides a relevant historical example. The functions of the League Secretary-General became part of the United Nations office. Compared with the League example, it had a broadened scope, but how broad, the constructors of the Charter at San Francisco did not fully foresee.

All three Secretaries-General constantly and consciously sought and accepted opportunities to expand and consolidate the influence of their office in matters of peace and security. In twenty years, the office of Secretary-General, novel in many respects and altogether untried in a world political situation comprising swift and violent change and the possibility of the destruction of human society, has in fact grown vastly in activity and influence. The record of the chief officer of the United Nations contains impressive examples of leadership, and failures as well, in the policy process of the organization.

By far the most rapid and profound increase in the influence of the Secretary-General resulted from tasks assigned to him by the Security Council and the General Assembly. He accepted the challenge of these assignments and had an important part in defining goals and means for peace-keeping efforts.

Once peace-keeping operations got underway, the Secretary-General provided a channel for specifically interpreting United Nations policy. His own executive office closely directed the operations. The Secretary-General usually determined when further instructions had to be sought from a deliberative organ, rather than waiting for a member government to raise questions. He negotiated with governments to give effect to his instructions. By such devices as personal visits, reports, and advisory committees, he built up some steady support and dependable political advice for his efforts. The governments which offered this support acted as his constituency in the deliberative organs and to some degree as his advisers when there was a question of seeking or making a policy change.

The peace-keeping assignments show the Secretary-General at his most influential, taking a leading role in both formulating the guiding policies and in conducting the operations themselves. But all the

Secretaries-General have attempted to take the initiative in actual or political international conflicts by suggesting solutions which require little administrative apparatus.

Peace-keeping operations and exploratory discussions in which he offers his services can be looked upon as the extremes among the influential possibilities open to the Secretary-General in matters of peace and security. Between these extremes the Secretary-General has negotiatory and observational duties given him by deliberative organs. They differ from his own unaided initiatives because of the official source of the formal instructions; they differ from peace-keeping operations in the nature of the politico-administrative tasks he is asked to undertake, for these include no use or suggestions of armed force. Because the Secretary-General serves as the principal United Nations negotiator in these instances, he naturally has a great influence on the proceedings. Moreover, he undoubtedly agrees wholly or in great part with the aims of the negotiations and has to consult member governments while his mandate is prepared. He therefore has both advice and support from member governments.

The Conditions of Influence

Certain favorable conditions encourage the expansion of activities by the Secretary-General in the field of maintaining peace and therefore contribute to the growth of the influence of the office. In part, the Secretary-General creates or augments these conditions.

The centrality of the office of Secretary-General in the political process and institutional complex of the United Nations gives it a special advantage in maintaining an alert and informed watch over developments within and bearing on the international organization. This centrality derives from the ministerial functions of the Secretary-General, his "special right" under Article 99 of the Charter and its implications, and from executive assignments given him by the deliberative organs. Beyond these essentially institutional factors, he is attributed a time-honored role as a confidential consultant available to governments.

Because the independence of the office from national policies has usually been successfully maintained, the member governments have some justification in viewing the Secretary-General as a disinterested person. This reputation has contributed to the effect of positive efforts by the Secretary-General. His duties and rights thus provide an initial group of conditions conducive to the exercise of influence.

The vaguer, complex configuration of world politics molds the influence of the office of Secretary-General. Conflicts posing issues of peace and security with which the Secretary-General may become concerned derive from political relationships in an international complex broader and deeper than the United Nations organization. Whatever the Secretary-General attempts or does in matters of peace and security relates to moves of actors who may appear in the United Nations arena but simultaneously take other roles elsewhere. When the parties to an issue of peace and security refuse to become involved with the United Nations, the influence of the Secretary-General usually remains minimal.

The nature of the actors, moreover, may affect the Secretary-General's approach to matters of peace and security. Small and middle-sized states probably react more sensitively to his attempts to influence than do the great and powerful states. Further distinctions in sensitivity of reaction to the Secretary-General's activities can be based on the strength of ideological orientations of governments and the openness of their decision-making processes. It seems likely that the Secretary-General has greater influence with governments following limited, pragmatic policies than those guided by expansive dogmas, and that he usually finds a better reception from governments with open, democratic decision processes.

In any case, the Secretary-General cannot act as if only his organization exists and has a determining effect in keeping the peace. If he is to discover favorable conditions for action, he must do so in the general context of world politics, which includes his organization.

The list of these favorable conditions begins with the support, or at least acquiescence, of the great powers in policies favored by the majority of other members of United Nations organs. This condition is a necessary one for field operations of any but the smallest scope. Permissive or positive attitudes on the part of the great powers were, for example, prerequisites for the formation of UNEF and ONUC and for their large-scale (in United Nations terms) operations. Such a great-power reaction bolsters the influence of even mild suggestions by the Secretary-General to parties involved in peace and security issues. An opposed reaction by a great power will very likely either negate or closely limit his influence. Sharp and uncompromising opposition by great powers to his attempts to exercise influence can result, as it did in both Korea and the Congo, in the undermining of his further personal effectiveness and can create doubt concerning the future viability of his office.

Governments, whether or not they are of great powers, must also be willing to deal with the Secretary-General if his influence is to be brought to bear. This implies that these governments must accept some commitment to the United Nations, its Charter and practices, and also respond positively to its recommendations, at least in relevant situations. This condition has frequently been present, as in the Palestine negotiations carried out by Hammarskjöld, or the diplomatic initiative by Thant in the West New Guinea case. It was not present when the Secretary-General was instructed to act during the Hungarian revolution, and consequently he had no effective influence.

In addition to these two sets of conditions, a broad international consensus which either positively favors the Secretary-General's actions or abstains from opposing them is necessary for the successful exercise of his influence. This consensus sometimes can be mustered or registered through proceedings of a deliberative organ which end in a demonstrative vote; at other times, it manifests itself only during consultations and may not be demonstrated formally and publicly.

In more graphic terms, the office of Secretary-General can be located at the apex of a triangle. One side represents a channel for influence on the Secretary-General and for his influence on individual governments, including those of the great powers and the parties involved in issues; the other side stands for the collectivity of United Nations members. The Secretary-General may exert influence directly or indirectly on either of the other points of the triangle. The length of the sides varies in particular situations and over time. By using the means at his disposal, the Secretary-General can help to shape the dimensions of the triangle.

The Technique of Influence

The Secretary-General has at his disposal a variety of techniques by which he can help to forge support and a consensus, and which have helped expand the influence of his office.

One set of techniques for exerting and building influence derives from the legal and moral undertaking of member governments in joining the United Nations. The Secretary-General can attempt to interpret these undertakings. When his interpretations are accepted, he exercises influence and helps to organize acquiescence or support and a broad consensus. He may call to the attention of concerned governments the provisions of the United Nations Charter, the past practices in accordance with them, and sometimes his own opinion regarding the application and relevance of these provisions and practices to a particular issue. He may urge governments—that is, try to persuade governmental leaders—to conform scrupulously to their commitments. He does so frequently in his *Annual Report*. More private and particular recommendations can be transmitted to governments through the multiple diplomatic and personal channels open to him. These include the corps of permanent representatives at headquarters, the conversations held with governmental and non-governmental visitors, and consultations during his own frequent travels. The press and other mass communications media can also be used as a means of contact with governmental elites.

A more direct, overt, and sometimes powerful means of influence depends on initiative by the Secretary-General to fulfill the aims of the United Nations. Article 99 offers an obvious but delicate possibility. The record of the office of Secretary-General has been characterized by a positive attitude toward the possibilities of influence growing out of Article 99. He has assidously consulted, collected information, and become involved in peace and security issues. The effect of Article 99 and its implications has been to deepen and extend the influence of the office of Secretary-General on United Nations activities in the peace and security field.

Allied to the Secretary-General's sensitivity to the political significance of Article 99 and its implications is his response to additional duties. The Secretary-General has always adopted the attitude that he was ready to serve the United Nations, its organs and members, with enthusiasm and energy within the purposes of the organization broadly conceived. Although a civil servant, he would be an active and positive one, rather than a clerkly and passive one. This attitude, once enunciated, makes it easily possible for deliberative organs to assign tasks to him and for him to pursue them in an intelligent and innovative fashion.

This willingness to serve, so explicitly and frequently stated by Hammarskjöld, has been matched with a willingness to seek the assignment and definition of additional duties. The Secretary-General has participated in planning the overall policies governing such duties, and has taken full responsibility for vigorous steps in carrying them out. His consultations and suggestions, open declarations of desirable courses, seaches for information and consensus, and interventions in deliberative organs, help to shape the policy of the organization. And in the absence of specific instructions, the Secretary-General alone decides on the policies which govern his office and his own official actions.

In this connection, Hammarskjöld provided a ready source of ideas for dealing with issues of peace and security. He left a record of innovation, represented by the "Peking formula," "preventive diplomacy," and the United Nations "presence," and of a magisterial hand in dividing complex problems into smaller, more tractable ones. Thant has shown considerable skill at producing useful approaches to issues of peace and security. Lie tried frequently but less successfully to act in a similar fashion.

In order to support his readiness to act and to preserve any influence gained from it, the Secretary-General must carry out high-quality administrative operations in emergencies. Even with the limited resources of the Secretariat, he must prove willing and able to carry out whatever assignments he seeks or is given. Rapid, decisive, and appropriate administrative actions have made it possible for the Secretary-General to create or retain at least some influence in peace and security situations.

The influence of the Secretary-General may cumulate. Hammarskjöld's successful negotiation with the Peking regime marked a turning point in the fortunes of the office. It created the expectation among governments that the office of Secretary-General had some unexplored usefulness, and that Hammarskjöld personally could manage peace and security issues with tact and effectiveness. It therefore served as a basis for the high degree of discretion and influence given him in the UNEF case. The same may be said of each successive negotiatory, observational, and peace-keeping assignment.

Accumulated influence adheres to the office of Secretary-General as well as to its incumbent. Thant has been able to act within broader limits than he might have in taking over from someone of less accomplishment and prestige than Hammarskjöld. The latter entered the office when its influence had sharply fallen away, and at first acted cautiously within narrow limits. Yet it seems clear that the cumulation of influence constitutes no irreversible process, especially in view of the background of world politics which condition the activities of the Secretary-General.

To some degree, the accumulated influence of the office of Secretary-General has been formulated into a doctrinal definition of its functions. This doctrine is based on precedent and on the energetic, initiating, policy-forming stance of each Secretary-General, which in itself is unusual for a civil servant.

The ability to refer to established precedents or well-articulated doctrine offers the Secretary-General a framework and an argument for the exercise and expansion of influence. The use of precedent and doctrine tends to reinforce their legitimacy. Thus, precedents and doctrine encourage the Secretary-General to attempt influential actions in matters of peace and security, and provide the member states with justifying argument for accepting such actions.

Despite a willingness to serve, an initiating stance, and a doctrine, the office of Secretary-General lacks the usual seeds of influence which elaborate administrative apparatuses and legal authority sow for high officials of national governments. The Secretary-General must instead rely on unending attempts to persuade member governments and their officials to use the United Nations and to be guided by its decisions. The crucial component of influence exercised by the office of Secretary-General frequently is nothing more than persuasion. It could hardly be otherwise in the diplomatic atmosphere, in the universe of intergovernmental relationships, in which the Secretary-General functions. Even were he to have additional formal, legal authority, it might have little value in determining the behavior of reluctant governments.

It must be taken for granted that at least a few member governments will always listen to the Secretary-General and take his views into account. A varying mixture of objective and subjective appreciations of the office by member governments comes into play. If the Secretary-General exerts influence, member governments must open the way to accepting it on the basis of past performance and estimates of future action. They must be ready to consider novel proposals for dealing with matters of peace and security and yet have some assurance that past successes have not altogether been discarded and that past failures are not to be repeated *in toto*. These are objective considerations. In addition, governments must subjectively find it possible to trust the office and its incumbent to act in a responsible and intelligent manner.

The persuasiveness of the Secretary-General therefore depends in some part—perhaps predominantly—on the perception that member governments have of the man who holds the office. This perception results not only from what the person in the office of Secretary-General does and says, but also from what he is presumed to be, what his personal characteristics connote, and what his personal capacity as civil servant and statesman might be. This is but another way of saying that the office of Secretary-General reflects the man who holds it. It also raises questions that now can be dealt with only speculatively and with a certain humility about one's ability fully to understand another man's mind and heart.

The personal intelligence, ingenuity, tact, courage, and stamina of the Secretary-General himself are important factors bearing on even the roughest calculation of the influence of his office, and must be counted along with the more impersonal components of world politics. The intelligence of the Secretary-General sets the boundaries of his understanding of political and administrative situations. His ingenuity leads him to initiatives, suggestions, and solutions devised appropriately to fit issues of peace and security with which he may deal. Together, his intelligence and ingenuity may even lead him to anticipate far in advance the possibility of international conflict and to plan ahead to meet it. His tact has an important bearing on how his efforts to exert influence will be received by member governments. Suggestions of arrogance or righteousness, mistakes in timing, and misjudgment of the intentions and prestige of governmental figures, can destroy any initiative by this international official who leans so heavily on the staff of persuasion. Bountiful courage is needed by the Secretary-General because of the exposed centrality and independence of his role; the frequently frustrating nature of his tasks, which include organizational and functional novelty in settings of violence or near-violence; and the likelihood of public criticism, not to say outright personal abuse, in return for his best-intentioned efforts. Finally, he needs stamina simply to endure his burden for long.

It is not likely that any man could bring to the office of Secretary-General the precise combination of personal qualities which would permit maximizing other factors leading to influence. Each of the Secretaries-General has had some of the human capacities needed to establish and exercise the influential possibilities of the office and to preserve it against attack and erosion. Lie acted with courage to develop and extend the original expectations for the office. Hammarskjöld set a remarkably high standard for himself, and to a great degree met it. He soon had renown in United Nations circles for foresight and analytical ability, a sense of timing, and courageous innovation. In defense of their office, both he and Lie resisted unrelenting onslaughts by the Soviet Union. Thant quickly restored much of the wavering confidence in the office and has shown ingenuity, tact, and courage in his conduct of it.

Each of the three Secretaries-General has, as could be expected, failed in some ways to reach standards of perfection. Both Lie and Thant have temerariously, perhaps unnecessarily bluntly, commented on national governmental policies. The former's proposals sometimes appeared to lack much intellectual depth. The high-minded Hammarskjöld on the other hand sometimes used language that could be read as a pontifical warning to less perspicacious statesmen. Lie often showed impatience with administrative detail, but Hammarskjöld personally took on over-heavy administrative and political burdens simultaneously.

The public impression made by Thant is perhaps less clear-cut and characteristic than that of his predecessors, but his words do have respectful governmental and nongovernmental audiences.

Hammarskjöld certainly achieved more fame than he ever admitted seeking. Whatever the weight of such observations, none of the three failed to use his office to extend and exert influence in matters of peace and security.

The Limits of Influence

The development and effects of the Secretary-General's influence have hardly been uniform or evenly paced. Nor do they warrant the conclusion that the scope of his office and influence must continue to expand without restraint or interruption. Very real obstacles project from the same legal, political, and personal factors which have operated in the past when his influence has been effective in spite of severe difficulties and handicaps.

The Secretary-General has fulfilled the expectation that he would be involved in handling issues of peace and security. But this has not permanently installed him on a plane of political equality with the other, deliberative, decision-making principal organs of the organization. Nor does he have the status of a member state. It is from them that he ultimately derives much of the prestige that permits him to exercise influence. He is elected by the members. He begins his term of office with the backing of the great powers, the other members of the Security Council, and the General Assembly. He cannot count on this backing as a permanent factor unless he avoids every controversial situation. Although he has an extraordinary individual status as head of a principal organ of the United Nations, still he serves the organization and its organs. They bear the overall legal and moral responsibility in matters of peace and security.

Even though the Secretary-General influences the decision-making organs in various ways, he does not in the final analysis make decisions for governments. He rather serves them when they have reached a consensus. If he can help them reach it, his role may be highly congenial to them. If they cannot find a consensus or if the Secretary-General insists on his own policies despite divisions in the deliberative organs, he may be faced with demands for his resignation or may have to threaten or offer to resign in an effort to clarify his position. He has ample opportunity incorrectly to estimate his standing, but few positive guidelines and precedents in making his estimate.

Even the employment of the formal powers under Article 99 is closely fenced in. Although the Secretary-General has the "special right" to bring any matter concerned with peace and security before the Security Council, his doing so commits the members of the Council to nothing. They may or may not agree even with his assessment of a matter as bearing on the maintenance of peace. He may send documents to the Council, speak before it, intervene in its discussions, and hold confidential consultations. But he can neither vote in favor of, nor veto, a resolution before it. Whatever his views, he is bound to follow its instructions while he remains in office. The same comment applies to questions of peace and security which he brings to the General Assembly.

Diplomatic initiatives by the Secretary-General depend for their effect on the receptivity of member governments to his taking an influential role and to the content of his suggestions. This receptivity in turn depends on governmental deliberations, which normally are largely beyond the influence of the Secretary-General. In some cases, the Secretary-General has no or almost no effect on the policies of governments. On other occasions, his suggestions and conciliatory efforts may coincide with or be designed to fit well enough into the policies of member countries so that his initiatives are welcomed.

It is true that the Secretary-General may act with a view to creating favorable conditions for his initiatives. But his capacity to do so can hardly be very great so long as governments guard their sovereignty and attempt to act as independently as possible of outside agencies and agents. The firm backing of a deliberative organ is more likely than his own efforts to enhance his persuasiveness. Yet even in this situation, some modicum of cooperation from the governments involved must be forthcoming if he is not to be halted at his first step.

Within his instructions from deliberative organs, then, and within the willingness of member governments to consider his suggestions, the Secretary-General may exercise influence in maintaining peace by means of conciliatory procedures. These are, however, narrow limits. For it can hardly be said that the Security Council or General Assembly habitually arrives at a deep, lasting, and far-reaching consensus on matters of peace and security, or that governments involved in such issues easily relax their stances and adjust their views.

Each peace-keeping assignment tends to extend the limits within which the Secretary-General's influence may operate. In carrying out such assignments, he may for considerable periods deeply affect the foreign relations of the governments where United Nations forces are employed. This may even lead to a voice in the internal management of such governments. Moreover, the presence of an armed force, even one which operates under narrow, peace-keeping instructions, still carries a threat of ultimate violence to work the will of the United Nations. To a considerable degree, the Secretary-General or his senior representatives on the spot furnish the immediate interpretation of that will. This crude factor of violence permits the Secretary-General somewhat more latitude in attempting to exert influence than would the normally delicate diplomatic procedures. His leverage may be further augmented by a civilian relief and reconstruction operation.

The extended limits of influence resulting from a peace-keeping assignment given to the Secretary-General are impressive only when compared to the narrow boundaries within which he usually works. He is still at the mercy of governments which contribute troops and supplies. Cooperation by governments can turn into recalcitrance or sabotage in such vital matters as the refusal to withdraw invading forces or objectionable persons from the affected area. The Secretary-General can do little about such developments.

The Secretary-General is especially vulnerable to attacks by great powers which disagree with his policies. Furthermore, a determined onslaught very likely will throw the entire organization into a crisis. Programs and policies recently considered highly important become doubtful. The psychological atmosphere becomes unconducive to advanced planning in keeping the peace and security as well as in other areas. The Secretary-General's own policies and suggestions adopted by deliberative organs begin to suffer from lack of support. His influence is reduced in accordance with the doubt about the future of the policies he represents.

The Secretary-General's direction of the internal administration of the Secretariat, which offers some support for his influence, also has severe limits. The top level of the Secretariat is staffed under the watchful eyes of member governments which agree to the principle of an international civil service and at the same time eagerly seek to have their own nationals appointed to high posts on representational grounds. This layer of the civil service should furnish an important base for the Secretary-General's efforts to help in maintaining peace. In fact, it has proved to be of only mixed utility.

In part as a reaction, the Executive Office of the Secretary-General has tended to preempt policy functions, especially in the peace and security area. The growth of this office provides the Secretary-General with a devoted and dependable immediate staff, but it also narrows the number of officials who gain policy-making and diplomatic experience and reduces the institutionalization of his work on peace and security issues.

Recruitment, appointment, and assignment of personnel rest largely in the hands of the Secretary-General. But even here, the limits of his authority and his use of it to foster influence on the policy-making process are subject to limitation. Opposition by the great powers may especially limit his internal direction.

In the allied function of budget-making, severe limitations also bear on the Secretary-General. His budgets in the first instance reflect policy decisions by the Security Council and the General Assembly in issues of peace and security. But the same limits which apply to his influence on policies for dealing with peace and security situations necessarily apply to budget proposals based on those policies.

Financing the budget is dealt with separately. It involves national governmental decisions in the fiscal field, over which the Secretary-General has minimal influence. A refusal to pay or failure to do so on time can place the Secretary-General in the invidious position of lacking financial resources to carry out policies he helped to design. The unwillingness of a great power—the usual source of large financial contributions—to support programs favored by the Secretary-General has especially limiting effects.

In the face of a refusal to pay contributions, the ingenuity of the Secretary-General cannot produce gold from paper documents. He may have but one response to financial stringency. That is to pare the programs for which funds are sought. While supporters of such programs may deplore reductions, the governments refusing to contribute will have achieved precisely what they sought. Only if the governments favoring such programs find means of contributing additional amounts can the Secretary-General maintain some of his influence in carrying them through.

Finally, the personal attributes, talents, and moral precepts of the Secretary-General limit his influence. No man, however brilliant, can turn all of the complexity and conflict of the universe of the Secretary-General into manageable simplicity and calm cooperation. His range of attention cannot encompass every political affair; his prescience cannot extend far enough to alert him to each future outcome of present actions; and his tact cannot cover all the inadequacies of others. His own morality, however poorly defined or ill-expressed, and that embodied in the United Nations Charter, must forbid him certain policies. The courses left open include impractical strategies and unfortunate tactics. All statesmen, including the three Secretaries-General, make mistakes. And like any political leader, the chief United Nations officer will almost inevitably find that some political opponents turn into personal enemies and that he cannot work harmoniously with some people. Were it to be otherwise, the Secretary-General would have to be recruited from among the angels.

The Future

There is little reason to expect that the limits now applying to the Secretary-General will suddenly vanish. The possibility that he will dependably be able to stimulate and direct peace-keeping operations under broad mandates seems particularly dim in view of recent experience.

Yet actions of the Secretary-General which fall more nearly within more traditional diplomatic rubrics seem likely to grow in the future. It is as a conciliator or mediator, where he can assume the role of honest broker, that the Secretary-General can best and most influentially prepare, through synthesizing views and projecting ideas, means for maintaining peace. His efforts can find the basis for the consent of member governments, if there is any, and his intelligence and tact can produce quite real results.

If diplomatic consultation and discussion disclose wide consent, the Secretary-General can on his own formal or informal initiative seek to have defined operational duties, such as investigatory or mediatory tasks, officially assigned to his office by the Security Council or the General Assembly.

Far more than the Secretary-General's "special right" under Article 99, it can be expected that the precedent of availability for service will form the basis of his future activities. Such an attitude is a prerequisite for both his activity as a conciliator and mediator and as a party concerned in matters of peace and security as a result of the "special right." Whether the administrative equipment for such a role will improve is impossible to foresee. The budgetary crisis, moreover, interferes with the ability of the office always to be ready to serve, because it suggests the possibility that the Secretary-General can be given assignments which he favors and influences, only to find himself checked by financial obstruction.

The United Nations will continue to require of its Secretary-General performance as a representative and link to various publics in member countries. He has been most successful in dealing with rather narrowly defined elites, diplomats for example, and probably will continue to speak and act in such a way as to interest and involve specialist groups.

Whatever its development in the future, the office of the Secretary-General will certainly remain a besieged and lonely one, literally and figuratively. From its height in the United Nations Secretariat building, the view to the east reaches over a grimy concentration of factories, past an expanse of dwellings, toward the mists of the Atlantic coast. To the west, the great windows of the building face the angular confusion of midtown New York. The rectilinear disorganization of the Manhattan skyline resembles one aspect of the work of the Secretary-General. At any time of day or night, he has before him a series of inscrutable but concrete problems. These range from the management of the building in which he works to the specific issues of a thermonuclear arms race.

The very orientation of the Secretariat building, open directly only to the east and west, symbolizes another fact which deeply affects the office of Secretary-General. Frequently, the political East and the political West have together produced heavy storms that crash against the office the way gales assault the surrounding city.

The influence of the Secretary-General extends to one of the United Nations buildings looking to the south. This is the General Assembly hall, where the host of new states from the south of the longtime capitals of international politics have made their presence felt. The view to the south has great significance for the Secretary-General, whose office has taken on new character with the lengthening of the United Nations membership list.

The mist that obscures the view to the East has not yet lifted and may become thicker because of problems generated around China, still the hulking pariah of the United Nations universe. The storms of North-South relationships, too, are unlikely to abate but rather to take on new and perhaps even more intractable attributes. Whatever happens, they will sorely test the man whose world centers on the thirty-eighth floor. His future actions will quite likely confirm the proposition that it is still impossible closely to chart the influence of the Secretary-General in advance.

The office of Secretary-General can now best be seen as concrete and particular, responding to the highly personal touch of its occupant and to the specifics of world politics at any one moment. It seems likely to remain so until both greater experience with the office and greater institutionalization of its functions take place. But whatever the future of the United Nations brings, the office of the Secretary-General can be expected to influence the work of the organization.

Appendixes

APPENDIX A

COVENANT OF THE LEAGUE OF NATIONS (*Excerpts*)

Article 6

1. The permanent Secretariat shall be established at the Seat of the League. The Secretariat shall comprise a Secretary-General and such secretaries and staff as may be required.
2. The first Secretary-General shall be the person named in the Annex; thereafter the Secretary-General shall be appointed by the Council with the approval of the majority of the Assembly.
3. The secretaries and staff of the Secretariat shall be appointed by the Secretary-General with the approval of the Council.
4. The Secretary-General shall act in that capacity at all meetings of the Assembly and of the Council.

Article 15

1. If there should arise between Members of the League any dispute likely to lead to a rupture, which is not submitted to arbitration *or judicial settlement* in accordance with Article 13, the Members of the League agree that they will submit the matter to the Council. Any party to the dispute may effect such submission by giving notice of the existence of the dispute to the Secretary-General, who will make all necessary arrangements for a full investigation and consideration thereof.
2. For this purpose, the parties to the dispute will communicate to the Secretary-General, as promptly as possible, statements of their case with all the relevant facts and papers, and the Council may forthwith direct the publication thereof.

APPENDIX B

CHARTER OF THE UNITED NATIONS
(*Excerpts*)

CHAPTER III. ORGANS

Article 7

1. There are established as the principal organs of the United Nations; a General Assembly, a Security Council, an Economic and Social Council, a Trusteeship Council, an International Court of Justice, and a Secretariat.

2. Such subsidiary organs as may be found necessary may be established in accordance with the present Charter.

CHAPTER XV. THE SECRETARIAT

Article 97

The Secretariat shall comprise a Secretary-General and such staff as the Organization may require. The Secretary-General shall be appointed by the General Assembly upon the recommendation of the Security Council. He shall be the chief administrative officer of the Organization.

Article 98

The Secretary-General shall act in that capacity in all meetings of the General Assembly, of the Security Council, of the Economic and Social Council, and of the Trusteeship Council, and shall perform such other functions as are entrusted to him by these organs. The Secretary-General shall make an annual report to the General Assembly on the work of the Organization.

Article 99

The Secretary-General may bring to the attention of the Security Council any matter which in his opinion may threaten the maintenance of international peace and security.

Article 100

1. In the performance of their duties the Secretary-General and the staff shall not seek or receive instructions from any government or from any other authority external to the Organization. They shall refrain from

any action which might reflect on their position as international officials responsible only to the Organization.

2. Each Member of the United Nations undertakes to respect the exclusively international character of the responsibilities of the Secretary-General and the staff and not to seek to influence them in the discharge of their responsibilities.

Article 101

1. The staff shall be appointed by the Secretary-General under regulations established by the General Assembly.

2. Appropriate staffs shall be permanently assigned to the Economic and Social Council, the Trusteeship Council, and, as required, to other organs of the United Nations. These staffs shall form a part of the Secretariat.

3. The paramount consideration in the employment of the staff and in the determination of the conditions of service shall be the necessity of securing the highest standards of efficiency, competence, and integrity. Due regard shall be paid to the importance of recruiting the staff on as wide a geographical basis as possible.

APPENDIX C

REPORT OF THE PREPARATORY COMMISSION OF THE UNITED NATIONS
(*Excerpts*)

CHAPTER VIII. THE SECRETARIAT

SECTION 2

B: THE SECRETARY-GENERAL

FUNCTIONS, TERM OF APPOINTMENT AND PROCEDURE OF APPOINTMENT

Functions of the Secretary-General

8. The principal functions assigned to the Secretary-General, explicitly or by inference, by the Charter, may be grouped under six headings: general administrative and executive functions, technical functions, financial functions, the organization and administration of the International Secretariat, political functions and representational functions.

9. Many of the Secretary-General's duties will naturally be delegated, in greater or lesser degree, to members of his staff and particularly to his higher officials. But the execution of these duties must be subject to his supervision and control; the ultimate responsibility remains his alone.

10. The Secretary-General is the "chief administrative officer of the Organization" (Article 97) and Secretary-General of the General Assembly, the Security Council, the Economic and Social Council and the Trusteeship Council (Article 98). Certain specific duties of a more narrowly administrative character derived from these provisions are indicated in the Charter (e.g., in Articles 12 and 20, and in Article 98, the last sentence of which requires the Secretary-General to present an annual report to the General Assembly on the work of the Organization) and in the Statute of the International Court of Justice (Articles 5 and 13).

11. Further specific duties falling under this head, many of which will no doubt be defined in the Rules of Procedure of the various principal organs concerned and their subsidiary bodies, relate to the preparation of the agenda and the convocation of sessions, the provision of the necessary staff, and the preparation of the minutes and other documents.

12. The Secretary-General also has administrative and executive duties of a wider character. He is the channel of all communication with the United Nations or any of its organs. He must endeavour, within the scope of his functions, to integrate the activity of the whole complex of United Nations organs and see that the machine runs smoothly and efficiently. He is responsible, moreover, for the preparation of the work of the various organs and for the execution of their decisions, in co-operation with the Members.

13. The last-mentioned functions of the Secretary-General have technical as well as administrative aspects. More particularly as regards the work of the Economic and Social Council and the Trusteeship Council, the expert technical assistance which the Secretary-General is able to provide, and which he himself must control, will clearly affect the degree in which these organs can achieve their purposes.

14. Under the Charter, the Secretary-General has wide responsibilities in connection with the financial administration of the United Nations; and it may be assumed that, under the financial regulations which will be established by the General Assembly, he will be made primarily responsible for preparing the budget, for allocating funds, for controlling expenditure, for administering such financial and budgetary arrangements as the General Assembly may enter into with specialized agencies, for collecting contributions from Members and for the custodianship of all funds.

15. The Secretary-General is the head of the Secretariat. He appoints all staff under regulations established by the General Assembly (Article 101, paragraphs 1 and 3), and assigns appropriate staff to the various organs of the United Nations (Article 101, paragraph 2). He alone is responsible to the other principal organs for the Secretariat's work; his choice of staff—more particularly of higher staff—and his leadership will largely determine the character and the efficiency of the Secretariat as a whole. It is on him that will mainly fall the duty of creating and maintaining a team spirit in a body of officials recruited from many countries. His moral authority within the Secretariat will depend at once upon the example he gives of the qualities prescribed in Article 100, and upon the confidence shown in him by the Members of the United Nations.

16. The Secretary-General may have an important role to play as a mediator and as an informal adviser of many governments, and will undoubtedly be called upon from time to time, in the exercise of his administrative duties, to take decisions which may justly be called political. Under Article 99 of the Charter, moreover, he has been given a quite special right which goes beyond any power previously accorded to the head of an international organization, viz: to bring to the attention of the Security Council any matter (not merely any dispute or situation) which, in his opinion, may threaten the maintenance of international peace and security. It is impossible to foresee how this Article will be applied; but the responsibility it confers upon the Secretary-General will require the

exercise of the highest qualities of political judgment, tact and integrity.

17. The United Nations cannot prosper, nor can its aims be realized, without the active and steadfast support of the peoples of the world. The aims and activities of the General Assembly, the Security Council, the Economic and Social Council and the Trusteeship Council will, no doubt, be represented before the public primarily by the Chairmen of these organs. But the Secretary-General, more than anyone else, will stand for the United Nations as a whole. In the eyes of the world, no less than in the eyes of his own staff, he must embody the principles and ideals of the Charter to which the Organization seeks to give effect.

Term of Appointment, etc.

18. The first Secretary-General should be appointed for five years, the appointment being open to renewal at the end of that period for a further five-year term. There being no stipulation on the subject in the Charter, the General Assembly and the Security Council are free to modify the term of office of future Secretaries-General in the light of experience.

19. Because a Secretary-General is a confidant of many governments, it is desirable that no Member should offer him, at any rate immediately on retirement, any governmental position in which his confidential information might be a source of embarrassment to other Members, and on his part a Secretary-General should refrain from accepting any such position.

Procedure of Appointment

20. From the provisions of Articles 18 and 27 of the Charter, it is clear that, for the nomination of the Secretary-General by the Security Council, an affirmative vote of seven members, including the concurring votes of the permanent members, is required; and that for his appointment by the General Assembly, a simple majority of the members of that body present and voting is sufficient, unless the General Assembly itself decides that a two-thirds majority is called for. The same rules apply to a renewal of appointment as to an original appointment; this should be made clear when the original appointment is made.

21. It would be desirable for the Security Council to proffer one candidate only for the consideration of the General Assembly, and for debate on the nomination in the General Assembly to be avoided. Both nomination and appointment should be discussed at private meetings, and a vote in either the Security Council or the General Assembly, if taken, should be by secret ballot.

Notes

ABBREVIATIONS IN NOTES

Annual Report	United Nations, *Annual Report of the Secretary-General on the Work of the Organization*
Preparatory Commission, *Report*	United Nations Preparatory Commission, *Report of the Executive Committee* (London, 1945)
Repertoire	*Repertoire of the Practice of the Security Council* (New York, United Nations Department of Political and Security Affairs, 1959)
Repertory	*Repertory of United Nations Practice* (New York, United Nations, 1955)
UNCh	*United Nations Chronicle*
UNCIO	*Documents of the United Nations Conference on International Organization* (New York and London, United Nations Information Organization, 1945–1946)
UNGA	United Nations General Assembly
UNOR	United Nations Official Records
UNORGA	United Nations, Official Records, General Assembly
UNORSC	United Nations, Official Records, Security Council
UNR	*United Nations Review*
UNYB	*Yearbook of the United Nations* (New York, Columbia University Press in association with the United Nations, 1952–1964; Lake Success, N. Y., United Nations Department of Public Information, 1946–1951)

NOTES

INTRODUCTION

1. Although the Charter of the United Nations speaks of the "appointment" of the Secretary-General, the process it prescribes can scarcely be distinguished from an election, since votes are cast for a candidate.

2. Such organizations as the World Health Organization or the United Nations Educational, Scientific and Cultural Organization typically place a supervisory council close to their Directors-General, thus adding a level to the policy process. The United Nations Secretary-General does not have this encumbrance.

3. The term "administrative" includes those functions which in United States usage are grouped under "executive."

Cf. Preparatory Commission, *Report,* pp. 74–75.

4. *Ibid.,* p. 75.

CHAPTER I. MODELS FOR SAN FRANCISCO

1. For a discussion of the nature and practices of international conferences, see Frederick S. Dunn, *The Practice and Procedure of International Conferences* (Baltimore, Johns Hopkins University Press, 1929).

2. Gerard J. Mangone, *A Short History of International Organization* (New York, McGraw-Hill Book Co., 1954), pp. 67–90. Leonard S. Woolf, *International Government* (New York, Brentano's, 1916), pp. 394–95 and *passim.* Francis P. Walters, *A History of the League of Nations,* 2 vols. (London, Oxford University Press, 1952), pp. 17–22.

3. Specific material in this section is drawn from: Leon Bourgeois, *La Pacte de 1919 et la Société des Nations* (Paris, Bibliothèque-Charpentier, 1919), pp. 206–8, 214. David Hunter Miller, *The Drafting of the Covenant,* 2 vols. (New York, G.P. Putnam's Sons, 1928), II., 3–15, 43–46. C. Howard-Ellis, *The Origin, Structure and Working of the League of Nations* (London, George Allen and Unwin, 1928), pp. 61ff, 163. Robert Cecil, Viscount Cecil, *A Great Experiment* (London, Jonathan Cape, 1941), pp. 89–90. Stephen M. Schwebel, *The Secretary-General of the United Nations: His Political Powers and Practice* (Cambridge, Harvard University Press, 1952) (hereafter cited as Schwebel, *The Secretary-General*), p. 4.

4. For a brief summary of these plans, see Egon F. Ranshofen-

Wertheimer, *The International Secretariat* (Washington, Carnegie Endowment for International Peace, 1945), pp. 13–16. On the functions of the Secretary-General, see Walters.

5. League of Nations, *Official Journal: Eleventh Ordinary Session,* Special Supplement No. 88, No. A.16.1930, pp. 3–4. Howard B. Calderwood, "The Higher Direction of the League Secretariat," *Arnold Foundation Studies in Public Affairs,* V., No. 3 (Winter, 1937), pp. 28–31.

6. League of Nations, *Official Journal,* 1936, p. 1139; and Schwebel, *The Secretary-General,* pp. 9–10, 215ff.

7. Walters, pp. 809–10.

8. See James T. Shotwell (ed.), *The Origins of the International Labor Organization,* 2 vols. (New York, Columbia University Press, 1934).

9. G.N. Barnes, *History of the International Labour Office* (London, Williams and Norgate, 1926). E. Beddington Behrens, *The International Labour Office* (London, L. Parsons, 1924). Paul Perigord, *The International Labor Organization* (New York, D. Appleton & Co., 1926). Francis Graham Wilson, *Labor in the League System* (Stanford, Cal., Stanford University Press, 1934).

10. Edward J. Phelan, *Yes and Albert Thomas* (London, Cresset Press, 1949), pp. 12–18. B. W. Schaper, *Albert Thomas: Trente ans de réformisme social* (Assen, the Netherlands, van Gorcum & Comp., 1959), pp. 210–14.

11. Article 12, Standing Orders of the International Labour Conference, Constitution of the International Labour Organisation (Geneva, International Labour Office, 1955), p. 32. Phelan, pp. 124–27.

12. *Ibid.,* pp. 143 ff.

CHAPTER II. THE MODELS MODERNIZED

1. Interview with Arthur Sweetser, October 11, 1961 at Washington. Ruth B. Russell, assisted by Jeannette E. Muther, *A History of the United Nations Charter: The Role of the United States 1940–45* (Washington, Brookings Institution, 1958), especially Chapter IX. Miss Russell's work has special value for its account of the work done in the Department of State and at the Dumbarton Oaks Conference. Royal Institute of International Affairs, *The International Secretariat of the Future: Lessons from Experience by a Group of Former Officials of the League of Nations* (London, 1944). *Proceedings of a Conference on Training for International Administration* (Washington, Carnegie Endowment for International Peace, 1944). See also the debate in the House of Lords during 1943 in which Drummond took part. *Parliamentary Debates,* House of Lords, Fifth Series, Vol. CXXVII (London, HMSO, 1963), pp. 182–255.

2. Russell, Chapters IX, XVI.

3. Material on the Dumbarton Oaks talks is drawn from *ibid.*, Chapters XVIII–XIX; and Schwebel, *The Secretary-General,* pp. 17–18.

4. The Dumbarton Oaks draft read as follows: "Chapter X. The Secretariat: 1. There should be a Secretariat comprising a Secretary-General and such staff as may be required. The Secretary-General should be the chief administrative officer of the Organization. He should be elected by the General Assembly, on recommendations of the Security Council, for such term and under such conditions as are specified in the Charter. 2. The Secretary-General should act in that capacity in all meetings of the General Assembly, of the Security Council, and of the Economic and Social Council and should make an annual report to the General Assembly on the work of the Organization. 3. The Secretary-General should have the right to bring to the attention of the Security Council any matter which in his opinion may threaten international peace and security."

5. Treatment of the problems of the office of Secretary-General and the Secretariat involved several committees of the San Francisco Conference, and gave rise to procedures too complex to be treated here. These committees included Committee II/1, I/2, III/1, and the Executive and Steering Committees. The account here is based on: *UNCIO,* III, V, VII, VIII, IX. Leland M. Goodrich and Edvard Hambro, *Charter of the United Nations,* Second and Revised Ed. (Boston, World Peace Foundation, 1949), pp. 492–503.

6. During this discussion, which took place in Committee II/1 on the basis of a report by a drafting subcommittee, the views of a League official were sought. In this unique instance, Alexander Loveday, who officially represented the Economic, Financial and Transit Section of the League, supported strengthening the Secretary-General but opposed the Uruguayan suggestion. *UNCIO,* VII, 162ff.

7. The Big Five, or the great powers, were the permanent members of the Security Council: China, France, the United Kingdom, the Soviet Union, and the United States.

8. This account relies mainly on the documents of the Preparatory Commission and the Executive Committee of the Preparatory Commission. See Preparatory Commission, *Report.* This document contains detailed reports and accounts of discussions. Also see the *Journal of the Preparatory Commission* (London, 1945) and the document series bearing symbol PC/EX/SEC/; and Preparatory Commission, Documents, Committee 6. The Pelt-Hill draft is contained in PC/EX/SEC/27, Sept. 29, 1945.

CHAPTER III. THE APPOINTMENT PROCESS

1. Since the membership of the Security Council was increased from 11 to 15 in 1965, the votes of four rather than two elected members have to be obtained.

2. Rule of 48 of the Security Council, UN Doc. S/96/Rev. 4, and Rule 142 of the General Assembly, UN Doc. A/4700.

3. *Repertory*, V, 112–13.

4. Trygve Lie, *In the Cause of Peace* (New York, Macmillan, 1954), pp. 4–10; Schwebel, *The Secretary-General*, p. 50.

5. *Ibid.*, pp. 49–53. Lie, pp. 15–16. UNORGA: First Session, First Part, *Plenary Meetings*, p. 610.

6. Lie, pp. 366–69, 385.

7. Verbatim transcript of press conference, Dec. 16, 1949, at New York. For further detail on the subsequent actions in regard to Lie's candidacy see: Schwebel, *The Secretary-General*, pp. 189–203. Lie, pp. 371–85. Thomas J. Hamilton, "The U.N. and Trygve Lie," *Foreign Affairs*, XXIX, No. 1 (Oct., 1950), pp. 76–77. UNORGA: Fifth Session, *Plenary Meetings*, p. 288.

For perceptive comments on Soviet tactics, see Alexander Dallin, *The Soviet Union at the United Nations* (New York, Praeger, 1962), pp. 99–100 and *passim*.

8. *New York Times*, Oct. 26, 1950.

9. Lie, p. 383.

10. For full account, see UNORGA: Fifth Session, *Plenary Meetings*, pp. 250–92; and UN Doc. A/1468.

11. UNORGA: Fifth Session, *Plenary Meetings*, pp. 291–92.

12. Lie, pp. 408–9.

13. On Lie's resignation and its immediate results, see: *Ibid.*, p. 412. UNORGA: Seventh Session, *Plenary Meetings*, pp. 187–88. Joseph P. Lash, *Dag Hammarskjöld: Custodian of the Brush-Fire Peace* (Garden City, N.Y., Doubleday, 1961) (hereafter cited as Lash, *Hammarskjöld*), pp. 10–11. Lash, who was well acquainted with Hammarskjöld's views, declares that Lie hoped for vindication of his work by being continued in office. At the same time, Lie's immediate staff acted as if there was no doubt about the decision. If Lash's view is correct, Lie attempted to force the General Assembly to back him; this represents a strong effort by the Secretary-General to influence the policies of the member states toward his office.

14. The following account is based on: Lie, pp. 414–16. Lash, *Hammarskjöld*, pp. 9, 12–13. Dallin, pp. 38–39. *UNYB*, 1954, pp. 43–44. Richard I. Miller, *Dag Hammarskjöld and Crisis Diplomacy* (Washington, Oceana Publications, 1961), p. 13. UNORGA: Seventh Session, *Plenary Meetings*, pp. 669–79.

15. Biographical and social material in this section is based on: Schwebel, *The Secretary-General*, pp. 53–55. Lash, *Hammarskjöld*, pp. 16–43. Richard I. Miller, pp. 15–17. Lie, pp. 418–19. Dankwart A. Rustow, *The Politics of Compromise* (Princeton, N.J., Princeton University Press, 1955), pp. 8, 202–6.

16. *Repertoire*, Supplement 1956–1958, p. 77. *UNORGA:* Twelfth Session, *Plenary Meetings*, pp. 174–76.

17. UNORSC, *901st Meeting*, pp. 2–19.
18. UNORGA: Twelfth Session, *Plenary Meetings*, pp. 174–76.
19. UN Charter, Articles 108–9.
20. On his candidacy, see *New York Times*, Sept. 19–20, 23, 26–27, 1961.
21. On these negotiations, see: *New York Times*, Sept. 23, 27, 29, Oct. 1, 4, 6, 7, 15, 1961. *Soviet Mission to the UN*, Press Release, Oct. 1, 1961. UN Doc. A/4794.
22. *New York Times*, Oct. 7, 9, 13, 15, 20–25, 27, and Nov. 3, 1961. *US Delegation to the General Assembly*, Press Release No. 3820, Nov. 1, 1961.
23. UN Doc. A/PV. 1046, Nov. 3, 1961.
24. "Scholar, Writer, Diplomat," *UNR*, VIII, No. 12, pp. 20–21. *New York Times*, Nov. 2, 1961. And interviews with informed persons.
25. On the reappointment of Thant see: *New York Times*, May 6, 1962, Sect. IV (Thomas J. Hamilton); and *ibid.*, Sept. 1, 17–18, Oct. 14, Nov. 19, 29, 1962. Verbatim transcripts of press conferences, June 5, August 2, and Sept. 17, 1962. UNORGA: Seventeenth Session, *Plenary Meetings*, pp. 951–63.
26. Verbatim transcript of press conference, Jan. 20, 1966.
27. Verbatim transcript of press conference, July 6, 1966.
28. UN Press Release SG/SM/557.
29. Verbatim transcript of press conference, Sept. 19, 1966.
30. UN Press Release SG/SM/564.
31. UN Doc. S/RES/227 (1966), and *UNCh*, III, No. 10 (Nov. 1966), p. 4.
32. UN Doc. S/PV.1329.
33. UN Doc. A/PV.1483.

CHAPTER IV. CONCEPTS OF THE OFFICE

1. Schwebel, *The Secretary-General*, p. 10. Hans Kelsen, *The Law of United Nations* (London, Stevens and Sons, 1950), pp. 136–37.
2. Schwebel, *The Secretary-General*, pp. 46–47.
3. Address to the American Jewish Committee, April 10, 1957, reprinted in Wilder Foote, *The Servant of Peace* (London, The Bodley Head, 1962), p. 128.
4. Address at Atoms for Peace Award Ceremony, Jan. 29, 1959, reprinted in Foote, p. 198.
5. *Introduction, Annual Report, 1957*, p. 3.
6. Address at University of Chicago Law School, reprinted in Foote, p. 225.
7. *UN Bulletin*, IX, No. 2 (July 15, 1950), p. 86.
8. *Introduction, Annual Report, 1951*, p. 3.
9. *Introduction, Annual Report, 1952*, p. 5.
10. *Introduction, Annual Report, 1949*, p. 9.

11. *UN Bulletin,* IV, No. 8 (April 15, 1948), pp. 303–4.

11a. Address to Consulative Assembly of the Council of Europe, May 3, 1966, *UNCh,* III, No. 6 (June, 1966), p. 57. Address to Algerian National Assembly, Feb. 4, 1964, *UNR,* XI, No. 3 (March, 1964), p. 14.

12. *UNR,* X, No. 6 (June, 1963), p. 48.

13. *Ibid.,* p. 50.

14. *UNR,* X, No. 7 (July, 1963), p. 57.

15. *Introduction, Annual Report, 1962,* p. 5.

16. *UNR,* X, No. 7 (July, 1963), p. 57.

17. *UNR,* X, No. 5 (May, 1963), p. 38.

18. *Introduction, Annual Reports, 1948–1964, passim.*

19. *Introduction, Annual Report, 1955,* p. 11.

20. *Introduction, Annual Report, 1956,* p. 2.

21. *Ibid.,* p. 3.

22. *Introduction, Annual Report, 1960,* p. 1.

23. *Ibid.,* p. 2.

23a. *Introduction, Annual Report, 1966,* p. 13.

24. *Introduction, Annual Report, 1949,* p. 11.

25. *Introduction, Annual Report, 1951,* p. 5.

26. *Introduction, Annual Report, 1954,* p. 11.

27. *UNR,* X, No. 1 (Jan., 1963), pp. 56–57.

28. *Introduction, Annual Report, 1962,* p. 3.

29. *Introduction, Annual Report, 1963,* p. 5.

30. Joseph P. Lash, "Dag Hammarskjöld's Conception of his Office," *International Organization,* XVI, No. 3 (Summer, 1962), pp. 542–43.

31. Foote, pp. 81, 84–85.

32. *Ibid.,* p. 94.

33. *Ibid.,* pp. 94–95, 98.

34. *Introduction, Annual Report, 1957,* pp. 3–4.

35. For the text of his remarks and the source of quotations in this paragraph, see UNORSC, *751st Meeting,* pp. 1–2.

36. *Ibid.,* pp. 2–20.

37. For the text of his address, see UNORGA: Twelfth Session, *Plenary Meetings,* pp. 174–75.

38. *Ibid.*

39. See especially *Introduction, Annual Report, 1960, passim.*

40. This term, more often than not, refers to the execution of instructions given to the Secretary-General by another organ and not to his own diplomatic initiative. An example would be the establishment by the General Assembly of the United Nations Emergency Force and its instructions to Hammarskjöld to employ it. Because it covers so much, the term describes little.

41. See Chapter VII, *infra.*

42. *Introduction, Annual Report, 1959,* p. 3.

43. *Ibid.*
44. *Introduction, Annual Report, 1960,* p. 4.
45. *Ibid.*
46. *Introduction, Annual Report, 1959,* p. 5.
47. I am informed that it also upset the delicate balance among the United Nations and the Specialized Agencies in administering the technical assistance program. Hammarskjöld was not permitted to expand the sphere of economic operations into the political field without meeting shocked and determined opposition from the directors of the Specialized Agencies. He overcame this opposition through persuasion and persistence.
48. *Introduction, Annual Report, 1947–1952, passim.*
49. *Introduction, Annual Report, 1949,* p. 14.
50. UNORSC, *70th Meeting,* p. 404.
51. Schwebel, *The Secretary-General,* p. 89.
52. Lie, p. 88.
53. Schwebel, *The Secretary-General,* p. 66.
54. "The International Civil Servant in Law and Fact." Address at Oxford University, May 30, 1961, reprinted in Foote, p. 346.
55. *UNR,* XI, No. 2 (Feb., 1964), p. 9.
56. *UNR,* X, No. 5 (May, 1963), p. 38.
56a. Statement at Queen's University, Kingston, Ont., May 27, 1965, *UNCh,* II, No. 6 (June, 1965), p. 103. Address at University of Denver, April 3, 1964, UN Press Release SG/SM/51.
57. UNORGA: Fifth Session, *Plenary Meetings,* pp. 291–92.
58. UNORGA: Seventh Session, *Plenary Meetings,* p. 535.
59. Some indications that the Soviet Union deeply disagreed with Hammarskjöld's views and mistrusted his motives could be found in the Soviet press. See the *New York Times,* July 16, Aug. 4, and Aug. 8, 1960, and Dallin, pp. 142–43. See also the Soviet statements regarding the Congo in UNORSC, *896th* and *897th Meetings,* and Hammarskjöld's reply in UNORSC, *901st Meeting,* pp. 2–19. Khrushchev's "troika" speech to the General Assembly may be found in UNORGA: Fifteenth Session, *Plenary Meetings,* pp. 68–84.
60. *Ibid.,* pp. 95–96 and *New York Times,* Sept. 27, 1960.
61. UNORGA: Fifteenth Session, *Plenary Meetings,* pp. 331–32.
62. Foote, pp. 349–49.
63. *Introduction, Annual Report, 1961.*
64. Lash, "Dag Hammarskjöld's Conception of his Office," p. 545.
65. *Introduction, Annual Report, 1961,* p. 5.

CHAPTER V. INTERNAL ADMINISTRATION

1. Preparatory Commission, *Report,* p. 86.
2. See remarks on this subject, in Lie, pp. 53–54.

3. Schwebel, *The Secretary-General,* p. 132. Lie, pp. 45–50.

4. Alvin Z. Rubinstein, *The Soviets in International Organizations* (Princeton, Princeton University Press, 1962), p. 281.

5. Dallin, pp. 97–98.

6. Schwebel, *The Secretary-General,* pp. 131–32. Sydney D. Bailey, *The Secretariat of the United Nations* (New York, Carnegie Endowment for International Peace, 1962), p. 70.

7. UNGA Resolutions 1446 (XIV) and 1559 (XV). UN Doc. A/4776 is the Committee's report, titled "Review of the Activities and Organization of the Secretariat." See also the separate statements by the Soviet, United States, British, and Colombian experts. The latter served as chairman. Annexes I, II, III, and IV.

8. UN Doc. A/4794.

9. For perceptive comments on the top level of the Secretariat, see Jean Siotis, *Essai sur le Secrétariat International* (Geneva, Librairie Droz, 1963), Part 3, especially Chapter III.

10. Lie, pp. 43, 175. Schwebel, *The Secretary-General,* pp. 133–34.

11. UN Doc. A/2022.

12. See UN Docs. A/2554, 2625, 2731, 2884; A/C.5/580; and UNGA Resolution 784 (VIII).

13. UN Doc. A/2731.

14. The fact that at first the special political affairs pair included a neat balance of Soviet and United States nationals had the effect of limiting the administrative effectiveness of the new arrangement, if for no other reason than the Soviet insistence on restricting terms of service for its citizens to short periods. Bunche was one of the original appointees to the new office and remained there continuously during the following years. Others have been Sir Humphrey Trevelyan, C. V. Narasimhan, and Omar Loutfi. See Andrew Boyd, *United Nations Piety, Myth, and Truth* (London, Penguin, 1962), pp. 169–70.

15. UN Doc. A/2745.

16. *Introduction, Annual Report,* 1960, p. 3.

17. See UN Doc. A/4776/Annex I; and A/4794.

18. *UNR,* IX, No. 1 (July, 1962), p. 1.

19. See authoritative comments by one of Thant's closest associates in C. V. Narasimhan, "Administrative Changes in the Secretariat," in Richard N. Swift (ed.), *Annual Review of United Nations Affairs, 1961–1962* (New York, Oceana Publications, 1963), pp. 1–20.

20. This is based largely on *United Nations Yearbooks, Annual Reports,* and UN Doc. ST/SGB/124.

21. *Annual Report, 1955,* p. 117. This arrangement was discussed by the Fifth Committee during the Ninth Session.

22. Because certain functions have been shifted in and out of the Executive Office, statistical comparisons can be rather meaningless. Nevertheless, 60 posts were assigned to the Executive Office as originally

conceived, but this was cut to 39 in 1947. In 1950 the number exceeded 50, including 16 staff members working on Specialized Agency coordination. Ten years later the total had receded to 31, but another 13 posts were assigned to the office of Under-Secretaries for Special Political Affairs. The number increased slowly after 1960, remaining below 40. See UNORGA: Second Session, *Fifth Committee, Annexes,* Annex 27, p. 249; UNORGA: Fifth Session, Supplement No. 5, *Budget Estimates* . . . , pp. 61–62; UNORGA: Fifteenth Session, Supplement No. 5, *Budget Estimates* . . . , pp. 20–21. In this connection, it is interesting to note the views of the Soviet member of the 1961 Committee of Experts, who pointed out that in the offices of the Secretary-General could be found seven of the thirteen Under-Secretaries at headquarters. UN Doc. A/4776.

23. Schwebel, *The Secretary-General,* p. 132.
24. Lie, p. 48, 175, 328.
25. *Ibid.,* p. 343.
26. UN Doc. A/4776.
27. UNORGA: Fifteenth Session, *Plenary Meetings,* p. 151.
28. *Ibid.,* p. 194.
29. Lash, p. 54.
30. See Conor Cruise O'Brien's revealing sketch of the "Congo Club," in his *To Katanga and Back: A UN Case History* (London, Hutchinson & Co., 1962), pp. 51–54. Lash, pp. 53–54.
31. *Ibid.,* pp. 54–55. Siotis, p. 225.
32. See, for example, Leon Gordenker: *The United Nations and the Peaceful Unification of Korea* (The Hague, Martinus Nijhoff, 1959), *passim;* and "Policy-Making and Secretariat Influence in the U.N. General Assembly: The Case of Public Information," *The American Political Science Review,* LIV, No. 2 (June, 1960), pp. 359–73.
33. Rule 6, UN Doc. S/96, Rev. 4.
34. *Repertoire,* p. 66.
35. *Repertory,* I, 143, and I, Supplement No. 1., 282.
36. Rules 13 to 15, Provisional Rules of Procedure of the Security Council, UN Doc. S/96/Rev. 4.
37. *Repertoire,* Supplement 1956–58, pp. 6–8.
38. Rules 7 and 18, Provisional Rules of Procedure of the Security Council, UN Doc. S/96, Rev. 4.
39. UN Doc. A/3936.
40. Cordier in Swift (ed.), p. 6.
41. UN Charter, Article 101.
42. See discussions in: Bailey, pp. 80–93. L. M. Goodrich, "Geographical Distribution of the Staff of the U.N. Secretariat," *International Organization,* XVI, No. 3 (Summer, 1962), pp. 465–82. Georges Langrod, *The International Civil Service; its Origins, its Nature, its Evolution* (New York, Oceana Publications, 1963), pp. 184–94. See also UN Doc.

A/5063, 5270; and *UNYB, 1961*, pp. 539–44. For an account of the debate on geographical distribution see UN Doc. A/5377. The instruction to the Secretary-General is contained in UNGA Resolution 1852 (XVII).

43. Walter Lippmann's interview with Khrushchev, reported in the *New York Herald Tribune*, April 17, 1961, p. 2.

44. Lie, p. 387.

45. A great deal has been written about this entire controversy. Much of it, as might be expected, is either tendentious or irrelevant. Another large portion concentrates on the legal relationship involved without much sensitivity to the tangle of political emotions, conceptions, and aspirations which caused the dispute. For useful accounts of the affair see: Lie, Chapter XXI. L. M. Goodrich, *The United Nations* (New York, Crowell, 1959), pp. 149–52. Langrod, pp. 212–32. UN Doc. A/2364. The account by Mohammed Bedjaoui, *Fonction Publique Internationale et Influences Nationales* (London, Stevens and Son, 1958), pp. 576–618, contains interesting material on the loyalty question in the Specialized Agencies as well as in the UN. The discussion here relies mainly on these sources and on the numerous relevant passages of the *Official Records* of the General Assembly.

46. For extended discussion and analysis of the budget process and financial implications, see: J. David Singer, *Financing International Organization: The United Nations Budget Process* (The Hague, Martinus Nijhoff, 1961). John G. Stoessinger, *Financing the United Nations System* (Washington, Brookings Institution, 1964).

47. See Schwebel, "A United Nations 'Guard' and a United Nations 'Legion,'" in William R. Frye, *A United Nations Peace Force* (New York, Oceana Publications, 1957), pp. 195–216.

48. UNORGA: Eleventh Session, *Plenary Meetings*, p. 343.

49. Rosner, pp. 163–67.

50. *Introduction, Annual Report, 1964*, p. 1.

51. UN Doc. A/C.5/843.

52. UN Doc. A/C.5/864.

53. UNGA Resolution 1731 (XVI); and International Court of Justice Reports, 1962, Advisory Opinion of July 20, 1963. For a discussion of the opinion, see Stoessinger, Chapter VI.

54. *Introduction, Annual Report, 1964*, p. 6.

55. For a short account of the Assembly actions, see Stoessinger, pp. 134–38.

56. UN Doc. A/C.5/974.

CHAPTER VI. THE SECRETARY-GENERAL AS UN REPRESENTATIVE

1. Preparatory Commission, *Report*, p. 87.

2. *UNYB* 1948–49, pp. 936–39; UNGA Resolution 258 (III). For

the Secretary-General's pleading before the International Court, see International Court of Justice, Pleadings, Oral Arguments, Documents, *Reparation for Injuries Suffered in the Service of the United Nations,* Advisory Opinion of April 11, 1949, pp. 43ff. See Manley O. Hudson, *The Permanent Court of International Justice* (New York, Macmillan Co., 1943), pp. 400–2, 486, 501, 503, 507, and 531, on League practice. See also International Court of Justice, Pleadings, Oral Arguments, Documents, *Effects of Awards of Compensation Made by the United Nations Administrative Tribunal,* Advisory Opinion of July 13, 1954, pp. 287–307.

3. See C. Wilfred Jenks, *The Proper Law of International Organization* (London, Stevens & Sons, 1962), p. vi.

4. For a discussion of some of the substantive views presented in the *Annual Report,* see Chapter IV, *supra.*

5. Goodrich and Hambro, p. 501. See also Rule 48, Rules of Procedure of the General Assembly, UN Doc. A/4700.

6. *Annual Report,* 1948, pp. xvii–xviii, and Schwebel, in Frye.

7. Cf. Schwebel, *The Secretary-General,* p. 67.

8. Preparatory Commission, *Report,* p. 102.

9. Robert H. Cory, "Forging a Public Information Policy for the United Nations," *International Organization,* VII, No. 2 (May, 1953), pp. 229–42. Leon Gordenker, "Policy-Making and Secretariat Influence in the UN General Assembly; the Case of Public Information." Richard N. Swift, "The United Nations and Its Public," *International Organization,* XIV, No. 1 (Winter, 1960), pp. 60–91.

CHAPTER VII. THE SECRETARY-GENERAL AND HIS "SPECIAL RIGHT"

1. Preparatory Commission, *Report,* p. 87.

2. H. G. Nicholas, *The United Nations as a Political Institution,* 2nd Ed. (London, Oxford University Press, 1962), p. 156.

3. Arthur L. Burns and Nina Heathcote, *Peace-Keeping by UN Forces, from Suez to the Congo* (New York, Praeger, 1963), pp. 24–25, 162–66.

4. Lash, *Hammarskjöld,* pp. 224–26. UN Doc. S/4300, April 1, 1960. *New York Times,* July 12, 1960.

5. UN Doc. S/4382, July 13, 1960; UNORSC, *873rd Meeting,* p. 21.

6. UN Doc. S/4381, July 13, 1960; and S/Agenda/873, Rev. 1, July 13, 1960. The President can practically dictate the provisional agenda if he wishes. Yakov A. Malik did so in August, 1950, during the Korean conflict. See Leland M. Goodrich and Anne P. Simons, *The United Nations and the Maintenance of International Peace and Security* (Washington, Brookings Institution, 1955), p. 99.

7. UNORSC, *873rd Meeting,* p. 1.

8. *Ibid.*, p. 3.
9. Rule 6, UN Doc. S/96/Rev. 4.
10. UNORSC, *873rd Meeting*, p. 4.
11. *Ibid.*, pp. 4–5.
12. UN Doc. S/1495, June 25, 1950. Lie, p. 328, Gordenker, *The United Nations and the Peaceful Unification of Korea*, pp. 203–10.
13. UNORSC, *473rd Meeting*, pp. 1–2; and Lie, p. 329.
14. UNORSC, *473rd Meeting*, p. 3.
15. Lie, p. 330.
16. UNORSC, *70th Meeting*, pp. 396–404.
17. UNORSC, *87th Meeting.*
18. Lash, *Hammarskjöld*, p. 81.
19. Preparatory Commission Doc. PC/EX/A/26, Sept. 25, 1945.
20. UN Doc. S/96/Rev. 4.
21. Preparatory Commission, *Report*, p. 26.
22. UNORSC, *29th* and *30th Meetings, passim.*
23. UN Doc. S/93; *Repertoire*, pp. 92–93. Lie, pp. 81–83. Schwebel, *The Secretary-General*, pp. 92–93. UNORSC, *33rd Meeting, passim.*
24. Schwebel, *The Secretary-General*, pp. 83–87, Lie, pp. 86–88; *Repertory*, V, 160.
25. Schwebel, *The Secretary-General*, p. 86.
26. UNORSC, *847th Meeting*, pp. 2–3.
27. Andrew W. Cordier, "The Role of the Secretary-General," in Richard N. Swift (ed.), *Annual Review of United Nations Affairs, 1960–1961* (New York, Oceana Publications, 1960), pp. 4–5.
28. UNORSC, *847th Meeting, passim.*
29. See discussion in Schwebel, *The Secretary-General*, pp. 92–103.
30. Article 11.
31. Preparatory Commission Docs. PC/EX/15, PC/EX/A/43, PC/EX/A/53/Rev. 1; and PC/EX/A/62.
32. *Repertory*, V, 159–62.
33. *Introduction, Annual Report, 1960.*
34. *Annual Report, 1959*, p. 26.
35. Gordenker, *The United Nations and the Peaceful Unification of Korea*, pp. 46–48, 224. Lie, pp. 325, 334–35.
36. Later the dispute on the ownership of the temples was brought to the International Court of Justice for adjudication.
37. UNORSC, *847th* and *848th Meetings, passim;* and UN Doc. S/4222 and 4236.
38. UN Press Release SG/868, Nov. 8, 1959; UN Office of Public Information, Note No. 2072, Nov. 6, 1959; and verbatim transcript of press conference, Aug. 13, 1959.
39. Lash, *Hammarskjöld*, p. 143.
40. UN Press Release SG/871, Nov. 15, 1959; and *Annual Report, 1960*, pp. 22–23.
41. Miller, pp. 251–53.

42. UN Doc. A/C.5/842; and UNORGA: 15th Session, *Fifth Committee,* p. 17.
43. UN Press Release SG/971, Oct. 18, 1960.
44. Little is known of the Guinea mission, which was abruptly ended by the government as part of its reaction to Hammarskjöld's policies in the Congo after Lumumba accused him of acting too gently.
45. UN Press Release SG/971, Oct. 18, 1960.
46. Speech to the Students Association, Copenhagen, May 2, 1959.

CHAPTER VIII. NEGOTIATION AND MEDIATION

1. *Introduction, Annual Report, 1959,* p. 2.
2. Address at Oslo, June 3, 1958.
3. *Ibid.*
4. Lie, pp. 158–59; and Schwebel, *The Secretary-General,* pp. 140–42.
5. The fullest available account is in Lie, pp. 199–218.
6. The following account and quotations are based on Lie, pp. 275–88, 300, 318–19. See also UN Doc. A/1304; UNORGA: 5th Session, *Plenary Meetings,* pp. 437–41; UNGA Resolution 494 (V).
7. UN Doc. S/3575 and 3605; and Lash, *Hammarskjöld,* pp. 68–76.
8. The Suez Canal case was developed in Security Council meetings documented in UNORSC, *734–738th Meetings.*
9. UNORSC, *735th Meeting,* pp. 16–17.
10. UNORSC, *738th Meeting,* p. 13. The meetings issued only communiqués. UNORSC, *739th–741st Meetings.*
11. UNORSC, *742nd–743rd Meetings;* UN Doc. S/3771; Lash, *Hammarskjöld,* p. 77; and John Robinson Beal, *John Foster Dulles, a Biography* (New York, Harper, 1957), p. 207.
12. UNORSC, *743rd Meeting, passim.*
13. UN Doc. S/3728.
14. *Annual Report, 1954,* p. xi.
15. Verbatim transcript of press conference, April 20, 1954.
16. UN Doc. S/PV. 962 and 961; S/4861 and 4862.
17. UN Doc. S/PV.963.
18. *New York Times,* July 21, 1961; UN Doc. S/4874, 4875, and 4885.
19. UN Doc. S/4885.
20. UN Doc. S/4894 and Add. 1.
21. UN Doc. S/PV.964.
22. UN Doc. S/PV.966.
23. *UNR,* VIII, No. 10 (Oct., 1961), pp. 12–14.
24. The account of the New Guinea negotiations is based on *UNR,* IX, No. 2 (Feb., 1962), p. 1; No. 6 (June, 1962), p. 2; and Nov. 9 (Sept., 1962), p. 4; and *Introduction, Annual Report, 1962,* pp. 2–3.
25. Information about negotiations in the crisis still remains fragmen-

tary, especially with regard to Thant's role. This account is based mainly on *UNYB, 1962,* pp. 101–12, and documentary references cited there.

26. See remarks of Alex Quaison-Sackey of Ghana, UNORSC, *925th Meeting,* p. 17.

27. *Introduction, Annual Report, 1963,* p. 1.

28. Harlan Cleveland, "Crisis Diplomacy," *Foreign Affairs,* XLI, No. 4 (July, 1963), p. 646.

28a. The most authentic account now available of Thant's negotiations appears in Emmet John Hughes, "A Man for All Nations," *Newsweek,* LXVIII, No. 24 (Dec. 12, 1966), pp. 40–41. For an example of his public pleas on Viet Nam, see statement of Feb. 12, 1965, in *UNCh,* II, No. 3 (March 1965), pp. 21–22. He described the general aims of his diplomatic probing in his press conference of Jan. 20, 1966; see verbatim transcript. The content of his proposals was described in his statement of July 16, 1966, in *UNCh,* III, No. 8 (Aug.–Sept. 1966), pp. 32–33. See also *Introduction, Annual Report, 1966,* p. 13.

29. UN Doc. S/1511.

30. UNGA Resolution 906 (IX).

31. UNGA: Ninth Session, *Plenary Meetings,* pp. 379–443.

32. Lash says that Hammarskjöld was anxious to revive the shrunken prestige of the office; *Hammarskjöld,* pp. 56–57.

33. UNGA: Ninth Session, *Plenary Meetings,* p. 422.

34. See Lash, *Hammarskjöld,* pp. 57–58.

35. UN Doc. A/2888.

36. UN Doc. A/2889.

37. UN Doc. A/2891.

38. Verbatim transcript of press conference, Dec. 30, 1954.

39. Lash, *Hammarskjöld,* p. 61. See his colorful account of the whole Peking negotiation, *Ibid.,* pp. 60–65.

40. UN Doc. A/2954.

41. UN Doc. A/2954.

42. *UNR,* II, No. 5 (Nov., 1955), p. 1.

43. UN Doc. S/3538.

44. UN Doc. S/3379 and 3432.

45. According to the apparently well informed account by Lash in *Hammarskjöld,* pp. 68–69.

46. *UNR,* II, No. 9 (March, 1956), p. 1.

47. Verbatim transcript of press conference, Feb. 27, 1956.

48. *UNR,* II, No. 9 (March, 1956), p. 1.

49. Verbatim transcript of press conference, Feb. 27, 1956.

50. UN Doc. S/3562.

51. Lash, *Hammarskjöld,* pp. 69–70; and Richard P. Stebbins, *The United States in World Affairs, 1956* (New York, Harper & Bros., 1957), p. 91.

52. UNORSC, *717th Meeting*, pp. 2–3.
53. *Ibid.*, p. 5.
54. UNORSC, *718th–720th Meetings.*
55. UNORSC, *719th Meeting*, pp. 9–10.
56. UNORSC, *722nd Meeting.*
57. *Ibid.*, p. 12.
58. Lash, *Hammarskjöld*, p. 549.
59. *New York Times*, April 7, 1956; and *UNR*, II, No. 11 (May, 1956), p. 1.
60. UNORSC, *723rd Meeting*, p. 10.
61. Complaints in UN Doc. S/3576, 3577, 3579/Rev. 1, 3580, 3581, 3582, and 3583.
62. UN Doc. A/3584.
63. UN Doc. S/3585, 3586, and 3587.
64. *New York Times*, April 11, April 13, and April 21; and verbatim transcript of press conference, May 11, 1956.
65. UN Doc. S/3593, 3594, and 3596.
66. UN Doc. S/3594.
67. *New York Times*, May 8–9, 1956; ; UNORSC, *723rd Meeting*, p. 3; and Stebbins, pp. 93–94.
68. UNORSC, *723rd Meeting*, p. 9; and UN Doc. S/3600/Rev. 1.
69. UNORSC, *723rd–728th Meetings.*
70. UN Doc. S/6651.
71. UN Doc. SC/RES/209.
72. UN Doc. S/6683.
73. See UN Doc. SC/RES/214 and 211.
74. UN Doc. S/6699 and Addenda.

CHAPTER IX. INVESTIGATION AND OBSERVATION

1. UN Doc. S/3690, 3726, and 3261; and UNORSC, *746th, 752nd–753rd Meetings.*
2. UN Doc. S/3730, 3730/Rev. 1, and 3733; UNORSC, *753rd–754th Meetings.*
3. UNORGA: Second Emergency Special Session, *Plenary Meetings*, pp. 1–88; UN Doc. A/3286, 3319, and 3325; and UNGA Resolution 1004 (ES–II). India's representative, V. K. Krishna Menon, did not have instructions and opposed any condemnation. He and other delegates later tried to excise what they considered prejudicial language from resolutions on relief.
4. UNGA Resolution 1004 (ES–II).
5. Verbatim transcript of Secretary-General's press conference, Nov. 12, 1956; UN Doc. A/3315, 3335, 3340, 3341, 3346, and 3347.
6. Verbatim transcript of Secretary-General's press conference, Nov. 12, 1956. UN Doc. A/3359. See also the brief comment in Arthur Lall,

Modern International Negotiation (New York, Columbia University Press, 1966), pp. 11–12.

7. UN Doc. A/3341, 3346, 3358, 3362, 3403, and 3414; UNORGA: Eleventh Session, *Plenary Meetings*, p. 170.

8. UNGA Resolutions 1127 (XI), 1128 (XI), 1129 (XI), 1130 (XI), and 1131 (XI); UN Doc. A/3435/Add. 6; and UNORGA: Eleventh Session, *Plenary Meetings*, pp. 515–25. This discussion includes a statement by the Secretary-General and an interesting comment on behalf of India by Krishna Menon.

9. UN Doc. A/3485; UNGA Resolution 1132 (XI); and UNORGA: Eleventh Session, *Plenary Meetings*, pp. 515, 819–71.

10. UN Doc. S/4007 and 4002; UNORGA, *823rd Meeting*, pp. 1–32; *824th Meeting*, pp. 14–23; and *825th Meeting*, pp. 14–23.

11. UN Doc. S/4028 and 4029; and *UNR*, V, No. 1 (July, 1958), pp. 37–38.

12. UN Doc. S/4029.

13. UN Doc. S/4038; and *UNR*, V, No. 1 (July, 1958), p. 56.

14. See his long statement in UNORSC, *827th Meeting*, pp. 11–13.

15. UN Doc. S/4040.

16. UN Doc. S/4052 and 4069.

17. UN Doc. S/4043; and UNORSC, *827th Meeting*, *passim.*

18. These and subsequent quotations from UNORSC, *827th Meeting*, pp. 11–13 and *passim.*

19. UN Doc. S/4050; and UNORSC, *829th–830th Meetings*, *passim.*

20. UN Doc. S/4054, 4055, 4056, and 4057/Rev. 1; and UNORSC, *831st Meeting*, pp. 1–3, *834th Meeting*, pp. 10–11 and *passim.*, *835th* and *838th Meetings*, *passim.*

21. UNORSC, *837th Meeting*, p. 4.

22. UN Doc. S/4059. The suggestion is reminiscent of Lie's suggestion that the provision for periodic meetings of the Security Council be employed.

23. UN Doc. S/4085.

24. UNORGA: Third Emergency Special Session, *Plenary Meetings*, pp. 4–5.

25. UN Doc. A/3876; and Lash, *Hammarskjöld*, pp. 123–24.

26. UNORGA: Third Emergency Special Session, *Plenary Meetings*, pp. 102–3.

27. UN Doc. A/3993/Rev. 1, and 3934/Rev. 1; UNGA Resolution 1237 (ES–III).

28. UN Doc. A/3934/Rev. 1.

29. *Ibid.*

30. UNORGA, Thirteenth Session, *Plenary Meetings*, pp. 9, 146; UNORSC, *846th Meeting*, p. 5; and UN Doc. A/3986 and 4056; S/4113, 4114, and 4116.

31. UN Doc. S/5298 and 5321.

32. UN Doc. S/5321; and UNORSC, *1038th Meeting,* pp. 1–2.
33. UN Doc. S/5412, 5447 and Add. 1 and 2, 5501 and Add. 1, 5572 and Add. 1; and *UNCh,* I, No. 2 (June, 1964), pp. 51–52, and I, No. 4 (Aug.–Sept., 1964), pp. 29–30.
34. *Introduction, Annual Report, 1964,* p. 8.
35. Principle IX, Annex, UNGA Resolution 1541 (XV).
36. Subsequently, Indonesia used the formation of the Malaysian Federation as a pretext for withdrawing from the United Nations.
37. UN Doc. S/PV/1196, 1198, 1200, 1202–1204, 1207–1209, 1212–1223, 1225–1228, and 1229–1233 record the Security Council discussions. A long list of reports from the Secretary-General was put before these meetings.
38. *Annual Report, 1966,* p. 35; UN Doc. S/7338 and Add. 1–9.

CHAPTER X. PEACE-KEEPING—POLITICS AND POLICIES OF FORCES

1. For more comprehensive discussions of peace-keeping forces see Lincoln P. Bloomfield (ed.), *International Military Forces* (Boston, Little Brown, 1964). D. W. Bowett, *United Nations Forces* (London, Stevens, 1964). Burns and Heathcote. On Korea see Leland M. Goodrich, *Korea: A Study of United States Policy in the United Nations* (New York, Council on Foreign Relations, 1956). On Suez see: E. L. M. Burns, *Between Arab and Israeli* (New York, I. Obolensky, 1963). Gabriella Rosner, *The United Nations Emergency Force* (New York, Columbia University Press, 1956). On the Congo see: Burns and Heathcote. King Gordon, *The U.N. in the Congo: A Quest for Peace* (New York, Carnegie Endowment for International Peace, 1962). Catherine Hoskyns, *The Congo Since Independence* (London, Oxford University Press, 1965). Ernest W. Lefever, *Crisis in the Congo: A U.N. Force in Action* (Washington, Brookings Institution, 1965). Colin Legum, *Congo Disaster* (Baltimore, Penguin Books, 1961). Conor Cruise O'Brien. Fernand van Langenhove, *Le Rôle Proéminent du Secrétaire Général dans l'Opération des Nations Unies au Congo* (Brussels, Institut Royal des Relations Internationales, 1964). No monographic studies of the West New Guinea and Cyprus forces have yet been published, and the principal sources of information are the United Nations Official Record, especially the *Annual Report,* and the *United Nations Chronicle.* On Cyprus, see also Rosalyn Higgins, "Basic Facts on the U.N. Force in Cyprus," *The World Today,* XX, No. 8 (Aug., 1964), pp. 347–50.
2. *Annual Report, 1960,* p. 1–2.
3. "Cyprus," *UNR,* XI, No. 2 (Feb., 1964), pp. 4–6.
4. UNORGA: First Emergency Special Session, *Plenary Meetings,* p. 1–44.
5. William R. Frye, p. 3; and Lash, *Hammarskjöld,* p. 84.

6. Philip Noel-Baker made what appears to have been the earliest public suggestion of a special police force for Suez. To his suggestion, Foreign Secretary Selwyn Lloyd replied in the House of Commons that he had been trying to do something of the sort for years. Prime Minister Anthony Eden soon remarked that the government would be glad to let an international organization take over the task of separating belligerents. Pearson was certainly informed of these comments. *Parliamentary Debates,* House of Commons, Fifth Series, DLVIII (London, HMSO, 1956), cc. 1563–1565. Canada, Department of External Affairs, *Statements and Speeches,* 56/35, p. 9. Anthony Eden, *Full Circle, the Memoirs of Anthony Eden* (Boston Houghton Mifflin, 1960), p. 605; Frye, pp. 2–4.

7. UNORGA: First Emergency Special Session, *Plenary Meetings,* pp. 54–78; and UNORGA Resolution 998 (ES–I). The Assembly also adopted an Afro-Asian draft, authorizing the Secretary-General to arrange a cease-fire and report within 12 hours. This resolution seems logically subordinated to the Canadian draft. See UNGA Resolution 999 (ES–I). See also Lall, pp. 327–28.

8. Frye, p. 8; and Lash, *Hammarskjöld,* p. 88.

9. UN Doc. A/3289.

10. UNORGA: First Emergency Special Session, *Plenary Meetings,* pp. 79–89; and UNGA Resolution 1000 (ES–I).

11. UN Doc. A/3291, 3296, 3299, 3304, 3306, 3307, and 3943.

12. UN Doc. A/3302.

13. *Ibid.*

14. UNORGA: First Emergency Special Session, *Plenary Meetings,* pp. 118–19.

15. Rosner, pp. 34–35; UNORGA, First Emergency Special Session, *Plenary Meetings,* pp. 125–26; and UNGA Resolution 1000 (ES–I).

16. UNORSC, *873rd Meeting,* p. 5.

17. UN Doc. A/3943. This document, put before the General Assembly in 1958, never was discussed beyond a preliminary statement by Hammarskjöld, who took the silence of the Assembly as approval. UNORGA: Thirteenth Session, *Special Political Committee,* pp. 63–64. By referring to the report in the Congo case, he implicitly sought direct approval of it.

18. J. Gerard-Libois and Benoit Verhaegen, *Congo 1960* (Brussels, Centre de Recherche et d'Information Socio-Politiques, n.d.), II, 541–43. Lash, *Hammarskjöld,* p. 227.

19. Gordon, p. 22. UN Doc. S/4382.

20. UNORSC *873rd Meeting,* p. 36.

21. UN Doc. S/4387.

22. See UN Doc. A/5170, and UNORGA: Seventeenth Session, *Plenary Meetings,* pp. 49–58, for basic documents and official discussions of them.

23. UNORSC, *1094th–1102nd Meetings.* The only specific discussion of the mandate took place in the 1102nd meeting, although evidence of the importance of the Secretary-General in negotiations can be found in many statements.

24. UN Doc. S/5571.

25. *UNCh,* I, No. 5 (Oct., 1964), p. 4.

26. UN Doc. A/3302 and Adds. 1–16. UNGA Resolution 1001 (ES–I).

27. Frye, pp. 23–28.

28. Lash, *Hammarskjöld,* p. 230. R. I. Miller, pp. 271–72.

29. UN Doc. A/3943.

30. UN Doc. A/3289 and 3304. Lash, *Hammarskjöld,* p. 88.

31. For an account of preliminary negotiations, see E. L. M. Burns, pp. 196–205.

32. *Ibid.,* pp. 217–18.

33. UN Doc. A/3375.

34. UN Doc. A/3943.

35. UN Doc. S/5634 and Corr. 1; and S/5653.

CHAPTER XI. PEACE-KEEPING—OPERATIONS AND ADAPTATIONS

1. UN Doc. A/3306, 3307, and 3310.

2. UN Doc. S/3384. *Parliamentary Debates,* Fifth Series, House of Commons, Vol. DLX, cc. 881–82.

3. E. L. M. Burns, pp. 195–227.

4. *Ibid.,* p. 230.

5. UN Doc. A/3297 and 3309.

6. UNORGA: Eleventh Session, *Plenary Meetings,* pp. 277, 323–24. E. L. M. Burns, p. 243.

7. UN Doc. A/3512.

8. UNORGA: Eleventh Session, *Plenary Meetings.* p. 982.

9. *Ibid.,* pp. 1052–1053ff.; UNGA Resolutions 1124 (XI) and 1125 (XI). E. L. M. Burns, pp. 248–50; and UN Doc. A/3527.

10. UNORGA: Eleventh Session, *Plenary Meetings,* pp. 1192–93.

11. *Ibid.,* pp. 1175–78, 1283, 1300, 1313–15. E. L. M. Burns, pp. 255–59.

12. Lash, *Hammarskjöld,* pp. 109–11.

13. UNORSC, *873rd Meeting,* p. 37.

14. UNORSC, *877th Meeting,* pp. 5–30, and *878th Meeting,* p. 29; and UN Doc. S/4389 and 4389/Add. 1.

15. UNORSC, *885th Meeting,* p. 7.

16. UNORSC, *884th Meeting,* p. 3.

17. UN Doc. S/4426. See also the Secretary-General's comments, UNORSC, *885th–886th Meetings.*

18. UNORSC, *887th Meeting,* pp. 6–7, and UN Doc. S/4417/Add. 9.
19. UN Doc. 4475/Add. 1–3.
20. *UNYB, 1963,* pp. 44–45.
21. *UNCh,* I, No. 5 (Oct., 1964), p. 7.
22. UN Doc. S/4405, 4417, and 4426.
23. UN Doc. S/4417/Add. 8.
24. UNORSC, *887th–889th Meetings.*
25. UNORSC, *896th Meeting,* pp. 14–21.
26. UNGA Resolution 1474 (ES–IV). See also UNORGA: Fourth Emergency Special Session, *Plenary Meetings, passim.*
27. *Ibid.,* p. 102.
28. UNORSC, *920th Meeting,* pp. 16–17.
29. See Hammarskjöld's statement, UNORGA: Fifteenth Session, *Plenary Meetings,* pp. 1370 and *passim,* for extended debate; and UNGA Resolution 1592 (XV).
30. UN Doc. S/4606.
31. See his statement, UNORSC, *928th Meeting,* pp. 11–18.
32. UN Doc. S/4741. For the debates preceding adoption of the resolution, see UNORSC, *933rd–942nd Meetings.*
33. UN Doc. S/PV.973–S/PV.982.
34. *UNCh:* I, No. 3 (July, 1964), pp. 3–15; I, No. 5 (Oct., 1964), pp. 3–20; II, No. 1 (Jan., 1965), pp. 23–28; and II, No. 4 (April, 1965), p. 3.
35. UNORSC, *896th Meeting,* p. 17; and UN Doc. S/4505/Adds. 1 and 2.
36. UN Doc. S/4940/Adds. 15–19. Burns and Heathcote, pp. 137–48. *New York Times,* Dec. 4 and 6, 1961.
37. *Ibid.,* Dec. 11–15, 1961.
38. *Ibid.*
39. *Ibid.,* Dec. 16–20, 1961; UN Doc. S/5038; and Gordon, p. 145.
40. *Ibid.,* pp. 162–64, 170–76; UN Doc. S/5053 and Addenda. J. Gerard-Libois and Benoit Verhaegen, *Congo, 1962* (Brussels, Centre de Recherche et d'Information Socio-Politique, 1963), pp. 347–69.
41. *New York Times,* July 8, 10, 19, 1962.
42. UN Doc. S/5053/Add. 11. Details of the plan and rumors of a scheme for military operations against Tshombé began to leak out of Washington at the same time. *New York Times,* Aug. 19, 1962.
43. UN Doc. S/5053/Add. 14.
44. *Ibid.*
45. *UNR,* X, No. 2 (Feb., 1963), p. 1.
46. Bowett, p. 559.
47. *UNCh,* I, No. 1 (May, 1964), pp. 5–7.
48. UN Doc. S/5240.

49. Lefever, pp. 127–30.
50. UN Doc. S/5428.
51. UNGA Resolution 1885 (XVIII).
52. UN Doc. S/4557.
53. Gerard-Libois and Verhaegen, *Congo, 1960,* II, 903.
54. UN Doc. S/4639.
55. UN Doc. S/4807 and Annexes. Benoit Verhaegen, *Congo, 1961* (Brussels, Centre de Recherche et d'Information Socio-Politiques, 1962), pp. 350–56.
56. Gordon, pp. 119–20. Burns and Heathcote, pp. 93–95. UN Doc. S/4908, 4911 and Add. 1 and 2, 4917, and 4923.
57. Advisory committees have been used in other contexts. The Advisory Committee on Public Information is one which has helped the Secretary-General make a more convincing case for his budget. See Gordenker, "Policy-Making and Secretariat Influence in the U.N. General Assembly: The Case of Public Information."
58. *Annual Report, 1957*, p. 2. See also: Sydney D. Bailey, *The Secretariat of the United Nations* (London, Stevens, 1962), pp. 59–60. Burns and Heathcote, pp. 175–76. Rosner, p. 192. Despite the comments, little is known of what was done and said in the meetings.
59. UN Doc. A/3302.
60. Rosner, p. 53.
61. UNORSC, *885th Meeting,* p. 5.
62. *Ibid.*, p. 23.
63. UNORSC, *887th Meeting,* p. 8.
64. UNORGA: Fourth Emergency Special Session, *Plenary Meetings,* p. 91.
65. *New York Times,* March 10, 1961, Jan. 9, April 24, Sept. 1, Oct. 13, and Nov. 7, 1962. UN Press Release Note No. 2091; and UN Doc. SG/1094 and 1393.
66. UN Doc. S/5420.
67. UNORSC, *901st Meeting,* p. 27; *905th Meeting,* p. 19; *906th Meeting,* p. 13; and UN Doc. S/4523.
68. For discussion of the proposal see UNORGA: Fourth Emergency Special Session, *Plenary Meetings,* pp. 37ff.
69. *Ibid.*, pp. 91, 95, 101, and 102.
70. UNGA Resolution 1474 (ES–IV).
71. UN Doc. A/4711 gives some information on the commission, about which little was made public. See also *UNR,* VII, No. 6 (Dec., 1960), p. 1.
72. UN Doc. A/4711.
73. *Ibid.*
74. The experienced Under-Secretary, Dragoslav Protitch.

CHAPTER XII. PEACE-KEEPING—CIVIL RAMIFICATIONS

1. "United Nations Administration of West New Guinea (West Irian)," *UNR,* IX, No. 12 (Dec., 1962), p. 26. For critical and informed comments see Paul W. van der Veur, "The United Nations in West Irian: a Critique," *International Organization,* XVIII, No. 1 (Winter, 1964), pp. 53–73.
2. *New York Times,* Aug. 29, 1950.
3. *Annual Report, 1961,* p. 39; and UN Doc. E/1851/Rev. 1.
4. UNORSC, *479th Meeting,* pp. 5–6.
5. *UNYB, 1950,* pp. 269–70; and *Annual Report, 1951,* pp. 40–41.
6. Gene M. Lyons, *Military Policy and Economic Aid: The Korean Case, 1950–1953* (Columbus, Ohio State University Press, 1961), pp. 21–23.
7. UNGA Resolution 376 (V). For an account of the General Assembly's discussions and United States aims, see Goodrich, *Korea: A Study of United States Policy in the United Nations,* pp. 126–36.
8. *Annual Report, 1951,* p. xiii.
9. UNOR, Economic and Social Council: Eleventh Session, Resumed, pp. 371–73; and UN Doc. E/1851/Rev. 1 and Add. 1 and E/1852.
10. *UNYB, 1950,* pp. 273–75; and UN Economic and Social Council Resolution 339.
11. Lyons, p. 27.
12. The following account is based on *ibid.,* pp. 32–35, 52–55, and Chapters VII–IX.
13. UNGA Res. 997 (ES–I).
14. UN Doc. A/3376.
15. Lash, *Hammarskjöld,* pp. 95–97; and *UNR,* III, No. 11 (May, 1957), p. 24.
16. UN Doc. A/3306 and 3307.
17. UN Doc. A/3376 and 3386.
18. UNORGA: Eleventh Session, *Plenary Meetings,* pp. 251–86.
19. *Ibid.,* p. 259.
20. UN Doc. A/3306 and 3307.
21. UN Doc. A/3492. "United Nations Team Clears Suez Canal," *UNR,* III, No. 11 (May, 1957), pp. 24–29.
22. Gerard-Libois and Verhaegen, *Congo, 1960,* I, 52–54.
23. Robert L. West, "The United Nations and the Congo Financial Crisis: Lessons of the First Year," *International Organization,* XV, No. 4 (Autumn, 1961), pp. 604–7; and Ritchie Calder, *Agony of the Congo* (London, Victor Gallancz, 1961), pp. 22–23.
24. Gordon, p. 63.
25. UNORSC, *873th Meeting,* p. 4.

26. UNORSC, *877th Meeting,* p. 3.
27. UN Doc. S/4405 and 4417/Add. 5.
28. *Ibid.*
29. *Ibid.*
30. UN Doc. S/4557.
31. Progress Report No. 12 on United Nations Civilian Operations in the Congo during September–October 1961, Leopoldville, pp. 1–2.
32. Progress Report No. 5 on United Nations Civilian Operations in the Congo, Leopoldville, p. 1.
33. UN Doc. General LEO/PROG/3, p. i; and Progress Report No. 11 on United Nations Civilian Operations in the Congo, pp. 35, 48; and Report of the United Nations Civilian Operations in the Congo, May 1, 1963.
34. UN Doc. General LEO/PROG/3, pp. i–iv.

INDEX

Abbreviations Used: GA General Assembly; SC Security Council; SG Secretary-General; UN United Nations.